THE BRITISH ARCHAEOLOGICAL
ASSOCIATION

CONFERENCE TRANSACTIONS
For the year 1985

XI

MEDIEVAL ART

AND ARCHITECTURE

at Exeter Cathedral

Edited by
Francis Kelly

1991

Previous volumes in the series

I. Medieval Art and Architecture at Worcester Cathedral
II. Medieval Art and Architecture at Ely Cathedral
III. Medieval Art and Architecture at Durham Cathedral
IV. Medieval Art and Architecture at Wells and Glastonbury
V. Medieval Art and Architecture at Canterbury before 1220
VI. Medieval Art and Architecture at Winchester Cathedral
VII. Medieval Art and Architecture at Gloucester and Tewkesbury
VIII. Medieval Art and Architecture at Lincoln Cathedral
IX. Medieval Art and Architecture in the East Riding of Yorkshire
X. Medieval Art, Architecture and Archaeology in London

Copies of these may be obtained from W. S. Maney and Son Limited, Hudson Road, Leeds LS9 7DL
or from Oxbow Books, Park End Place, Oxford OX1 1HN

ISBN Hardback 0 901286 27 3
Paperback 0 901286 26 5

British Library Cataloguing-in-Publication Data
A catalogue record for this book is available from the British Library

PRINTED IN GREAT BRITAIN BY W. S. MANEY AND SON LIMITED
HUDSON ROAD, LEEDS LS9 7DL

CONTENTS

Preface

The Conference in 1985 was a lively and successful one for which the University of Exeter deserves much credit. The contributors to these *Transactions* have been uniformly co-operative in their long-delayed production. I am confident that they have made a valuable and scholarly contribution to the study of the Cathedral for many years to come.

The *Transactions* could not have been printed without the considerable funding which they have attracted and for which the Association is very grateful indeed. This most generous support has come from: the Dean and Chapter of Exeter Cathedral, the Exeter Cathedral Preservation Trust, the Claude and Mary Pike Charitable Trust, the Francis Coale's Fund, Lady Craufurd, The British Academy, the Council for British Archaeology, Devon County Council, Exeter City Council, the Universities of Exeter, Warwick and California Santa Cruz and from anonymous gifts.

Once again the *Transactions* contain a single bibliography in an attempt to provide a uniform research tool.

Readers should note that some of the material in the articles has been printed in reduced type in an attempt to reduce costs.

The Editor wishes to thank especially Linda Hind of W. S. Maney and Son (our printers) for her cheerful and patient efficiency.

The Documentation of Exeter Cathedral: The Archives and their Application

By Audrey Erskine

Exeter Cathedral is well known for the extent of archival documentation surviving among the capitular records relating to its fabric and fittings in the medieval period, and this is certainly notable though by no means complete. There are, however, various other later sources of information among the chapter's records, so this paper aims first to provide a brief review of the whole extent of such material up to the early 20th century; and secondly to make some general observations on the nature and content of the medieval fabric accounts and their application to the building.

The fabric fund

In the administration of most great churches a specific fund was habitually set aside for the building and maintenance of the fabric and furnishings, and no other cathedral church in Europe built before 1350 has more extensive earlier records surviving of accounts of such a fund than Exeter. The Norman cathedral on the site was begun in the early 12th century, and there is no written record of the progress of its building. But it was extended and transformed from the 1270s onwards, and for this latter work a series of accounts of the fabric fund survive from 1279, though there are numerous and important gaps in the subsequent series and many of the surviving records are damaged, defective or in part illegible. The medieval fabric accounts begin with a unique and incomplete memorandum roll of receipts and payments dated 1279–87, though not every year is covered by it. From 1299 the annual rolls of account of the *custos* of the fabric begin: there is internal evidence that the 1299–1300 roll is the second account of a series which began at Michaelmas 1298. From 1299 to 1353 there is a sequence of these accounts, sometimes continuously for several years at a time, sometimes with several years missing between them. But after 1353 there is a serious break of eighteen years, and the series is not renewed until 1371; thereafter until 1467 there is a reasonably full sequence, though with a few years' break between many of them. After this the yearly rolls are meagre in quantity, and are for the years 1479–80, 1486–7, 1493–4, 1505–7 and 1513–14 only, which is the end of the survival of the series. The section of the series from 1279 to 1353 has been edited in a fully extended calendar form in English (with Latin terms retained),[1] the later section from 1371 to 1514 was transcribed by Dr D. F. Findlay.[2]

An interesting late medieval record of the fabric chest (*cista fabrica*) exists from 1482 until well into the 16th century.[3] Though it says nothing about the state of the fabric, it contains lists of quantities of lead, timber, boards, stone, wax and plaster in stock every year and also shows that the chest was the repository for monies deposited in coin; and incidentally that the chapter borrowed from it for other purposes, including loans on security to various citizens of Exeter.

From 1514 there is a long gap in the series of fabric accounts proper, though the survival in the Bodleian Library of a fragment of a stray Exeter fabric account from Michaelmas 1548–Michaelmas 1549 indicates that the accounts continued to be kept in the previous roll form of membranes of parchment through the 16th century and have now been lost. In consequence there is a dearth of direct information about Reformation changes in the fabric and fittings of the church. The accounts themselves do not resume until well after the Restoration, by then in volumes, and there is a complete series in this form from 1672 to 1936.[4] But they are not a very informative or helpful source, as payments were in the main to named contractors against their bills without details of the nature of the work performed. However, to supplement them there are two fabric order books, in which estimates are noted and which are therefore much more specific, dated 1812–20 and 1908–29. The great 19th-century reorganisation of all ecclesiastical property, which involved the transfer to the Ecclesiastical Commissioners of the estates of the Exeter chapter by 1862, resulted in a change in the chapter's financial organisation, and produced yearly fabric 'solutions',[5] statements which make a formal summary of receipts and expenditure running from 1862 to 1925.

Numerous documents exist which are subsidiary but directly related to the fabric accounts (though not for the medieval period) but even among these the 16th century remains largely a blank. Much more survives, however, from the Restoration period onward, concerning the bells and organ, including Loosemore's estimate for materials for his new organ in 1665; estimates for the glass of both the east and west windows in the mid-18th century and after, including those of Peckitt of York; James Meffin's account for repaving the choir; another for sanding and repainting the bishop's throne and one for work on Bishop Stapledon's tomb, together with a few general surveyors' accounts of the late 18th century.[6] It is, however, after 1798 that there is a wealth of vouchers[7] supporting the formal accounts, due to a reform in the accounting system introduced about that time which lasted until about 1829. They cover the restoration work carried out under the direction of John Kendall, an Exeter mason and carver of monumental statuary, who was head of a local firm of masons and devoted a great part of his time to work on the cathedral from c. 1805 to 1830. Many details can be gleaned from his estimates and bills, particularly in relation to the restoration of the west front and image screen. At this period, part of the receipts of the capitular timber fund were applied to the fabric, and in supplementation of these vouchers an account book of 1810–31[8] records payments to John Kendall and others for work on his new altar screen, some close improvements, the chapter house, the cloisters, the organ and alterations to monuments. After 1830 the vouchers were not preserved with so much care, though some exist for many years during the 19th century but of much more miscellaneous character.

There are no very exhaustive records from the Scott restoration of 1870–7; a group of accounts[9] are chiefly with Scott's contractors and give little direct information about the work. One original Scott drawing, his projection of his intentions for the choir, and two more original plans signed by him for designs for the choir stalls[10] do remain, but little else. Though there are summary accounts for special restorations after Scott's time, they are equally uninformative. The west front restoration of 1906 and after was funded by a public appeal, and the surviving papers are rather relating to the appeal than the work, and unfortunately casts of mouldings and photographs said to have been made at that time are no longer to be found.

Other fabric sources in the capitular archives

Various other classes of the capitular records contain information, sometimes in much greater detail than that of the fabric accounts themselves, about the fabric and fittings of the cathedral.

The obvious and most important series is that of the Act Books[11] of regular capitular business: the earliest is c. 1379 to 1435, there is then a break until the beginning of the 16th century, another unfortunate loss over the late 16th century, then a series from the beginning of the 17th century without break, except for the Commonwealth period 1646 to 1660, until the present time. These volumes are the prime source for agreements and orders relating to work of various kinds on the cathedral building. An example of outstanding interest is the chapter's agreement with Robert Lyen, alias Glasyer, of April and May 1391[12] about the repair of window glass and his contract to glaze the great east window using both new and ancient glass; this is much fuller information than is to be found in the meagre record in the fabric roll. Two interesting post-medieval examples throw light on the condition of the sanctuary area of the cathedral in the late 1630s. Most of the stone wall of the great 14th-century reredos designed by Thomas of Witney, which had been stripped of its ornament in the Reformation period, was still in place, and in 1638 a contract was made with William Cavell, 'lymner', to paint a new design for an altar screen directly on to this bare stone. The adjoining sedilia, also part of Witney's scheme for the sanctuary area, had been much damaged in the same period, and, as a result of a specific injunction received from Archbishop Laud in 1639, following his metropolitical visitation, the chapter immediately ordered its repair. It is referred to as 'the monument of King Edward the Confessor' which 'shall with all convenient speed be repaired by Peeke and Pope, and each of them shall have x.s. a week for their work.'.[13]

An increased amount of information about the chapter's audit procedure is to be found in the 18th-century Chapter Acts, and after an order made in January 1754/5 laid down that no bills were to be paid for any work done without order of chapter,[14] fuller details of work ordered and bills to be paid were entered into the Acts. These often supplement the bare entries in the volumes of fabric accounts, particularly in the period of Dean Jeremiah Milles's campaign of 'Improvements' to the cathedral and its furnishings between 1762 and 1784. Supplementary to the summaries of accounts at audit included in the Chapter Acts yearly from the early 19th century onwards is a series of Surveyors' Reports prepared for presentation to the audit which run in a very full though not entirely complete series from 1817 to 1948, a record continually indicating the preoccupation with the recurring problems of the north and south towers and the west front and image screen. Included with these are a few reports by eminent architects invited by the chapter from time to time to give advice. Gilbert Scott made one in 1869 concerning the whole cathedral building, with emphasis on the south tower, though later reports from such experts as G. F. Bodley and John Pearson are specifically related to particular problems such as the west front. A report on the condition of the timber roof of the cathedral made by Sir Francis Fox in 1923 which found the whole roof to be slipping was followed by a complete roof-strengthening operation in 1923 and 1924, the engineers' plans for which survive complete.[15]

Other medieval sources include some charters of the late 13th century which throw light on the state of progress of the building of the extreme eastern chapels and Lady Chapel.[16] There is also a considerable quantity of medieval accounts of various funds subsidiary to the common fund of the cathedral, and miscellaneous information relating to the fabric can be found in some of these. For example, the accounts of payments for obit celebrations,[17] which run from the beginning of the 14th century, include some details of the payments made by canons of their contributions to the new fabric and decisions made by the chapter about the organisation of the fabric fund. Similarly the accounts called 'debt rolls' (rotuli debitorum),[18] which record arrears of payments due at the Michaelmas audit, sometimes mention incidentally items which do not necessarily appear in the fabric accounts, such as payments for new organs in 1430–1,[19] and in 1434–5 a new 'entreclos', money for repairing the ornaments of the church, and new desks for the Lady Chapel.[20]

It is only during the Commonwealth period that major references to the state of the cathedral building are to be found elsewhere than in the church's own records. No records were kept between 1646 and 1660, and it is in the city records of the mayor and commonalty of Exeter[21] that there is information about making the wall at the crossing which divided the church into two separate meeting houses (one for Presbyterians, one for Independents), the sale of the cloisters, the melting down of the organ pipes and similar matters. At the Restoration, cathedral fabric accounts as such were not kept immediately, and detailed entries for taking down the wall and the restoration of the cathedral to its proper uses are noted for several years in what are called 'extraordinary payments' accounts[22] (extraordinary, that is, in the sense that the payments were not regular quarterly or annual ones), before specific fabric books were begun in 1672. In the later 17th century, repercussions of what was done during the Commonwealth were still apparent, resulting in arguments about the building being raised during Bishop Lamplugh's visitation in 1676.[23] Doors had been made in the cathedral during the 'time of the late Troubles', some of which had been filled in again; but there was particular discussion of a north-east door, which the Treasurer in particular wished to be preserved (chiefly because his residence was built up against the wall of the cathedral just outside it, so it saved his legs a good deal) on the grounds that 'it was not indecent in itself nor prejudicial to anyone'.

More careful attention began to be paid to the organisation of the cathedral's accounts from the late 17th century, so there are far fewer possibilities of finding information about the fabric and furnishings in the more general capitular archives from then on. It is in newspaper reports that details not to be found elsewhere are often noted in the 19th and early 20th centuries, as for instance in the account of the re-opening of the building after Scott's restoration of 1870–7, or about the Temple Memorial west window at the beginning of the 20th century, when there was some controversy about the removal of the Peckitt glass.[24]

Modern records

This brief general review has aimed to provide a conspectus of the scope of the capitular records relating to the cathedral fabric roughly up to the beginning of the last war, before the bomb damage of 1945. Little or no attempt has been made to refer to record sources elsewhere, to the survival of photographs or to published works on the cathedral. It may therefore for completeness be mentioned that there is a collection of prints of the cathedral in the Cathedral Library, and though it cannot claim to be entirely comprehensive it of course includes John Carter's great survey published by the Society of Antiquaries in 1797. And an attempt is being made to collect a file of record photographs, the earliest of which go back to the late 1860s. Besides the relevant entries in the chapter minute books, the post-war record is largely in the office of the cathedral surveyor. But the extensive and accumulating records of recent and progressing conservation programmes, including reports, surveys, plans, photographs and conservators' records, are being compiled and assembled by the Exeter Museums Archaeological Field Unit, for eventual deposit with the capitular archives.

THE CONTENT OF THE MEDIEVAL ACCOUNTS

The accounts of the warden (*custos*) of the fabric fund of Exeter Cathedral during the Middle Ages[25] are drawn up in the normal medieval form of charge and discharge, first the receipts then the expenditure for the year from Michaelmas, a balance made and submitted to audit. The warden accounted for the purchase of materials, the payments of salaries to successive master masons and other fees which might arise, the wages of craftsmen (by name) and labourers, the cost of transportation of materials, the care of tools, the provision of scaffolding, and all the other requirements of a building operation. The accounts, on rolls of membranes sewn head to tail, are written in highly abbreviated Latin, though using numerous French and English terms, in varying degrees of legibility. The obvious fact which must always be borne in mind is that the warden did not aim to provide any description of the building, the accounts were compiled for audit by contemporaries who understood their conventions, and his aim was to keep track of his complicated wages bill and also to put down sufficient detail in his accounts to indicate work in progress and the cost of materials in order to get his sums right. In fact, the modern historian of the medieval building and its furnishings is entirely in the hands of an individual warden in the manner in which he dealt with details. These wardens were not professional accountants — they were normally recruited from among the vicars choral or chantry priests of the establishment. They lacked formularies to aid them in accounting practice such as a manorial bailiff would have to guide him, so within the charge/discharge framework they drew on their own experience. Such medieval building accounts which generally survive differ considerably in layout, detail and terminology from one church to another, and within this single Exeter series they differ also from one period to another in vocabulary and layout, quite apart from the differences from time to time of the nature of the work performed. Moreover, the preoccupations of the accountants are with the details which gave them the most trouble; for instance, up to 1330 (after which most stone was acquired direct from contractors at the local quarries), there is almost more about transport, the repair of carts and oats for the horses than there is about the actual process of building. The application of the fabric fund was also within closely defined limits: nothing will be found in the accounts about the deanery house, the Bishop's Palace or the residentiaries' houses (with the sole exception of the building of a house for the Treasurer[26]), though there are references to the chapter house, the water supply of the close, and all the buildings and sheds needed as workshops, storage and the residence of the workforce. There are few or no references, either, to the making of tombs and monuments, since these were normally paid for by executors, and it was not the practice to take these payments into the receipts of the fund and so enter their expenditure under the outgoings.

The fabric accounts survive as a very much broken series, and to account for some of the gaps it has been suggested that no accounts were kept for some years because no work was in hand. The evidence of the accounts themselves does not, however, support this view. They are the records of a fund which had always some receipts, however small, to be shown, and arrears brought forward from a previous year are to be found at the head of the next extant following account after a break. The only period in the whole history of the fund when it can be stated with certainty that no specific fabric accounts were kept is 1646 to 1672, first because of the dissolution of the chapter during the Commonwealth and then in the immediate post-Restoration period, which was one of vigorous reorganisation both of the finances and of the building of the cathedral during which all available resources were applied to immediate necessities. In the medieval period it is *before* the Black Death period that a few years are missing and, though meagre, they were kept continuously from January 1347 to 1353. In the earlier 14th century, the lack of any entries which can be interpreted as referring to the minstrels' gallery must mean that this was constructed during one of the gaps in the records which consequently provide no reliable guide to its date. Even more tantalising is the lack of any entries which can be interpreted as referring to the lower range of the west front image screen. Theories have been put forward that separate yearly accounts may have been kept for this particular major work which have been lost. It is true that there is a precedent for this, as separate accounts were kept over 1316–22 for what is called 'the tabulature of the high altar', but these are not self-contained with their own receipts section, they are subsidiary to the usual fabric accounts of the relevant years which transfer funding to them.[27] So some trace of special accounts for the image wall would surely appear somewhere if they ever existed, and documentary evidence arguing from the lack of entries would appear to point to the beginning of its construction to have been during the general gap in the records after 1353.

THE INTERPRETATION OF THE MEDIEVAL ACCOUNTS

Since the mid-18th century, when Dr Charles Lyttelton, then dean of Exeter, gave a valuable account of the sequence of building of the cathedral,[28] the medieval fabric accounts have been a quarry for various writers giving an account of the building. Dr George Oliver[29] published some abstracts from them in 1861 and these have been widely used as source material ever since. However, the use of abstracts can be dangerous, and although admittedly the accounts themselves are far from solving all problems, deductions about the full significance of particular entries which are not themselves completely specific must take all possible aspects of their context into consideration if any reasonable degree of authority is to be accorded to the documentation. So a few examples drawn from the earliest range of records, those of the main building period 1279 to 1353, here follow to illustrate the importance of context.

The bishops and funding

The bishops of Exeter from Bronescombe to Grandisson are popularly credited with being great 'building bishops' responsible for the extension and reconstruction of the cathedral between c. 1270 and 1360. It is of course a historical commonplace which hardly needs comment that the responsibility of diocesans, whatever their largely unrecorded opinions on architecture, was to the funding rather than the design of building works, which was the province of the directing architect, while the administration of the actual fund was the responsibility of the dean and chapter.[30] Even so, a superficial reading of the receipts sections (many of which are defective) of the accounts of the period credits Bishop Walter Stapledon with surpassing munificence from his personal fortune towards the building programme. Vastly generous though he was, he only equalled the generosity of his immediate predecessor Bishop Thomas Bitton. Bitton is shown to have contributed £124 18s. 8d. yearly to the fabric fund, exactly twice the total contribution made by the dean and canons (undoubtedly a specific though unrecorded arrangement with them). Stapledon continued this contribution at the same figure until 1326, and in 1310 acknowledged the generosity of his predecessor by appropriating the church of Westleigh to the support of the hospital of Clyst Gabriel particularly to honour the memory of Bishop Thomas *pro immensis subsidiis fabrice ecclesie nostre* which he had made in his lifetime.[31] In 1326 Bishop Walter discontinued the yearly grant, clearly because the choir and presbytery were then complete and ready for the dedication of the high altar, substituting a lump sum gift of 1,000 marks; this was indeed very generous, but he could not have forseen his own death at this juncture, so presumably he did not intend any further yearly contributions. From these general considerations if follows that it is inaccurate to credit Bishop Stapledon with specific personal responsibility for any particular furnishing and the standard reference to 'Stapledon's reredos' for instance, is inaccurate, for though there are separate accounts for its construction these were kept only for convenience and not on account of separate funding for the project.

The cathedral craftsmen

Some unsupported supposition has entered into the postulation of an Exeter school of stone-carvers, based on general stylistic rather than documentary evidence, but it is in fact very difficult to connect particular work with particular men, in spite of the pay lists of craftsmen by name. A study of stone-carving in the cathedral[32] suggests that changes in the style of corbels and roof-bosses in the cathedral 'can only mark the arrival of a new master mason in the Exeter workshop' and that 'the leading mason during this phase seems to have been a man named William from Montacute in Somerset'. Later it is remarked that William of Montacute remained a leading figure among the sculptors, though displaced by a certain Richard Digon in 1313. However, the relevant entries in the accounts between 1301 and 1313 show a different picture: William of Montacute certainly does appear as an experienced mason, at the highest rate of pay, for three weeks in Michaelmas term 1301; four weeks in Christmas term and seven weeks in Midsummer term 1303, and one week in Michaelmas term 1312; he is mentioned as performing task work in one term of 1312, carving at least one great corbel and one great boss, but at no other time. Richard Digon, described as a stone-carver, carved two large bosses at task in the Easter term 1312, and the wages list of that year show that he worked for eight weeks in the Easter term and the whole of the Midsummer term, but does not appear in the record at any other time before or after 1312–13.[33] This example illustrates the fact that while the sequence of master masons, the architects in charge, are known with certainty, not enough is known in sufficient detail to be able to discuss specifically the achievements of other individuals or 'schools'. Howard Colvin summarised the situation when saying (after remarking on the sequence of master masons) 'among their subordinates there is much less certainty — the accounts lend no support for the idea recently adduced about Chartres (at an earlier period) that medieval masons were organised into self-contained teams which moved *en bloc* from one job to another like a swarm of bees'.[34]

The New Work of 1353

In the final section of the last account surviving before the very unfortunate break in the records of eighteen years, there is a heading dated May 1353, 'The beginning of the New Work of the church of the blessed Peter before the Great Cross', and there follows a record of nineteen weeks of work, involving timber, stone, centerings, and a little scaffolding, costing in labour and materials about £20. These entries have frequently been interpreted as indicating the commencement of the roof vaulting of the nave. If this is true it is a highly significant section for dating the whole work of the nave, but if its full context is taken into consideration this interpretation can be shown to be to a very high degree unlikely.[35]

First, the term 'New Work' as applied to an integral part of the building is anachronistic even after 1310, when the fabric of the eastern extension, that is the rebuilding of the presbytery and choir was completed; in that year the chapter decided that two fabric funds, one for new fabric and one for old fabric, were unnecessary and there was to be in future one fund and one Work. From 1310 to 1326 the main endeavour was directed under the direction of Thomas of Witney to the elaborate furnishing of this part of the building, and the term New Work disappears from the headings of the accounts. The dedication of the high altar in 1328 was the final acknowledgement of the completion of the New Work.

Secondly, the situation in the period from 1326 to 1342, the date of the last appearance of Thomas of Witney as master mason in the records, was entirely favourable to the completion of the nave under his direction. Bishop Stapledon had donated 1,000 marks in 1326, and Thomas of Witney invested much of this large sum in stockpiling a great store of materials, particularly stone, for the nave work, and in 1331 a considerable stock of timber was donated by Bishop Grandisson from his Chudleigh estate. Receipts were reasonably high during this period, varying between £175 and £125 a year, so there was money to pay labour, plenty of materials and the master mason available, though perhaps only on a visiting basis, to direct. Moreover, there was no need to build outer walls, as the existing walls were retained up to window level, and by 1334 the great Corfe marble columns of the nave were in position. Although there is a break in the surviving records from 1335 to 1339, there is no reason to suppose any deficiency of funding during that interval, for in 1340, the next surviving account, receipts were £198, and in 1342, Thomas of Witney's last recorded year of office, receipts were still £135.

Finally, after another short break in the accounts until late 1346, if the series of accounts 1346–53 are reviewed, it is clear that even before the effects of the Black Death could have been very marked, only restricted works on a small scale were in hand: in 1346–7, receipts were £47 and work was on the porches; in 1346 the chapter had made an agreement with the mayor and commonalty about water supplies, and pipe-laying was the major preoccupation of the next few years, which could be carried out by unskilled labour at a time when the mortality had affected the supply of skilled craftsmen. By 1352–3 there was no resident master mason — Richard Farleigh received a consultant's fee of 20s. and was present for only a week and a half; the term 'New Work' is in this very account also applied to a small job of making benches for the choir, and there is no sign whatever of resources of money, labour or materials for any major project even if it was to continue into 1354 and after, when we have no accounts to testify. Though it would be rash to hazard a suggestion of what the 'New Work' of 1353 was, the background evidence, although negative, lends great cumulative weight to the rejection of the identification of it as being the nave roof-vault. All indications combine to support the conviction that Master Thomas of Witney was the architect of the whole nave as well as having completed the choir and its furnishings in Exeter Cathedral while he was master mason there.

REFERENCES

1. D&C Exeter 2600–2635, fabric accounts, 1279–1353, for a full edition of which see Erskine (1981) and (1983).
2. D&C Exeter 2636–2704 /1–11, fabric accounts, 1371–1514, an edition of which was presented as a PhD thesis by D.F. Findlay to the University of Leeds in 1939. A photocopy of the text (but not of the introduction) is available in Exeter Cathedral Library.
3. D&C Exeter 3680, 1482–1549.
4. D&C Exeter 3776/1–13, of which 3776/4 and 8 are Fabric Order Books.
5. D&C Exeter 7000, a group in date order.
6. D&C Exeter 4671–4678 (bells, 1582–1726); 4683–4693 (organ, 1664–1819); 4662–4670 (windows, 1761–7); 4695 (throne, c.1763); 4707 (monuments, undated); 4710/1, 2 (paving, 1762); 4712/1–20 (reports by Arthur Bradley, surveyor, 1745–53).
7. D&C Exeter 7001, a large group of bundles of vouchers and miscellanea in (broken) date order from the late 18th century to 1906.
8. D&C Exeter 7081.
9. D&C Exeter 7170/51/1–6.
10. D&C Exeter Plans 1/1.
11. D&C Exeter 3550–95/1–6, 3596/1–12, 3597/1–8 (and continuing), Chapter Acts and Chapter Minutes, 1383–20th century to date. From 1660, the series is unbroken and in strict date order.

12. D&C Exeter 3550, f. 70. See Chris Brooks and David Evans (1988), Appendix I, for a full transcription.
13. D&C Exeter 3557, 112–13 and 155–6. For a fuller account of the painted altar screen, which was paid for by Archdeacon William Helyar, see Audrey Erskine (1988), 57–8. Archbishop Laud's orders, which also enjoined further expenditure on the fabric, were received by the chapter on 20 June 1639, ibid., 59.
14. D&C Exeter 3569, 36.
15. D&C Exeter 7003, Surveyor's Reports, a (broken) series in date order; D&C Exeter Plans 4/1, plans by Archibald Dawney, constructional engineer, 1923.
16. Erskine (1983), 317–22.
17. D&C Exeter 3673–772.
18. D&C Exeter 2705–66, a (broken) series of rolls of accounts, 1332–1509.
19. D&C Exeter 2731.
20. D&C Exeter 2735.
21. The archives of the city of Exeter are preserved in the Devon Record Office. Relevant extracts from the City Chamber Acts etc. are quoted in William Cotton and Henry Woollcombe, *Gleanings from the Municipal and Cathedral Records relevant to the History of the City of Exeter* (Exeter, 1877), 141–84.
22. D&C Exeter 3787 and 3788.
23. D&C Exeter 3691, Visitation Book, and 4724–5, related groups of correspondence.
24. Files of newspaper cuttings are preserved in the Cathedral Archives.
25. The section which follows is based on Erskine (1981), xiv–xvi, and Erskine (1983), ix–xviii.
26. D&C Exeter 2661, fabric account for 1402–3.
27. Erskine (1981), 87–145.
28. Charles Lyttelton (1797).
29. George Oliver (1861), 379–91. See Erskine (1981), xvi–xvii and Erskine (1983), xxv, for a fuller account of the use of the fabric accounts by previous writers.
30. See Erskine (1983), ix–xiii, on the funding of the work.
31. D&C Exeter 1932.
32. Michael Swanton (1979), 19, 22.
33. For entries in the accounts relating to William of Montacute, see Erskine (1981), 63, 177, 178, 180, 191; and to Richard Digon, ibid., 67, 192, 193.
34. *Journal of the Society of Archivists*, vol. 7 no. 6 (October 1984), 390.
35. The discussion of the nave vault which follows is an amplification of Erskine (1983), xxxv–xxxvi.

A Note on the Building Stones of the Cathedral

By John Allan

The geology of Devon is amongst the most complex and varied in Britain,[1] offering medieval masons a remarkable range of building stones.[2] The cathedral displays only a restricted selection of the types of stone visible in the country's other medieval buildings; the slates, sandstones, shales and limestones of the South Hams and central and west Devon, for example, were almost entirely eschewed. Nevertheless more than a dozen stone types were used in the medieval structure (Exeter Volcanic, Permian and Triassic sandstone, Salcombe, Beer, Portland, Purbeck marble, grey lias, Ham Hill, Caen, ?Quarr, Heavitree breccia, south Devon slate) drawn from fourteen documented[3] and at least four undocumented[4] quarries (Fig. 1). Post-medieval improvements in transport, particularly the arrival of the railways, allowed the use of stone from more distant quarries: Bath (Avon),[5] Doulting (Somerset),[6] Ketton (Northamptonshire),[7] Weldon (Northamptonshire),[9] Lepine (Marne, France),[9] and St Maximin (Oise, France),[10] bringing the total to about 20 stone types from at least 26 different quarries. Only the medieval stones will be discussed here.

The Exeter Volcanic series

In the Exe Valley and the area to the north-west of the city lies a series of isolated outcrops of volcanic lava of Permian date,[11] known locally as *trap*. One such outcrop, at Rougemont on the edge of the walled city, is believed to have been the principal source of volcanic stone used in the Roman and early medieval city,[12] although this quarry receives no mention in the fabric rolls. Other quarries are known at Dunchideock, Westown, Budlake, Spencecombe, Heazille Farm (near Rewe), Poltimore, Killerton, Posbury, Knowle, Pocombe, Silverton and Thorverton (Fig. 1). In each of these quarries the stone varies considerably, as surviving faces show. In a single quarry the colour may vary from light grey to dark purple, the texture from very vesicular to hardly vesicular, in some places with pronounced veins of quartz or calcite.[13] The vesicular trap can be dressed as a freestone, and was commonly used for ashlar in medieval buildings in the Exe Valley, although its texture is too coarse for intricate carving. This was commonly regarded as the best-wearing kind of this building stone, being least prone to spalling.[14] A few blocks of this sort will be seen in the exterior of both the Romanesque church[15] and the 14th-century fabric[16] but its principal use was in filling the webs of the vault,[17] particularly in the nave. The fabric rolls record the purchase of large quantities of stone from Silverton between 1301–2 and 1350;[18] several references specify that this was used for the vault[19] where the lightness of the vesicular stone would have been an advantage. When only moderately veined, trap could also be dressed for ashlar and was employed, for example, on the internal face of the south-west staircase of the nave. Being hard-wearing, it was used for stair treads, replacing the use of the less robust Salcombe stone seen in the Norman stairs of the transeptal towers. Some volcanic blocks which served this purpose are of impressive size – up to 0.28 × 0.95 × 0.30 m. By contrast veined volcanic stone cannot easily be dressed, but, being readily available locally, was used to fill wall cores. The fabric rolls provide continual references to the carriage of stone from Barley, the hill on the opposite side of the Exe, where such stone was dug from at least two large quarries, one near modern Barley House, the other nearby at Pocombe. The latter was until the last century well-known locally for a very hard trap with prominent and irregular quartz veins, but that was not the only type quarried: some was slightly vesicular.[20] Between 1299

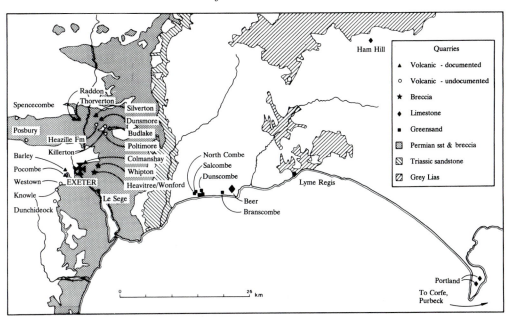

FIG. 1.   Sources of building stone at the cathedral

and 1325–6 the fabric rolls record the purchase of nearly 12,000 loads of stone from Barley, over 2,000 loads being supplied in some years (1301–2, 1306–7, 1325–6).[21] Strikingly, references to Barley almost cease after 1325–6, perhaps in part because a great store of this stone had been accumulated, in part because the re-used Romanesque fabric provided much of the stone for wall cores in Grandisson's nave. The other documented volcanic stone quarries are Raddon, which supplied 2,071 feet of stone whose total cost was £12 11s. 0d. in 1394–5,[22] and Colmanshay, a minor quarry whose site has been located in the Longbrook Valley, Exeter,[23] and which provided 350 loads of stone between 1341 and 1347.[24] It has been suggested that these loads were used in the spandrels above the nave vaults,[25] but the identification is doubtful.

Permian and Triassic sandstone

In the Exe Valley and at various points along the coast from the Exe estuary eastward to Budleigh and Salcombe are outcrops of red, pink or white Triassic and Permian sandstone. Both white and pink bands are sometimes seen on a single block, so they evidently had a common source. This stone was used in 11th- and 12th-century buildings in Exeter.[26] Blocks of a distinctive hard, crystalline red sandstone of this type can be seen beside the robbed responds of the nave aisles and in the west external face of the south tower. Although these have long been noted by earlier commentators, the quite widespread use of Permo-Triassic sandstone elsewhere in the cathedral seems to have escaped attention. A scatter of white sandstone blocks, which at a casual glance might be mistaken for weathered Salcombe stone, can be seen in the blind arcading of the north tower (Fig. 2, level B) and in the internal wall face of the same tower (Fig. 2, level B). Isolated blocks of both white and pink sandstone of this type have been noted during recent repairs to the south tower. It is less

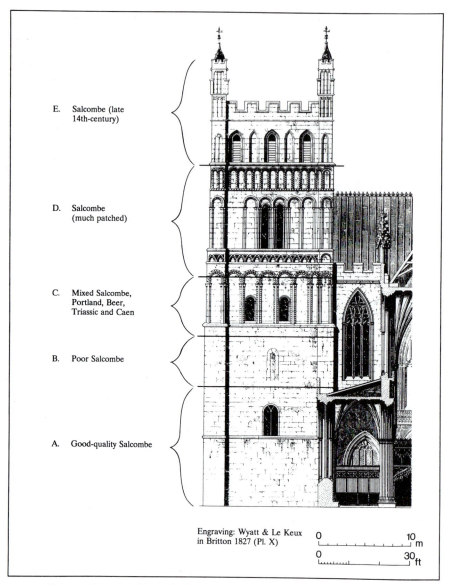

E. Salcombe (late
    14th-century)

D. Salcombe
    (much patched)

C. Mixed Salcombe,
    Portland, Beer,
    Triassic and Caen

B. Poor Salcombe

A. Good-quality Salcombe

Engraving: Wyatt & Le Keux
in Britton 1827 (Pl. X)

FIG. 2.   Exeter Cathedral, the geological succession in the north tower

common in the Decorated building but was used, for example, in some of the plain walling of the spandrels above the nave vaults.

Salcombe stone

The facework of the cathedral consists predominantly of Salcombe stone, a coarse sandstone of the Upper Greensand varying in colour from pale green to yellow and dark orange. It also varies both in durability (the green stone being the hardest) and in texture. On the coastal area around Salcombe several quarries exploited this stone; abandoned workings are to be seen at North Combe, South Down, Dunscombe and Branscombe. The best building stone was said to be that found on the hillsides about half a mile inland; carriage from the quarries to the beach must have been a difficult business, since the descent is very steep. Hope[27] calculated that on average quarrying of Salcombe stone cost 2d. per ton, transport from the quarry to the beach another 3d., sea transport to the quay at Topsham a further 2d., but road haulage from Topsham to Exeter a further 9d. North Combe was the largest quarry, working the hard green beds; it has long been abandoned. South Down was re-opened in the 1850s, when the quality of its stone was said to be below average.[28] One quarry at Dunscombe was worked briefly in the 1930s, when stone was still removed by pick and bar and wedge.[29] A second Dunscombe quarry was re-opened in 1979 to provide ashlar for the cathedral's south tower.[30] When the old quarry face was cleared, rows of pick-marks, presumably of medieval date, were visible. Here a total depth of between 5 m and 6 m of stone was quarried, in eight beds varying in depth from c. 0.35 m to c. 0.95 m. The best was at the bottom.[31] Salcombe stone is virtually the only freestone in the fabric of the early Romanesque church, which consistently used the hard-wearing varieties, now weathered to light grey or grey-green. In the north tower this material was succeeded by the extensive use of Salcombe stone of considerably poorer quality (Fig. 2, level B), more orange in colour and crumbly and shelly in texture. Material of this sort was recently quarried at Dunscombe: it required considerable care during quarrying to avoid splitting. In the upper portions of the north tower and the south tower this poorer stone is less evident. It was, however, used once again in Grandisson's time: massive blocks of this sort, up to 0.6 m deep and over 1.2 m in length, can be seen on the upper storey of the north porch, the northern nave buttresses and St Edmund's chapel (Pl. XXIIIA, B). Salcombe stone is to be seen throughout the Decorated church; with the growing use of Beer stone, its popularity waned after the mid-14th century but it was used extensively in the reconstruction of the upper storey of the north tower in the 1390s.

Despite its popularity at the cathedral (no doubt brought about by the fact that Salcombe was an episcopal manor), Salcombe stone seems not to have been widely used elsewhere. The local churches of Sidbury, Sidmouth and Salcombe employed it, and so did some buildings in the Exeter area,[32] but it was evidently much less popular than Beer stone.[33] One reason for this may have been the considerable depth of overburden: layers of flint and clay, often 7 m in thickness, overlie the beds. Once this is removed, the top bed encountered in some quarries, known locally as 'curly stone', is hard and full of fossils, and cannot be cut with a saw. Only after the removal of that layer can quarrying begin.

Beer stone

Beer stone is a chalk, pale grey when damp, white when dry. Unlike Salcombe stone, it was quarried principally in a single underground shaft. Writing in the 1830s, de la Beche[34] described the quarry as extending 180 yards into the hillside, with eight workable beds, varying in hardness from soft to very hard, most of them between 16 and 24 in. (0.41 m–0.61 m) in thickness. A total depth of about 12 ft (3.6 m) of stone was then worked. Within living memory a total depth of about 13 ft (4 m) of stone was quarried, the widest bed being about 4 ft (1.3 m) thick; four-foot cubes of stone, each weighing about four tons, were commonly extracted. The largest blocks then removed weighed over twenty tons. These were cut with a saw, contrasting with the earlier extraction of stone by pick. Although Beer stone is sometimes seen in 12th-century work in Devon,[35] it was hardly used in the

Romanesque cathedral.[36] It was employed in the earliest stages of the reconstruction of the east end of the church (e.g. for bases, corbels and mouldings in the Lady Chapel) but to a lesser extent than Caen or Salcombe stone. Small quantities were used in the structure of the presbytery and choir (e.g. for window tracery in the clerestory). Its ease of carving and fine texture made Beer stone the obvious medium for elaborate carving, so the sedilia, pulpitum and altar screen[37] were worked almost entirely in this stone. In the course of the early 14th century Beer stone played an increasingly important role at the cathedral, particularly with the reconstruction of the nave, as both the structure and the fabric rolls indicate (Fig. 3). The first reference to Beer stone in the fabric rolls is in 1316–17;[38] Hope calculated that they record the use of a total of 2,020 tons of this stone at the cathedral in the years before 1342.[39] With the reconstruction of the nave this material played an increasingly important role, being used for all bosses, all ribs, most arch mouldings and nearly all window tracery.

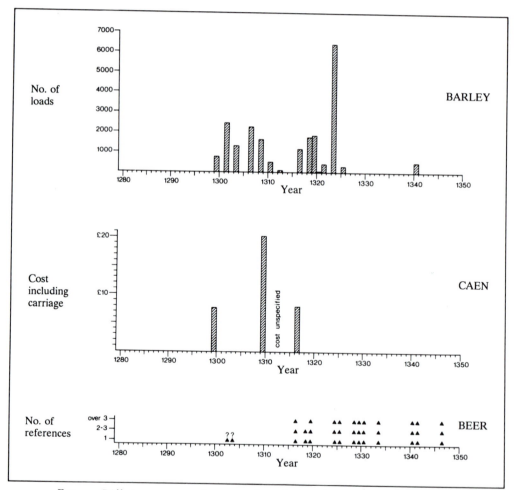

FIG. 3.   Differing patterns of consumption of selected building stones, recorded in the cathedral fabric rolls (Source: Erskine (1981); (1983))

The image screen of the west front consists entirely of Beer stone, and all the 15th-century tracery of the cathedral and chapter house is also in this material. By this time Beer stone had become by far the most popular freestone used in Devon.

Heavitree stone

A few kilometres to the east of the medieval city and now engulfed in its modern suburbs in the areas of Whipton, Wonford and Heavitree were quarries exploiting the coarse red breccia of Permian date known locally as Heavitree stone. Characteristically it consists of a red sandstone matrix in which are angular inclusions of volcanic trap, chert and quartz porphyry, sometimes interleaved with fairly pure red sandstone. The beds are *c.* 0.3–1.0 m thick at Wonford, but at Heavitree beds of 2–2.6 m are recorded.[40] This stone is not suitable for sculpture but can be quarried in large blocks. It is not found in the fabric of the Romanesque or Decorated cathedral and seems to have come into use in the mid-14th century. The earliest evidence for its use is the purchase of small quantities of stone from Wonford in 1340–1,[41] followed by its use in repairs to the city wall at Eastgate in 1347.[42] By the end of the 14th century the quarries were clearly being worked on a large scale. The cathedral used a total of some 3,942 horseloads of stone from Whipton in 1393/5, principally if not entirely for the reconstruction of the belfry tier of the north tower, whose inner faces and staircase are entirely of this stone.[43] In that work the Heavitree stone was concealed behind facework of Salcombe stone. However it was employed for the exterior of the heightened walls of the chapter house in the reconstruction programme following the fire in 1413. Heavitree stone became the predominant building stone of the Exeter area in the 15th and 16th centuries, surviving in use until at least the mid-19th century. Lysons' description of the Heavitree quarry in 1809[44] records that by that time it was a quarter of a mile in extent and 90 to 100 ft (27–30 m) in depth, the principal bed being 6 to 8 ft (1.8–2.4 m) in thickness. The stone is variable in quality, the best being a durable conglomerate, the worst a crumbly sandstone. Most beds are, however, prone to quite rapid weathering.

Purbeck marble

The use of the fossil-rich green-brown Jurassic limestone of Purbeck has received much attention,[45] and will be mentioned only briefly here. Its earliest use was for the mid- to late 12th-century bishops' tombs. In the Decorated cathedral it was used for all piers, the capitals and bases of the piers and triforia, and for many attached shafts. At least one altar slab was subsequently purchased.[46] The fabric rolls indicate that finished articles were normally purchased; by contrast most other quarries were supplying unworked stone. Much of this stone used at Exeter has a characteristic greenish colour. Gilbert Scott made extensive repairs to the cathedral's Purbeck marble in 1870–7, using a stone of a greyer hue than the medieval work.

Portland stone

The fabric rolls record the use of the hard, white and rather shelly Jurassic oolite of Portland in only a single year (1303–4), when a bargeload of Portland stone was imported, followed by eighteen great stones for bosses and sixty-one capitals and bases.[47] The use of this material in the medieval cathedral was, however, far more widespread than the documentary evidence indicates. In the Romanesque church it first appears in the middle stages of the north tower, datable to the mid-12th century (Fig. 2, level C).[48] In the Decorated church there are a few isolated blocks of Portland stone throughout the eastern portions of the church (e.g. in the stair turret of the chapel of St John the Evangelist). It is occasionally seen in the plain walling of the presbytery, choir and crossing but was used more extensively in the nave. Quite large quantities of this stone are visible in the north porch, the upper portions of St Edmund's chapel and the west front (Allan and Blaylock below, Pl. A). In the restoration of the cathedral it was in regular use at least from the beginning of the 19th century;[49] it was widely recognised as being 'very superior for exposed positions ...'.[50] It was, however, more expensive than Beer stone. For example in 1813 it cost 10s. 6d. per foot compared with 8s. for freestone; the latter presumably came from Beer.[51]

Minor south-western sources

The soft *blue-grey lias* of the sort used at Glastonbury and Wells, which could be quarried on the border of Devon and Dorset around Lyme Regis, was used only once at Exeter: the capitals and shafts of the early 13th-century chapter house were of this material.

The golden-brown shelly Jurassic limestone of *Ham Hill* was likewise rarely used in south Devon[52] and, given the long and hilly journey from the Somerset quarry, it is perhaps surprising that this stone was employed at all. The oft-quoted records of its employment for the altar steps, four bosses and an unspecified purpose in 1301–2[53] could account for all the known usages of this stone at the cathedral. The plinth formerly supporting the Bishop's Throne was of this material[54] and there is an odd isolated block in the triforium of the north choir wall, but it has not been noted elsewhere.

The *dark grey slate* of the South Hams, much used as roofing slate in medieval Exeter, was quite commonly employed to level courses of ashlar or pack vertically between blocks. Thin slabs can be seen, for example, on the upper portions of the south tower. They provide some of the earliest instances of the use of this material.

On the external face of the east wall of the chapels of St Catherine and St Andrew is to be seen a very shelly grey limestone; to the writer's knowledge it is the only instance of the use of this stone at Exeter. This may be *Quarr stone*.

Caen stone

The fine-grained cream or pinkish-coloured limestone of Caen (Normandy) was far less commonly used in the south-west than the south-east of England, and examples of its employment in Devon are not common. It is absent from the primary Romanesque fabric, first making its appearance in the middle stage of the north tower (Fig. 2, stage C). There are also a few blocks in the middle and upper stages of the south tower, probably datable to *c.*1150–80. Prolific use of Caen stone is characteristic of the earliest fabric of the reconstruction of the eastern limb of the cathedral. In the chapels of St Andrew and St Catherine it was employed extensively for plain walling (for example in the west wall and around the altars) for shafts, arch mouldings and probably for much of the infilling of the vault. The use of Caen stone extends into the adjacent choir aisle to the east, possibly indicating the extent of work carried on contemporaneously with the chapels. Much of this stone is also to be seen in the Lady Chapel, for example, in the lower parts of the north wall and the piers between the Lady Chapel and the chapel of St John the Evangelist. There is a scatter in the presbytery, choir and tower crossing; it was used, for example, for some of the corbels supporting the galleries in the towers, for some choir bosses, and for some bosses, ribs and webs of the transeptal vaults. However, by the time the construction of the nave was in hand Caen stone supplies evidently dwindled with the flood of Beer stone shipments (cf. Fig. 3). It is not to be found in the nave vault, although a scatter of Caen blocks is to be seen in the west front and St Edmund's chapel (Allan and Blaylock below, Pl. A).

ACKNOWLEDGEMENTS

I am particularly indebted to Peter Dare, former Chief Mason of the cathedral, for sharing over a number of years his remarkable practical knowledge of the cathedral's building stones. His intimacy with them is such that he can distinguish stones not only by their colour and texture, but, for example, by their smell when being dressed, or the taste of their stone dust. I also wish to thank my colleagues Stuart Blaylock of Exeter Museums Archaeological Field for much useful discussion, Piran Bishop for drawing Figs 1–3, and Pam Wakeham for preparing the typescript.

REFERENCES

1. For a concise summary see Durrance and Laming (1982), with full bibliography.
2. For recent discussions see Clifton-Taylor (1989); Beacham (1990).
3. Barley, Beer, Branscombe, Caen, Colmanshay, Ham Hill, Portland, Purbeck, Raddon, Thorverton, Salcombe, Silverton, Whipton, Wonford.
4. The sources of grey lias, Triassic sandstone, ?Quarr stone and south Devon slate.
5. Bath stone was used from the 1830s, for example on the west front (Allan and Blaylock below). Scott used it in the 1870s, for example in his new staircase to the pulpitum. Bath stone from Combe Hill Quarry was used in the reconstruction of St James' chapel after the bomb damage of 1942, from Monks Park Quarry in the flying buttresses on the south side of the nave in 1968, and from Box in the north nave aisle in 1972 (Hope (n.d.), 24/1–2).
6. For the use of a particularly coarse variety of this stone on the west front see Allan and Blaylock below. It was also used on the external face of the east window and in the replacement of many choir and nave finials of c. 1895–1914.
7. Ketton stone was used after c. 1906 on the west front (Allan and Blaylock below). Extensive repairs to the south tower were also in this stone.
8. Weldon stone was used on the exterior of St James' chapel after 1942 (Hope (n.d.), 38/1). It may also be identifiable in repairs to the south tower.
9. Some Lapine stone, acquired via Chichester Cathedral, was employed in the corbel table above the great west window in 1972 (Gundry (1972)).
10. Stone from St Maximin was used to provide new weatherings in the north tower in 1971 (Gundry (1972)).
11. Durrance and Laming (1982), 106–11; Ussher (1902), 55–87; Tidmarsh (1932).
12. E.g. Howard (1933), 331–2.
13. The geological study of the Exeter Volcanic Series has been greatly advanced in recent years, allowing the products of specific outcrops to be identified. The volcanic stone of the cathedral is now in need of re-examination in the light of this work.
14. E.g. Pickard (1933), 323.
15. For example at the base of the north wall of the north tower.
16. For example on the north-west buttress of the nave (visible from the leads of the image screen).
17. This stone was also used on the inner face of the spandrels of the arcade walls, above the vaulting cones.
18. Erskine (1981), 18, 84–7, 95–7, 156; (1983), 222, 232, 242, 258–77, 315. The name could have referred to quarries at Heazille Farm, or Dunsmoor Farm, or beside Silverton village or at Ruffwell.
19. Erskine (1981), 82–5, 89, 92, etc.
20. Ussher (1902), 60–1. Both the veined and vesicular types can still be seen in the surviving quarry faces at Pocombe.
21. E.g. Erskine (1981), 13–23, 33–5.
22. Findlay (1939), roll 2654, 16. The date is given wrongly by Hope (n.d., 28/0).
23. The location of the quarry was established by Erskine and Hope (Hope, n.d., 28/2). This quarry would have provided volcanic trap rather than the sandstone mentioned by them (Erskine (1983), xv; Hope (n.d.), 28/2). See Ussher (1902), 25.
24. Erskine (1983), 264, 266, 277.
25. Hope (n.d.), 28/2.

26. E.g. Exeter Castle Gatehouse, St Nicholas Priory west range, Exe Bridge.
27. Hope (n.d.), 36/1–3.
28. Cornish (1932), 31.
29. Ibid.
30. Gundry (1972).
31. Records made by Stuart Blaylock, 1983.
32. Cowick Barton (the large 14th-century coffin from this site, now displayed at St Nicholas Priory, is of Salcombe stone); St James Priory (the 12th-century capitals from this site, now in the Royal Albert Memorial Museum, Exeter are of this stone); St Nicholas Priory (some of the 12th-century architectural fragments at St Nicholas are of Salcombe stone); St Mary Arches church (where it is used in the nave piers); Polsloe Priory (restricted use for shafts and shaft bases).
33. As the above examples illustrate, however, recent excavations have shown that its use was more extensive than is apparent from standing structures. A few further fragments were recorded at Buckfast Abbey and Torre Abbey (for example in the nave arcade at the latter site).
34. De la Beche (1839), 487–8.
35. E.g. Alphington church font; Axminster church.
36. Excepting a few blocks in the north face of the north tower (Fig. 2, level C).
37. If that is the derivation of the canopy now placed against the north wall of the chapels of St Catherine and St Andrew.
38. Erskine (1981), 88. Hope ((n.d.), 25/3) records an entry for 300 Beer stones in 1302–3 and the carriage of Beer stones in 1304 but these references do not appear in Erskine's edition and are no longer legible.
39. Hope (n.d.), 25/6. Hope's calculations here (and elsewhere) are not beyond dispute. In some instances it is impossible to be certain that several successive entries in the fabric rolls do not record successive stages in the carriage of a single load. In other instances there are uncertainties about the identification of the quarry.
40. Ussher (1902), 23–4.
41. Erskine (1983), 263–4.
42. Erskine (1983), 284.
43. Findlay (1939), roll 1653, 10–13; roll 2654. The total is that of Hope (n.d.).
44. Lysons (1822), ccxliii.
45. E.g. Dru Drury (1948); RCHME (1970), vol. II (south-east), pt 1, xi–xli; Leach (1978); VCH/*Dorset*, II, 331.
46. In 1381–2 (Hope (n.d.), 34/3 for details). Towards the western end of the north choir aisle lies a massive rectangular Purbeck marble slab measuring 1.54 × 3.58 m in plan, on which survive traces of at least one cross close to a corner. This appears to be a medieval altar slab.
47. Erskine (1981), 33, 35. The then cathedral mason, Peter Dare, was able to identify eighteen choir bosses of Portland stone when scaffolding was erected to clean the high vaults in 1982. The stone had previously been employed for some of the largest bosses in the presbytery (e.g. Prideaux and Holt Shafto (1910), no. 77).
48. For its use in 12th-century contexts in Dorset, e.g. at Wareham, see RCHM (1970), vol. II (south-east), pt 1, xl.
49. Allan and Blaylock below, 108–9.
50. D&C Surveyor's Report, March 1813.
51. D&C Fabric Vouchers, 1813.
52. Exceptions include the freestone of Cullompton church tower.
53. Erskine (1981), 18–20, 22, 24.
54. As the masons who dismantled it before the Second World War recall.

The Romanesque Cathedral of St Mary and St Peter at Exeter

By Malcolm Thurlby

SYNOPSIS

This paper re-examines the evidence for the lost Romanesque Cathedral begun in 1112 or 1114. The structural archaeology is analysed in the light of art-historical parallels and, while a definitive reconstruction is not attempted, its place in English Romanesque architecture is more clearly defined. Certain key aspects of the design emerge, such as the presence of rib-vaults in the aisles, the absence of a traditional crossing and the use of pointed arches. The paper argues for an apse-ambulatory plan with polygonal radiating chapels and for large columnar piers in the arcades.

INTRODUCTION AND DOCUMENTATION

The Cathedral of St Mary and St Peter at Exeter has attracted considerable attention from architectural historians. Interest has focused on the late 13th- and 14th-century fabric and in particular on its role in the genesis and development of the Decorated style.[1] Study of the Romanesque building, which was commenced by Bishop Warelwast in 1112 or 1114, consecrated in 1133 and finally completed by Bishop Henry Marshall (1194–1206), has been minimal by comparison, which is not altogether surprising considering that the later medieval remodelling has retained only the lower sections of the aisle walls and the transept towers from the original fabric, and even they are not untouched by later hands.[2] However, in the reworked fabric there are important clues as to the appearance of the 12th-century structure. This information is supplemented with some reused Romanesque fragments and a report on the apsidal foundation found during Scott's restoration of 1870 to 1877.[3] While there is not sufficient evidence for a definitive reconstruction of the Romanesque cathedral, at least certain aspects of its appearance will be made clear, which will lead to a more complete understanding of its place in English Romanesque architecture

PLAN OF THE ROMANESQUE CATHEDRAL

The lower section of the nave aisle walls has been retained from the Romanesque fabric, albeit reworked in places. The exterior of the fifth bay of the north aisle preserves most completely its original 12th-century appearance with a shallow chamfered plinth, which stands two courses above the later bench, and regularly coursed ashlar rising to the sill of the 14th-century window. The bay width of 18 ft 3 in. is defined by the pilaster buttresses measured centre to centre.[4] This Romanesque bay division is still visible on the interior of the south nave aisle wall where the original responds have been cut back leaving a clear break in the stonework which is also marked by the use of red sandstone which is found interspersed throughout the Romanesque nave and transepts.[5] The placement of these responds demonstrates that the rhythm of the present nave arcade does not correspond with its Romanesque predecessor, although both comprise seven bays.[6] The 18 ft 3 in. bay is also employed in the present choir, with the exception of the short western bay, which suggests that the Romanesque bay rhythm is preserved. Indeed, certain details indicate that the core of the Romanesque fabric may be retained in the narrow bay and two full western bays of the choir. The wall in these two western bays is 8 in. thicker at arcade level than in the bays

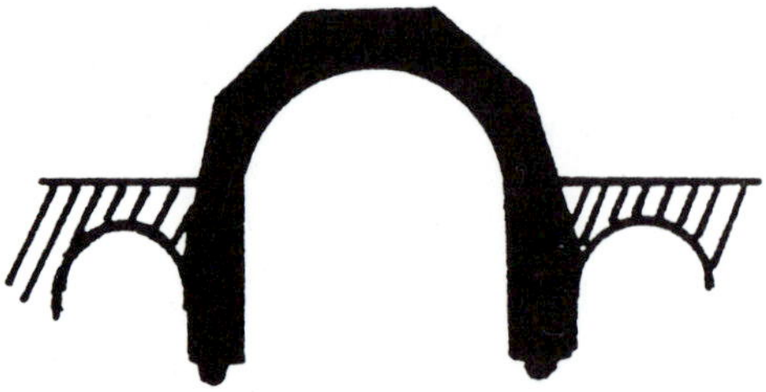

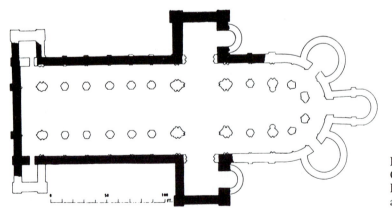

FIG. 1. Exeter Cathedral, plan of Romanesque east end, redrawn after Bishop and Prideaux

further east; the pier diameter is 5 ft 2 in. against 4 ft 6 in. The inner faces of the larger piers are in line with the piers to the east, with the result that the 8 in. increase projects into the aisles. This has caused problems in the third bay from the west where the 'thin' arch is supported to the west by a 'thick' pier. The discrepancy has been resolved by allowing the rear arch mouldings to die into recessed stilted springers.[7] The change in thickness is witnessed in the clerestory where the shafts carrying the formeret in the two western bays descend to the base of the clerestory, whereas in the thinner third bay the shaft supporting the inner order has to be corbelled out above the arch of the wall passage (VIIID). The greater thickness of the two western bays can also be appreciated in the depth of the clerestory window jambs, while at this level on the exterior the thinning of the wall to the east of the second bay is marked by the asymmetry of the buttress between the second and third windows.[8] In addition to these changes the two western bays of the arcade are set apart by the inclusion of a tall plinth beneath the arcade, the latter also being present from this point on the aisle walls above which there are remains of Romanesque masonry to the level of the window sill.

The above observations should be read in connection with the information that when the choir was being repaved in Scott's restoration between 1870 and 1877, Mr Edwin Luscombe, the Clerk of the Works, recorded that 'at the line of the first step east of the pulpit traces of the foundation of a wall of five-sided apsidal form were found'.[9] This led Bishop and Prideaux to reconstruct a polygonal apse to the presbytery in which other details of the plan were taken from Lethaby who conjectures solid walls to the east of the break in the present arcade, and enclosed apses to the aisles (Fig. 1).[10] Against this Radford noted that 'A central apse of this form would be unparalleled in contemporary English architecture', and therefore suggested that the foundations 'could well have been part of a sleeper wall of an arcade separating the east end of the choir from an ambulatory and radiating chapels'.[11] His

FIG. 2. Exeter Cathedral, plan of Romanesque church, after Radford

reconstruction of a semicircular apsidal arcade of five bays and three radiating chapels is based on Norwich Cathedral, which plan he follows for the horseshoe-shape of the eastern radiating chapel, while he substitutes a hypothetical slightly more than semicircular form or those to the north-east and south-east (Fig. 2).[12] Radford is quite correct in observing that there are no examples of five-sided apses flanked by enclosed apsidal terminations to the aisles in English Romanesque architecture, but Bishop and Prideaux's reconstruction of the east end of Romanesque Exeter cannot be dismissed quite so easily. At Anglo-Saxon Deerhurst a five-sided apse is flanked by square porticus which, when viewed from the exterior, would have appeared not dissimilar to the Exeter apse flanked by enclosed apses.[13] After Deerhurst polygonal forms in planning continued to be popular in the West Country School of Romanesque Architecture, in which a precise parallel for the five-sided form is found at Dymock (Gloucestershire).[14] These parallels give give credence to Bishop and Prideaux's reconstruction, but no more than that. Indeed, within this school there is evidence to support Radford's idea of an apse-ambulatory plan, albeit in slightly modified form. The apsidal division of the 'nave' and the ambulatory of the crypt of Gloucester Cathedral takes on a five-sided plan.[15] This in turn serves as a foundation for the former three-sided termination to the main arcade of the choir which was carried on columnar piers. So, if a five-sided foundation served a three-sided apse at Gloucester, then the same is possible at Exeter, although given the absence of a crypt at Exeter one would expect a five-sided foundation to be built for a five-sided apse.[16]

There is one feature which lends credence to the reconstruction of the Romanesque cathedral with an apse-ambulatory plan with radiating chapels. I refer to the right-angled section of rubble wall with random ashlar quoins which is exposed in the outer face of the south wall of St James's chapel off the south choir aisle (Pl. VA). The chapel suffered bomb damage in 1942 which revealed masonry from the Romanesque fabric.[17] I should like to suggest that the angled rubble wall in question represents the southern extremity of a polygonal south-east radiating chapel of the Romanesque cathedral which was recased in the construction of St James's chapel and subsequently left exposed in the reconstruction after the 1942 bomb damage.[18] The rubble masonry with random ashlar quoins relates to the east gate of Exeter Castle (illustrated in BAA CT VIII, Pl. IX B), while the location of the

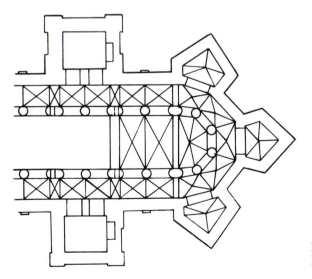

FIG. 3.   Exeter Cathedral, plan of
Romanesque east end and 'crossing'

90 degree angle accords happily with the reconstruction of a chapel along the lines of the former Romanesque polygonal south-east radiating chapel at Worcester Cathedral (Fig. 3).[19] The dimensions of the Exeter chapel would have been greater than at Worcester, but the relatively large scale,although unusual finds parallel at Norwich Cathedral. Here, as at Exeter, the extreme north–south dimension of the chapel — from the ambulatory side of the entrance arch to the outer wall of the chapel — is the same as the width of the main span of the choir.

Among the reused Romanesque material in St James's chapel was a substantial fragment of a large multi-scalloped capital now set against the east wall of the cloister (Pl. VD).[20] Radford has observed that it would have topped a column 5 ft 6 in. in diameter, but he notes that the thickness of the Romanesque wall at Exeter is over 6 ft and therefore he concludes that this capital probably did not come from a huge columnar pier of the type common in West Country Romanesque churches in which, he adds, there is no parallel for the square abacus. Instead he believes that

It must have belonged to a column addorsed against a pier and forming the respond of the arch. The size and shape of the column make it probable that this was not one of the arches of the arcade, but a main arch, such as those of the crossing or that on the chord of the apse. The latter position is more probable.[21]

However, the juxtaposition of a huge demi-columnar respond and a capital with a square abacus is also unparalleled in the West Country. Therefore, contrary to Radford, it seems to me that placement atop a columnar pier would be an acceptable solution for the capital in question, and one that may be explained with reference to a Norman type of capital used, for example, on the minor piers in the nave at Jumièges, where the shaft is somewhat thinner than the wall above.[22] This type of capital is found not uncommonly in England, as in St John's chapel of the Tower of London where, as at Jumièges, the arcade wall is thicker than the shaft of the columnar support.[23] Then in the West Country later reflections of this arrangement are found in the nave arcades of St Mary Arches at Exeter and St Germans Priory (Cornwall), in the north nave arcades at North Petherwin (Devon) and St Breward (Cornwall), in the south nave arcade at St Clether (Cornwall), in the chancel at Ledbury (Herefordshire), and in the nave arcades of St Mary Arches at Exeter and St Woolos at Newport (Monmouthshire).[24] Given such an arrangement at Exeter the apparent discrepancy between the 5 ft 6 in. shaft and the slightly over 6 ft wall is explained.

On the relationship of the transept towers with the Romanesque fabric Radford has reconstructed a full crossing surmounted by a tower. This would involve having short transept arms of the same height as the nave and presbytery connecting with the towers which would therefore be integrated fully into the transept space as they are today (Fig. 2). Conversely Lethaby has continued the regular Romanesque bay rhythm through the 'crossing', thus separating the towers from the main body of the church by the side aisles with which they would have communicated through two arches of similar scale as the main arcade (Fig. 4). Allan and Jupp have demonstrated that the level of the roof abutting the transept towers was lower in the 12th century than today, for the present roof cuts the first level of blind arcading on the inner faces of the towers.[25] Radford's case for a full crossing is therefore seriously weakened, and by implication Lethaby's notion of the continuation of the main arcade from the presbytery through the choir to the nave becomes distinctly credible. Whether the towers would have communicated with both adjacent aisle bays or only the one to the west in order to provide greater isolation for the altar in each space must remain an open question. A similarly moot point is the scale of the arch leading to the tower; it may have been relatively large as in the north tower at Yarnscombe (Devon) and the south tower at High Bickington (Devon), or low and narrow as at East Down (Devon).[26]

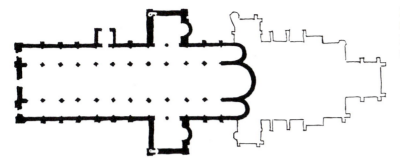

FIG. 4. Exeter Cathedral, plan of Romanesque church after Lethaby

One further aspect of Lethaby's plan has to be addressed, for he does not take into account the thickness of the tower walls in continuing the uninterrupted rhythm of the 18 ft 3 in. bay through the tower area. These walls must be given careful consideration for they caused problems in the later medieval remodelling. In the choir the thickness of the tower wall is expressed by the narrow bay to the east of the crossing, but to the west the first bay of the nave arcade has been elongated to encompass the thickness of the west wall of the towers. Given a window designed to fill the bay the result of this scheme is that the easternmost light of the aisle window is blind because it overlaps the west wall of the tower (Pl. VE). I should like to propose that that narrow choir bay reflects the essence of the original Romanesque arrangement for the piers aligned with the tower walls, which would then permit the reconstruction of two regular bays through the tower area as shown in the sketch plan (Fig. 3). Rather than being conceived in the manner of the present contracted bay, parallels with other major West Country Romanesque churches suggest that the piers aligned with the tower walls would have been designed as single elongated unit. The crossing piers at Gloucester, Tewkesbury, Pershore, Hereford, Shrewsbury, Great Malvern and Sherborne are all elongated on the east–west axis. Of these the eastern crossing piers at Tewkesbury provide the closest parallel for Exeter because they were originally pierced with low arches communicating between the choir and choir aisles (Pl. VC). Reference should also be made to the nave piers of Leominster Priory (Herefordshire) which are similarly pierced by narrow arches.[27]

ELEVATION OF THE ROMANESQUE CATHEDRAL

For the elevation of Romanesque Exeter there is little evidence in either the present choir or nave, so reference must be made to the towers to work with the hypothesis that the elevation of the nave and choir is reflected in the proportions of the towers. The validity of this methodology has been demonstrated by Richard Gem in his reconstruction of Lanfranc's cathedral at Canterbury, and may be checked against extant structures such as Durham Cathedral and St Étienne at Caen.[28] At Exeter the Romanesque window in the west wall of the north tower therefore reflects the placement of the Romanesque aisle windows (Pl. VE). Because the top of this Romanesque tower window comes close to the top of the present aisle windows it is plausible to suggest that the height of the present main arcade reflects the height of the 12th-century original. This theory is supported with reference to the interior east wall of both towers. In each case the centre of the wall is occupied with a richly moulded pointed arch opening into the eastern chapel (Pl. VIA, B). Above the arch in the north tower is a single row of unmoulded voussoirs, and this feature is repeated in the south tower except that the voussoirs only occupy the upper range of the arch — between about ten and two o'clock — the lower parts being flanked by regularly coursed masonry. After a short distance above the unmoulded voussoirs of the south tower arch there occurs a similar range of voussoirs forming a relieving arch. However, the apices of the two arches are not aligned, which would be unusual if they had been conceived as part of a single design. While lack of alignment alone does not provide conclusive evidence for the attribution of the arches to separate building campaigns, other details prove that they were created at different times. The trajectory of the extrados of the voussoirs of the relieving arch continues to either side of the chapel arch as a suture in the masonry, outside which the stonework belongs to the Romanesque fabric. The second and third stones below the left springer of the relieving arch interrupt this suture and yet do not form continuous courses with the Romanesque ashlar outside the suture. Therefore it follows that the suture must pre-date the arch to the chapel and most likely represent the extrados of a Romanesque arch (Pl. VIb, E). The evidence in the north tower validates this theory, for above the chapel arch there is a similar suture — but without the voussoirs of the relieving arch used in the south tower — and here it is cut at about two o'clock by a single horizontal stone that courses with the masonry to the side of the chapel arch but not with the Romanesque masonry outside the suture (Pl. VIA). The existence of these pointed arches in the Romanesque fabric implies that a chapel appended to east wall of each tower. However, there is no indication of a roof line of a former chapel on either tower and therefore it seems likely the arches formed a large altar niche in the thickness of the wall like the examples in the transept towers at Ottery St Mary (Devon) (Pl. VIc) and the north tower at Stoke-sub-Hamden (Somerset).[29] This reading is also supported by interpreting the references in the building accounts of 17 November 1285 and 16 February 1286/7 to throwing down the wall under in the arch of St Paul's tower (north) and St John's tower (south) respectively as opening out the altar niches in the east wall of both towers to provide access to the new chapels on the east of the towers.[30] Given the use of pointed arches in the transept towers it is fairly certain that the same form would have been used for the main arcades throughout the building.

The proportions of the regular aisle bay are exactly right for the reconstruction of quadripartite rib-vaults, the plan of which is determined with reference to two keystones found in the wall of St James's chapel after it was damaged in the air raid of May 1942 (Pl. VID).[31] In the use of rib-vaulted aisles Exeter conforms with numerous contemporary British buildings such as Durham, Selby, Lindisfarne, Winchester, Gloucester, Southwell, Peterborough, Romsey and Dunfermline.[32] Of these Winchester and Dunfermline provide general parallel for the Exeter profile of a torus flanked by shallow narrow hollows.[33]

On the form of the aisle responds Bishop and Prideaux report that 'Mr Luscombe also informs us that the base of one of these (nave) responds which was uncovered *in situ* showed the section to have been that common in the very late Norman period' (Fig. 5).[34] Contrary to Mr Luscombe's opinion that we are dealing with a common late Norman section, I do not know of a precise parallel for the type. It is true that the flat central element of the pilaster flanked by quadrant rolls occurs in the presbytery of Hereford Cathedral, in the chancel at Dymock (Gloucestershire), in the apse at Kilpeck (Herefordshire) and in the four western bays of the nave at Lessay (Manche).[35] Of these only Kilpeck and Lessay preserve the original Romanesque fabric above the pilaster. At Kilpeck the responds carry the single ribs of the apse vault while at Lessay they receive the ogives and a transverse rib of the high vault.[36] If the function of the Exeter respond was analogous to Kilpeck then it would have carried a broad transverse rib with the ogives supported on adjacent corbels, a juxtaposition not uncommon in English Romanesque architecture.[37] On the other hand it is possible that the Exeter respond worked in a similar manner to Lessay, with the quadrant rolls reflecting the ogives of a quadripartite rib-vault in each bay while the central section of the pilaster received the transverse rib.[38] Indeed, the narrow central section of the Exeter respond would

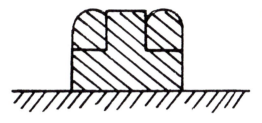

FIG. 5. Exeter Cathedral, section of Romanesque respond in nave south wall, redrawn after Bishop and Prideaux

be better suited to this function than its broad counterpart at Lessay. The Exeter respond also differs from Hereford, Dymock, Kilpeck and Lessay in projecting further from the plane of the wall; the quadrant moulded angles represent just half the thickness of the respond at Exeter, whereas they frame the entire projection in the other examples. It is therefore possible that the front of the respond carried the vault ribs while the back supported wall arches of substantial form like those in the north nave aisle at Gloucester.[39] This comparison serves to emphasise the anomalous nature of the Exeter respond, for at Gloucester the individual elements of the responds are stepped in plan with the result that each arched member of the vault springs unencumbered by its neighbour. The compact design of the Exeter respond would result in the ogives springing immediately in front of the wall arches and alongside the transverse rib. Such a scheme would be unparalleled in British Romanesque architecture, but given the great variety in vault design in the period the possibility of this configuration should not be ruled out.[40] I believe, however, that a more probable scheme may be devised with reference to the choir aisle and first nave aisle responds in the church of the hospital at St Cross (Pl. VIIc).[41] At St Cross the transverse arch and diagonal ribs spring from capitals on a half shaft and nook shafts respectively, while immediately behind the ogives there is a narrow wall arch which springs from the same abacus as the ogive. The central shaft of the respond is corbelled out just below the string-course at the level of the window sill. The plan of the respond at base level therefore analogous to its counterpart at Exeter. The proportions and details are different — the projection of the back section of the pilaster at St Cross is but a fraction of that at Exeter, the front flat section of the pilaster at St Cross is much broader than at Exeter — but it is undeniable that the introduction of a corbelled central shaft to the Exeter respond to carry the transverse rib or arch would greatly relieve the crowding on what would otherwise be a relatively tiny surface.

It is difficult to be conclusive about the form of the vault for the aisle behind the elongated piers which we have reconstructed in front of the tower walls at Exeter. It is possible that the narrow bays were vaulted in a manner similar to the wester bays of the choir aisles of Romanesque Tewkesbury. Although the Tewkesbury vaults were rebuilt in the 14th century clear evidence remains for the use of a barrel-vault behind the elongated eastern crossing piers.[42] There was no respond between this barrel and the groin-vault immediately to the east — that is the groin-vault behind the westernmost main arcade arch of the choir. Therefore the barrel would have read as an extension of the western severy of the groin-vault. Something similar might be imagined at Exeter in which the severy of the aisle rib-vault nearest the elongated pier would have been extended in the form of a barrel behind these piers. There is, however, a problem with this theory for Exeter because in the west bay of the south choir aisle there remains part of a blocked Romanesque(?) arch just beneath the wall arch of the present vault (Pl. VIIA). Obviously it cannot be a blocked window because the wall at this point abuts the east wall of the south tower. It would therefore seem to be the remains of an unmoulded pointed Romanesque blind arch like the moulded round-headed one in the west bay of the north choir aisle at Gloucester Cathedral (Pl. VIIB). If this reading of the blind arch is correct then the vault in this bay — and presumably the narrow bays in the nave — could not have been a barrel but was probably a narrow rib-vault.[43]

For the upper storeys of the elevation at Exeter we must return again to the towers. Initially these are most easily read on the south tower in the two lower ranges of blind arcading which represent the gallery or triforium and the clerestory. On the north tower the division between the ground and first storeys is not marked by a string-course, but close examination reveals a blocked window in the centre of the east and west walls which would correspond to the level of the gallery/triforium. These windows should be read in connection with those on the first storey of the south and north faces of the SW and NW towers at Southwell Minster as a general reflection of the first storey of the elevation, and not taken as evidence that there were windows lighting a gallery. Indeed, it is very unlikely that there were ever windows lighting a gallery at Exeter, for as Allan and Jupp have indicated

the external buttresses of the tower descend to 9m above floor level. The roof level must have been below this point; there is hardly room for a tribune.[44]

The clerestory is marked by the second row of blind arcading on the south tower, which is at the same level as the first row on the north. In both cases there are windows enclosed in the blind arcades on the east and west faces of both towers, one on the south tower, and two on the north. The base of the Romanesque clerestory is also marked by the chamfered string-course above the doorway leading on to the roof of the north choir aisle from the west end of the present north choir clerestory passage.

For the external appearance of the Romanesque nave and choir at Exeter the above evidence is not difficult to interpret; the aisles were divided by pilaster buttresses into bays of 18 ft 3 in. and had single round-headed windows in each bay like the extant window in the west wall of the north tower. Above that the aisle roof sloped steeply to the base of the clerestory, marked by the string-course at the bottom of the first row of blind arcading on the north tower, and the string dividing the first and second rows of blind arcading on the south tower. The height of the clerestory is then probably marked by the top of the first blind arcade on the north tower, second on the south.

In their reconstruction of the Romanesque 'crossing', Allan and Jupp offered two alternatives for the design of the aisle roof between the towers.[45] On the south side they reconstruct a transverse roof on walls built up to gallery level, while on the north the aisle roof continues uninterrupted behind the towers. A compromise between the two schemes would seem to be the most likely solution. There is no evidence for Romanesque walls having been built behind the towers at gallery level. Allan and Jupp's south side reconstruction must therefore be dismissed. On the other hand it is improbable that the aisle roof would have continued straight through from nave to choir in that it could have resulted in a serious build up of leaves or snow next to the tower wall. This problem would have been avoided by the construction of a transverse roof behind each tower at the same level as the aisle roof.

The internal appearance is not so easily determined. Three possibilities seem to be open. In the first place we might envisage an elevation similar to that reconstructed by Richard Gem for Romanesque Worcester with a main arcade carried on drum piers, a relatively squat gallery and a clerestory with wall passage.[46] In contrast to Worcester, however, Exeter almost certainly had pointed arches for the main arcade, although whether this form would have been carried through to the gallery is a moot point; the only two extant West Country Romanesque examples of galleries above pointed main arcades, the west bay of the nave of Leominster Priory (Herefordshire) and the nave of Malmesbury Abbey (Wiltshire), have round-headed arches in the gallery.[47] It is of further interest that at both Leominster

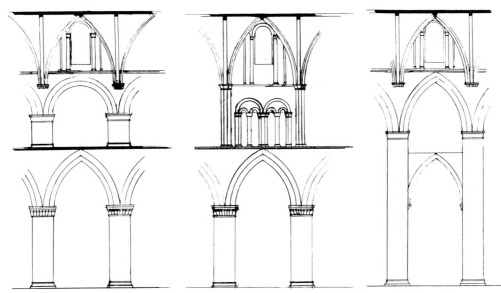

FIG. 6.   Exeter Cathedral, reconstruction of Romanesque elevation with (A) a gallery,
(B) a triforium and (C) grant order

and Malmesbury there are no windows at gallery level and that the roof over the gallery
extends from the top of the aisle wall to the clerestory (Fig. 6, A). A similar arrangement of
the roof is also witnessed above the nave aisles of Gloucester Cathedral. Here, however,
there is a low triforium rather than a false gallery with the result that the floor level in the
clerestory passage is well below the top of the aisle roof.[48] The reconstruction of the
Romanesque elevation of Exeter with a triforium rather than a gallery does have a certain
appeal in as much that the Gothic elevation may be read as a reflection of its Romanesque
predecessor (Fig. 6, B). The final possibility for the 12th-century elevation which involves
the giant order is as intangible as it is fascinating (Fig. 6, C). Given the use of the giant order
in the choir and transepts of Tewkesbury Abbey, in the nave of Romsey Abbey, and
throughout Oxford Cathedral, plus the large number of other possible examples detected
by Richard Halsey, the claim for Romanesque Exeter to be included in this group does not
seem unreasonable.[49]

There is no evidence in the fabric of the cathedral with regard to the original covering of
the nave and choir. However, in view of the tradition of vaulted main spans in Romanesque
churches in the west country, there is good reason to suggest a high vault for the choir, if not
for the nave. It is now generally agreed that the great Romanesque abbey churches at
Tewkesbury and Pershore were vaulted throughout, while at Gloucester the choir and nave
had high vaults.[50] The nave of Chepstow Priory was groin- or rib-vaulted which implies that
the choir would also have been vaulted.[51] At Hereford Cathedral the choir was vaulted and
at Malmesbury Abbey rib-vaults covered the choir and transepts.[52] Then there are many
smaller buildings which have, or had, vaulted chancels.[53] Therefore, given the use of
rib-vaults in the aisles at Romanesque Exeter, a high rib-vault may be reconstructed in the
choir.

There remains to be discussed the ornamentation of the superstructure of the towers. The
Romanesque love of design variety is immediately evident in that detailing of one tower is
not exactly matched on the other. However, the family resemblances between the ornament

are close enough to suggest that construction of both was in hand at the same time.[54] An obvious general parallel for rich tower decoration in the West Country School of Romanesque Architecture is the crossing tower of Tewkesbury and specific details seem to confirm links with this area of Gloucestershire.[55] The triple stepped shafts of the third layer of arcading on the north transept occur on the apse of Dymock,[56] while in the penultimate arcade of the south tower the extremely unusual capitals with straight plain sides are paralleled in the respond capitals of the transverse arches in the Gloucester chapter house (Pl. VIID, E). The form of the shafts of this section of arcade and the fluted design of some of the capitals suggest another comparison which is significant with regard to date. The keeled roll flanked by chevron at right angles to the wall surface is found in triforium of the choir at St Cross where we also find fluted capitals.[57] The church of St Cross was probably commenced by Henry of Blois after his return from exile in 1158 and so a date in the 1160s seems entirely plausible for these features at Exeter.[58]

SOURCES OF THE ROMANESQUE DESIGN

Numerous parallels presented above have already placed Exeter in the context of the West Country School of Architecture, but exemplars for the towers and the pointed arches have to be discussed. Towers like those at Speyer can be quickly dismissed as a source for Exeter, for, although they flank the choir, they simply hold stairvices whereas at Exeter we are dealing with tower chapels.[59] In this respect the tower chapels at S. Abbondio, Como are closer, but unlike Exeter they are not separated from the choir by aisles.[60] More interesting are examples of towers at the ends of transepts like Saint-Michel-de-Cuxa and Angoulême Cathedral, although whether there is any connection between these examples and Exeter is a moot point.[61] Closer, I believe, are the tower chapels flanking the choir beyond the aisles at Saint-Benoît-sur-Loire, which appear to be ultimately related to Fulbert's Cathedral at Chartres, and more immediately to the choir of the abbey church of Marmoutier near Tours.[62] However, tower chapels flanking the aisles are found closer to home at Anselm's Cathedral at Canterbury where the main arcade also continued across the entrance to the east transepts.[63] Whether Canterbury owes anything to the French examples or simply reflects an insular development is difficult to decide. Certainly we must record the former existence of tower chapels in the Anglo-Saxon Cathedral at Canterbury, as well as at St Mary's, Wareham (Dorset) and Tredington (Warwickshire).[64] These pre-Conquest examples, however, are all specifically double-storey chapels, which was not the case at Exeter.

One aspect of the design which is almost certainly of French inspiration is the pointed arch. Of the two major regions for the use of this form, Burgundy and south-west France, the latter seems to be the most likely source for Exeter, given the connections between the West Country School of Romanesque Architecture and the west and south-west of France.[65] While pointed arches occur frequently in Romanesque churches in the west and south-west of France, dated examples remain the exception, especially before the 1112/14 start of Exeter. The earliest example may be in the west bay of the domed church of Saint-Étienne-la-Cité at Perigueux, normally dated to the late 11th century because it is stylistically earlier than Angoulême Cathedral which was in building in 1105.[66] Of the domed group, Cahors Cathedral, which was consecrated in 1119, serves as another early dated example of the pointed arch in the region.[67] Outside the domed group an interesting candidate for influence on Exeter is the church of Saint-Pierre at Beaulieu (Corrèze) which was probably commenced around 1100.[68] Here the main arcade, the crossing and the arches to the transept chapels are pointed and of two unmoulded orders just like the crossing arches at Crediton.

INFLUENCE OF THE ROMANESQUE CATHEDRAL AT EXETER

The most obvious and concerted influence exerted by Romanesque Exeter on parish church design in the West of England is in the transeptal placement of towers. Ottery St Mary (Devon) follows the cathedral in having two towers, while elsewhere in Devon a further fifteen churches have either a north or south tower placed transeptally.[69] In Cornwall there are eight transept towers and a further seventeen in Somerset.[70] Perhaps the most interesting, if tentative, case of the influence of the Exeter towers is in Ireland, at Cormac's Chapel at Cashel (1127–34) (Co. Tipperary). Roger Stalley has demonstrated that the design of the chapel depends strongly on West Country models.[71] However, he observes that

the chapel was probably designed for a small Benedictine community, dependent on the Scottenkirche at Regensberg, a link which may explain the Germanic appearance of the square towers flanking the chancel arch.[72]

Stalley may well be correct in his assessment but, given the numerous West Country links for the chapel, Exeter becomes a prime candidate as the source for the towers.

The juxtaposition of red sandstone and limestone found in nave aisles responds at Exeter also occurs in the north respond of the chancel arch at Meavy (Devon), in a reset portal at Paignton (Devon) and in the gateway of Plympton Priory (Devon) where green sandstone is also used.[73]

The reconstruction of pointed arches at Romanesque Exeter makes good sense in that it provides a source in the major building in the area for the remarkably regular occurrence of this form in 12th-century churches in Devon. Pointed arches communicate with the axial tower at Branscombe, the west tower at Cookbury, Meeth, Northlew and Sidbury, the north tower at Yarnscombe and the south tower at Braunton and High Bickington, while at Northlew the west doorway is also pointed. Pointed arches are used in the north nave arcade at North Petherwin, for the crossings at Colyton and Crediton, and the former crossing tower at South Brent. The stylistic connection between Crediton, High Bickington and Exeter may then be furthered with reference to the beak-spur bases of the nook shafts at Crediton crossing and the south doorway and south jamb of the former chancel arch at High Bickington, which are closely parallelled in two loose nook shaft bases preserved in a room behind the minstrels' gallery at Exeter.[74] In Cornwall reflections of Romanesque Exeter Cathedral are seen in the pointed arch to the west towers at St Gennys, Tintagel, Crantock and St Martin-by-Looe, and the unmoulded pointed arches in the 12th-century fabric of St Germans Priory (Cornwall) (Pl. VB).

In sum: it is to be regretted that we do not have the evidence for a definitive reconstruction of the Romanesque fabric of Exeter Cathedral. Nevertheless, certain essential aspects of the design have been determined, including the use of rib-vaulted aisles, the absence of the traditional crossing and the use of pointed arches, while it seems likely that the main arcades were carried on large columnar piers in the tradition of West Country Romanesque buildings and the east end terminated in an apse ambulatory plan with polygonal radiating chapels like Romanesque Worcester. The popularity of the pointed arch in Romanesque churches in Devon and Cornwall is obviously to be seen as a reflection of Exeter, as is the occurrence of transeptally placed towers in the region into the later Middle Ages.

ACKNOWLEDGEMENTS

I should like to thank Peter Dare, former Master Mason of Exeter Cathedral, and his successor, David Price, for giving me unlimited access to the upper parts of the cathedral and for answering numerous questions regarding the fabric. Eric Fernie and Richard Gem kindly read a penultimate draft of the text and offered valuable suggestions. I have also benefited from discussing various aspects of the building with John Allan, Stuart Blaylock, Richard Halsey, and Roger Stalley.

Research for this article was made possible in part through a generous grant from the Social Sciences and Humanities Research Council of Canada. Funding towards its publication was generously made available by the Council for British Archaeology.

REFERENCES

1. Bony (1979), 16–18; and Virginia Jansen's paper in these *Transactions*.
2. Dugdale (1819), refers to the 'Chronicle of Exeter Cathedral preserved among Archbishop Laud's manu-scripts at Oxford' which gives 1112 as the foundation date of the cathedral; D. W. Blake (1972), 15–33, esp. 32, n. 52 refers to the 1112 date recorded in the Exeter Chronicle (Exeter Cathedral Dean and Chapter MS 3625), and the 1114 date given in the Annals of Tavistock (Bodleian Library MS Digby 81, f. 88). The foundation and consecration dates of the cathedral are discussed by Blake (1972), 28–9, and F. Rose-Troup (n.d.). On the Romanesque fabric see: J. Hellins (1892), 120–5; P. Addleshaw (1899), 23–4, 50; Lethaby (1903), 167–76; Bishop and Prideaux (1922), 24–9; Clapham (1934), 48 and 61; B/E *South Devon* (1952), 132; Boase (1953), 94; Radford (1960), 28–36; Hope and Lloyd (1973), 5–7, 11–12, 37; Allan and Jupp (1981), 141–5; McAleer (1984), 71–6.
3. Bishop and Prideaux (1922), 25.
4. This is the only bay in which the Romanesque pilaster buttresses are preserved, but the chamfered plinth continues through the north nave aisle — interrupted by later buttresses and the north porch — round the north (St Paul's) tower to St Paul's chapel, and reappears in the second bay from the west (excluding the narrow bay) or the north choir wall. The Romanesque bay size is normally given as 18 ft 6 in. but the width of each pilaster buttress is 47 in. (3 ft 11 in.) and the distance between them is 172 in. (14 ft 6 in.) which gives a centre-to-centre bay size of 18 ft 3 in. The pilasters project 9 in. from the plane of the wall.
5. In the north nave aisle the later reworking of the Romanesque responds is more thorough than in the south aisle; one stone of the first respond survives; the place of respond 2 is covered by a wall monument to John MacDonald; respond 3 is replaced by the stair to the minstrels' gallery; there are signs of patching for respond 4 but nothing for 5 and 6. Also in bays N4 and N6 there is a Romanesque chamfered plinth above the Gothic bench which also appears in S2, S3, S4 (restored), S5, S6 (partly restored) and S7.
6. The evidence for the west front of the Romanesque nave is discussed by McAleer (1984), 71–6. Peter Dare, the former Master Mason of Exeter Cathedral, kindly pointed out to me that during restoration work on the west front evidence of the *c.* 1200 façade was revealed on the present south buttress and in the angle between this buttress and the back of the figurated screen. The evidence takes the form of three recessed quatrefoils with moulded frames set flush with the wall surface which originally formed part of a crenellated design. The quatrefoils are set on the south and west faces of the buttresses and in the angle of the south and former southernmost buttress facing west at the level of the canopies of the upper range of 14th-century statues on the screen façade. Perhaps they indicate that behind the 14th-century screen there is still the core of the original façade. The quatrefoils are neither wider nor deep enough to have held figures but it is significant that quatrefoils frame figures and busts on the tomb of Bishop Henry Marshall (d. 1206) in the cathedral. Parallels for the use of quatrefoils across angles on a façade are found at Wells and Salisbury, while a contemporary use of moulded recessed quatrefoils is on the upper storey of the south-west transept of Ely Cathedral.
7. Hope and Lloyd (1973), 15, pl. 2. This discrepancy is most obvious in the doubling of the soffit roll springers.
8. On the north clerestory the west face of the buttress projects 10½ in. from the outer plane of the window jamb, but 19½ in. on the east face. On the south clerestory the west face projects 10 in. and the east face 19 in.
9. Hope and Lloyd (1973), 5.
10. Bishop and Prideaux (1922), 25–6; Lethaby (1903), 168, fig. 2. Lethaby's reference to the discovery of the aspidal east end of the Romanesque north choir aisle reported in the *Saturday Review* is refuted by Bishop and Prideaux (1922), 26.
11. Radford (1960), 34.
12. Fernie (1976), 77–86.
13. Taylor and Taylor (1965), figs 85 and 89. A reconstruction drawing of Deerhurst in its 10th-century state is given by Klukas (1984), 81–98, fig. 2.
14. The term West Country School of Romanesque Architecture is adapted from Harold Brakspear's article on early Gothic architecture in the region (1931), 1–18. West Country School is used in broadest geographical sense to group buildings like St Germans (Cornwall), Chester Cathedral and St John, Ewenny Priory (Glamorganshire) and Cormac's Chapel at Cashel (Co. Tipperary) with the south-west Midlands group of Worcester Cathedral, Gloucester Cathedral, Tewkesbury Abbey and Pershore Abbey. A plan of Dymock is given Gethyn-Jones (1979), p. 23. Polygonal plans are used in the West Country School of Romanesque Architecture for the radiating and transept chapels at Worcester [Gem (1978), 15–37, fig. 10]; the main apse

and radiating and transept chapels and St Peter's Abbey (now Cathedral) at Gloucester [Wilson (1985), 52–83, figs 1 and 5]; the apse of the choir at Tewkesbury Abbey [*BAA CT*, (1985), frontispiece]; the apse of the castle chapel at Ludlow [Clapham (1934), 111, fig. 36]; and the tower naves of Ozleworth (Gloucestershire) and Swindon (Gloucestershire) [Clapham (1934), 111, fig. 37].

15. Clapham (1934), 65, fig. 22.
16. Richard Gem believes that 'it is difficult to envisage why free-standing piers should have been set on a polygonal sleeper wall rather than a semicircular one — unless the sleeper were laid out thus to facilitate the parallel alignment of a polygonal ambulatory wall' (comment on draft of text, 29 February 1988).
17. Hope and Lloyd (1973), 17–18, 40–2.
18. St James's chapel was commenced before 1279 because the fabric account for 30 September of that year records expenditure 'For 3 windows for the chapel of St James by order of the steward' [Erskine (1981), 2]. Drury (1947), 19, tells us that 'The clearance of the debris (of St James's chapel) also revealed some interesting wall surfaces which suggested that there were at one time corridors or rooms connecting the so-called prison, later known as the flower room, with the Bishop's Palace. In rebuilding the south wall, these surfaces were carefully preserved and steps were taken to leave them permanently exposed'. I should like to thank Mr P. W. Thomas, Assistant Librarian of Exeter Cathedral for this reference.
19. Gem (1978), 21–6.
20. Radford (1960), 28.
21. Ibid.
22. Musset (1974), pl. 31. B/E *South Devon*, 132; Webb (1956), 210, n. 34; and Hope and Lloyd (1973), 12; Halsey (1985), 27, all equate the Exeter capital fragment with a columnar pier of the main arcade. Bilson (1922), 112, observes that the columnar piers in Durham choir are 6 in. less in diameter than the thickness of the wall.
23. B/E *London: The Cities of London and Westminster*, 3rd edn (1973), pl. 4.
24. On St Germans nave see Spence (n.d.), 9; see also Furneaux (1849), 82–9 and Gem (1973), 289–91. For Ledbury see RCHM *Herefordshire*, II. *East* (London 1932), pls 136 and 137. The nave of Exeter, St Mary Arches is illustrated in B/E *South Devon* (1952), pl. 14a. On St Woolos see Morgan (1885), 279–96, esp. 287. A similar capital with multiple scoring on the scallop faces as at Exeter is preserved on a short section of reconstructed shaft outside the north porch at South Petherwin (Cornwall). The multiple scoring of the scallop faces also appears on the round capitals in the crypt of St Nicholas's Priory, Exeter.
25. Allan and Jupp (1981), 143, fig. 2a. The form of the roof between the towers and the main body of the church is discussed below (p. 26).
26. It is suggested below (p. 28) that the use of pointed tower arches in these buildings reflects Romanesque Exeter.
27. On Leominster see: RCHM *Herefordshire*, III, *North-West* (London 1934), plan opp. 111; pl. 135 interior nave to east. The east bay of the nave of Wimborne Minster (Dorset) is not without significance in connection with the narrow bays at Exeter in that it is narrower and less tall than the bays to the west, its arch is plain rather than being ornamented with chevron and it is further differentiated in being supported to the west by an elongated pier rather than on the cylindrical piers which are used in the rest of the nave. It is argued that Romanesque Exeter used pointed arches; therefore the use of this form in the Wimborne nave may be seen as a distant reflection of Exeter. Wimborne nave is illustrated in B/E *Dorset* (1972), pl. 12.
28. Gem (1982), 1–19, esp. 5–7. For Durham see Billings (1843), pls VII, XII and XXV; for Saint-Étienne at Caen see Musset (1975), pls 1–3, 11, 14–15.
29. At Ottery St Mary the exterior wall of each tower steps back immediately above the window of the altar niche. There is a small altar niche in the east wall of the Romanesque north tower at Yarnscombe (Devon).
30. Erskine (1981), 7. This is not the traditional interpretation of these references which are normally taken to pertain in each case to the removal of a wall beneath the present arch leading into the tower thereby opening up the towers to their present transeptal form [Dugdale (1819), 516–7; Lethaby (1903), 168–9; Hope and Lloyd (1973), 14; Allan and Jupp (1981), 147; Erskine (1983), xxvii]. However, the traditional interpretation does not take account of the aisle and 'crossing' of the Romanesque fabric which would have still been extant at the time. Because the roof between each tower and the main body of the church was at aisle level (see below, p. 26), the tall arches which open up the towers to full transepts only make sense in connection with the construction of the present crossing. Had they been built 1285–6/7 then they would have had to be blocked above the level of the Romanesque aisles until the present bays between the crossing and the towers were built. My reading would also account for the removal of the altar in St Paul's tower in 1285 [Erskine (1981), 7] as a necessary measure before opening up the altar niche into a chapel.
31. Radford (1960), 28–30. These keystones and two rib fragments are preserved in a room behind the minstrels' gallery.
32. On the evidence of an engraving after Hollar the nave aisles of Old St Paul's, London, were rib-vaulted [Dugdale (1818) between 108 and 109]. The stepped plan of the shafts on the face of the nave arcade piers

also suggests that the nave was planned for a high vault (I should like to thank Richard Gem for drawing my attention to Old St Paul's in connection with Romanesque vaulting).

33. More refined versions of this rib profile remain popular into the 1160s and 1170s.

34. Bishop and Prideaux (1922), 26.

35. For Hereford Cathedral presbytery see Thurlby (1988); the Dymock responds are illustrated in Gethyn-Jones (1979), pl. 55b and c; for Kilpeck apse see RCHM *Herefordshire SW* (London: HMSO, 1931), pl. 167; for the west bays of Lessay nave see Musset (1975), pl. 82.

36. The Dymock respond probably carried a single order arch between the chancel and the aspe. On Hereford Cathedral see Thurlby (1988), 185–9.

37. The juxtaposition of a shafted respond for the transverse rib/arch with corbels for the diagonals is found in English Romanesque architecture at Warwick, St Mary, crypt; Beaudesert (Warwickshire), chancel; Berkswell (Warwickshire), crypt; Stoneleigh (Warwickshire), chancel; Leonard Stanley (Gloucestershire), chancel; Cambridge, Holy Sepulchre, nave aisle; Upton (Buckinghamshire), chancel; Durham Cathedral, nave high vault and chapter house; Rievaulx Abbey, chapter house; Conisborough (Yorkshire) castle chapel; Oxford Cathedral choir aisles.

38. Analogous alignment of the lateral and central members of vault responds occur in: the second and third responds of the south nave aisle at Romsey Abbey where the bases and capitals of the lateral columns are set diagonally; in the chapter house at Much Wenlock Priory in which each element is composed of two half shafts separated by an angular fillet and the capitals for the diagonal ribs are set diagonally [Boase (1953), pl. 72a]; in the chapter house at Forde Abbey (Dorset) where the paired shafts carrying the transverse arch and single shafts supporting the ogives are recessed in line with the wall and the capitals for the ogives are not set diagonally [RCHM *Dorset*, I, *West* (London 1952) 240, pl. 194] and in the closely related chapter house at Bindon Abbey (Dorset) where the Forde scheme is repeated except for the substitution of diagonally set bases and capitals for the lateral columns [RCHM *Dorset*, II, *South-East*, Part 2 (London 1970), 404–6].

39. Bilson (1899), 305, fig. 19.

40. Transverse and diagonal ribs spring from single capitals in the gatehouse of St Augustine's, Bristol and in the chancel at Rudford (Gloucestershire).

41. Kusaba (1983.

42. Halsey (1985), 16–17.

43. There is no evidence in the nave aisles for responds relating to the north-west and south-west elongated piers. Therefore if a narrow rib-vault was used behind these piers, the ribs would have been corbelled out.

44. Allan and Jupp (1981), 145.

45. Ibid., 145, fig. 3b.

46. Gem (1978), 15–37. Also see the nave of Shrewsbury Abbey [Cranage (1912), 866–92]. The evidence for a clerestory passage at Shrewsbury is provided by a 1658 drawing of the north side of the abbey published in Owen and Blakeway (1825), pl. opp. 58, in which the passage is shown in the ruined west wall of the north transept. The height of the blocked windows in the towers at Exeter indicates that the clerestory would have been taller than its counterpart at Shrewsbury and in this regard closer to Worcester. The Romanesque choir of Gloucester is not without interest in this connection in that the columnar piers of the main arcade and the squat gallery may be seen as a source for Exeter. Wilson (1985), 69–72, reconstructed a three-storey elevation with a high groin-vault in the 11th-century choir of Gloucester, while I have argued for an elevation without a clerestory and a barrel-vault springing from just above the gallery [Thurlby (1985b), 45–7]. Wilson's observation that the presence of 12th-century string-courses high up on the parts of the west angle stair turret which jut into the north transept preclude the existence of a barrel-vault as at Tewkesbury and Pershore, disproves my assumption that the Gloucester transepts were barrel-vaulted. I also overlooked the evidence in the north-east stair turret of the north transept for the former existence of an opening to a clerestory passage in the east wall which matches the opening from the south-east turret of the south transept to the clerestory passage in the east wall of the south transept. Moreover, in the north-east stair turret just below the level of the opening to the east clerestory passage there is a passage into the north wall which is blocked after a short distance. From the steep downward slope of the barrel-vault of this passage it is plausible to suggest that it linked with the passage across the north wall of the transept to which access was gained from the north-west staircase at the same level as the nave triforium [Thurlby (1985b) 46, fig. 5]. The existence of a clerestory with wall passage in the east walls of the transepts does not necessarily mean that the same scheme was used in the choir — compare Durham, for example. I would therefore maintain my comparison between the fragment of upper level blind arcading immediately to the west of the westernmost clerestory window on the north side of the choir and this motif at Tewkesbury and Pershore. Because it is connected with a high barrel-vault in the latter two monuments, it is plausible to suggest the same scheme in the Gloucester choir. Whether the Romanesque fragments reused in the 14th-century remodelling of the south transept and choir belongs to Serlo's time or to the 12th-century is a moot point, and therefore at the present state of research they should not be used in a reconstruction of the 11th-century design.

47. On Malmesbury: Brakspear (1913), 399–436, pl. LI.

48. *BAA CT*, VII (1985), pl. X.

49. Halsey (1985), 27–8.

50. Thurlby (1985a), 5–17; Thurlby (1985b) 36–51; Wilson (1985) 52–83. The debate on the form of the Romanesque choir high vault at Gloucester Cathedral and the case for wood-roofed transepts is presented above, n. 46.

51. Lynam (1905), 271–8. Lynam reconstructs groin-vaults but ribs are equally possible.

52. Thurlby (1988), 185–9; Wilson (1985), 82 n. 96. It has been suggested that the nave of Leominster Priory was intended for a series of domes along the lines of churches in the Perigord and Angoumois [Smith (1963), 97–108]. If this was the case then the choir of Leominster would also have been vaulted.

53. The presbytery of Ewenny Priory (Glamorganshire) has a rib-vaulted eastern bay and a barrel-vault to the west [Thurlby (1988), 281–94]. At Cormac's Chapel, Cashel (Co. Tipperary) the choir is rib-vaulted and the nave is barrelled [Stalley (1981), 62–5, 80]. A barrel-vault is still extant in the choir at Kempley (Gloucestershire) and there is evidence for the former existence of one in the choir at Halesowen (Worcestershire) [Thurlby (1984), 37–43, in which plate 4 is printed upside-down]. Four-part rib-vaults are, or were, used in the choirs at Coln St Dennis, Hampnett, Hazelton, Leonard Stanley and Rudford (Gloucestershire), at Devizes, St John, and Devizes, St Mary, and at Compton Martin (Somerset). At Kilpeck (Herefordshire) ribs are used in the semicircular apse. At Avening and Elkstone (Gloucestershire) four-part rib-vaults are used in the choir and under the axial tower. There is a barrel-vaulted axial tower at Langford (Oxfordshire) and what can only be described as a barrel-vault with applied ribs in the axial tower at Christon (Gloucestershire). There is clear evidence for a former Romanesque groin-vault under the former axial tower at Dymock (Gloucestershire).

54. There are numerous design differences in the Romanesque west towers at Lincoln Cathedral and yet, like Exeter, they were probably executed in the same building programme.

55. Clapham (1934), pl. 12.

55. Gethyn-Jones (1979), pl. 50b.

57. Kusaba (1983), pl. I–74.

58. Ibid., 62, 66.

59. Conant (1966), fig. 88.

60. Chierici (1978), 174 (plan), pl. 57 (exterior from east).

61. On Saint-Michel-de Cuxa see Durliat (1964), 40–6, pl. 2; for Angoulême Cathedral see Daras (1961), 70–90. Lethaby (1903), 111, refers to Angoulême and Geneva Cathedral in connection with the Exeter towers.

62. For Saint-Benoît-sur-Loire see Berland (1980), 100 (plan) pls 1 and 2 (exterior from north-east). On Fulbert's Chartres see Hilberry (1959), 561–72; on Marmoutier: Lelong (1976), 704–34; Lelong (1979), 241–7. See also Gardner (1984), 86–113, esp. 94–5. Of interest here is the priory church of Saint-Denis at Nogent-le-Rotrou (Eure-et-Loire) which has been introduced in connection with West Country Romanesque Architecture by Richard Halsey in his discussion of the sources of Tewkesbury [Halsey (1985), 25–6, pl. VB]. Because the upper parts of the fabric of Nogent-le-Rotrou have been destroyed we cannot be sure whether there were towers over the transepts as at Exeter, but in the absence of this evidence we should record that the standard elevation continues across the entrance to the transept arms with enlarged piers opposite the transept walls just as proposed for Exeter.

63. For Anselm's choir see Woodman (1981), 47, fig. 26. In discussing Romanesque Exeter, Richard Halsey [(1985), 34, n. 82] says that 'It perhaps followed the Glorious Choir at Canterbury in having a continuous arcade that ran across the "transept", really lateral, tower chapels'. Old Sarum is often discussed in connection with the Exeter towers: Clapham (1934), 48, 61; Boase (1953), 116; Webb (1956), 42; also see RCHM *City of Salisbury*, I (London 1980), p. 15, plan opp. 15. However, Richard Gem informs me that the evidence for the former existence of transeptally placed towers at Old Sarum is very weak. Another candidate for transeptally placed towers is Shaftesbury Abbey on the evidence of the transept walls being thicker than the other walls of the church [RCHM *Dorset*, IV, *North Dorset* (London 1972), plan opp. 58]. Unlike Exeter, however, these spaces at Shaftesbury would have been entered through a wide, crossing-like arch. I should like to thank Richard Halsey for drawing my attention to Shaftesbury.

64. Fernie (1983), 96–7, 106.

65. Thurlby (1985a), 9–10; Smith (1963), 97–108.

66. Secret (1968), 37–44, esp. 41.

67. Durliat (1979), 281–340.

68. Maury (1974), 45, 47–87.

69. Transeptally placed towers occur in the following churches in Devon: Abbotsham, Ashreigney, Barnstaple, Beaford, Bishop Tawton, Braunton, Burrington, East Down, Fremington, High Bickington, Ilfracombe, Mortehoe, Pilton, Shirwell and Yarnscombe.

70. In Cornwall see Blisland, Bodmin, Duloe, Lawhitton, Mawgan-in-Pydar, St Enodoc, Saltash and Veryan. In Somerset: Barwick, St Philip and St Jacob at Bristol, Butcombe, Creech St Michael, Cucklington, East Coker, Ilton, St Michael Church, Sampford Brett, Somerton, Stoke-sub-Hamden, Tintinhill, Upton Noble, Wanstrow, Wellington, West Camel, Weston-in-Gordano and Yarlington.
71. Stalley (1981), 62–5, 80.
72. Ibid., 62.
73. B/E *South Devon*, 205, 224, 243.
74. Radford (1960), pl. II.

The Design and Building Sequence of the Eastern Arm of Exeter Cathedral, *c.* 1270–1310: A Qualified Study

By Virginia Jansen

The eastern arm of Exeter Cathedral was rebuilt from c. 1270–1310. Despite surviving fabric accounts, the archaeology and sequence of building contain many puzzles, compounded by the variety of medieval building practices. By 1279–80 construction was under way on at least the aisle and eastern chapels, and by 1285 building extended throughout the periphery of the eastern arm — aisles, eastern chapels, and the Romanesque transept. By 1288–91 the central presbytery (four eastern bays) had been begun. Originally the elevation design had two storeys separated by the steep splays of the clerestory window sills. In 1318 this was remodelled to correspond to the three-storey elevation with superposed triforium and clerestory passages already built in the choir bays (three western bays of the eastern arm), c. 1304–12. Evidence suggests three masters at work, the last of whom is the documented Roger, who probably introduced the three-storey elevation. Exeter Cathedral combines contemporary Court-related details, especially from London and Wells, with older forms from the north-east and Cistercian architecture to developed Decorated design in all its richness.

INTRODUCTION

In the second half of the 13th century when the chapter of Exeter began rebuilding its cathedral, Gothic architecture in Britain was rapidly changing. The use of French elements, particularly the large tracery window, altered the way in which British masons regarded architectural design.[1] Much of this change, generally beginning with the rebuilding of Westminster Abbey in 1245, occurred within the milieu of the royal court, but the picture is complex.[2] Not only are there cases of independent influence from France, but certain provincial sites acted as secondary centres of dissemination, in which other interpretations of architecture were added to the transmitted ideas. Exeter Cathedral, built over several decades in this period, shows a variety of forms which seems to have resulted from several factors — from the length of time spent in building, from different designers at work, and from requirements of the various sections of the cathedral. Yet Exeter Cathedral is surprisingly unified, partly because of the sensitivity of successive designers to existing portions and partly because of the segmented nature of the ground plan (Pls I and IV, plan at front of volume). A study of the architecture of the eastern arm — the work east of the nave including the 13th-century remodelling of the transept — is most easily examined in two parts: first, the chronology of the work with investigation of specific sources of individual details, and second, the place of the several designs in the history of English architecture, including the extent and character of the work of the different master designers.

Even if some of the conclusions proposed in this paper may prove unexpected, it presents no sweeping reversals of the traditional chronology established by previous 20th-century writers on Exeter Cathedral.[3] It attempts, however, to define the sequence more precisely, to account for as much evidence as possible, and to compare the work at Exeter more extensively with contemporaneous building in order to assess its significance within English architecture. Since the results offered depend upon interpretation of small changes observed in the fabric and of three kinds of evidence, one cannot claim certainty, and it is hoped that future historians may be able to take the examination further.

At first glance Exeter Cathedral would seem to present a nearly model specimen for the architectural historian. It is a well-documented church: much useful material on chronology, materials, workmen, and patrons can be gleaned from the fabric accounts.[4] An abundance of detailed changes in the tracery patterns and vaulting bosses provides material for establishing a sequence of construction. Little of the fabric has undergone substantial restoration. Yet numerous puzzles in the chronology of the building sequence of the eastern arm remain. In the crucial early years of the work, from *c.* 1270 to 1299, fabric accounts are missing or fragmentary;[5] some of the documents lack the specificity necessary to pinpoint locations, or references are made to features such as window patterns which were either remodelled later or no longer survive. A second system for establishing chronology, derived from the 'archaeology' of the fabric, is difficult to use because of three factors — interruption of coursing by the insertion of later monuments, replacement or reshuffling of original stones, and the likelihood of irregularity and variety in the building practices at Exeter. A third system of information, the weakest since it relies so extensively on interpretation, uses a chronology constructed from the presumed development of architectural forms, particularly of tracery designs. Although still an important tool, its use requires thoughtful revision when integrated with other material. But discrepancies in and uncertainties about the information of the documents, stones, and art historical interpretations remain, producing a kind of jigsaw puzzle at a monumental scale. In fact, the study of the rebuilding of the eastern arm of Exeter Cathedral becomes a model instead of the various ways in which architectural historians practise their vocation and of the problems that such methods may produce.

The interaction of these various kinds — or systems — of information allow different conclusions to be suggested. Such unstable interpretation is true for medieval building practices and architectural design, about which we know little, especially — and this is the important point — in application to any single example. Gothic practices were probably more flexible than historians generally acknowledge, and a more detailed examination of medieval construction practices, supply, and the building trade still needs to be undertaken. A few considerations in advance will alert the reader to the fragile workings of exposition on Exeter Cathedral to follow.

During the Middle Ages a variety of building practices existed concurrently. For example, long sections of walls might be laid out horizontally, or circumscribed portions built up to a height. Vertical elements such as shafts and springers might be constructed of larger stones, at times before the walls. Tracery might be built before the wall above to help serve as the centering or it might be added any time after the surrounding wall was built. Supply and size of stones could be irregular because of uneven beds in quarries, transport requirements, numbers in the workforce, and funding from the patron's coffers. Features of embellishment, such as tracery patterns or bosses, could be designed and carved well in advance of installation or just before, set in later or built with the masonry. They may be conceived by different designers, working in more traditional or more modern patterns, more local or not. Forms may be altered to suit a particular location or requirement (e.g. to accommodate the represented subject). When historians select one of these several practices, it commonly means that they are working from a particular hypothesis about artistic development, because there rarely exists in the Middle Ages enough evidence to prove a statement and to apply it generally.

EARLY WORK

The two-storey chapels off the presbytery aisles

Surviving remnants of the fabric accounts and other documents provide evidence that rebuilding had begun by 1279–80. Work was proceeding in several places along the borders of the Norman building simultaneously — in the two-storey chapels of St James and of St Andrew (off the south and north aisles of the presbytery respectively), in the eastern chapel of St Gabriel, on the south side, and by the altar of St Edmund at the north-west end.[6] In addition, Norman material reused in the 13th-century masonry of the chapel of St James and its adjoining choir wall indicates that part of the Norman east end had been demolished.[7] Thus, by 1279–80 it seems that the rebuilding of the entire eastern arm had been planned, the site had been prepared, and at least the layout of the entire presbytery had been indicated.[8] When the decision to rebuild was taken is unknown, but surely several years before 1279.

The earliest-looking work appears in the two-storey chapels off the aisles, where the simplest bar tracery pattern at Exeter is found in the upper storey (Pl. II). The pattern of two lancets surmounted by an oculus occurs throughout England. The robust handling is similar to windows in many small churches of the 1260s and '70s, as at Etton (Northants.) or, more locally, to one section of the pattern found in the stairway to the chapter house at Wells (Pl. XA).[9]

This early-looking tracery pattern might suggest that rebuilding began here, as a convenient attachment to the Norman fabric in an isolated section, but several points indicate that the work is probably not earlier than other parts of the east end. The *summary account* (see note 5) and other documents cite work not only on these chapels in 1279–80, 1287, and probably in 1284–5, but also on several other portions of the eastern arm by 1285: the Lady Chapel, the eastern side chapels, and the transept.[10] The profiles of the capitals and bases in these aisle chapels show the standard Exeter mouldings of the eastern arm (see Figs 3.3 and 3.5 in R. K. Morris's article, p. 63). What appears to be the same sculptor has been identified in work of the chapel and other dispersed locations.[11] The blind tracery of the aisle of this bay has a pattern closely similar to that of the adjacent aisle window (Pl. VIIIc), and on the exterior the courses at spandrel level (beginning about the third course above the tracery capital) run through continuously. Although the tracery pattern and what might be called its 'archaic' handling suggest work of several years earlier, the coursing of the walls indicates that these chapels (at least at spandrel level on the north side) were built at the same time as the presbytery aisles east of the chapels.[12]

Like the tracery of the stairway at Wells, the simple windows of the aisle chapels make dating by tracery pattern more complicated than usually acknowledged, and suggest that the method of dating by formal evolution of design needs to be reassessed. Historians now recognize that patterns had a longer life than previously supposed, even in buildings connected with the highest levels of patronage. There are many reasons for the forms of such features as tracery not fitting a 'predictable' chronological pattern.[13] At Salisbury, the classic pattern of the chapter house (1280s) continued the tradition of the earlier design of the cloister.[14] Was the simple pattern of the stairway at Wells perhaps used for a less important space, denoting a functional entrance in contrast to the elaborate chapter house? At Exeter, may the theme of a small-sized, less important unit have been played out in the upper tracery of the aisle chapel? An unequivocal response is now impossible, but solutions other than simply a presumed evolution of forms need to be suggested.[15]

Several points, however, indicate that the first work on these chapels came early in the rebuilding, contemporary with work on the eastern chapels. Caen stone found in the ribs in this chapel is used throughout the earlier work on the eastern arm of the cathedral, but not in the intermediate aisles. Quarr stone used on the exterior here is found almost nowhere else in the cathedral save for a few courses in the eastern side chapels, such as the sill of the chapel of John the Evangelist.[16] Thus, whereas there is archaeological evidence for a progression in the work from the two-storey and the eastern chapels to the aisles, the spandrel coursing shows they were built together. Any time-lag must have been small, perhaps not more than half a decade. The chapels were most probably designed and begun in the 1270s, whereas work on them was coming to a close in 1285–7 — if the reference to the 'tower beyond the exchequer' applies to St Andrew's — when construction was proceeding throughout the periphery of the eastern arm.[17]

The eastern chapels — the first stage

Citing St Gabriel's chapel adjacent to the Lady Chapel on the south side as 'almost newly constructed' in 1280, a grant by Bishop Bronescombe confirms that work was under way there in the 1270s.[18] In 1289 work on the eastern side chapels was still continuing, while in 1285 an aumbry in the vestry of the Lady Chapel was recorded, denoting that the walling below the windows was finished by this date.[19] A period of ten years spent on these chapels seems long, but the delay in construction could be explained by work going on over a broad extent of the site, with no particular press to finish up one part before the whole eastern arm could be made usable, or perhaps Bronescombe or his clerk was expressing an optimistic view, meaning that surely the chapel would be almost finished very soon.[20] In any case, the architectural details of these chapels raise many problems.

The tracery patterns in the side windows of the eastern chapels — that of St Gabriel on the south and of St John the Evangelist on the north — show a pattern based on subdivision, a kaleidoscopic composition of circles crowded by small trefoils. The multitude of circles, by c. 1280 a familiar formula, is much like that in a window at Grantham (west front, north aisle, perhaps c. 1280), which was surely derived from the east front of Lincoln.[21] In the Exeter triplets of the sub-unit, however, the central lancet separates the lateral oculi (Pl. II). This stepped triplet pattern resembles windows found often in western England, for example, Lichfield (nave aisle, 1265 sqq.), Acton Burnell (Salop, c. 1270s), and St Wer-burg's, Chester (south aisle, presbytery, c. 1280). Outside the west the pattern was used in several places such as Old St Paul's (aisle tracery, 1270s), where rounded trilobes similar to those at Exeter fill in the corners.[22] Based on this range, a date for these lateral windows in the late 1270s or c. 1280[23] would seem plausible, but the design of the window in the eastern wall needs to be taken into account.

The tracery on the east side of these chapels describes such a marked change in pattern and in method of designing that it is difficult to imagine that both windows are con-temporary (Pl. VIIIA). The eastern pattern introduces the advanced geometric design seen throughout the main sections of the eastern arm. The central oculus has grown to overwhelming proportions, the subsidiary forms are uninscribed, and a central lancet creates a five-light window. This design destroys the symmetrical balance of the older, classic patterns of the Westminster workshop and probably reflects new designs from France, which seem to have been taken up first in London at Old St Paul's in the 1270s.[24]

This change in form raises questions about chronology: whether the eastern design was invented later (but presumably before 1288–91 when construction on the central presby-tery had begun);[25] whether the tracery for the lateral windows had already been carved earlier; whether different designers were at work; or, whether different patterns were used in the same chapel as thought appropriate to fill varying widths (a practical solution) or to create different effects (a signifying response). As with the upper windows of the aisle chapels, these questions suggest that tracery patterns cannot be used uncritically as date-indicators, but that other considerations need to be taken into account, particularly in a small chapel where it seems unlikely that adjacent windows would be designed at different times.

The highly irregular coursing of these chapels is ambiguous also so that evidence from the stones provides few clues in understanding the sequence of construction. In places the stones are coursed through, but the arch surround is not continuous with the wall which itself rarely ties into the stones of the vaulting shafts (Pl. IXA). The vertical mullions and springers of the tracery are also rarely laid evenly with the wall until the third course of the springing of the window arch where the coursing becomes regular, as is normally the case throughout the eastern arm. In the west wall between the chapels and the retrochoir, the courses rarely fit smoothly either with the jambs of the doorways to the retrochoir or with the piers of the arch to the Lady Chapel. These disjunctions could be explained by assuming that the work in this period was going on in a slow, piecemeal fashion by a small crew dependent upon sporadic financing before the large-scale operation of the central presbytery with its uniform architecture,[26] but some construction practices also need to be addressed.[27]

The process of building the wall itself offers further grounds for deliberation. Although in many medieval buildings the vertical vaulting shafts and horizontal walling are evenly coursed through, such consistency occurs infrequently in the early work at Exeter.[28] An alternative practice appears at Exeter, where the vaulting shafts in the eastern chapels are generally not coursed with the wall but built with Caen stone, perhaps cut to size in France, whereas the walling uses local, Salcombe Regis, stone.[29] The external sills of the western lateral windows of the Lady Chapel overlap the sills of the side chapels (Pl. IXB), but at spandrel level the stones course through between these and the Lady Chapel. Thus, it seems that the eastern chapels were built to a certain height (perhaps just above the sill and maybe by the date of Bishop Bronescombe's document of 1280), then left unfinished, possibly awaiting either or both the design and carving of the tracery. After 1289 when the chapels were cited as still under construction, certain sections — perhaps the spandrels and vaults — may have been set in place.[30]

Given the ambiguity of the evidence, it is not possible to be certain about the windows of the eastern side chapels. What one might say is that logic of construction tied to a few connections between walls and vaulting shafts suggests that these two adjacent windows of the side chapels were built and probably even designed together, perhaps sometime in the early 1280s, despite their differences in stylistic patterns.

Below the windows the wall arcading, which links construction at the lower level throughout the eastern chapels, poses similar problems about the sequence of the east end (Pl. IXA and Fig. 1.4). The cusped arches and geometric motifs in the spandrels may be generally compared to the aisle dado at Old St Paul's of c. 1256 sqq.,[31] whereas the forms of the piscina and sedilia in the Lady Chapel correspond to slightly later monuments (Pl. IXD and Fig. 1.5). The gable surmounting an arch with an oculus in the tympanum nearly replicates that on Bishop Aquablanca's tomb in the north arm of the transept at Hereford, dated to c. 1268.[32] The cinquefoil-cusped arches of the sedilia also appear at Hereford (north porch and tomb of St Thomas Cantilupe, both possibly in the 1280s) and in numerous locations throughout England.[33]

In the tomb recesses of the two western bays of the Lady Chapel the trefoils of the arcading become sharply pointed, filling out the surface of the spandrels more completely than in the eastern bay (at right of Pl. IXD and Fig. 1.6). While these suggest the sinuous court forms of the late 13th and early 14th century,[34] they occur in an archaeological context of c. 1280–5; the simplest solution would be to assume that they were inserted

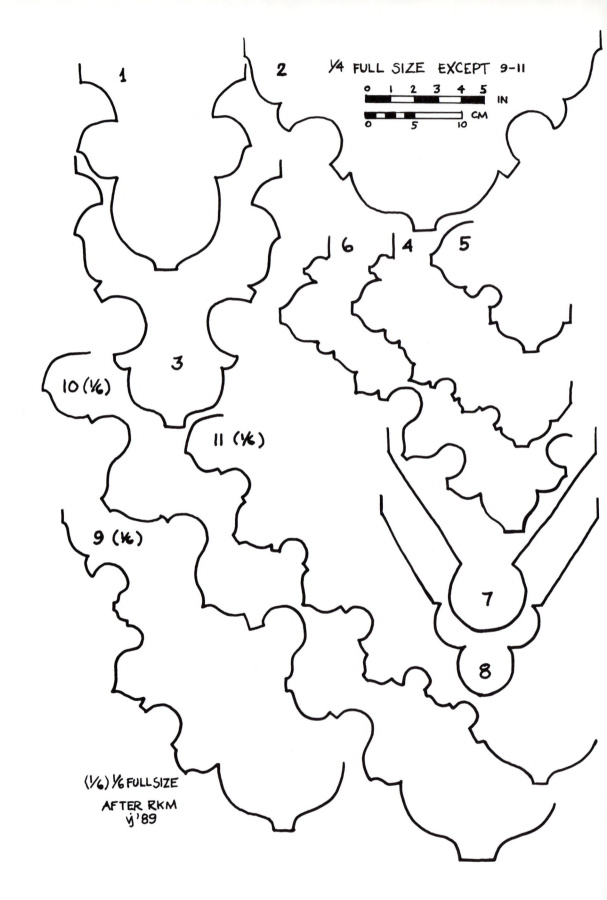

1

2

¼ FULL SIZE EXCEPT 9-11

0 1 2 3 4 5 IN

0 5 10 CM

6   4   5

3

10 (⅙)

11 (⅙)

9 (⅙)

7

8

(⅙) ⅙ FULL SIZE

AFTER RKM
vj '89

later.[35] A few of the courses, however, appear to continue through both bays so that these sharper forms may be contemporary with the less pointed ones. Because of the different cutting of stones for walls, shafts, and arches, however, it is singularly difficult to be sure about the matter, even though on the exterior the coursing beneath the sills is generally regular except for some discontinuities in the buttresses.

The retrochoir

The retrochoir is perhaps the most difficult section of the work to date (Pl. II). Both the bosses and the tracery show forms expected of a date early in the sequence of construction. The windows show the classic formula of the four-light subdivided pattern, resembling tracery at Lincoln Cathedral (east front, one section, perhaps designed in the 1260s), Salisbury (chapter house, probably of the 1280s), and Wells (stairway to the chapter house, Pl. XA).[36]

The retrochoir occupies a pivotal position in the sequence of construction, as its western side forms the eastern arcade of the presbytery. Its joints are confusing to read as the chantry chapels of the 16th century hide much of the walling and mask the change in alignment between the side chapels of the Lady Chapel and aisle walls of the presbytery. The north and south walls are aligned with those of the aisles, but project some three feet beyond the north–south periphery of the eastern chapels. Moreover, the main mullion of the retrochoir windows has the same moulding as those of the presbytery aisles — a single roll finishes the chamfer, unlike the double roll of the eastern chapels (Figs 1.7, 1.8).[37] Irregular coursing in the western walling of the eastern chapels raises doubts whether the retrochoir was built simultaneously with these chapels, and the arrangement of the roof for drainage at the intersection between them and the retrochoir suggests that at least the upper walls and vaults of the retrochoir were built later, although at the level of the parapet all these walls are coursed continuously.[38] Thus, the retrochoir tracery pattern, which has the appearance of the second earliest design, was probably not the next executed, or even the next conceived. Of course, it is possible that the tracery was drafted or carved earlier and simply fitted later with the windows of the aisles, although the mouldings and alignment argue against it.[39] On the other hand, one might decide that for a less significant location (markedly clear when viewed from the exterior) a simplified version was selected of the more complicated pattern constructed in the lateral windows of the eastern chapels — and meant to be seen in conjunction with it. In such a case, the traditional pattern would have been seen to mediate between the repetitive richness of the eastern chapels and the vibrant invention of the presbytery aisles (Pl. II), a hierarchical layout appropriate to medieval patterns of thought. Such usage would imply that once forms became common, they entered into a general mason's stock and could be called upon to fit a variety of needs. If so, despite its appearance, this tracery would have been designed and executed in the early to mid-1280s, at the same time as the tracery of the easternmost bay of the presbytery aisles. If it was any earlier, this revision would only advance its date by a few years.

FIG. 1.   Exeter Cathedral, selected mouldings of eastern arm (at ¼ full size unless otherwise noted; based on R. K. Morris, Warwick Archive of Moulding Drawings)

1–3 vaulting ribs: St Andrew's chapel diagonal and transverse ribs, Lady Chapel (cf. also presbytery vault). 4–6 arches: eastern chapels wall arcade, Lady Chapel sedilia and tomb recesses. 7–8 mullions: presbytery aisle, eastern lateral chapels. 9–11 arches (⅙ full size):   eastern transept chapel entrance arch, arch between Lady Chapel and lateral chapel (cf. presbytery arcade but with additional penultimate filleted roll), eastern chapels entrance arch from retrochoir

The presbytery aisles

While work was continuing on the east end, some building was also undertaken on the presbytery aisles.[40] Two seams in the wall below the windows may attest to a break in construction — in the second bay from the east of the aisles on the north and in the first bay on the south.[41] The latter is especially clear, for the masonry juts out a few inches, showing a problem in alignment (Pl. IXc). The tracery of these bays is unusual, revealing the experimentation typical of the 1280s, before the designer — or a different artisan — took up the patterns seen repeatedly throughout the rest of the eastern arm.[42]

I have found only one indirect comparison for the easternmost design, the east window of the Easby refectory.[43] Its structure is similar, but the oculus in the head produces a different effect. The comparison is distant. It is unlikely that there was a direct link. It probably reflects parallel development and illustrates the inventiveness of many designers in this period.

Undoubtedly related to the second Exeter window however is the contemporary example in the Bishop's Palace chapel at Wells derived from the east window of St Etheldreda's chapel, Holborn, of *c.* 1284–6.[44] Because the Wells design is so clearly related to St Etheldreda's and the evidence at Exeter discussed below suggests construction of these walls by the mid-1280s, it is difficult to determine which — Wells or Exeter — might be earlier and which might have influenced the other; but in any case a date from the mid-1280s seems reasonable for both. What is more remarkable is the proximity in date of all three windows. Clearly there were very close architectural relations among Exeter, Wells, and London.[45]

The window of the third bay, a near relative to the east window of the lateral eastern chapels, shows an older-looking version of the pattern found in the west bay of the Lady Chapel (Pls II, VIIIA). The design seems closest to the clerestory tracery of the wide choir bay at Old St Paul's, under construction in the late 1270s or early 1280s.[46]

In the next Exeter bay, the fourth west from the retrochoir, the tracery appears only internally over the arch to the aisle chapels (Pl. VIIIc). The sharper pattern includes 'Y' tracery and is most closely related to the designs of the Exeter Lady Chapel and Merton College chapel, Oxford (1289–94), both of which probably postdate this example (Pls II, Xb). The type of design is connected with the work of St Etheldreda's, Holborn (*c.* 1284–6, Pl. Xd), which epitomises this new phase in tracery.[47] At Exeter the third and fourth windows mark the beginning of a period of more uniform tracery designs. For example, the designs of bays six and seven of the choir aisles repeat the patterns of the third and fourth bays (of the presbytery) respectively, and in the clerestory the choir windows copy the tracery of the presbytery (Pl. II), which follows closely the patterns of the Lady Chapel.

The dating of these presbytery windows within the sequence of building is problematic. The coursing of the spandrel level continues through from the two-storey aisle chapels eastward without a break. (But then, throughout the entire eastern arm the parapet appears to be continuously coursed.) If the 1285 entries in the *summary account* refer to finishing work on the north aisle chapel as discussed above, then the coursing means that these walls date from this time.[48] And so would the tracery, unless one assumes that it was designed and inserted after the walls had been built. But coursing seems generally continuous between the tracery and jambs, and comparisons with the tracery at St Etheldreda's and the Bishop's Palace chapel at Wells support reasonably well a date of, or even before *c.* 1285 for these windows, even if this seems early in the context of current knowledge.[49] The eastern tracery might even be earlier, if the break in the second bay below the window divided the designing of the first window from the others. At this stage, however, it must be emphasised that these speculations are tentative.

The tracery of the choir aisles probably did not follow directly despite its similarity in design to the windows of the presbytery aisles. Since these aisles were roofed in 1306–7 and the glass installed in 1308, a more likely assumption would be that the tracery was made as the choir was constructed.[50] Such a lag would mean that the older patterns were chosen for the sake of conformity to the earlier work (as in the case of the Salisbury chapter house), rather than that these windows were designed immediately after the presbytery aisles.

Remodelling of the Romanesque transept

In 1285–7 the *summary account* documents remodelling of the transept, including windows, which were renewed in 1319–21,[51] but there is no evidence that the transept chapels were worked upon until later. In 1310–11 an entry refers to the roof 'over the chapel of St Paul's tower' (south arm), whereas other entries mention windows 'of the new chapels' without specifying which chapels, but probably the transept chapels were meant.[52] However, numerous entries in the fabric accounts of 1319–21 date the tracery to this later time (Pl. VIIIB).[53] The arch mouldings vary more in composition than vocabulary from the standard Exeter types (Figs 1.9, 1.10), but it is unclear what conclusion should be drawn.[54]

THE LARGE-SCALE CAMPAIGN: COMPLETION OF THE EASTERN ARM

At some point work moved from slow, piecemeal building on the periphery to a large-scale campaign, in which construction proceeded quickly so that the entire eastern arm was completed in about a generation. When did this occur and why? Unfortunately, from 1288 to 1298 (inclusive) there remain no fabric accounts whatsoever.

As we have seen, by the second half of the 1280s work was under way in several places throughout the eastern arm — the eastern chapels, retrochoir, presbytery aisle walls and chapels, and transept. Although these sections illustrate a determined effort toward rebuilding the cathedral, they remain segments. Are they enough for tradition to name Bishop Quinil (1280–91) '*primus fundator novi operis*'?[55] Would it not be more likely that Quinil is credited because he left a sizeable endowment (probably at or near his death in 1291) to the fabric which may have provided funding for almost a decade? If so, *c.* 1291 would mark a sharp turn in the work of the cathedral in which the slow rate of building gave way to full-scale construction, now with a large crew backed up by a steady supply of building materials.[56] Probably beginning with whatever connections were needed for completion — maybe still the arches to the aisle and eastern chapels and the blind tracery over the arches of the aisle chapels — work proceeded with the completion of the Lady Chapel and the retrochoir, as first the presbytery and then the choir went up — by 1302 and 1309–10 respectively.[57] Formal differences underlie the distinction between the first building of the periphery and the later construction of the major campaign, and confirm a new situation.

The Lady Chapel: the second stage

Above the wall arcading where the socles of the shafts become polygonal in contrast to the round socles below, the Lady Chapel must date from a later period (Pls II, IXD).[58] In contrast to the more rounded forms of the earlier work, architectural detail, particularly the tracery, displays a precious sharpness, which continues into the clerestory and fourth and fifth bays of the aisles. The earlier, regular subdivided tracery alternates with a sharper 'Y' design,[59] and the elements have become acutely pointed, revealing that the masons are using

D

forms of the late 1280s and '90s. In this instance, comparisons with dated buildings suggest a developmental sequence which some of the documented work at Exeter bears out.[60]

At the east end of the Lady Chapel a seven-light window contains a rich mixture of forms including mouchettes or 'fish-bladder' shapes (Pl. I), which we know of earliest in Britain at St Etheldreda's Holborn (east window, mid-1280s).[61] More closely related to Exeter, however, is the east window of Merton College chapel, Oxford (1289–94); the oculus with double-cusping, the pointed quatrefoil, the 'Y' tracery are the same.[62] The side windows of the Lady Chapel are also directly related to tracery in the three-light lateral windows at Merton College chapel (Pls II, XB). The tracery motifs of curved triangle and 'Y' tracery are similar to ones in the chapter houses at Wells (c. 1295–1300), although the ogee arches at Wells signify that it is stylistically later than the designs at Exeter and Merton College.[63]

The combination of several of the Exeter motifs with sharp 'Y' tracery had appeared earlier at St Etheldreda's, where the west window is closely analogous to the eastern window of the Exeter Lady Chapel (Pl. XD).[64] All the Lady Chapel tracery patterns, drawn freely from a large repertory of geometric forms, indicate a very late stage in the development of geometric design, before the adoption of ogee arches from the 1290s on radically changed tracery design. At Exeter a date no earlier than the late 1280s to the mid-1290s seems reasonable, based on the internal relative chronology and formal development of tracery design. The roofing of the Lady Chapel in 1304 suggests a *terminus ante quem*, whereas the 1289 grant citing the lateral chapels as still under construction provides a probable *terminus post quem*.[65]

What is also significant about the comparative evidence for the Lady Chapel and the presbytery aisles is the picture that is emerging in this period of the closest interconnections among the London workshops and other sites: Oxford, Wells, Exeter, and elsewhere. It seems as if nearly every mason and patron knew of all the significant building in England and at times farther afield — perhaps even in the design stage. There seems to have been a free exchange of and experimentation with architectural design. Indeed, in a cathedral far from London headed by Bishop Quinil, a cleric of local background, the work reveals an up-to-date knowledge of architecture. This fact sets the design of the presbytery elevation in an even more surprising light and implicitly underscores a discussion of the meaning of its forms, to be addressed below.

The clerestory windows

Further examination of the windows in the clerestory, the glass for which the fabric accounts date to 1302–4, discloses no really new designs (Pl. II).[66] Here a stock vocabulary, derived from the patterns and sources of the Lady Chapel, is mixed and re-integrated with more modern touches, such as mouchette fillers and more complicated cusping. For example, the easternmost clerestory window is a three-light version of the intersecting type seen at St Etheldreda's, Merton College chapel, and the Bishop's Palace chapel at Wells. The second clerestory window is particularly close to the western windows of the choir of Chester (possibly c. 1295–1300), and those in the north chapel at Ledbury (perhaps early 14th century).[67] The repetition indicates either that the master's designs had crystallised or that a new master was keeping to the compositions already in use.[68] In either case, since tracery no longer provides grounds for speculation about the sequence of building and since the preservation of the fabric accounts for the majority of years following 1298 establishes the chronology, we can turn to analysing the architectural features of the central presbytery and assessing the place of Exeter Cathedral in late 13th-century English architecture.

HISTORICAL POSITION OF ARCHITECTURAL DESIGN

Ground plan and architectural details of the central presbytery

The ground plan of Exeter Cathedral follows the Old Sarum type, developed in the 12th and early 13th centuries in southern and western England. The stepped levels at the east end contrast with the steep front typical of north-eastern England. The specific series to which Exeter belongs has a projecting Lady Chapel flanked by side chapels, with an ambulatory-retrochoir separated from the presbytery by arches.[69] Begun at Old Sarum or Romsey, this type appears later at Winchester, Salisbury, St Albans, and Wells.[70] Aisle chapels, located at the division between presbytery and choir where at Salisbury an eastern transept is placed, occur earlier at Southwell and Pershore and, later, at Wells.

Unlike the plan, which responds to liturgical and planning requirements, the architectural details of the eastern periphery reveal, as we have seen, a close and continuous acceptance of successive court-related forms. In contrast to these, the effect of the central vessel of the presbytery reflects little of court idiom (Pl. IV). Such a difference suggests consideration of what was appropriate for the main vessel of the church as opposed to its subsidiary units, especially if, as seems likely in view of the tracery patterns, the second designer was at work both in the side and the central aisles. The difference may also be due to an independent attitude toward the nature and meaning of court art which was concerned more with highly developed and refined decorative forms than with robust, monumental expression.[71] This character derives from the handling of specific elements, such as piers, vaults, corbels, mouldings, and elevation design.

The clustered piers of both the retrochoir and presbytery arcade have a long ancestry, particularly in the north-east and in Cistercian architecture, for example, at Byland, Beverley, Lincoln (nave and Angel Choir), and Chester in the north and Midlands, and in the west at Much Wenlock and Tintern (Pl. Xc). The retrochoir pier is a variant with distinct major and minor shafts, as often found in Lincolnshire churches, in the main transept at Beverley, and in the nave of Tintern, which must date after Exeter.[72]

In the arcade of the church the designer multiplied the number of shafts around the core to sixteen. In appearance the piers resemble again predominantly north-eastern precedents such as those at Kirkstall, Beverley (eastern transept), Rievaulx, and, in the last half of the 13th century, at Bridlington Priory, Sweetheart Abbey, and farther south St Albans feretory.[73] The Bridlington piers have the same smooth diagonal format with multiple shafts (twelve) in coursed stone, but the exceptional Beverley (c. 1230) and St Albans (c. 1270?) piers and the standard Rievaulx (c. 1225) pier — all with sixteen shafts, emphasized diagonal shafts, and moulded capitals — provide the nearest comparisons.[74]

Although it lacks duplicates, the remarkable high vault of Exeter has precedents. It is the richest, the most developed of tierceron vaults and as such stands at the end of a line of development. The design was used in a form similar to Exeter's in the nave of Lincoln (c. 1220 sqq.) and the presbytery of Ely (1234–52), but they lack two pairs of lateral tiercerons (Fig. 2).[75]

Thereafter, the pattern was used in court circles when the northern master, Robert of Beverley, vaulted the monks' choir of Westminster Abbey in 1262–9. The design was probably repeated at Old St Paul's (c. 1280s).[76] A nearly contemporaneous vault in the chapter house of Wells (1290s–1306) has two pairs of tiercerons, making it closest to the Exeter design.[77] Based on a stylistic sequence of tracery patterns, the Wells vault may date just a few years later than Exeter's, which was completed by 1301. These comparisons place the Exeter vault in both a Midlands and a court context.

Pevsner calls the Exeter vault the '*nec plus ultra* of an existing style, the style of 1250–60, rather than … the creation of a new style',[78] for about the same time as the Exeter vault,

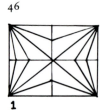
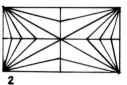

Fig. 2. Diagrams of vaults

1. Exeter Lady Chapel. 2. Exeter presbytery. 3. Lincoln nave, Ely presbytery. 4. Westminster Abbey choir (east nave bays), Old St Paul's (based on Wren). 5. Wells chapter house

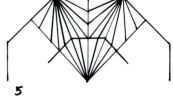

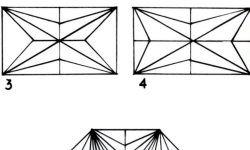

court architects were moving in another direction and produced the lierne vault. But neither the use of the tierceron vault nor the clustered pair at Exeter can be considered retrogressive, especially in view of the master's demonstrated awareness of recent developments in tracery. Since used at Old St Paul's the tierceron vault was both current and traditional, appropriate for the high vault of a cathedral church.[79] Rather, it would appear that the master wanted to revive forms from the earlier 13th century in order to create a different kind of architecture, in which the emphases were on richness of pattern and unity throughout the choir. The third pair of lateral tiercerons, those which no other extant vault has, leaves no wide gaps on the surface; the design produces a continuous, unified texture congruent with the multiple elements seen throughout — with tracery patterns, piers, mouldings, and the richly carved, numerous large corbels and bosses.

These last details of the architecture confirm the Midland-northern strain in the work. Large decorative corbels, associated with clustered piers, are seen at Ely, York (south transept arm), the Lincoln Angel Choir, York St Mary's, and the north arm of the transept at Hereford.[80] The richness and multiplicity of the nave arcade mouldings resemble earlier northern building at, e.g. Rievaulx[81] and Whitby, although the shallow hollows, where no strong shadows mark divisions sharply and where light flickers over undulating surfaces, are also a feature of late 13th-century art. This quality contrasts with the outlined orders in western churches such as Pershore, Wells, and Chester (north choir arcade).

Elevation design

In the two designs for the elevation, other sources were influential. The first design, in existence for only about a generation, can no longer be seen today, but remnants visible on

FIG. 3. Exeter Cathedral, reconstruction of original elevation of presbytery

the presbytery wall disclose that the original design contained two storeys without a wall passage.[82] There are no 13th-century English cathedrals with a two-storey design, but it exists in smaller churches (e.g. Southwell, Pershore) and Cistercian architecture, both with and without a wall passage. The latter type can be seen at, e.g. Buildwas, Abbey Dore, and just before Exeter, the choir of Tintern (1270–87; Pl. Xc). The evidence at Exeter suggests that the zone now occupied by the triforium may originally have started as large deep raking splays at the base of the sills of the clerestory windows. Parallels for this treatment may be found at the Cistercian Abbey Dore and, on a smaller scale, at Tintern (also Cistercian), and also in the clerestory splay at Hereford in the north arm of the transept (1260s).[83] Although three storeyed, the Hereford elevation provides a significant comparison not only because of date and architectural connections, but also because the splay is tall and very steep, as that at Exeter would seem to have been. Three or four courses above the triforium sill a line across the masonry suggests that some kind of slope existed rather than a flat rear wall with sill floor of the kind normally found in examples with passages such as at Pershore, Southwell, and Netley. On the basis of the existing clerestory sill, a steeply-raking splay of about

65 degrees is projected. About two feet above the main arcade would have been a set back from which the sill-splay rose (Fig. 3).[84] A line surviving in the masonry seems to pinpoint this intersection. When the triforium was added in 1318, the slope of the splay would have been built up above this line to form the wall behind the triforum, whereas below it, the roughened masonry indicates that the wall was cut back to allow for the depth of the blind arcade.[85]

With a two-storey elevation the Exeter presbytery possessed a far different character. Although many similarities suggest that the elevation may have been based on that of Tintern, the large clerestory gave Exeter a boldly different effect and should be considered the motivating force behind the design. With its moderate height in the normal English manner, which allowed greater visibility to the richly sculptural architecture, the Exeter pattern modernised the elevation. The two cavernous voids of the arcade and clerestory produced a balanced pattern, aptly labelled 'an architecture of large holes'.[86] A middle storey might have distracted from the repeating series of arches — of arcade, clerestory, and vault. Instead, the proportions of the broad, rectangular space set the dominating tone of an architecture of dignity and mass in which elaborated details of piers, mouldings, corbels, tracery, and ribbed vaults added luxuriance. Without the strong horizontal of the triforium band, the clerestory windows register vigorously, filling the whole width of each bay accentuated by the fan-like torque of the vaulting. As with the plain surfaces in the spandrels and aisle walls, the raking splay provided a foil to the multiple lines of the arcade mouldings and the diverse patterns of the tracery and ribs, providing areas of restraint against their networks, and it brought the mullions visually forward to play an equal role in the design.

If the two-storey elevation fitted in so well with the character of the architecture, why was the elevation altered so soon after the bays of the choir were built? The radical change reveals a different judgement about church design, and was probably effected either by a new patron, i.e. a new bishop, or by a new master mason. The chronology, however, does not fit the accession of a new bishop, and it is unlikely that a seated bishop would sustain the cost ensuing from a change of mind half-way through the work.[87] It seems more probable that there was a change in master mason, who was able to argue for the new design. A master would hardly have designed two radically different elevations to stand side-by-side, nor does it seem likely that he would have been able to justify a change in his own scheme in mid-construction. If so, the new mason should be the Roger, documented at Exeter in 1297. Since the annual fabric accounts survive extant beginning only in 1299, we do not know when he arrived, but it must have been after the two-storey elevation had already been built in the presbytery.[88]

Along with the change in elevation, Roger added a clerestory passage in the thicker wall of the western choir bays, thicker presumably because the wall included remnants of the Norman fabric, although none has yet been found in the upper levels. More significant is the effect of the triforium and balustrade of quatrefoils. By substituting them for the splay, Roger eliminated the previous contrast of richness and restraint in order to supplement the Decorated quality of the tracery, arcade, and vault.[89] He accentuated the breadth and flow of the horizontal and increased the complication of line already apparent in mouldings, ribs, and tracery. The pattern of many openings created a constant flickering of texture.

Roger's design — two superposed passages in an elevation of short triforium and tall clerestory — followed a pattern new to the Decorated style in England. It was derived from the elevation at St Werburg's, Chester (now Chester Cathedral), which seems to have been based on a Burgundian pattern brought to the north-west by Edward I's Savoyard masons.[90] Its influence even went beyond England, for probably from Exeter the design passed to Brittany — to Quimper and to Tréguier.[91]

Was Roger one of the masons in North Wales, passing through Chester, the main supply centre for the Edwardian castles, before going to Exeter? Such conjecture would tally with Richard Morris's observation that many of the mouldings from the workshops of the North Welsh castles were transmitted to the south-west.[92]

The masters and summary of architectural phases

The architecture of Exeter Cathedral reflects the complexity of the many currents in British Gothic architecture in the last half of the 13th century. Exeter's forms seem less connected to indigenous traditions of the south-west than to other models. It shares court-related features with contemporary buildings in the region and beyond, unsurprising in a period in which many clerics held royal appointments. At Exeter the court-connected work derives from two periods — the forms of the 1270s and 1280s reflect the court style of the 1260s, whereas the later work bears the imprint of the court style of the 1280s and '90s. On the other hand, the dominant effect of the interior of the church is northern, originally with a Cistercian-inflected design. Such a mixture of features seems best explained by postulating three different master masons at work, the last of whom would be the documented Roger, if my speculation should prove correct.

The first master, the designer who drew up the plan for the whole eastern extension perhaps in conjunction with Bishop Bronescombe, may have been an older man trained in the court work of the 1260s in one of the western regional centres of court influence, such as Hereford or Lichfield. He designed the plan in accordance with buildings he may have known, since the plan of the east end and aisle chapels exhibits elements of the west and south. The forms of his wall arcading, tracery, and mixture of attached and detached shafts reflect the style of Westminster and the earliest work of Old St Paul's as known in the west. He would have been active at Exeter in the 1270s and probably the first years of the 1280s.

The second man, perhaps active from the early 1280s to the mid-1290s, might have originally come from the Midlands or the north — he certainly was aware of that architecture — but he knew the most recent court work keenly, e.g. at Wells the work of Bishop Burnell, chancellor of England from 1274–92, and Merton College chapel in Oxford. Bishop Quinil (1280–91), a local cleric, may even have acquired such a mason through Burnell.[93] However, this master was radically inventive, combining the textural richness of the British tradition, particularly that of the Midlands and the north with the ideals of strength and restraint of northern and Cistercian architecture and the modernity of new court forms. He gave Exeter the distinctive, impressive character visible today, and thus deserves Pevsner's title, 'the Master of Exeter'.[94] If his two-storey elevation did not survive long, it was because the design was ahead of its time, for in the 14th century this elevation became the preferred pattern, allowing the openness and spaciousness of late medieval architecture.

Although we cannot be certain where his work begins, he was surely responsible for at least the upper parts of the Lady Chapel and the presbytery. Since the east five-light window of the eastern side chapels seems to lead into the tracery of both the aisles and the Lady Chapel, he might have taken charge at this point. The absence of wall arcading in the presbytery aisles and the use of polygonal bases in their windows hint that he was at work here, perhaps by c. 1282–5.

Before Master Roger took charge, at least by 1297, the greater part of the presbytery elevation must have been constructed. This work would set Roger's arrival, possibly from the north-west, in or just prior to 1297. The provision of a house implies that he was already a known master.

CONCLUSION

Thus the forms of Exeter Cathedral, in the south-west of England, suggest an architectural axis connecting the south-west with the Midlands and the north — an axis around which court-influenced ideas pivoted.[95] In many ways Exeter is heir to the large early 13th-century churches of the north-east, but the second master, although agreeing that this was a proper model of how a great church should look, glossed it with a northern and Cistercian restraint and unity of texture.[96] Essentially this contrast between richness and reserve — between changing tracery patterns and varied stones, on the one hand, and the repeated elements of piers, mouldings, vaults, on the other — gives Exeter its particular tone. At least indirectly, the instigator of this character was probably Bishop Quinil; such a conjecture would best answer the question: Why would this cathedral in the south-west have looked to the north-east at this time? Although the master mason gave ideas their physical existence, the bishop-elect who was at Lincoln for the translation of St Hugh in 1280 may have thought that the impressive, luxuriant architecture of Lincoln was the appropriate model for a cathedral church. That hypothesis need not take away from the second master's ingenuity nor does it wholly explain his art, for he freely and skilfully combined elements from several traditions — Midland, northern, Cistercian, and court — to produce a remarkable design.[97]

Exeter also plays a role in the dissemination of up-to-date court forms and the beginnings of the Decorated style. On the outside, the richly varied tracery forms of the very large windows, the crenellated battlements, and the pinnacles and flying buttresses announce a new manner of building. On the inside, the use of fine, undulating mouldings and multiplied units in the piers, the triforium, and the vaulting herald the fluent rhythms of the new style, which also appears in the chapter house of Wells. Supplemented by the naturalistic foliage sculpture, the play of light and shade without bold contrasts activates the space which seems to model the surface of the wall. By combining the linearity of the French-inspired geometric style with the older insular tradition of plasticity, the masters at Exeter Cathedral created an interplay of richness in depth and pervasive, mobile space which was at once characteristically Decorated and entirely English.

ACKNOWLEDGEMENTS

This research was supported in part by faculty research funds granted by the University of California at Santa Cruz and the Arts Division Research Committee. Grateful thanks are due the Dean, the Very Reverend R. M. S. Eyre, and Chapter of Exeter Cathedral and the accommodating cathedral staff who made studying the cathedral a pleasure. Very special thanks go to the former master mason, Mr Peter Dare, who kindly spent a good deal of time informing me of building practices and thoughtfully considering many questions, even after his resignation. Mr Dave Price, now master mason, and his wife continued the response to my enquiries. Mrs Audrey Erskine, the Cathedral Archivist now retired, patiently discussed problems on several occasions and read a draft of this paper. I have profited often from helpful discussions with Professors Jean Bony and Jean Givens as well as Drs Richard K. Morris and Pamela Blum, all of whom kindly read the manuscript and advised me on many points. Here I would also like to acknowledge my greatest debt to Jean Bony for his energetic guidance of the first research I undertook on Exeter Cathedral in 1968–9, and for his continuing instruction over these many years. As a small return I dedicate this work to him with warm appreciation for always sharing his time, knowledge, and thoughts most generously.

REFERENCES

1. Bony (1979).
2. Bony (1979), 10, passim; Colvin (1983), 129–39.
3. Lethaby (1930), Bishop and Prideaux (1922), B/E *South Devon* (1952), and Erskine (1983), xxvi–xxix.
4. Erskine (1981; 1983).

5. The earliest account records exist only as a summary in a fragmentary state; e.g. expenses are summarised only for 1279–81 and 1285–7; Erskine (1981), xi. No rolls have been preserved from 1287–99. Referred to hereafter as *summary account*.

6. Erskine (1981), 2–3, and (1983), 317. On St Edmund's Chapel see the paper by Philip McAleer in this volume. The two-storey chapels of St James and of St Andrew have been also termed 'transeptal chapels', but to reduce confusion with the chapels of the transept I shall refer to them as the aisle chapels as Erskine does. They do not form an east transept (B/E *South Devon* [1952], 132). The chapels beyond the retrochoir east of the aisles, I shall refer to as eastern side, or lateral, chapels, referred to as 'NE and SE chapels' in B/E *South Devon* (1952), 135 and passim.

7. C. A. Ralegh Radford (1960), 28 and 32 proposed that the large capital now on view in the cloister area belonged to a respond. Hope and Lloyd (1973), 12, based on Everett and Hope (1968), 181, suggested that the Norman east end was nearly demolished from the start of the Gothic rebuilding, but Radford and Bishop and Prideaux (1922), 44, believed that the main part of the choir remained in use, as I think likely. Evidence of Romanesque walling remains in the Gothic choir (west bays), as previous authors observed, and in the sixth bay on the south side at the bench level of the aisle changes, although no Romanesque stones are seen farther east. Hope and Lloyd (1973), 12, hypothesised that foundations to level the slope of ground south and east of the Norman choir might have taken Norman stones. However, the location of the major joint between the older work of the presbytery and the newer choir, as easily seen in formal differences and well documented in the fabric accounts, argues for a substantial portion of the Romanesque choir standing until the Gothic choir was built, as was often the case elsewhere. There is also a seam between the north aisle two-storey chapel at the west and the adjoining eastern choir bay. See further Malcolm Thurlby's contribution in this volume.

8. Erskine also recognised the extent of the work (1983), xxvii.

9. The oculi of the Exeter windows may have contained cusping, indistinct in a photograph of *c.* 1873 (National Buildings Record) but Buckler's drawing of 1807 (British Library MS Add. 36361, ff. 84v–85r) shows them without.

    The dating of the Wells stairway is disputed, ranging from *c.* 1265 to after 1286; Morris (1984), 200–3. A document of 1286 refers to a 'new structure long ago begun' (*nova structura iam diu incepta*), presumably the chapter house and its complex; Colchester and Harvey (1974), 205, n. 33, and Robinson (1931), 162. Although the tracery uses a pattern typical of a date up to *c.* 1270, the naturalistic foliage of the capitals and the connections in foliage design and mouldings with the chapel of the Bishop's Palace of the early 1280s indicate that at least the upper part of the stairway may be dated to the 1280s, if not to post-1286. The lower part with the round plinths common to the Early English style and the corbel figures might well fall earlier; there appears to be irregularity, possibly a break, in the masonry between the plinth and the socle of the bases of the vaulting shafts. A lower break in the masonry is the one Armitage Robinson noticed (work cited above, 162). The lowest parts of the chapter house complex, which include the undercroft and its entrance passage, have capitals, mouldings, and stiff-leaf corbels which reveal an earlier stylistic layer than that of the staircase windows. The passage to the undercroft might be dated to the 1250s (Morris [1979], 15), or possibly 1260s, perhaps after 1263 when profits were restored to the fabric (Robinson, [1931], 159); details reveal that it is distinctly later than remains of Bishop Jocelin's palace of the *c.* 1230s.

10. Erskine (1981), 2–7. The *summary account* refers to the ironwork of two windows in the west face of 'the tower beyond the exchequer' in 1284/5. If this entry refers to the upper windows as Erskine reasonably argues, then these windows were being installed at this date; Erskine (1983), xxvii and (1981), 6. Even with this specificity, however, we cannot claim assurance in this matter. The entry is problematic, for 'the tower beyond [*ultra*]' has to be understood as 'the tower *above*' if the entry is to refer to this aisle chapel, an uncommon but known usage. Second, there are not two windows in the west face of this chapel, nor are there windows *above* the exchequer room: the upper windows are those *of* the exchequer. The 'tower beyond' could refer literally to the tower of the transept (so considered by Bishop and Prideaux [1922], 36 and implied by Allan and Jupp [1981], 144), but neither does this tower have two Gothic windows in the west face. Moreover, since this one is called St Paul's in the accounts, the absence of name suggests that a tower other than that of the transept was meant. The accounts are tantalising, but they cannot be pressed into the kind of specific use that the architectural historian would wish. However, on the south side in the corresponding chapel of St James (the vestry), carpenters are documented in 1285 (Erskine [1981], 6, and [1983], xxvii, n. 4) and other work including 1,000 tiles was paid for in 1287 indicating a nearly finished state (Erskine [1981], 7).

11. Givens (1985), 100–6, 113, and her forthcoming study, 'The Sculptor of St James's at Exeter Cathedral', in which she locates this work and interprets the sequence of construction in light of the fabric accounts.

12. On the south side the explosion of a bomb during World War II destroyed most of the evidence; see Radford (1960), 28–30; Hope and Lloyd (1973), 12. The external eastern joint of the north aisle chapel is almost completely hidden by the projecting chapel, but the lower wall below the window sill is coursed evenly with the wall of the aisle. Adjacent to the two-light window above, the coursing goes through at the corner, but

irregularities occur near the window, due either to the setting in of the window or to a break in work, probably the latter. At the west these chapels were built against the aisle wall of the Norman church, parts of which were still standing up to the spandrel level of the aisle window of the choir, indicating that the chapels preceded the building of the Gothic choir aisles.

13. See above, p. 36.

14. Both the chapter house and cloister were planned together, but construction lagged over several decades; Blum (1991), 22–37. For a French example, see Bonde and Maines (1987), 47.

15. One cannot always seek methodically a single answer in dealing with a multivalent society. For some time literary theory has favoured instability in and plurality of interpretation; some recognition of shifting or slippage might well be brought into art historical discussion.

16. Information about the stone supplied by Peter Dare, 1987. Since the somewhat varied profiles of the vaulting ribs use the same vocabulary, they provide no conclusive evidence for dating (Fig. 1.1, 1.2, 1.3).

17. See above, n. 10. The present tracery in the ground storey of St Andrew's chapel was probably renewed after 1657, when the heads of the lights were remade according to Bishop and Prideaux (1922), 106, whereas earlier the chapel of St James had 'Y' tracery such as may be seen in the chapel of St Edmund, noted also in Erskine (1983), xxviii, n. 1, and Bishop and Prideaux (1922), 33 (note) as well as shown in a photograph of c. 1873 and an engraving, Kendall (1842), Pl. XIV. See also the paper by Philip McAleer, to whom I am grateful for the reference to Kendall. In the reconstruction after World War II it seems that the tracery in St James's was restored after the 'Gothic survivalist tracery' of St Andrew's. The medieval 'Y' tracery of St James's was unlike anything in the eastern arm, and I suspect later than the original rebuilding, most likely redone in c. 1319, when forms of glass for the exchequer, transept, and chapel of St Edmund were recorded (Erskine [1981], 109, or less likely in 1310–11 when iron for 'windows of the new chapel[s]' — not otherwise specified — was paid for; Erskine [1981], 52–6). The lateral window of St Andrew's is clearly inserted, perhaps in c. 1319.

18. Erskine (1983), 317.

19. Erskine (1981), 6; Erskine (1983), 317–18: a grant of 1289 cites the chapels as 'under construction'.

20. Richard Schneider, York University, Toronto, reminded me that documents do not present unbiased facts and must also be interpreted.

21. Illustrated in Bony (1979), Pls 38 and 32 and *BAA CT* (1986), Pls XXA and XVIA.

22. Other examples at Dunsfold (Surrey), Meopham (Kent), the chapter house of Southwell (late 1280s), etc. Ultimately the arrangement derives from the north gable tracery of the transept at Westminster Abbey, finished by 1259. The dating of Old St Paul's is discussed by Bony (1979), 11, n. 15, and Morris (1990). The cusping in the Exeter window varies in older illustrations, but otherwise the tracery is well documented.

23. The *summary account* records for 1280 'a certain window on the south side' without stating which one; Erskine (1983), 3.

24. Bony (1979), 11, finds the large central motif in several locations in France, e.g. Agnetz, c. 1250, and St-Quentin, after 1275. A sharper version appears at St Etheldreda's, Ely Place, Holborn, London, c. 1284–6 (west window, Pl. XD). The five-light window with a large central motif may have first appeared in Britain in the wide eighth bay of the aisle of Old St Paul's or the east gable window at Lincoln, both perhaps in the 1270s.

25. See below, p. 43.

26. Cf. Bishop and Prideaux (1922), 34; Morris (1984), 202. Givens (1985), 109, cites as also less homogeneous the sculpture of the eastern chapels in contrast to that of the retrochoir and presbytery.

27. Contemporary masons insist that upon efficiency in building; they maintain that leftover stone would be used so that irregular coursing may not be evidence of a break in construction. Discontinuity may have been caused by haphazard availability of stones from the quarry and stockpiles. Such practices would be especially true of small-scale, poorly-financed operations. Erskine (1983), xii, confirms that the accounts show 'little was wasted'. Cf. Kimpel (1977), 197.

28. Kimpel, (1977), 197, 201.

29. Cathedral masons Price and Dare in conversation, 1987; Dare suggested that the tooling marks were produced by what is now known as a 'French drag', a tool not used by English masons as far as he knew.

30. In 1301–2 the fabric accounts imply no substantial time-lag between the carving and setting of bosses in place, but they may record only the difference in this case between the rapid campaign of the central presbytery and the piecemeal work of the periphery; Erskine (1981), 18–24. Givens (1985), 110, accepted the late 1280s as possible for the bosses. In her forthcoming article, 'The Exeter Fabric Accounts as a Record of Medieval Sculptural Practice', she discusses problems of the relationship between carving and installation. See also Anna Hulbert in her lecture to the Exeter Conference, printed in this volume.

31. Morris (1990), 76, 79. Compare the arcading to the undated wooden choir screen at Old Shoreham and the spandrel trefoils to the rounded ones at Lincoln (Angel Choir, c. 1256), to pointed ones at Notre-Dame, Paris

(transept south arm, 1259–67), just before Old St Paul's; this illustrates how quickly new motifs from France were being taken up in Britain; see Bony (1979), 10.

32. Illustrated in Bony (1979), Pl. 21. Cf. also the doorway to the chapter house undercroft at Wells (c. 1250s–64 sqq.), and, in France, the tomb of Abbot Adam at St-Denis, and in the 1260s the vestibule at St-Germer and the Porte Rouge, Notre-Dame, Paris.

33. E.g. most relevant for Exeter: Lincoln Angel Choir wall arcade (c. 1256), Wells stairway tracery lights (1280s, Pl. XA), Lichfield west façade (perhaps c. 1280), Salisbury chapter house dado arcade (1280s), Merton College chapel, Oxford sedilia and piscina (1289–94). Richard K. Morris dates the Hereford work in 'The Remodelling of the Hereford Aisles', JBAA, 3rd series, XXXVIII (1974), 36, although I would put the north porch slightly earlier because of the different type of capital and the relationship to the north transept arm (also noted by Morris). The moulding motif of roll with fillet and three-quarter hollow in the sedilia arch (Fig. 1.5) occurs also at the Lincoln Angel Choir, Old St Paul's, St Etheldreda's, Holborn, and Merton College chapel, the last illustrated in Morris (1978a), Fig. 4A.

34. For example, Exeter sedilia and bishop's throne, Merton College chapel tracery; see Bony (1979), 10–11, 22–3.

35. See above, p. 38.

36. Illustrated in Bony (1979), Pls 32 and 92.

37. Observed by Peter Dare, 1987.

38. Peter Dare, (pers. comm., 1985 and 1987): possibly the vault was built later to allow material to be hoisted up to the eastern gable wall (completed in c. 1304), after which the retrochoir vault would have been finished, the break in work perhaps revealed by the change in stone above the springing.

39. Restoration seems not to have touched the windows, save possibly for minor variance in the foiling of the oculi (Buckler's drawings, British Library MS Add. 36361, f. 101v and 104v; Carter, [1797b], Pl. IVA).

40. Cf. Bishop and Prideaux (1922), 38.

41. Such discontinuities may however signify little more than irregularities in supply and labour. Another break in coursing occurs in the stair tower of the chapel of St John the Evangelist between the bottom courses and the sill; the significance for the sequence of construction is unclear.

42. See also Georgina Russell's paper on the subject in this volume.

43. Illustrated in B/E Yorkshire: The North Riding (1966), Pl. 20b.

44. Latter illustrated in Bony (1979), Pls 71 and 63–4 respectively. The earliest known British examples of intersecting tracery are found at Old St Paul's (east front gable, 1280s; Morris [1990], 88); Durham Chapel of Nine Altars (late 1280s; Bony, [1979], 12); and Newstead Abbey (west front, perhaps 1280s). Georgina Russell (1986), 83–9, proposes the Newstead pattern as reconstructed by Peter Kidson for the west façade of Lincoln, although I would question her date of c. 1242–4 as separating Lincoln too long from the other examples; see also Russell (1980), 87–9 and her paper on the original east window at Exeter in this volume. Finding scattered examples from the 1280s–90s throughout England indicates how rapidly and widely motifs were spread in this period.

45. As well as Oxford (Merton College chapel) and Hereford; see Morris (1990). Clerical connections between Exeter and Wells also abound; e.g. Thomas Bytton, canon of Wells since 1269 and dean of Wells since 1284, became bishop of Exeter in 1292; Robinson (1927), 25–9. Robinson cites further interrelationships. Between 1270 and 1310 five deans of Wells were canons at Exeter, and in the 1280s five canons of Wells also held stalls at Exeter.
    Bony (1979), 17, dates the Wells chapel before Exeter, and the clear affiliation of Bishop Burnell with the court would tend to support this. Since the dates for Exeter given here are earlier than previously supposed, the relation may have to be reversed, however, or else Wells may need to be considered as built 'nearer to 1280', as suggested in Draper (1981), 19.

46. Morris (1990), 88. Cf. also, although less closely, the west window of St Etheldreda's (Pl. XD).

47. Bony (1979), 11; 'Y' tracery in bar is seen early at Hereford Cathedral (transept north window, c. 1268) and Amiens (interior, south transept arm, late 1250s-early 1260s). A different line based on 'Y'-formed arches is found in the 1240s, e.g. at Lincoln and York. Deriving from St-Urbain at Troyes or that milieu, the motif of the large pointed trefoil occurs at Old St Paul's (choir triforium, from the late 1270s-early 1280s; Morris [1990], 88; illustrated in Bony (1979), Pl. 28).

48. Erskine (1981), 5–6 and (1983), xxvii, and above, n. 10. The glass in these windows was inserted in 1304, about a decade later than the proposed date of design and installation of the tracery, and at this time some glass was bought for the chapel of St James as well; Erskine (1981), 35.

49. If so, the workshop of St Etheldreda's rather than the built chapel might be the source for these designs. The date of the fourth aisle tracery design could be later, but tied to the time when the arch below was inserted, between c. 1285 and 1291; see n. 58.

50. Erskine (1981), 38, 41, 44.

51. Erskine (1981), 108, 127–9, and Morris in this volume and Morris n. 74.

52. Bishop and Prideaux (1922), 47–8; Erskine (1981), 52–6.
53. Erskine (1981), 106–9. The jambs in the chapel of St Paul are coursed continuously with the wall so that possibly only the inner tracery and head were renewed. The design of the eastern windows are similar to Dorchester Abbey (Oxon.) and Sta Catalina in Barcelona (Bony [1979], 12–13, Pls 75–6).
54. Round plinths in these chapels are like those found in the early work of the eastern arm.
55. Obit accounts, Erskine (1981), xiii.
56. These suppositions are based on the discussion in Erskine (1981), xiii. The 15th-century *Chronicon Breve Exoniense* gives 1288 for the beginning of the church rebuilding, but it seems to be unreliable for 13th-century events. One might even infer from the document of 1289 referring to the eastern chapels that continued small-scale work meant no full operation was yet in progress. Since the rebuilding in fact began under Bishop Bronescombe, Bishop Quinil must have provided a very large amount of funding in order to be called '*primus fundator novi operis*', a title which 20th-century historians would probably apply to Bronescombe. In addition to Quinil's largesse to the fabric while he was living, evidence discussed by Erskine makes it seem likely that an especial donation occurred at his death, which could have called forth the honorary label. The *summary account* made for 1279–87 hints at 1288 as the starting date, however. And possibly, as Mrs Erskine cautioned (pers. comm., 1989), the title may indicate simply Quinil's role in regard to the 'new work', a term developed for accounting purposes in his time rather than signify the rebuilding of the eastern arm.
57. Erskine (1981), 24–6, and 48–9, e.g. corbels and vaulting bosses were painted and the roof was leaded in 1302, while in 1310 the choir stalls were removed; in 1311 the choir was paved, Erskine (1981), 54. The accounts record the dedication of the church in 1312; Erskine (1981), 63.
58. Bishop and Prideaux (1922), 35, noted that the eastern buttresses are bonded in only above the sill, but there is enough regular coursing in the general disjunction, particularly on the north side, to question such a statement. E.g. the plinths are bonded through whereas irregularities in the adjoining buttresses of the southeast angle suggest a lack of concern for regular coursing. Round socles are found in other earlier Exeter work — of the eastern side chapels, the chapels off the aisles, the retrochoir, and the vaulting responds of the aisles (as well as the presumably later chapels of the transept). Polygonal socles occur at the base of the rere-arches of the aisle windows and on the jambs of the entrance arches to the eastern chapels from the retrochoir and to the aisle chapels from the aisles. In the latter case the arch seems inserted; its arch moulding compares only to those of the entrance arches from the retrochoir to the eastern chapels, which differ from all other arch mouldings at Exeter (Fig. 1.11). But in a few places in the Lady Chapel, both polygonal and round bases are carved in one stone. Polygonal socles may be comparatively dated in relationship to St Etheldreda's, *c.* 1284–6 (Morris [1990], n. 114), and Merton College chapel, 1289–94.
59. This difference does not seem to derive from the width of the wall. The two types of arches are used at Merton College chapel (Bony [1979], 12), which gives a comparative date of *c.* 1289–94 for the Exeter work. 1289 accords with the Exeter document citing the eastern side chapels as incomplete and generally with the beginning of the central presbytery campaign. Stylistically the tracery could be dated as late as the years before 1304, when the roof of the Lady Chapel was leaded (Erskine [1981], 35). As here, dates should be given more accurately to reflect a range in chronology rather than the earliest time possible for dating a design, as suggested by a date preceded by *circa*.
60. For example, the sequence of St Etheldreda's, Holborn, to Merton College chapel, Oxford.
61. Illustrated in Bony (1979), Pls 63–4.
62. Illustrated in Bony (1979), Pl. 72. the pattern with a centre oculus containing multiple trefoils, usually six, is characteristic of the 1290s; it is found at Guisborough, Lincoln (cloister), and Ripon (illustrated in Bony [1979], Pl. 88); the general type appears at Exeter in the blind tracery to the aisle chapels (*c.* 1285–91). the multiplication of small units seems to have occurred first in Britain in the clerestory at Old St Paul's, probably in the late 1270s or early 1280s; see Bony (1979), 72, n. 15, Morris (1990), 88 and n. 140.
63. Illustrated in Bony (1979), Pls 172, 265.
64. Bony (1979), 11, where similarities to French examples are discussed. Also typical of courtly motifs of this period are crenellated battlements and the square external profile of the Lady Chapel. Crenellation is found on all of Bishop Robert Burnell's works; Bony (1979), 17.
65. Erskine (1981), 35 and (1983), 317–18.
66. Erskine (1981), 24–8, and installation in 1304, Erskine (1981), 35.
67. Jansen (1975), 200–1. For Ledbury, see B/E *Herefordshire* (1963), 216.
68. B/E *South Devon* (1952), 136 and 138.
69. The ground plan might reflect Sarum liturgical practices. Robinson (1931), 168, states that Bishop Brewer had installed Sarum chapter organisation at Exeter already in 1225, but no precise record of the liturgical observation in this period exists. By the 14th century, however, Bishop Grandisson's (1327–69) modifications to the customs reflected the Use of Sarum, as Audrey Erskine informed me in 1985. Hope and Lloyd

(1973), 11, propose the likelihood that Bishop Bronescombe attended the consecration of Salibury in 1258 and thereafter introduced Salisbury features to Exeter; they note both plans have seven bays in the eastern arm to accommodate the canons. I would make any connection between the plans on the basis of liturgical practice, however, not on a bishop's attendance.

70. Hearn (1971), 187–208.

71. Cf. Bony (1979), 13, 17–18, where he evaluates the term 'provincial' in a positive light.

72. The earlier Tintern choir pier (1270–87) has the same format but the diagonal shafts are detached. For Lincolnshire piers see Dean (1979), 101–3.

73. For recent discussion of clustered piers see Hoey (1984), 214, 220–1, and idem (1987), especially 249–55.

74. Hollar represents the sixteen shafts of the Old St Paul's pier as a series of projections and recessions unlike the evenness of the clustered Exeter pier so that the former, whether it took the form of a combination of coursed and detached shafting or of all coursed marble, as Richard K. Morris (1990), 82, proposed, seems less directly relevant to the latter. Sixteen-shafted piers composed of a mixture of detached and coursed shafts exist elsewhere, e.g. throughout Lincoln and in the York transept, but the two series should be kept separate despite the related desire to elaborate the shafting. See further Hoey (1987). Continental examples of the sixteen-shafted pier exist, too, such as the crossing piers at St Elisabeth, Marburg, but here the design is articulated with hollows in the Rayonnant manner rather than the continuous planes of the standard clustered type.

75. The narrower vault of the Lady Chapel has two pairs of lateral tiercerons, rather than three, and is cited by Morris (1990), n. 74, as the first known example of this increase in tiercerons.

76. Morris (1990), 80.

77. The vault in the Bishop's Palace chapel at Wells (1280s) has only one pair of tiercerons in each direction.

78. B/E South Devon (1952), 138.

79. The master cast the vaults of the aisles as simple quadripartite ones as if to underline the point, perhaps using a hierarchical system, which I have suggested might be considered in interpreting tracery design.

80. In the late 13th century Chester has smaller foliage corbels. Hoey (1987), 257, discusses other examples connected with clustered piers.

81. Illustrated in Bony (1979), Pl. 105.

82. Bishop and Prideaux (1922), 41; B/E South Devon (1952), 136; Bony (1979), 17. Everett and Hope (1968), 186–7, give the change in dimensions of the diameter of the piers from 4 ft 6 in. (presbytery) to 5 ft 2 in. (choir). Because there is not sufficient width for a wall passage in the triforium now, it would seem unlikely that there had been enough space in the first design.

83. Large splays also exist at, e.g. Cistercian Pontigny, 12th-century Creully St Martin (Calvados), and on the interior of west façades at Byland and Wells and of the transept façades at Westminster.

84. These measurements which vary slightly from bay to bay have some margin of error. Thanks are due to Richard K. Morris for helping to measure the slope.

85. In 1318 38 marble columns were ordered; Erskine (1981), 98. I owe the suggestion of the diagonal splay to Jean Bony.

86. Bony (1979), 7.

87. Bishop Quinil died in 1291, a date when work on the central presbytery may have been begun, and Bishop Bytton in 1307, at which time the choir was nearly finished (by 1310). Thus, the elevation was changed during Bytton's episcopacy and not at his accession to the see.

88. Everett and Hope (1968), 189, also came to the conclusion that the change in elevation is Roger's, but the supposition that the designer of the presbytery was another master counters Lethaby (1903), 175; Bishop and Prideaux (1922), 7; and Harvey (1984), 257, who consider that Roger was probably the designer of the entire eastern arm. Erskine (1981), xi, provides evidence of Roger's presence in 1297. In 1280/1 a Master R. appears in the accounts (Erskine [1981], 3–5), but there is no way of establishing his identity with Roger, which, contrary to Erskine (1983), vi, and Harvey, ibid., I find unlikely for the reasons discussed above.

89. Late 13th-century quatrefoil balustrades existed also at Guisborough and York, but probably not Chester; see Jansen (1979), 242, n. 54.

90. Bony (1979), 14, Pl. 81, and following him Jansen (1979), 229–30. Any connection with Wells, where the same two-dimensional pattern occurred, must be ruled out: the construction of the middle storey is different, and all relationships point elsewhere, either to contemporary or to Midland–northern sources.

91. Jansen (1979), 242, n. 55; Bony (1958), 51 (Fig. 15).

92. Richard K. Morris (1978a), 27 and 31. A detail connects Exeter and Chester further — the use of double hollow chamfer mouldings in the triforium arches (Fig. 4.7 in R. K. Morris's article, and Jansen [1975], Pl. 85); see also Jansen (1982), 46–7, and (1975), 176, 181–3.

93. Quinil, however, often made short trips to London; Hingeston-Randolph (1889), xxi.

94. B/E South Devon (1952), 138.

95. The west-southwest and Midland-north axis seems to be apparent in other ways, too; cf. Morris (1979), 26, on the pervasive type of the base at Exeter, and Givens (1985), chapter IV, on naturalistic foliage at Exeter, York and Southwell.
96. A further detail helps to confirm the connection: both Exeter and the Lincoln Angel Choir as well as the chapter house of Wells have bundles of five vaulting shafts, whereas three is the norm in other churches of this period. Bony (1979), 13, discusses connections between the Cistercians and court architecture.
97. As discussed above, many of the elements had been combined before in this period, but in different ways, e.g. at Old St Paul's and Tintern; these buildings enlarge the context for the architecture at Exeter.

Thomas of Witney at Exeter, Winchester and Wells

By Richard K. Morris

Master Thomas of Witney is one of the best recorded architects of the 14th century, and the nave and fittings at Exeter Cathedral are his most famous works. Audrey Erskine's excellent edition of the fabric accounts indicates that he held the position of master mason at the cathedral for at least twenty-six years, from Michaelmas 1316 until Midsummer 1342.[1] Moreover, his career as a whole (fl. 1292–1342) has been skilfully pieced together by John Harvey, based primarily on documentary sources,[2] and these works by Erskine and Harvey form the essential background for this paper. Suffice it to reiterate here that Master Thomas probably hailed from Witney in Oxfordshire, and is documented in a junior capacity at St Stephen's Chapel, Westminster, 1292–4. Then, after a gap in his recorded career and before moving to Exeter, he appears as a resident of Winchester in or before 1311 and in charge of work on the cathedral presbytery there. Besides these buildings, a good case can be made for his involvement at Wells Cathedral; and it has also been suggested that he is connected with works at Malmesbury Abbey and Merton College, Oxford.[3] With regard to Exeter, it will be pertinent here to assess more closely his work at Winchester, as well as to give some consideration to the stylistic evidence for the attribution to him of parts of Wells and Malmesbury.

The primary aim of this paper is to examine the architectural detail of work at Exeter Cathedral in Witney's period, and especially the mouldings, to see if the documents provide a valid frame of reference for following the style of a master mason. If the documentary evidence was lost, would we still recognise that Witney had worked at the cathedral? If he had an identifiable style, to what extent could he impose it on a building already half complete at his arrival? How do his designs for the detail of the liturgical furniture compare with those for monumental architecture? And for works executed in stone with those in wood? These are some of the issues to be addressed below.

It is best to commence with the furnishings of the eastern arm, for these have long been acknowledged as the most distinctive examples of his style and ingenuity as a designer. In a stroke, he ushered in the full-blown fantasy of Decorated style, rooted in his previous experience with the Kentish masons working for the court. The works attributed to him present every possible variation on the ogee arch — nodding, haunched, depressed (e.g. the throne, pulpitum, sedilia, and the Stapledon tombs, Pls XIA, B, C; XIIB, C, XXVIA); though simple ogee arches had appeared at Exeter shortly before his arrival, in the choir-stalls of John of Glaston and elsewhere.[4] He also introduced lierne vaults at a moment when they were still a novelty nationally (pulpitum, sedilia, St Edmund's chapel, Pls XID, XIIA, XXIIID),[5] and the throne and sedilia reveal a delight in complicated geometry, especially canopies designed on a geometrical plan (Pl. XIIB).[6]

The earliest of the furnishings is the bishop's wooden throne (1313–19),[7] for which Robert de Galmeton was chief carpenter and about which Master Thomas de Winton ('Thomas from Winchester') gave advice in 1313. It is clearly very important for the purpose of this paper that one accepts that this Master Thomas is identical with Thomas of Witney,[8] and that he designed the throne — either in 1313, as an outside consultant, or immediately upon his appointment as master of the works in or before 1316.[9] In fact, Harvey's examination of the documentary evidence proves conclusively that Witney had been engaged previously at Winchester, and this is corroborated by the stylistic evidence to be considered later. Moreover, it can be demonstrated that the throne is the seminal work for the architectural detail of the other fittings designed and made during Witney's period as master mason: especially the pulpitum (1317–25) and the presbytery sedilia (c. 1316–26),[10] both in stone.

The mouldings of all the relevant furnishings and fittings are illustrated in Figures 1 and 2. The initial impression of the profiles may be one of variety, but closer inspection reveals a number of distinctive common elements. Variation of detail is to be anticipated in a situation where several experienced craftsmen were engaged on the works, as the accounts indicate.[11] Indeed, it may be more than coincidence that two skilled masons with names implying that they came from outside the area — John de 'Baunebiri' (?Banbury) and Robert 'Atteboxe' (?Box near Bath) — first appeared at Exeter in the same year as Witney.[12] Had they travelled with him from his previous job, perhaps Winchester Cathedral? None the less, the shared elements in the furnishings suggest the hand of one master designer behind the scenes, who must surely be the master mason, Thomas of Witney. The salient points of comparison are as follows:

a) *Arch soffits*: The main arches employ a distinctive double moulding for the soffit, the upper one defining the arch and the lower one the cusping (Figs 1.1, 1.6, 1.9A–B and Pl. XIIA).

b) *Undulating mouldings*: The throne and pulpitum arches follow exactly the same design, with the lower profile combining pear and wave mouldings (Figs 1.1, 1.6B). These are both mouldings which Witney seems to have introduced to the cathedral workshop, for they are not found in those parts of the church which pre-date his arrival (see e.g. Figs 3.9–11). Small wave mouldings also appear on the piers of the pulpitum (Fig. 1.5C), and though these components are in Purbeck marble and were supplied ready-cut from Corfe,[13] the template was probably designed in the cathedral workshop under Witney, rather than at the quarry.[14] This procedure can definitely be demonstrated with the Purbeck marble bases of the pulpitum (see (e) below). The wave moulding was never to be a major characteristic of his work, but certainly he shows a predilection for undulating shapes in his architectural mouldings at Exeter and elsewhere, as will be seen later (e.g. Fig. 5).

c) *Filleted capitals*: Some of the capitals of the throne and pulpitum use a roll and fillet moulding in this context for the first time at Exeter (Figs 2.2–3A). Previously, the design of capital favoured in the cathedral since the late 13th century placed a keel moulding in this position (Figs 3.1, 3.3A), but this moulding is discontinued in all the works attributed to Witney except for the capitals of the sedilia (Fig. 2.4).

d) *Bead mouldings*: Probably the most distinctive and personal detail is the introduction of an additional bead moulding (or occasionally a fillet) at the necking of most of the capitals of the throne, pulpitum and sedilia (Figs 2.2–5B). The main exceptions are the front capitals of the pulpitum, which are the only ones executed in Purbeck marble, and probably represent a standard component from the Corfe quarries (Pl. XIB). They are quite similar to those which the Canon family had been supplying to the cathedral previously (cf. Figs 2.1, 3.3), and are of a conventional design for the period.[15] It is very significant for the attribution to Witney that the capital with the additional bead at the necking appears, perhaps for the first time in England, in the undercroft of St Stephen's Chapel, Westminster, where he was employed in the 1290s.[16] Given this early usage in the south-east, the ultimate source is

FIG. 1.   Exeter Cathedral: furnishings and monuments (Witney)

1–3. Pulpitum: main arch (det.), transverse arch, vault rib.   4. Bishop's throne: rib (timber).
5. Pulpitum: pier (det., Purbeck).   6. Throne: canopy arch (det., timber).   7. R. Stapledon tomb: recess arch.   8. Bishop Stapledon tomb: recess arch.   9. Presbytery sedilia: arch.
10. St Andrew's chapel: north canopy, arch

4. Courtesy of John Allan

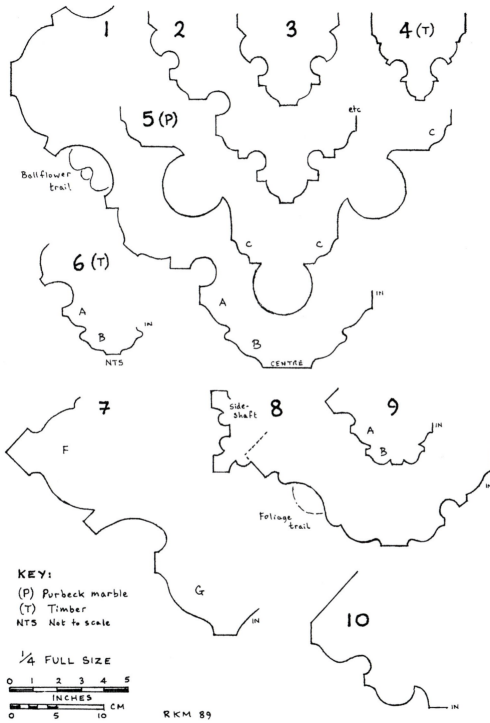

KEY:
(P) Purbeck marble
(T) Timber
NTS Not to scale

¼ FULL SIZE

INCHES
CM

RKM 89

E

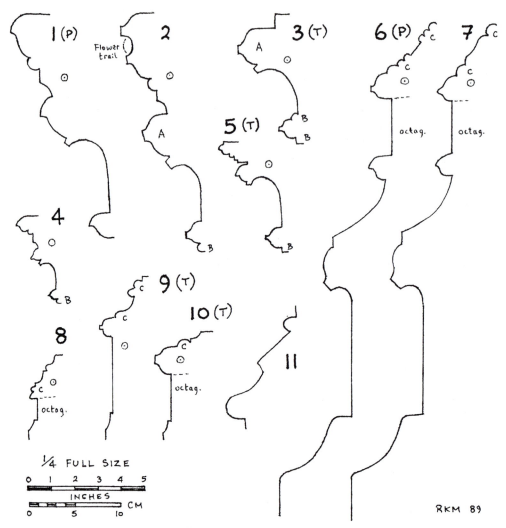

FIG. 2.   Exeter Cathedral: furnishings and monuments (Witney)

1–2. Pulpitum: west capital (Purbeck), east capital.   3, 5. Bishop's throne: capitals (timber).
4. Presbytery sedilia: capital.   6–7. Pulpitum: west base (Purbeck), east base.   8. Sedilia:
base.   9–10. Throne, bases (timber).   11. R. Stapledon tomb: plinth

3, 5, 9, 10. Courtesy of John Allan

probably in French Rayonnant architecture,[17] but it appears that it was also popular with craftsmen like Witney who worked in wood: the easier carving quality of wood encouraging extra embellishment. The main distribution of this unusual feature lies in the south of England from the 1290s onwards including the wooden choir-stalls at Chichester and Winchester Cathedrals.[18] This is the area in which Witney is most likely to have been employed before his move to Exeter, where he introduced the device in the capitals of the wooden throne. At Winchester, he worked alongside the Norfolk carpenter, William Lyngwode (1308–c. 1310), who used the detail in his choir-stalls there, and it is interesting that its other main distribution is in East Anglia.[19]

e) *Elaborate bases*:   A fondness for extra bead mouldings and a general fussiness in design character-ises most of the bases of the throne, pulpitum and sedilia (Figs 2.6–10; and cf. Figs 3.4–5). Harvey is surely correct in emphasising the tall and ornate bases of the pulpitum as a particular feature of Witney's work.[20] Though the west bases are of Purbeck marble (Pl. XIc), they are unlikely to be a design of the Corfe marblers because their profile is virtually identical to the east bases, which are in freestone and a product of the cathedral workshop under Witney (cf. Figs 2.6, 2.7).

f) *Symmetry, hollows and prominent fillets*:   Hollow mouldings and some fillets had inevitably been incorporated in arch profiles from the inception of the rebuilding of the cathedral (e.g. Fig. 3.9B–C), but the furnishings show a new symmetry in their disposition and a greater use of fillets, particularly exemplified in the heavily moulded arches of the pulpitum (Figs 1.1–2). The ribs of the miniature vaults of the pulpitum and throne also exhibit these characteristics (Figs 1.3–4), but are less helpful in characterising his work; the throne rib is a miniature version of one of the rib profiles already employed in the high vault of the choir, completed *c.* 1310 (cf. Figs 1.4, 3.10).

g) *Omission of scroll and keel mouldings*:   In the arches of all the furnishings, scroll and keel mouldings are discontinued, which had been a feature of arch designs in the cathedral workshop up to this time (e.g. Figs 3.9, 3.11A and D; cf. Figs 1.1, 1.2, 1.6, 1.9).

h) *Foliage spandrels*:   In addition to the moulding comparisons, a memorable feature of the pulpitum is the exquisitely carved foliage in its cusped and sub-cusped spandrels (Pl. XIA); and exactly the same idea appears in the throne, in the tympana of the gables of the main canopy, rather hidden by the ogee arches in front of them (Pl. XIIB, bottom). The usage in a gable suggests a link in design, if not in execution, with the excessive foliage in the cusped and sub-cusped tympana of the north aisle tomb recesses in St Thomas's church, Winchelsea (1312 sqq.),[21] virtually contemporary with the Exeter throne. And the ultimate source may well be the foliate spandrels of Lyngwode's choir-stalls at Winchester, a year or two earlier.[22]

The foregoing analysis has avoided the two other extant monuments in the eastern arm which date from Witney's period: the tomb of Bishop Stapledon (d. 1326)[23] and that in the north choir aisle attributed to his brother, Sir Robert Stapledon (d. 1320). Their architec-ture feels heavier than the style of the fittings and they present fewer points of comparison, lacking pinnacled canopies and such moulded elements as bases and capitals (e.g. Pl. XIIc). None the less, the detail of the bishop's tomb inclines one to accept that its design is also from Witney's hand. Comparison of the arch moulding with the canopy arches of the sedilia and throne reveals obvious similarities, especially the broad filleted profile of the soffit (cf. Figs 1.6, 1.8, 1.9). Moreover, the exaggeratedly depressed shape of the ogee arch and of its sub-cusping, together with the hollow moulding delicately carved with foliage tendrils, is very reminiscent of the treatment of such features on the façade of the pulpitum (Pl. XIA).

Sir Robert Stapledon's tomb (Pl. XIIc) relates less precisely to Witney's style, and is harder to assess in this context. The recess appears to combine local workmanship based on the cathedral workshop with ideas typical of the Decorated style at Witney's previous work place of Winchester. Elements of the arch moulding bear comparison with the arches already discussed (cf. Figs 1.7, 1.8), and the undercut wave moulding is used at Winchester Cathedral in the clerestory of the east bay of the presbytery, surely by Witney, as well as elsewhere at Winchester (cf. Figs 1.7G, 7.7).[24] The heavy and slightly crude appearance of the overall design relates to a series of local tomb recesses at Modbury and elsewhere in Devon,[25] but Witney also favoured robust mouldings for monumental architecture (e.g. nave, north porch, Pl. XIIIB and Fig. 5.7), though less so in his furnishings. One other feature of the tomb worthy of comment is the carved heads on the cusping (Pl. XIIc), which are unusual in stonework but more common in woodwork. The idea might already have been known in the cathedral workshop,[26] but could well have been derived from Lyngwode's choir-stalls at Winchester by way of Witney: angel busts appear in this position on the Exeter throne.[27]

The liturgical furnishings of Bishop Stapledon's episcopate, and his own tomb (and perhaps that of his brother), demonstrate that a new designer had arrived at Exeter, with fresh ideas. The details would lead us to this conclusion, even if the accounts had not survived. This cannot be said, however, for the main architecture of the cathedral undertaken in Witney's time. The elevations of the transept arms and the nave (Pl. XXXIVD) are virtually identical in design and detail to that of the choir. This need not surprise us in the transept, which was well on the way to completion before his arrival. Even in the nave it should be remembered that the east bay was finished as part of the programme for the eastern arm, and therefore stood as a model for work on the rest of the nave, which commenced in earnest after 1328. In fact, the indications are that the components for this bay had been carved, and largely put into place before he appeared as Master Mason in 1316.[28]

None the less, it is remarkable that templates with designs dating back to the 1280s and 1290s were retained for the mouldings of the main features of the nave: arcades, triforium, windows and ribs. In particular the mullion profile still employed in the 1330s in the nave aisle and clerestory windows had been in use at Exeter for fifty years, and was completely outdated (Fig. 3.6).[29] Minor modifications of detail which did take place are virtually indiscernible, such as the substitution of fillets for bead mouldings in the diagonal ribs of the aisle and high vaults in the six new bays of the nave (cf. Figs 3.10, 4.10E).[30] This equates with the preference for fillets observed in his furnishings, and in small changes in the capitals of the nave clerestory and vault springings (cf. Figs 3.2, 4.2–3). Unfortunately, these mouldings are not sufficiently distinctive to provide a conclusive answer to the vexed question of the date of the high vault, and though their evidence would not contradict a completion date in his time,[31] it is sounder at this juncture to leave the matter open.[32]

Away from the main east/west elevation, however, there are two areas in which the moulding profiles bear witness to Witney's personal contribution: the corbelled-out triforium passages under the towers, and the various major doorways of the nave. The reason for his intervention is presumably because such features had not existed in the fabric as rebuilt up to then, and therefore completely new templates were needed.

The triforium passages are corbelled out from the east and west walls of the transept end bays, and are additions to whatever work was done in this area in 1285–7.[33] They are not mentioned in the accounts, but one of the mouldings provides a vital clue to their date. The edge of their balconies, at the foot of the balustrade, is carved with the distinctive sunk chamfer (Fig. 4.8), and all the circumstances suggest that this moulding was introduced at Exeter by Witney. It had been used slightly earlier at Winchester Cathedral in the feretory east arcade, for which he was almost certainly responsible (Fig. 7.3), and also for some of the contemporary Decorated work in the transept there.[34] Then, at Exeter, sunk chamfers form the arches of the blind triforium arcade added to the presbytery, as the accounts tell us, in c. 1318.[35] The arches are a different design to those of the pre-existing triforium in the choir (cf. Figs 4.6, 4.7; Pl. XIIB), though the reason for the change is unclear. Perhaps Witney felt that this shallower moulding was visually more appropriate for the thinner walls of the presbytery.[36] Interestingly enough, he did not use it for the triforium of the six bays of

FIG. 3.   Exeter Cathedral: eastern arm (pre-Witney)

1–3. Capitals: Lady Chapel, choir vault, main arcade (Purbeck).   4–5. Bases: main arcade (Purbeck), Lady Chapel.   6–7. Choir aisles: mullion, window jamb.   8–9. Arches: choir aisle window rere-arch, main arcade (⅙ scale).   10–11. High vault: ribs

10. Courtesy of John Allan

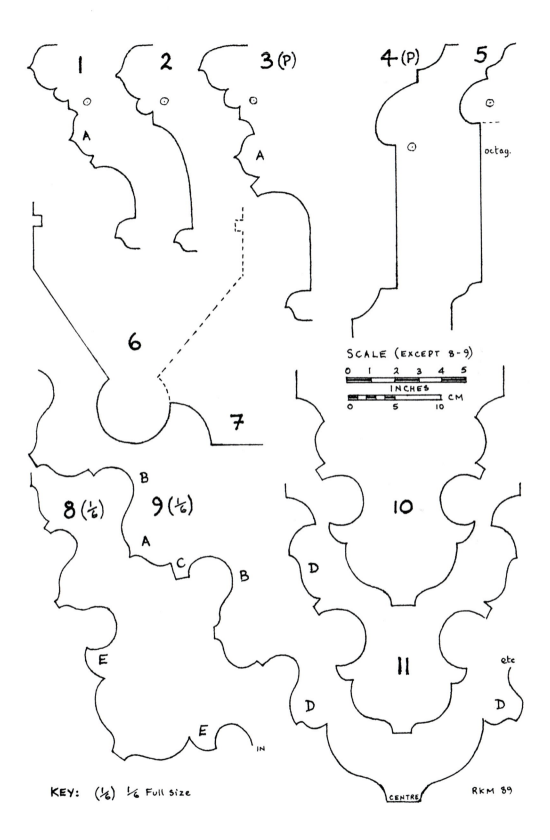

1

2

3 (P)

4 (P)

5

octag.

6

7

SCALE (EXCEPT 8-9)

0 1 2 3 4 5
INCHES

0 5 10
CM

8 (⅙)

9 (⅙)

B

A

C

B

10

D

E

B

11

D

etc

E

D

IN

KEY: (⅙) ⅙ Full size

CENTRE

RKM 89

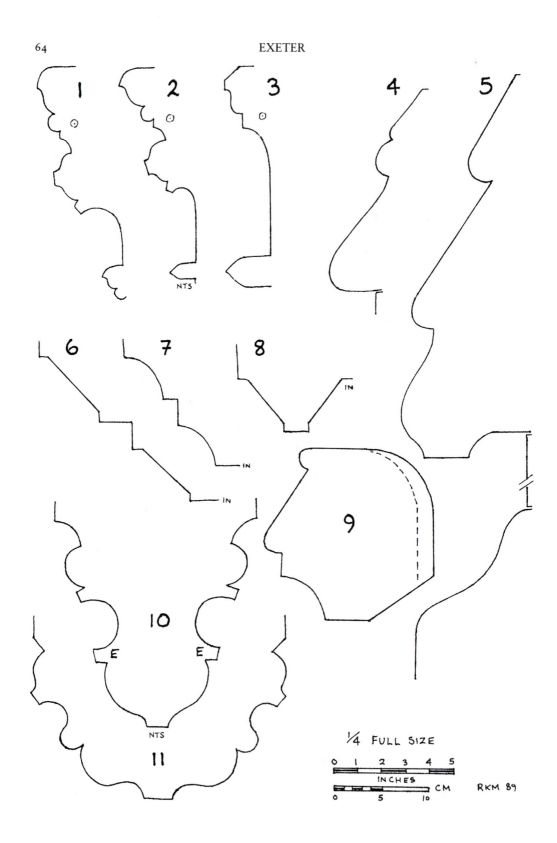

1

2

3

4

5

NTS

6

7

8

IN

IN

IN

IN

9

10

E E

NTS

11

¼ FULL SIZE

0 1 2 3 4 5
INCHES
CM
0 5 10

RKM 89

the nave done in his time, and therefore the moulding is characteristic only of his early years at Exeter, fresh from Winchester. Thus, the triforium balconies in the transept end bays should belong to *c.* 1316 or the years directly following, when we know that work was in progress to complete the upper parts of the transept arms.[37]

About ten years later, *c.* 1328/9, Witney designed the various portals of the nave, which can be attributed to him especially by analogy with his work in the east bay of Winchester Cathedral presbytery, as well as with the fittings at Exeter. The portals in question are those of the north porch, the three west doors (but not their porches), and the south door in the west bay of the nave originally leading to the cloister.[38] Also to be grouped with them for stylistic reasons are the arch leading to St Edmund's chapel, the large archway (now blocked) in the east wall of Bishop Grandisson's mortuary chapel, and probably the rere-arch of the nave west window.[39] As the arch in the Grandisson chapel is identical in its mouldings to the outer frame of the central west door (cf. Figs 5.4, 5.5; Pl. XIIIA), there seems little doubt that it was originally intended to be an exterior entrance to the chapel, which presumably would have been located inside the nave against the west wall, and that it belongs to *c.* 1330.[40] On the other hand, the arch to St Edmund's chapel looks earlier for stylistic reasons. It still includes beaded rolls, a moulding established in the cathedral workshop before his arrival (cf. Figs 3.8, 5.1E), as well as the undercut wave moulding, which he employed in the furnishings of the eastern arm (*c.* 1317–26) but not elsewhere in the nave work (Fig. 5.1G). As the accounts of 1318–19 record work on St Edmund's chapel, it is possible that this entrance arch was knocked through the north wall of the Romanesque nave at about this period, in advance of the major reconstruction of the nave after 1328.[41]

A representative set of profiles from the nave portals group is drawn in Figure 5, and the homogeneity of their style is self-evident. Some features are familiar from the fittings of the eastern arm, such as broad roll and fillet mouldings used for the soffit of arches and elsewhere (e.g. Figs 5.1, 5.4, 5.6, 5.9A); capitals with a filleted bell and an extra bead at the necking (Fig. 4.1); and foliage decoration in deep hollow mouldings (e.g. Figs 5.2, 5.4B and Pl. XIIIA). In particular, a curious 'opening up' of a roll and fillet moulding to create a hollow for flower tendril ornament emphasises the close design relationship between the arch of the north porch door and the freestone capitals of the pulpitum (Figs 5.7C and 2.2; and Pl. XIIA, bottom centre and top right). In addition, the profiles indicate a fondness for large bead mouldings (e.g. Figs 5.2, 5.4D), often continued into a counter-curve to create a noticeable ogee (e.g. Figs 5.3, 5.4, 5.7H); an idea apparently of Kentish and, ultimately, French Rayonnant origin.[42] In general there is an interest in 'round-nosed' mouldings (e.g. Figs 5.7, 5.9J), in bold undulating lines, and in rather asymmetrical shapes created out of roll and fillet mouldings (e.g. Figs 5.2, 5.3, 5.6–8K).

Three things stand out about the style of this group. First, the general contrast with the mouldings and detail of the lower parts of the west screen front, especially of the south and central porches, and the Grandisson chapel as built (Fig. 6, and cf. Figs 4.1, 4.4, 4.11 and 5.2, 5.4). The documentary evidence and the comparison with other buildings, particularly the presbytery of Wells Cathedral, leaves little doubt that these works on the west front are

Fig. 4.   Exeter Cathedral: architecture (mainly Witney)

1–3. Capitals: north porch door, nave clerestory (West bay), nave vault (bays 2–4). 4. West front: centre door, base.   5. North porch: plinth.   6–7. Triforium arches: presbytery (Witney), choir, etc. (pre-Witney).   8. Transept, tower bays: triforium balconies, cornice. 9. Triforium: balustrade, coping types (pre-Witney).   10–11. Vault ribs: nave aisles (bays 2–7), north porch

in the style of Master William Joy, and are his documented work of the 1340s.[43] In the centre porch, for example, the break is obvious between Witney's heavier filleted mouldings of the west door (Pl. XIIIA, left) and the delicate bowtell shafts, capitals and bases of the porch itself and of the entrance to the Grandisson chapel (Pl. XIIIA, right). The use of a rare pellet ornament on the latter, and on some of the lower statue niches of the front, is seen again in the nave on the miniature architecture of the famous minstrels' gallery, which was therefore probably carved in this post-Witney period as well.[44]

Second, one needs to account for the apparent contrast between the bulk of these ponderous, curvaceous mouldings and the more delicate, decorative profiles of the fur- nishings (cf. Figs 1, 5). The fact that they share a number of design similarities with the furnishings suggests that the explanation does not lie in a change of designer, but rather that Witney consciously fostered the differences to emphasise their respective contexts: the heavier ones for monumental architecture and the lighter ones for fittings. Exactly the same sort of contrast is to be seen between the fittings and architecture in the feretory bay of Winchester Cathedral, where he was previously engaged. And this leads on to the third point, namely that the main traits of his architectural mouldings at Exeter are surely derived from those at Winchester.

No definite date is known for the start of work on the rebuilding of the eastern arm of Winchester Cathedral,[45] but its internal elevation is directly related to that at Exeter, especially in the use of the pierced balustrade (Pls XIIID and XIIB, top), and must be close to it in time. It is known that this feature was first introduced at Exeter in the choir, c. 1300–10,[46] so it is generally accepted that its usage there precedes that at Winchester. One might even speculate as to whether the transmission of the idea was through Witney's visit to Exeter in 1313. Not only the overall design of the balustrade but also the profiles of the hand-rail are very similar in both buildings (cf. Figs 4.9, 7.8). Furthermore, in the feretory bay at Winchester, the design of the apertures for the clerestory passage and the profile of the adjoining clerestory window jambs both could be derived from the work of Master Roger (c. 1296–1310) and Master William Luve (1310–c. 1313) in the choir and transept at Exeter (cf. Figs 3.7, 7.6).[47] In other words, a date around 1313 would fit well for the start of work at the clerestory level in the east bay at Winchester.

What is certain, from the evidence assembled by John Harvey,[48] is that by c. 1310 Witney was an established resident of Winchester and engaged by the cathedral priory on a work which must surely be the rebuilding of the feretory bay linking the presbytery and the retrochoir. For purposes of comparison with Exeter, the relevant work of this period (c. 1310–15) focuses on the north-east arcade of the presbytery (Pl. XIIID), the feretory screen (Pl. XIIIC) and the east arcade of the wall above it.[49] The Decorated pier and the bases of the north-east arcade[50] are standard and rather anonymous designs in Purbeck marble, also employed in the main elevation at Exeter since the late 13th century (Figs 3.4, 7.5).[51] The other features, however, are more interesting, and warrant closer scrutiny.

In the profiles of the north-east and east arcade arches of the feretory (Pl. XIIID), we re-encounter the heavy curvaceous style of mouldings which characterised Witney's nave portals group at Exeter. The main relationships between them are mainly self-explanatory

FIG. 5.   Exeter Cathedral: nave arches (Witney); ⅙ scale
1. St Edmund's chapel: entrance (det.).   2. Nave, south aisle, west bay: cloister door.   3, 5. West front, centre door: interior, exterior (dets).   4. Grandisson chapel: east arch.   6. West front, north and south doors: interior.   7–8. North porch: exterior jamb/arch, interior.   9. North porch entrance: jamb/arch.

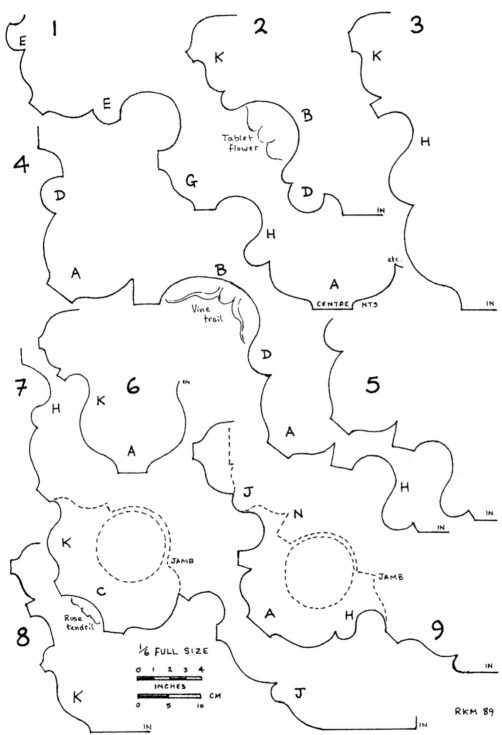

1

E

E

2

K

B

Tablet
flower

D

3

K

H

4

D

G

H

A

B

Vine
trail

D

A

CENTRE NTS

etc.

IN

IN

7

6

H K

IN

A

5

A

H

IN

J

N

K

JAMB

C

Rose
tendril

8

K

9

A H

JAMB

IN

J

K

⅙ FULL SIZE

0 1 2 3 4

INCHES

CM

0   5   10

IN

IN

RKM 89

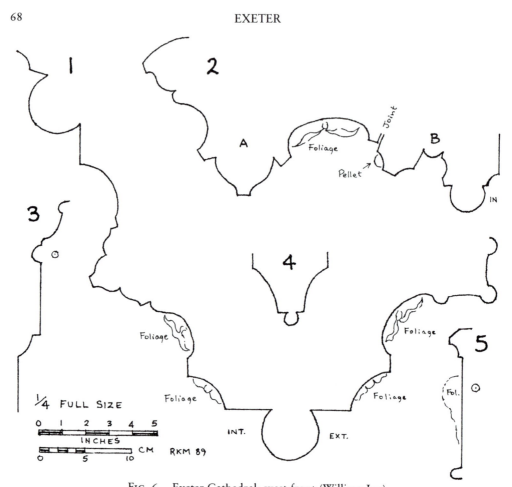

FIG. 6.   Exeter Cathedral: west front (William Joy)
1. Centre porch: vault respond and entrance jamb.   2. Grandisson chapel: door arch/jamb.
3–4. South porch: base, vault rib.   5. Centre porch: vault respond capital

from a comparison of the drawings (cf. Figs 7.1–2 and 4.11, 5.1, 5.3, 5.6, 5.9), and some arch profiles of the Exeter fittings are also relevant (e.g. Fig. 1.1, 1.2, 1.7, 1.8). One needs to allow for the appearance of bead mouldings in some of the later profiles at Exeter, in place of fillets. In the case of the north-east arcade arch, particularly telling points of comparison are the 'squashed' roll and fillet moulding for the soffit (Fig. 7.1A: cf. Bishop Stapledon's tomb arch, Fig. 1.8); and the asymmetrical double fillet moulding for the central order (Figs. 7.1B: cf. north porch door, Fig. 5.7C). Moreover, the relationship to the hoodmould of the curvilinear profile at the top of the arch (Fig. 7.1C) could be the germ of the idea for the unusual treatment of the interior frame of the north porch door at Exeter (Fig. 5.8K); and we have already seen how ogee and undulating mouldings in general were favoured by Witney. The ogee moulding with fillets is also the basis of the feretory east arcade arch (Fig. 7.2C), and the very rounded, almost vegetal quality of the roll and fillet moulding of the soffit recurs in the west door frames at Exeter (cf. Figs 7.2D and 5.6A).

Several other traits of the mouldings are of import for his style. The capitals of the clerestory rere-arch (significantly only in the feretory bay) have the characteristic extra bead moulding at the necking. In the capital of the north-east arcade, a filleted profile replaces the more usual scroll moulding for the bell,[52] and both these traits also occur in the vault corbels of the elaborate chapel in the east aisle of the north transept.[53] For the capitals of the feretory east arcade, a pear moulding is used instead for the bell (Fig. 7.4E), a moulding which went on to enjoy a wider currency at Exeter especially in the furnishings (e.g. Figs 1.1, 1.6B). The Purbeck piers of the east arcade incorporate prominent sunk chamfer mouldings (Fig. 7.3), which we have seen as a characteristic of his early work at Exeter, but its inclusion in a pier design is very distinctive. Not only does the sunk chamfer originate in the king's works in North Wales, but only three other instances for piers are known, and they all have royal connotations — in the choir arcades of Chester Cathedral (west bays, c. 1291–1305), of the London Greyfriars (1306 sqq.) and of Holy Trinity church, Kingston-upon-Hull (c. 1320 sqq.).[54] The London Greyfriars church, begun by the royal mason, Walter of Hereford, is the most likely source for the Winchester piers, and suggests that Witney[55] wanted the smartest, most fashionable forms from London for the prestigious setting of the feretory.

Below this arcade stands the highly ornate feretory screen (Pl. XIIIc), which previous authorities have correctly linked to the stone furnishings at Exeter,[56] and indeed all the signs are that it is the work of Witney — or perhaps one of his team. I introduce this slight qualification, because it is possible that Witney was primarily a structural and architectural specialist,[57] and that similar decorative details in some of the fittings attributed to him could actually have been determined by one or more skilled carvers who followed him from Winchester to Exeter.[58] With regard to date, stylistically the screen could belong to the period immediately preceding the Exeter fittings (i.e. c. 1310–15), but one should keep an open mind as to whether it might be a slightly later work of the 1320s, a date which could be substantiated by the main comparisons for the moulding profiles (see further below).

Regardless of these niceties of interpretation, the connection of the Winchester screen with the Exeter furnishings is clear. The delicate ogee arches have been compared to those of the pulpitum (Pls XIA, XIIIc), and the haunched form of the arch reappears in the main canopies of the bishop's throne. Like the Exeter furnishings, and the tomb of Bishop Stapledon, the screen is studded with a wide repertoire of foliage ornaments, including roses, tablet flower and ballflower tendril (Pl. XIIIc). In this context, the sculptured canopy reset against the north wall of St Andrew's chapel should be considered (Pl. XIID), for it bears a remarkable general likeness in its ogee arch and trefoiled gable to the feretory screen, even though the carving is not quite of the same exquisite quality. The idea that it was originally intended for the high altar reredos has been resurrected recently,[59] and if this were so, it might be one of the first works recorded in the altar accounts of 1316 sqq. Its mouldings are not really typical of Witney's furnishings at Exeter, though the double roll and fillet form somewhat resembles the soffit profile of the north-east arcade arch at Winchester (cf. Figs 1.10, 7.1F), and therefore may confirm its early date.

The mouldings of the feretory screen reveal convincing links with his work at Exeter. Fillets and extra beads characterise the stringcourses, and the asymmetrical treatment of the main roll and fillet moulding on the upper stringcourse (Fig. 8.1A) may be compared with various hoodmoulds used for the nave doors at Exeter (Figs 5.2, 5.3K). Bishop Stapledon's tomb provides the closest parallels for the lower string-course (Fig. 8.2B),[60] and for the arch and sideshaft profiles of the tabernacle work, especially the way in which hollows containing floral decoration are demarcated with bead mouldings, as also found on some of the nave doors (cf. Figs 8.3–4, 1.8, 5.2). Delicate bead mouldings were, of course, a feature

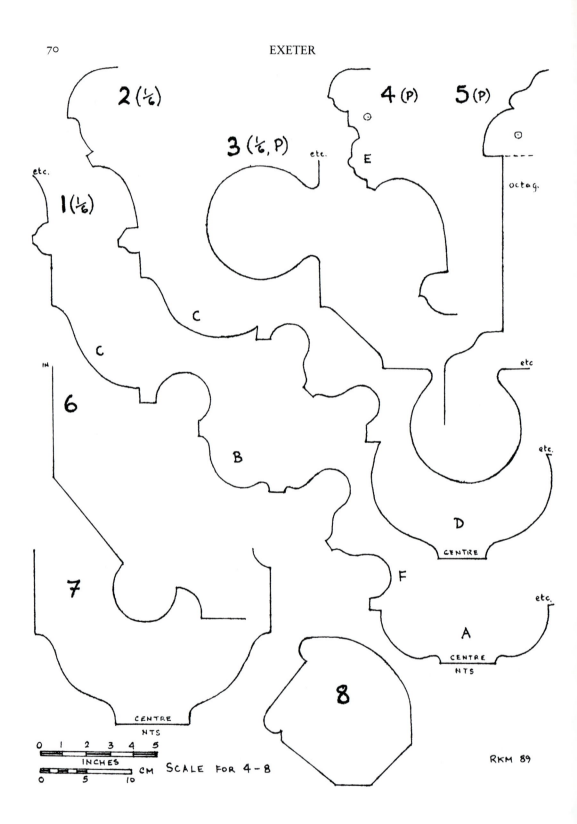

RKM 89

of the Exeter furnishings (e.g. Figs 2.6–7), but the observation that most of the links are with Bishop Stapledon's tomb (after 1326) and with the nave doors could support an argument that the feretory screen is a work of the 1320s, on a return visit to Winchester by Witney or one of his craftsmen.

As a tailpiece to this consideration of Winchester, it is of potential significance for fleshing out the bare bones of Witney's career to note that a number of the mouldings he had employed there appear marginally earlier at St Thomas's, Winchelsea. In the extant fabric of the church, usually dated c. 1290–1312, one can find beaded and filleted capitals, and sunk chamfer and pear mouldings.[61] In particular the profile of the main arcade arches looks to be transitional between the design of the undercroft ribs at St Stephen's Chapel, Westminster (where he had previously worked), and the feretory bay arcades at Winchester (Figs 7.1–2).[62] Some of these features, especially the pear moulding, continue in the monuments and fittings of the south aisle, generally dated after the foundation of an Alard chantry there in 1322.[63] It is well known that the architectural character of St Thomas's church, standing as it does in a royal new town, is very close to the style of Kentish masters working at court, such as Michael of Canterbury. Yet the names of the craftsmen involved here have gone unrecorded. From the evidence presented above, it seems quite possible that Witney was engaged in an important capacity at Winchelsea at some time between his disappearance from the Westminster accounts in 1294 and his reappearance at Winchester, c. 1310. And that Witney, or a craftman involved in his furnishings at Winchester and Exeter, continued to remain intermittently involved at Winchelsea with the various monuments of c. 1312 and c. 1322.

This paper has concentrated so far on the study of mouldings, and it has been shown at Exeter how relatively little opportunity was afforded to Witney to design new profiles for the architecture. The same is not true, however, of window tracery, and without doubt his greatest achievement in the field of architectural design at the cathedral is the display of tracery patterns in the nave windows (Pls III, XIVa, b). Given the conservatism of their mullion profiles, there is no implicit proof in the fabric that all the windows are his, but the documented progress of work on the nave implies that they would have been executed during his master masonship,[64] and the stylistic antecedents of some of them equate well with what is known of his earlier career.

The virtuosity of the windows is dazzling, for we are in the presence of the most varied display of non-flamboyant tracery patterns in the later Decorated period. The fact that the designs emphasise geometrical and crystalline qualities, rather than bold ogee curves, reflects his connection with the Kentish masons working at court and in the south east, and a continuing interest in continental Rayonnant. This is especially evident in the great west window (Pl. XXXIVd), in which the five-part organisation of the centre rose is clearly related to the slightly earlier window of St Anselm's chapel in Canterbury Cathedral (1336).[65] A smaller version of this idea may be seen in one of the clerestory designs (Pl. XIVa, top left), and other motifs in the clerestory, such as the 'mouchette wheel' and the 'propeller' pattern, are right up-to-date with some of the latest tracery designs on the continent (Pl. XIVb, top left, and XIVa, top right).[66] The best explanation for this cosmopolitan modernity is Witney's known involvement with court masons early in his

FIG. 7. Winchester Cathedral: feretory bay

1. North-east arcade arch (⅙ scale).   2–3. East arcade (⅙ scale): arch, pier (Purbeck).   4. East arcade: capital (Purbeck).   5, North-east arcade: base (Purbeck).   6–8. Clerestory: window jamb, rere-arch, balustrade coping (interior)

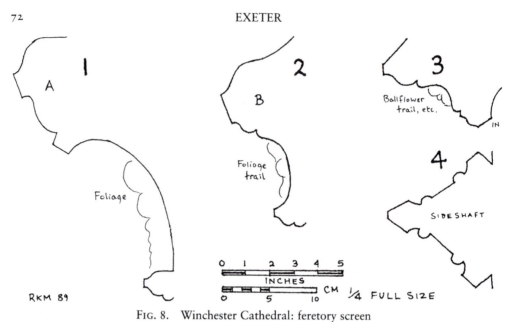

FIG. 8. Winchester Cathedral: feretory screen
1–2. String-courses: upper, lower. 3. Arch/gable. 4. Sideshaft

career which probably established enduring professional relationships with Kentish designers, whose work shows a familiarity with continental architecture.[67] In the south-east, designs related to the hexagonal, stellar form of the clerestory propeller pattern appear in the miniature blind tracery of the north aisle tomb recesses at St Thomas's, Winchelsea (*c.* 1312 sqq.), and in the rose window of the former great hall of the bishop of Winchester's palace at Clink Street, Southwark.[68] Of course, it is possible that one or both of these designs might be by Witney himself, and it should be noted that another version of the propeller pattern appears in the rose window of the north transept gable at Winchester Cathedral. Certainly Winchester is an important link in the distribution of this unusual pattern, which tends to substantiate his connection with it.

However, as John Harvey has pointed out, the most distinctive window tracery employed by Witney at Exeter consists of a series of cusped trefoils set in curved triangles.[69] One side of each triangle is omitted, to create what we shall term a 'fishscale' pattern, seen in its simplest form in the aisle windows of bays 2 and 4 of the nave (Pl. XIVA, lower right) and in the bishop's throne (Fig. 9.1). A characteristic detail is that the trefoil is kept intact within the fishscale frame, supported on a small 'eye' or dagger (e.g. Pl. XIVc lower).[70] The precursors of the fishscale pattern are likely to be the impaled trefoils and delicate curved triangles which appeared in the 1270s and 1280s in the east arm of Old St Paul's Cathedral, London, the greatest building of its generation and on which numerous masons from the home counties and beyond would have worked.[71] Subsequently, a more ornamental version of the curved triangle with split-cusping appeared in the south-east, as in the diaperwork of sections of Prior Eastry's choir screen at Canterbury Cathedral (1304 sqq.), and the aisle windows of St Thomas's, Winchelsea (before 1312).[72] Without doubt, he was familiar with these examples, but it was not until his work at Exeter that the fishscale pattern developed from them.

The case for personal attribution to him rests particularly on the evidence of the bishop's throne, where the motif appears seemingly for the first time, in the openwork tracery of the superstructure (Pl. XIIB, centre Fig. 9.1). On this basis, its inclusion in the great end windows of the transept arms implies that they are also to his design and followed very shortly afterwards (Pl. XIVc). Some minor details of their mouldings corroborate this attribution.[73] On stylistic grounds, these cannot be the windows which were 'opened out' in the towers in 1285–7, and though only the completion of the north transept window is specifically mentioned in the accounts, c. 1321,[74] it is probable that both windows belong to Witney's early years at Exeter. Typologically the south window ought to come first, in that it makes only limited use of single fishscale units, and it should be noted in passing that its transom, which has sometimes been considered an early example of its kind, is actually an insertion of the 15th century.[75]

Then, in the north transept window, a fuller appreciation emerges of the decorative use of the motif, in the tracery beneath the sub-arches (Pl. XIVc). Here, individual fishscale units are made to converge and diverge, though the trefoils within them remain on the same axis (Fig. 9.2); and this sense of two-directional movement pervades the more elaborate five-light design in bay 6 of the nave clerestory, dating from the 1330s (Pl. XIVB, top right, Fig. 9.3).[76] Thus, the greater pattern-making potential of fishscale tracery is revealed at Exeter, and it is this development which is the most obvious link with the windows of the nave clerestory of Malmesbury Abbey, and the Lady Chapel windows at Wells Cathedral (Pl. XIVD).

There is not space here to give more than an outline of either of these works, focusing on their tracery and vault patterns as they relate to Exeter. At Malmesbury, the date is unrecorded and the visual information is limited. The main facts are these. The mouldings of the windows show definite links both with the clerestory of Winchester Cathedral presbytery (Witney) and with work of c. 1320 and later at St Mary Redcliffe, Bristol (north porch and south aisle, the latter associated with Master William Joy).[77] The nave vault belongs with the remodelling of the clerestory, and the undulating moulding of its unusual rib profile relates especially to designs in the presbytery at Wells (c. 1326 sqq., mainly by William Joy), but is also reminiscent of a few details in Witney's work in the nave at Exeter.[78] Thus, the attribution to Witney on the basis of the window tracery finds some substantiation in the mouldings, but the evidence is not incontrovertible, and there is more than a suggestion of a link with his younger colleague and successor, William Joy. This has important ramifications for the date of the Malmesbury work, which is likely to be later than some commentators, including myself, have imagined.[79] Most of the moulding parallels hint at the years around or after c. 1320, and if Witney is to be credited with the work, the early 1320s is more than a possibility.[80]

For the date of the Wells Lady Chapel, we are, in contrast, embarrassed by such a wealth of evidence that in recent years two chronologies have been proposed for its erection: c. 1310–19 and 1323–6.[81] Moreover, on stylistic grounds alone, the case for Witney's involvement there is compelling, especially in the use of his brand of fishscale tracery and of highly ornate bases, to which one could add the style of the lierne vaults and some other features.[82] This being so, it is evident from what has been said above that 1323–6 will accommodate the other known facts of his career better than c. 1310–19, an argument to which the detail of the window tracery lends support. For this, it will be necessary to return briefly to Malmesbury. There, the original design for the more easterly windows of the nave clerestory followed exactly the side units of the Exeter north transept window, as Brakspear has convincingly demonstrated (cf. Figs 9.2, 9.4).[83] Whereas from the fourth bay onwards a new rendition of the pattern appeared, in which two sides of the curved triangle were omitted to produce a multi-directional effect (Fig. 9.5). The latter is the form adopted for the Lady Chapel windows at Wells, with very minor variations (Fig. 9.6; Pl. XIVD),[84] and one may regard this as the third and final stage in the development of the design: having evolved from uni-directional through two-directional (Figs 9.1–2). On this basis, the Lady Chapel windows are unlikely to be earlier than the 1320s and, given the change of pattern half-way through the clerestory at Malmesbury, it may be that work at the latter started before Wells, then continued concurrently with it.

The patterns of the vaulting of the Lady Chapel and retrochoir are also helpful in supporting an attribution to Witney. At Exeter, Malmesbury and Wells, we have the most important surviving group of early lierne vaults in England, in which a certain logic in their development and a consistency in some of their features justifies assigning all of them to one designer. The yardstick for this analysis must be the Exeter pulpitum (1317 sqq.), Witney's first datable use of decorative vaulting, and which shows him to have been working at an early date with what were to become the two main characteristics of Decorated lierne vaults — the lozenge or 'kite' shape (used in the west and east bays of the pulpitum, Pls XID, XIIA) and extra diagonal ribs to create a mesh pattern (in the east bay, Pl. XID).[85] These characteristics are brought together in one design in the high vault at Malmesbury, a mesh of one-bay diagonal ribs in which the central lozenge motif of the pulpitum east bay (Pl. XID) is rotated through 90 degrees, and the smaller lozenges straddling the ridge rib (Pl. XIIA) are incorporated within them.[86] Its design is thus perfectly explicable as a creation of Witney's mind around 1320; probably his first major 'net' vault, which would explain its rather experimental feel.

The Lady Chapel vault at Wells represents the next and most important step in this development, incorporating most of the essential features of the pulpitum vaults, adapted to the polygonal plan of the chapel and carried to a new pitch of sophistication.[87] The single central lozenge intersected by diagonal lines at Exeter (Pl. XID) is multiplied to eight similar units, radiating out from the centre point. A particular trick of Witney's at Exeter, the use of the lozenge to prevent the transverse ridge rib from meeting the centre boss (Pl. XID), is repeated here more consistently to stress the centrifugal star pattern. Furthermore, the potential of the short two-bay diagonal ribs in the pulpitum vault (Pl. XID) is realised by disposing the tierceron ribs like two-bay diagonals, in contrast, for example, to the contemporary octagon at Ely where the tiercerons are deployed in an orthodox manner. Thus an overall mesh of lines is created in the Lady Chapel vault, which is such a successful and significant aspect of the design, as Jean Bony has diagnosed.[88] In sum, the vault is a natural extension of the ideas latent in the Exeter pulpitum, and its attribution to Witney seems reasonable, the moreso because its unusual domed construction integrates the timber roof with the stone vault structure.[89]

Equally important for the future is the creation within its pattern of smaller lozenges as the basic unit of the mesh pattern, each completely open and unimpaired by other lines. The germ of this idea is again present in the east bay of the Exeter pulpitum, within the central lozenge (Pl. XID), and its development in the Wells Lady Chapel leads to the vault pattern of the centre bay of the retrochoir at Wells (before 1329), in which open lozenges again interrupt the line of the ridge ribs;[90] and to the vault of St Edmund's chapel, Exeter (after 1328), in which just one central open lozenge serves the same purpose (Pl. XXIIID).[91] Thus, the St Edmund's chapel vault is an updated version of the pulpitum east bay (Pl. XID), and is explicable by Witney's experience at Wells in the meantime.[92]

On the other hand, the mouldings at Wells cannot be related so directly to his work at Exeter. It comes as a surprise that the famous, elaborate bases of the Lady Chapel and the retrochoir piers are not from the same template as those at the Exeter pulpitum

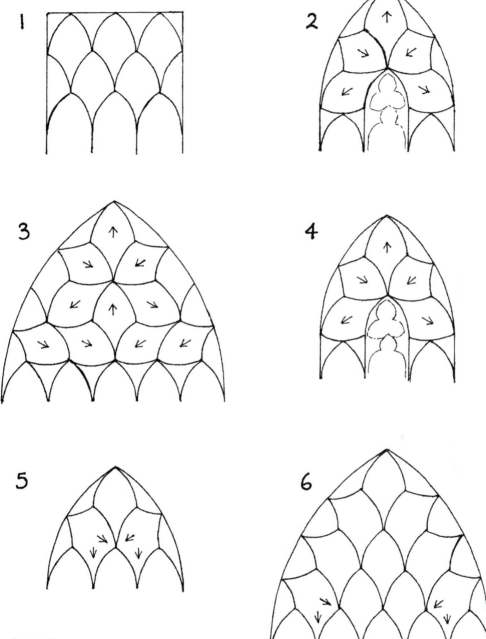

RKM 89

FIG. 9.   Fishscale tracery (Thomas of Witney): patterns of the frames (not to scale)

1. Exeter: bishop's throne.   2. Exeter: North transept, north window (det.).   3. Exeter: nave clerestory, bay 6.   4. Malmesbury: nave clerestory, bays 2–3 (reconstruction). 5. Malmesbury: nave clerestory, from bay 4.   6. Wells: Lady Chapel

F

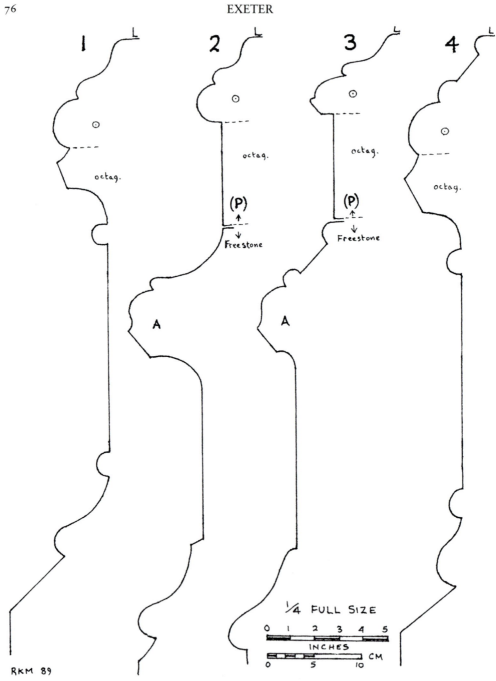

RKM 89

FIG. 10.   Wells Cathedral: bases

1. Lady Chapel: west piers.   2. Retrochoir (part Purbeck).   3. East chapels: corner piers
(part Purbeck).   4. Presbytery: north-east and south-east piers

(cf. Figs 2.6–7, Fig. 10). Indeed they bear little specific resemblance to each other except for the prominent canted demi roll-and-fillet of the sub-base (Figs 10.2–3A). None the less, the overall form is so unusual that it would be remarkable if most of them were not the work of the same designer.[93] As for the other mouldings in the eastern arm at Wells, their variety and unusual design raises complications of attribution which require more research, in which the author is currently engaged. However, there are also indications that traits of the Lady Chapel mouldings influenced certain details of the work in the later 1320s/early 1330s at Exeter. For example, the central feature of the retrochoir base (Fig. 10.2A) relates to the string-course on the south side of Bishop Stapledon's tomb,[94] and to the tall plinth (Fig. 4.5) of the north porch entrance.

The major job which drew Witney's attention away from Wells by 1329 was the resumption of work on the nave at Exeter at that time, lasting through the 1330s. Thus, an association with Exeter Cathedral which had begun by 1313 was to endure almost thirty years until 1342, when he disappears from the records and is presumed to have died, aged about seventy.[95] It has been shown that the early years of his long career included not only his recorded presence at St Stephen's Chapel, Westminster (1292–3 and 1294), but also a familiarity with other works around the turn of the century associated with court masons — St Thomas's at Winchelsea and the London Greyfriars; and he may well have been engaged on these. In particular, the stylistic links between Winchester and Winchelsea suggest that he worked at the new church of St Thomas, before his appearance at Winchester, c. 1310; for we know that by 1311 Witney had prospered and was a man of some substance.[96]

His main assignment at Winchester in the years directly preceding 1316 was a tricky one, namely to create an architectural link between the early Gothic retrochoir and the Romanesque east end by demolishing and rebuilding the feretory bay. Presumably a completely new presbytery was planned at this stage, but as the stylistic evidence shows that Witney's work is restricted to the east bay and that the other bays are rebuilt in a recognisably different style, it appears that only the Romanesque apsidal bay was demolished in this first phase of the programme. When he left for Exeter in or before 1316, the link bay was probably structurally complete except for the window tracery, but the remainder of the work looks to belong to the 1330s or later and to relate to the style of William Joy. The circumstances surrounding Witney's departure at this seemingly critical juncture are uncertain. The death of Bishop Woodlock of Winchester in 1316 may well have been a factor, but perhaps also Bishop Stapledon of Exeter, to use a contemporary cliché, made Witney an offer which he could not refuse.

The opening years of his tenure of the master mason's post at Exeter (1316–c. 1324) are the best documented and understood of his career. The lure of the job must have been, first, the commission to design and produce the sumptuous set of liturgical furnishings in wood and stone for the eastern arm. Second, he was provided with a rent-free house near the cathedral, but at the same time was evidently not restricted from taking on other commissions.[97] During these years he may, for instance, have returned briefly to Winchester to design the feretory screen; and in the early 1320s, he may have appeared at Malmesbury to advise on the new clerestory and vault. It must be remembered, however, that the chapter at Exeter continued to pay his fee in every quarter for which accounts survive right up to 1342, so that officially they retained first call on his services.[98] None the less, for five or more years (c. 1323–9), he appears in effect to have had enough time to concentrate on Wells, and other projects in this period could have included the rebuilding at Malmesbury still in progress (c. 1325–30).

The relevant dates recorded at Exeter and Wells coincide with an almost suspicious tidiness, but they are in agreement with the evidence provided by the development of his ideas in vaulting and tracery design. In 1322, the crossing tower of Wells is complete and the way is clear for the Lady Chapel work. In 1323, a mason of his name witnesses a document in Wells. From Midsummer 1324, he gives up his rent-free house in Exeter. In 1327, the lay subsidy records a wealthy mason resident in Wells, apparently Witney. In 1329, William Joy is appointed master of the fabric at Wells, following the resumption of work on the nave at Exeter with Witney as master mason: the new eastern arm there had been dedicated in 1328.

Witney's last dozen years at Exeter are more enigmatic. The responsibilities of design and supervision of the new nave would hardly have required the unbroken attention over this period of a master of his seniority, and he was probably no longer regularly in residence. He did not re-avail himself of the rent-free house at Exeter, and where he was based is unrecorded, though in or near Wells is a possibility. He was (in modern terms) nearing retirement age and it is questionable how much new work he would wish to undertake at this time. If he had developed some sort of partnership with William Joy, then he may have continued to give advice at Wells in the 1330s, especially on constructional matters like the remodelling of the choir bays and the insertion of the reinforcing arches around the crossing. He had a wide experience in this field, from the feretory bay at Winchester to the inserted triforium in the Exeter presbytery.[99]

'A dearly loved member of our household and a valuable and willing servant . . . whose industry is of special value for the repair and in part new building, by his skill, of the fabric of our church of Exeter.' This is Witney's contemporary testimonial, from two letters of recommendation written by Bishop Grandisson in the years 1328–30.[100] The typical understatement of a medieval grandee talking about a craftsman: patronising and modest. With hindsight and with a different set of values, we can appreciate that Witney was quite simply one of the outstanding independent architects of the 14th century. He was a talented designer and engineer in wood and stone, who built up a large practice in the south and south-west of England, and introduced the full vocabulary of Decorated style to the area. Today his achievement is best appreciated by standing looking west into the nave at Exeter — one of the finest interior spaces which has come down to us from the later Middle Ages.

ACKNOWLEDGEMENTS

I am particularly grateful to the following for advice and assistance with my research for this paper. At Exeter — the Dean, the Very Reverend R. M. S. Eyre; Mr Lloyd, the Cathedral Head Verger; Mr Peter Dare, formerly Master Mason at the Cathedral; Mrs Audrey Erskine, the Archivist, Exeter Cathedral Library; Mr James Allan of the Royal Albert Memorial Museum; and Mr Stuart Blaylock of Exeter Museums Archaeological Field Unit. At Winchester — Mrs Corinne Bennett, Architect to the Dean and Chapter; and Mr J. H. Lamplugh, the Cathedral Administrator. At Wells — the late Mr Linzee Colchester, former Honorary Cathedral Archivist. At Salisbury — the Dean, the Very Reverend S. H. Evans; and Mr Roy Spring, Clerk of the Works. At Malmesbury — Mr H. E. Rose, Malmesbury Abbey PCC. To Dr John Harvey I owe a special debt for his pioneering research on this subject and for several discussions about it, even if my conclusions are not entirely in agreement with his own. Mr Peter Draper and Dr Christopher Wilson have kindly supplied photographs for the illustration of this paper. The necessary research was partly funded by a grant from the Society of Antiquaries of London Research Fund, and my attendance at the 1985 conference was subsidised by a grant from the University of Warwick Conference Grant Fund.

REFERENCES

1. Erskine (1981), 72–173, and (1983), 213–72, for transcripts of the accounts; Erskine (1983), xx–xxi, for a summary of Witney's involvement at Exeter; and Erskine (1983), xxx–xxxiii, for an exemplary résumé of works at the cathedral during his time as Master Mason. For information, it should be noted that the

accounts generally refer to him simply as 'Master Thomas', and the earliest entry (Michaelmas 1316) calls him 'Master Thomas the mason' (Erskine (1981), 77). The first reference to him as 'Master Thomas de Witteneye' is for Easter, 1317 (Erskine (1981), 82).

2. The most recent account is in Harvey (1984), 338–41.

3. Work cited in n. 2 above, 340. It is very possible that Witney received early training in Oxford, as Harvey suggests, but there is nothing distinctive about the detail in the works in the crossing and sacristy of Merton College chapel to provide a specific link with Witney later in his career (except possibly the wave moulding in the entrance arch to the intended nave aisles, Warwick Archive OME.752); so Oxford has been omitted from further discussion in this paper.

4. For John of Glaston's work of 1309–10 sqq., see Tracy (1986), 99–103. In addition, ogee arches occur in the tracery of the east windows of the transept chapels of St Paul and St John Baptist (completed 1310–11); those in the chapel of St Andrew are more problematic, and have been suggested to be 17th-century alterations (Bishop and Prideaux (1922), 105–6). For the date of the transept chapels, see Erskine (1981), 50–6 (the only specific reference is to St Paul's chapel, 54), and the arguments put forward in Bishop and Prideaux (1922), 47–8.

5. The earliest surviving examples of lierne vaults elsewhere include the undercroft vault of St Stephen's Chapel, Westminster Palace, perhaps designed before 1298, when Witney was working there, but probably not executed until c. 1320: they bear a very close resemblance to the lierne vault used in the west bays of Exeter pulpitum (Pl. XIIA). Also the choir vault of Pershore Abbey (after 1288), which is a heavier design and, from the style of the bosses, seems unlikely to belong later than c. 1315–20.

6. For a plan of one of the sedilia canopies, see Morris (1943), Fig. 3. Masons working for the court show an interest in complicated geometrical design especially in castle planning in North Wales and elsewhere during Edward I's reign: see Maddison (1978). The use of triangular designs is also found in the Geddington cross (Northamptonshire), apparently one of the Eleanor crosses commissioned by the king in the 1290s. The latter is especially pertinent as a source for Witney's canopy work at Exeter.

7. Erskine (1983), xxx.

8. As do Erskine (1983), xx; and Harvey (1984), 337 ('Winton, Thomas of').

9. The only reference in the accounts to the actual making of the throne is in 1317 (Erskine (1981), 85), which may imply that the design had not been worked out in every detail as early as 1313, when the timber was selected and felled.

10. Erskine (1983), xxx–xxxi.

11. For example, the accounts specifically tell us of three craftsmen involved with the bishop's throne — Thomas de Winton/Witney (Erskine (1981), 71), and the local master carpenter, Robert de Galmeton, and 'his associate' (Erskine (1981), 85). Also, the altar account of 1316–17 (No. 2612A), which is especially relevant to the sanctuary fittings, includes several craftsmen whose high degree of skill is indicated by their remuneration — John de Baunebiri, Robert and Thomas Atteboxe, Robert Payne, Peter de Dene, E. de Nyweton, J. de Eston; see Erskine (1981), 196–7. For the main accounts, Erskine (1983), xxi, suggests that the position of mason in charge (the master's deputy) is indicated by the mason heading the wages list, and she notes that in Witney's early years, Robert Forde presumably fulfilled this role (1317–22).

12. Erskine (1981), 196 sqq. Baunebiri (Banbury) was a particularly skilled carver, because he is singled out in the 1318–19 altar account for extra payment 'for 3 vaults carrying the canopy of the high altar at task'; Erskine (1981), 111.

13. Erskine (1983), xv. The assertion in Bishop and Prideaux (1922), 17, that the stones for the piers were delivered uncarved is disproved by the observation made in the next note.

14. The Purbeck marble piers of the east face of the reredos at Beverley Minster, Yorkshire (Warwick Archive BEV.931), are identical to those of the Exeter pulpitum, and obviously were cut from the same template, indicating some repetitive production in pre-cut components from the Corfe quarries. The same is true of the Purbeck marble bases of both monuments (Fig. 2.6 and Warwick Archive BEV.938), but in this case there is clear evidence that the design originated in the cathedral work (see main text). As the Exeter commission appears to be earlier than that for Beverley (payment to William Canon for the 4 'columns' was made in 1319 — Erskine (1981), 107), presumably the Canon family of Corfe re-used Witney's templates for the other job (with his permission?). Certainly the accounts do not justify the assertion in Prideaux and Shafto (1910), 123, that William Canon was 'the builder and carver' of the pulpitum; see Erskine (1981), 107, for the actual wording of the reference.

15. See Morris (1979), 20.

16. Illustrated in Morris (1979), Fig. 16R.

17. E.g. Morris (1979), Fig. 16H (St-Urbain at Troyes, 1262–6).

18. Illustrated in Tracy (1987), Fig. 2, 5–7; see also the choir-stalls at St Mary's Hospital, Chichester; ibid., Fig. 1, 1–2. Except for St Stephen's Chapel, the detail appears to be rare in the works of the Kentish masters at court.

19. For Lyngwode at Winchester, see Tracy (1987), ch. III. Examples in East Anglia include the capitals of the cloister of Norwich Cathedral (1297 sqq., Warwick Archive NOR.804), and of the sedilia in the Lady Chapel at Ely Cathedral (1321 sqq., Warwick Archive ELY.320). The potentially early date of its usage at Norwich makes its appearance at Winchester in the works of both Lyngwode and Witney perhaps more than coincidental. Had Lyngwode also been employed earlier at St Stephen's Chapel, and was this the common source for both Norwich and the south of England? Or is its introduction in the Norwich cloister actually later than 1297, and a result of Lyngwode's visit to Winchester and his encounter with Witney? Work on the cloister east walk is thought to have continued as late as c. 1325–7; see Fernie and Whittingham (1972), 32–3.

20. Harvey (1984), 340. For the English context for these ornate bases, see Morris (1979), 29. It is interesting that the accounts acknowledge the elaboration of these bases by mentioning their 'sub-bases' as well (Erskine (1981), 107); compare with the payment for the presbytery triforium bases in which, correctly, bases only are listed (Erskine (1981), 98).

21. See Gee (1979), 38 sqq. and Pl. VIIIA.

22. Illustrated in Tracy (1987), e.g. Pls 64, 67.

23. His tomb probably dates from the late 1320s/c. 1330, as it appears to have been added to the reredos of the high altar (completed c. 1326), and therefore unlikely to have been prepared before his unexpected death in the same year; see further Morris (1943) 124–5.

24. For the Decorated architecture at Winchester Cathedral, see Russell (1983), whose reference numbers for the transept windows I have followed (also applying them to the transept chapels). The undercut wave is used there also in the transept chapels for the frame of South 2 (Warwick Archive WIN.506) and the soffit of an anonymous early 14th-century tomb recess in the north wall of North 3 (Warwick Archive WIN.925). Plain wave mouldings are another feature of the Decorated work in the transepts, for mullions (North 4, South 2) and for the ogee canopies of the tabernacles in North 2 (Warwick Archive WIN.503, 504, 514, 916).

25. At Modbury church, the two tomb arches in the south transept use Witney's sunk chamfer moulding. The tombs are consciously showy, like the recess in the chancel of Bere Ferrers church, also in south-west Devon — see Pevsner (1952A), Pl. 45(a). The evidence implies that these are all by one or more local masons who had gained experience in the cathedral workshop: the accounts show that Devon and Somerset names predominate in the workforce (Erskine (1983), xxiii). I am extremely grateful to Hugh Harrison of Herbert Read Ltd for drawing my attention to Modbury and providing photographs of the tombs.

26. The idea of prominent globular decorations on the tips of the cusps (foliage, not heads) is already present at Exeter before the end of the 13th century in the tomb recesses (non-ogee) of the Lady Chapel.

27. See Tracy (1987), Pls 52, 60, for the Winchester stalls; and ibid., Pl. 235, for the Exeter throne canopy. An early source in the south of England for this idea is the chapter house at Salisbury Cathedral of the second half of the 13th century, where heads are carved in stone on the octofoil cusping of the windows.

28. See particularly the style of the bosses in the east bay of the nave and aisles; Prideaux and Shafto, (1910), chapter VI. Bishop and Prideaux (1922), 48–51, interpret the accounts as indicating that the vault bosses of the east bay were painted in 1317, and that the glazing was installed by 1319, thus marking the completion of this work; for the text of the relevant accounts, see Erskine (1981), 82 (Easter 1317) and 109 (Midsummer 1319).

29. See Morris (1979), 1–3, for the national context.

30. Though some bead mouldings are retained in the high vault for the *tas-de-charge* stones (observation based on the south side of the nave) and for the transverse arches.

31. As argued most recently in Erskine (1983), xxxiii, though the evidence from the the capitals suggests that the process may not have been as 'continuous and logical' as she implies (see next note).

32. I am mindful of the example of the contemporary nave of Worcester Cathedral; see Morris (1978b), 127–37. At Exeter nave, if one assumes that the capitals which continue to include some scroll mouldings (e.g. Fig. 4.2) are earlier than those which favour more 'blunt-nosed' forms (e.g. Fig. 4.3), then there is a suggestion that the west bays (especially bays 6 and 7) were ahead of the centre bays (especially 3 and 4) by the time work had reached vault springing level. This could be equated with the implication from the accounts that quite a lot of attention was focused on the west end as soon as work commenced on the nave in 1329; and/or with the structural completion of the west gable by 1342, when it was being embellished — see further Bishop and Prideaux (1922), 70–1, and Erskine (1983), xxxii–xxxiii. The one potentially useful clue from the mouldings is that the rather crude profile of the 'blunt-nosed' capitals supporting the vault springers in the centre bays might be equated with the style of Master William Joy, documented at the cathedral 1346–7 (cf. Figs 4.3, 6.5). If so, the vault could not have been completed in Witney's time. It could be argued, however, that the simplification of these capitals is merely a sign of speeding up work on the nave in the 1330s to expedite its completion. For the context of 'blunt-nosed' capitals, see Morris (1979), 22–3. One additional resource which might assist in unravelling the date of the nave vault is the wealth of masons'

marks found on the ribs, which could be compared, for example, with the 14th-century marks at Wells (the subject of a recent unpublished study by Lance John — information kindly supplied by Linzee Colchester).

33. For more detail about the conversion of the south transept tower, see Allan and Jupp (1981), 145–7.

34. E.g. for the surrounds of transept windows North 1 and South 2, illustrated in Russell (1983), Pl. XXVc, D. For the national context for the sunk chamfer moulding, see Morris (1978a), 29 sqq.

35. The payment for the Purbeck marble components ('columns', bases and capitals) for the presbytery triforium is recorded in the Midsummer term, 1318 (Erskine (1981), 98); payment for painting '19 heads in the new galleries' (i.e. one side of the presbytery triforium) follows in the Christmas term, 1319 (Erskine (1981), 104). It does not seem to have been noted previously that some of the marble bases in the east bays (e.g. on the south side) appear to be Early English bases of the first half of the 13th century, reused. Were the Canon family of Corfe offloading some old surplus materials? Or were some of these bases reused from elsewhere in the cathedral, perhaps from the cloister area, where work began on a new east walk in 1318?

36. For the difference in wall thicknesses, see Everett and Hope (1968), 185–9.

37. See especially Allan and Jupp (1981), 147.

38. The loss of the cloister itself is unfortunate, as the east and north walks were one of the major works undertaken at Exeter during his period as master mason; see Erskine (1983), xxxi. It would be interesting to know the evidence for the reconstruction, in Brakspear's plan of the cathedral (Bishop and Prideaux (1922), opp. 186), of the north walk vault as a grid of two-bay diagonal ribs, similar in principle to the pattern of the nave vault at Malmesbury, attributed to Witney.

39. I have been unable to obtain a measured drawing of the west window rere-arch.

40. For the dating evidence for works on the west end of the nave, see Erskine (1983), xxxii; though the two windows 'in the new chapel' are unlikely to be the west windows of the chapel as existing, as these belong with the work of William Joy, c. 1346–7.

41. For the documentary evidence, see Erskine (1981), 108–9; see also McAleer in this volume. The vault is likely to be later, however, probably after 1328 judging by the boss illustrated in Prideaux and Shafto (1910), 181, No. 360; though not necessarily as late in Grandisson's episcopate as implied in Bishop and Prideaux (1922), 86.

42. See further Morris (1978), 38.

43. For William Joy, see Harvey (1984), 164–5. In the work done under his supervision, some mouldings from the Witney period were physically reused, e.g. the present string-course under the north springing of the tunnel-vault in the Grandisson chapel, almost certainly removed from the jambs of Witney's centre door and reused horizontally. Other designs bear a resemblance to Witney's work, such as the small wave mouldings on the tomb recess arch in the east wall of the Grandisson chapel, which had appeared earlier on the piers of the pulpitum (Fig. 1.5c); but the other mouldings of the recess indicate that the whole feature dates from Joy's period. However, the assignment of some other features is more complicated, e.g. the Grandisson chapel door (Pl. XIIIA, right), of which the outer frame recalls both the ogee arches and mouldings of the pulpitum (Pl. XIA, and cf. Figs 1.1, 6.2A), and could be later Witney-period work reused; but the mouldings of the inner frame, separated by a masonry joint, must be Joy's (Fig. 6.2B).

44. The pellet ornament on the Grandisson chapel door occurs on the mouldings which can be assigned stylistically to Joy; see n. 43. I have been unable to obtain any moulding profiles from the minstrels' gallery or make a close inspection of its front, which would require a scaffold, so the pellet ornament is the best visual evidence available at present to date it. However, the observation that it appears to have been carved later than most of the work on the nave need not necessarily mean that the idea of a gallery was an afterthought; for this, the best evidence is the implication of the accounts (see Erskine (1983), xxxii–xxxiii, and also Bishop and Prideaux (1922), 73 sqq.). Pellet ornament, and canopies similar in feel to those of the minstrels' gallery, appear in the reredos at Christchurch Priory (Hampshire), usually dated c. 1350.

45. For the 14th-century work on the eastern arm see especially Willis (1846), 43–50; Woodman (1983): Russell (1983): Tracy (1987), ch. III: and corrections of Woodman in P. Draper (1986), 68–74. Most authorities have followed Willis's suggested starting date of c. 1320, except Rannie (1966), 17; John Harvey in his more recent works, e.g. Harvey (1984), 339; and Tracy (1987), 21. I concur with their date of c. 1310. The comparison by Willis of the Winchester mouldings with 'those of the lantern and other works at Ely . . . carried on from 1322 to 1328' is not in my view sufficiently precise to substantiate his date of c. 1320; Willis (1846), 48. For the profiles, see Willis (1846), 76–7, and for Ely, Stewart (1868), especially Pl. 8. I also agree with Draper that no large interval of time need be postulated between the north-east and east arcades of the feretory, as suggested in Woodman (1983), 88.

46. Erskine (1983), xxviii–xxix.

47. In fact, for the six apertures (or entrances) to the passage sections in the feretory bay, three designs are used: 1) continuous chamfer for the shoulders and lintel (3 examples, see Pl. XIIID), as used for Master Roger's

choir bays at Exeter; 2) chamfer for shoulders only (2 examples), as used at Exeter for the inner bays of the transepts (west side only) and the nave east bay, probably by William Luve; 3) pointed arch (1 example), no parallel at Exeter. For Master Roger and Master William Luve at Exeter, see Harvey (1984), 191 and 257 ('Roger the Mason II'), and Erskine (1983), xix–xx. The roll and chamfer mullion profile (Fig. 7.6) which forms the basis of the window jamb design is not unique to Exeter in the late 13th century, and had already been used in central southern England not only at Merton College chapel, Oxford (c. 1289–94), but also at Winchester itself, where the mullions of transept window South 2 are probably of about the same date (Warwick Archive WIN.508, 509). None the less, the jamb design of the Winchester clerestory is closest to that at Exeter (Figs 3.7, 7.6). The original window jambs survive in the north-east and south-east windows of the feretory bay (Pl. XIIID).

48. Harvey (1984), 339–40: the exact date is uncertain of the agreement between 'Master T. of W.' and the prior 'to undertake the work of the presbytery at the joint cost of the bishop and the priory'. It is 'likely to be of 1316, but may be a good deal later than some lost agreement with the bishop — the documents relating to joint works involving a bishop and a priory or chapter usually start with the bishop. So there could be an initial date for the Winchester work *before 1316*' (John Harvey, personal communication, 1 April 1985, his underlining, citing Goodman's index to the lost Winchester documents). This is made the more likely by the other facts cited in Harvey (1984), and by the appearance of Witney as resident master mason at Exeter in 1316.

49. In Willis (1846), Fig. 19, these features are piers K(B), A(D), BD(I), and arches HK(C), AB(E), CD(J); the letters in parentheses are used in Woodman (1983), Fig. 1. Good illustrations of the pertinent features are in Woodman (1983), Pls V–VII.

50. Willis (1846), Fig. 19, pier K; the west pier, M, of the south-east arcade, and its bases, are also the same, but the arch above was rebuilt later in the 14th century and is not relevant here.

51. A minor difference is that the sub-bases of the main arcades at Exeter are circular in plan, whereas they are octagonal at Winchester: another hint that Exeter predates Winchester (cf. Figs 3.4, 7.5).

52. The profile of the capital is illustrated in Willis (1846), Fig. 37, G.

53. Chapel North 2; Warwick Archive WIN.510, 918. The mouldings and carvings of this chapel appear to belong stylistically with the work in the feretory bay.

54. For the sunk chamfer's origins, see Morris (1978a), 29–31. For Chester, see Jansen, (1979), 223 sqq., especially 228. For the London Greyfriars and Hull, see most recently; *Age of Chivalry* (1987), 73 and 228. A fragment of a pier from the London Greyfriars, which is the same design as the Winchester piers (Fig. 7.3), is in the Museum of London, carved in freestone, although the documents indicate that Purbeck marble was ordered, as at Winchester. I am grateful to Nicola Coldstream and Christopher Wilson for drawing my attention to this example during the conference.

55. In support, one may note that Witney had been engaged earlier on the royal work of St Stephen's Chapel, Westminster, and it is not impossible that he may have been employed at the London Greyfriars, 1306 sqq. There is a gap in his recorded career here, before his appearance at Winchester.

56. Russell (1983), 94; Tracy (1987), 21.

57. For example, see the argument forwarded in Tracy (1987), ch. III, that it was Witney who sorted out the structural problems with William Lyngwode's choir stalls at Winchester. Note also his implied carpentry skill in selecting timbers for and designing the amazing structure of the Exeter bishop's throne; and the handling of such difficult architectural commissions as adding the false triforium to the presbytery bays at Exeter, and the rebuilding of the junction bay between the retrochoir and the presbytery at Winchester.

58. E.g. perhaps John of Banbury, who left Exeter after 1319; see further nn. 11, 12.

59. Sekules, in this volume. For earlier suggestions to this effect, see Bishop and Prideaux (1922), 112. Alternatively, the canopy might have been part of an original scheme for the reredos (?c. 1313), abandoned in favour of a more sophisticated work (?after 1316).

60. The profiles of the comparable string-courses of Bishop Stapledon's tomb are illustrated in Morris (1943), Fig. 2, A and F.

61. See Warwick Archive WIA.103, 120, 202, 502, 508. In addition, the main arcade base, WIA.203, relates to the plinth profile of the Robert Stapledon recess at Exeter (Fig. 2.11).

62. Winchelsea arcade arch is illustrated, more or less accurately, in Bond (1906), 669. A detail of the rib profile from St Stephen's Chapel is illustrated in Morris (1978a), Fig. 6D.

63. The arch profile of the eastern recess in the south aisle is illustrated in Morris (1978a), Fig. 56. The western recess has a double pear moulding for the soffit of the arch, very reminiscent of the soffits of the Exeter pulpitum and bishop's throne (Fig. 1.1, 1.6A–B). In this context, it is worth noting the comments in Gee (1979), 39, that the general forms of the western tomb 'suggest a mason who had been accustomed to working on stone screens for statuary, such as reredoses'. This was exactly the sort of work in which Witney and his masons were engaged at Exeter in this period.

64. Especially the evidence concerning timber for the roof in 1332 and 1338, and for the completion of the west gable in 1341–2; Erskine (1983), xxxii–xxxiii. It may be objected that he was at least in his sixties when these fine tracery patterns were designed; but Le Corbusier was the same age when he started Notre-Dame-du-Haut at Ronchamp, and Michelangelo was in his seventies when he took over at St Peter's in Rome.

65. Illustrated, for example, in Hill (1986), 42.

66. Mouchette wheels are used in the clerestory of bays 5 (Pl. XIVB) and 7. For some other British examples, see Etherington (1965), 176–7 (group 29); to which should be added the nave aisle windows of Beverley Minster and the second stage windows of the west towers of York Minster. Continental examples include the nave of Bayonne Cathedral in Gascony (begun 1302, but tracery likely to be considerably later), the Lagrange chapels at Amiens Cathedral (1373–5), and Hal church (1341/2–1409) and Antwerp Cathedral in the Low Countries; as well as miniature tracery in the canopies of Flemish-made memorial brasses, e.g. the Walsoken brass at Kings Lynn (Norfolk) c. 1349. The propeller pattern is used at Exeter in bays 2 and 4 of the nave clerestory (Pl. XIVA), and is the basis for the west gable window. On the continent, the pattern was already in use especially in the Rhine valley area by the early 14th century, in workshops at Cologne and Strasbourg; but contemporary experiments with related forms can also be seen in northern France, e.g. Rouen Cathedral, south transept window.

67. For similarities in moulding types between the south-east and the continent, see Morris (1979), 34 and Fig. 18 (region I).

68. The Southwark window may also be related to Exeter in the way that its centrepiece is formed by a series of radiating cusped panels, a motif employed in the nave east bay clerestory windows, work directly preceding Witney's arrival; and then in his end window of the north and south transepts (Pl. XIVc). The Southwark window is illustrated in B/E, *London 2: South* (1983), Pl. 10.

69. Harvey (1984), 340, 'cusped spherical triangles'.

70. This differentiates the feature from almost all other examples of fishscale tracery, such as a small group of examples in the West Midlands, e.g. Lichfield Cathedral, choir aisles; Shifnal and Munslow (Shropshire); Kingsland (Herefordshire). However, for one design in this area, the two-light infirmary windows of Haughmond Abbey (Shropshire), the motif of the eye is used — a work with no other obvious connection with Witney; though the matter needs further research. Shifnal is illustrated in Bony (1979), Pl. 155; and for the West Midlands, see also Morris (1982), 55.

71. See further R. K. Morris (1990). Witney's fondness for the curved triangle in tracery design is evident in other nave windows which are not fishscale pattern (e.g. Pl. XIVA, top right, and XIVB, bottom left; as well as the west gable window).

72. Both examples illustrated in Bony (1979), Pls 160, 149.

73. Capitals with beaded necking are used for the rere-arch of the north window (Warwick Archive EXE, 554); and the profile of the actual rere-arch of the south window, with its prominent bead moulding and asymmetrical roll and fillet moulding, looks likely to have been detailed by Witney — for the profile, see Allan and Jupp (1981), Fig. 4, top right.

74. Erskine (1981), 129: Christmas term, 1320–1, 'iron-work for the great window in St Paul's tower', and glass is also included in the same entry. Preparations for the completion of the transept arms are indicated by the carving (1317–18) and priming (1319–20) of the bosses for both wooden vaults, though only for the south transept (St John's tower) do we have evidence for roofing (1319) and the erection of the vault (1322 sqq.); for relevant references in the accounts, see Erskine (1981), 97, 105, 117, 129, 141, 147, and for discussion see Allan and Jupp (1981), 147. Regarding the work of 1285–7, modifying St Paul's and St John's towers, recorded in the 1279–87 summary account (Erskine (1981), 6–7), both the small amount of money expended and stylistic considerations cast doubt on how much of the work visible in the transepts today relates to these entries.

75. The south window is illustrated in Allan and Jupp (1981), Pl. IVA. The form of the transom and its sub-cusping is virtually identical to that employed in the Perpendicular style refenestration of the chapter house c. 1460 (Brooks and Evans (1988), 123), and the interior capitals and profiles of the mullions are also closely related; all pointing to a major repair of the lower parts of the window in the mid-15th century, probably as a result of storm damage. It should be noted that the exterior profile of the south window mullion is simpler than that illustrated in Allan and Jupp (1981), Fig. 4.

76. The other nave clerestory window to employ fishscale tracery is the three-light window in bay 3 north, behind the minstrels' gallery, where the pattern is uni-directional and contained within a larger curved triangle.

77. With regard to Winchester (feretory bay), the shaft and the chamfer moulding of the jamb of the clerestory rere-arches are the same sizes as those at Malmesbury, and their arches use wave mouldings; Warwick Archive MAL.653, 654, and WIN.225, 226 (Fig. 7.7). The link with Bristol is the stepped chamfer mullion, used at Redcliffe in the north porch and the nave south aisle, Warwick Archive MAL.652, and BRR.600, 683; see Morris (1979), 8–11 and Fig. 13B.

78. The rib is Warwick Archive MAL.657. At Wells, see the presbytery main arcade arch, the clerestory window mullion (interior profile), and especially the clerestory window frame in the choir bays; Warwick Archive WEL.201, 220, 214. For Exeter, see figure 5.6–8κ.

79. In particular, the naturalistic foliage carving of some of the vault bosses has been cited to indicate a date no later than the early 14th century; for example, Draper (1981), 25. In fact, close inspection of the bosses suggests that the naturalism is more imagined than real. The leaves are wrinkled and bubbled, a sign of mature Decorated carving style, which would not deny a date in the 1320s; the more so if one accepts that the Wells Lady Chapel belongs in this decade (see further below, main text).

80. In suggesting that Malmesbury may precede Wells, Draper (1981), 25, implies that the appearance of fishscale patterns at Lichfield makes this form of tracery unhelpful in establishing a sequence. But the analysis presented here indicates that the type of fishscale tracery developed in the south-west (Fig. 8.2–6) has no parallel elsewhere, and that it is possible to argue for stylistic evolution in the windows attributed to Witney.

81. For a review of the arguments, see Morris (1984), 194–207, especially 203–6. Since writing that review, my own research on Witney has led me to modify some of my views, and in particular to agree that Peter Draper's late date for the Lady Chapel appears more compatible with what we know of Witney's career.

82. Especially the application of polygonal and triangular geometry in the plan of the Lady Chapel and retrochoir, recalling the design of the Exeter furnishings and of Witney's fondness for equilateral triangles in his tracery designs. In addition, there is the documentary evidence for a 'Thomas le Masun' and 'Thomas Mascon' in Wells in 1323 and 1327 respectively; cited in Harvey (1984), 340, and for his fullest account of Witney at Wells, see J. H. Harvey, 'The Building of Wells Cathedral II: 1307–1508', in Colchester (1982), 80 sqq. Harvey's evidence for attributing the remodelling of the Wells crossing tower (1315–22) to Witney is too circumstantial for consideration here, though it warrants further investigation, which I am currently pursuing.

83. Brakspear (1913), 415–16; though c. 1316–21 is the date of the Exeter window, not 1280 as stated in his footnote.

84. In the multi-directional fishscale units, a second side is actually retained, but with such a narrow profile that it does not make a major contribution to the reading of the pattern (Pl. XIVD). Other variations are the omission of the small cusped dagger in each unit, and the use of cinque-cusped heads for the main lights (Pl. XIVD), both for the only time in work attributed to Witney. Cinque-cusped heads were more of a tradition at Wells in the later 13th century than at Exeter.

85. See also Bock (1961), 313–17.

86. Illustrated in Bock (1962), Fig. 14(a); see also n. 38 above with regard to the lost Exeter cloister vaults.

87. Illustrated in Colchester (1982), Pl. 31. Witney had already shown interest at Exeter in designing a vault on an irregular polygonal plan: the miniature vaults in the seven-sided sedilia canopies are adapted from the vault pattern of the west bays of the pulpitum.

88. Bony (1979), 48–9 and Fig. 7.

89. Repairs in 1978 revealed that some bosses on the transverse ridge ribs were fixed to the frame of the timber roof. Witney, of course, had shown his skill in both stone- and timber-work at Exeter.

90. Illustrated in Draper (1981), Pl. VII (right).

91. Illustrated in Prideaux and Shafto (1910), Fig. 8. For discussion of dating, see above, n. 41.

92. The influence of the Exeter pulpitum at Wells may also be seen in the vaults of the east transepts (before 1329), which are an extension of the pulpitum west vault design with the distinctive feature of the omission of main diagonal ribs; illustrated in the Courtauld Institute of Art photographic archive, Wells Cathedral, Pl. 1/10/82.

93. It may be significant that the west bases of the Lady Chapel are the least like the Exeter bases, but the closest to the east bases of the presbytery (cf. Fig. 10.1, 10.4): a possible sign of the involvement of William Joy in some details in the Lady Chapel area.

94. Illustrated in Morris (1943), Fig. 2, A.

95. There is a gap in the accounts, 1342–6, so the exact date is unknown. It seems likely that he died elsewhere, in contrast to his predecessor, Master Roger II, whose death in 1310 was commemorated by the local Kalender guild; Erskine (1983), xix, and Harvey (1984), 257.

96. Harvey (1984), 339.

97. Harvey (1984), 339. For all subsequent documentary references to Witney in this article, see ibid., 339–41.

98. Gaps in the yearly accounts occur in 1322–3, 1326–8, 1329–30, 1332–3, 1334–40 (see Erskine (1981), viii); but there is no reason to think that he did not continue to receive his regular fee in these years.

99. See further, n. 57.

100. Harvey (1984), 339–40, translated from passages in Hingeston-Randolph I (3 vols, 1894–9), 218, 225.

Some Aspects of the Decorated Tracery of Exeter Cathedral

By Georgina Russell
with an Appendix by John Allan

Anyone who looks at Exeter Cathedral can see that the fenestration is an important element of the Decorated work. Like Hardwick Hall, the building could be described as 'more glass than wall'. This was an effect which the original designer must have consciously sought. Indeed the only constraints on window size must be the result of two no doubt conscious decisions made by client and/or designer. The first of these two was to limit the overall height of the new work so that the choir vault is only some 22 m from the ground, in contrast for instance to that of Westminster Abbey, which is 31.2 m high. One may surmise that the cathedral authorities originally intended to keep the Anglo-Norman nave, which may well have been the height of the present nave and choir.[1] They certainly decided to harmonise the levels of the top of the main arcade and the bottom of the clerestory with those of the pre-existing fabric.[2] The second decision was to reuse the foundations of the previous presbytery, with extensions eastward but no alteration to the overall width.[3] The first decision set a maximum limit to the height both overall and of individual features, such as windows both at aisle and clerestory level, while the two decisions combined prescribed the proportions of the choir height:width in section. If one adds to these a third decision to have a two-storey elevation, one will find that the size and proportions of the high east window are roughly prescribed.

In the following paper I shall consider four topics. First is an investigation of the sort of designs that were employed in the windows, from the point of view of geometry and how the windows fit into the wall space; the second is an examination of the overall scheme of the windows; the third is a hypothetical reconstruction of the tracery originally in the high east window over the altar; and the fourth is a brief consideration of the whole scheme in the context of other window schemes of the period in England from 1250 to 1330.

1. THE WINDOWS OF THE RETROCHOIR, PRESBYTERY AND LADY CHAPEL

As Professor Jansen points out above (see p. 43), there is no break in window tracery detail corresponding to the break in design of the triforium. On the other hand, however, there is a sharp contrast between the three pairs of windows (that is, paired north-south) of the retrochoir and the eastern chapels immediately beyond it on the one hand, and all the rest of the windows and the presbytery and Lady Chapel on the other hand. (Fig. 1; the former group is labelled nIII, nIV, nV, using the Corpus Vitrearum numbering system, in which 'n' stands for north aisle, while 'N' refers to North clerestory. See Introductory plan.)

In the first place, the three pairs referred to have equilaterally arched heads; this, combined with the designer's evident determination to make his windows fill the width available, produces some rather odd results. A good example is the east window of St John the Evangelist's chapel (nIII) off the north-east corner of the retrochoir (Pl. XVA) where the width of the aisle provided wall space for a five-light window. If one bears in mind that the main lights in this part of the building are all approximately 770 mm wide, that the apex could not be allowed to rise above the vault,[4] and that the sill level must have been predetermined for the whole of this part of the building, economies had to be made in the height of the main lights. To achieve this the springing-point for the window head is, in so far as one can be precise in the absence of a detailed survey, more than eight courses lower than that of the Lady Chapel windows (nI, nII) alongside it, while the sill is dropped merely by the depth of the sill itself. As a result, the head of the window alone is more than one and a half times as high as the main lights, while the area taken up by the main lights forms a horizontal rectangle approximating in proportion to the Golden Section. This is in marked contrast to the norm, which varies between a perfect square and a vertical rectangle, while the standard ratio of height of head to main lights is $1:\sqrt{2}$.

The adjacent north window (nIV) of this same chapel is even more extreme in its proportions (Pl. II, third window from the left), since in that case there was deemed to be enough room for six main lights of the standard width. The apex of the equilaterally arched head was set two courses higher in partial compensation, so that there is a gap of barely two courses below the corbel table, while the window-sill is kept at the same level as for the neighbouring east window. (Incidentally,these two sills are both lower than nVI–VIII.) Even so, the area occupied by the main lights below the springing point is here equivalent to two squares set horizontally while the area given over to the head of the window is greater than that occupied by the main lights. One can also see how much stonework there is in the head in proportion to the area of glass; this is particularly noticeable from the inside. Patching above the apex of the window might be 'read' as a *pentimento*, suggesting that the head of the window might once have been more acute.

The third window design of the trio (nV, Pl. II, fourth window from left) in the retrochoir area may have had its sill altered when Bishop Speke's chantry was inserted below it, but the head seems to have been untouched. The available width between buttresses allowed for only four main lights; here again the designer seems to have opted for a maximum glazed area, since the springing-point for the head has been set much higher than that of its neighbour to the east, in order to have the apex at a reasonable depth of three and a half courses beneath the corbel table.

Examination of these three pairs of windows, and possibly also the windows of the eastern 'transeptal' chapels, leads one to conclude that they represent the work of a different designer to the one responsible for the windows of the presbytery proper (nVI,VII, VIII, etc.) and of the Lady Chapel (nI, nII).

The latter have in common many features which set them apart from the previous group. For a start, all the sills, springing-points and apices of the windows are on a level with their neighbours, unlike the unsatisfactory variations in the group described above (Pl. II). Their apices and springing-points seem to be taken from nV. Secondly an overall pattern is laid down of five-light designs for the aisles and four-light designs for the clerestory (except in the narrow eastern bay of the latter). Thirdly, the effects of variation in bay widths and the somewhat squat proportions of each bay are absorbed through a masterly use of obtuse two-centred arches for the heads of the aisle windows. The radii for the arcs of a regular two-centred arch are normally equal to the total width of the window minus one light-width, but this can be varied considerably. In some aisle windows the squatness of proportion is mitigated because of the fact that a two-centred arch can be flatter (more obtuse) than an equilateral arch, consequently the springing-point can be higher, and this in turn means that the main lights can be taller. The effects of variation in bay-width can be absorbed by varying (or 'cheating' with) the striking-points for the arcs. An instance of this is the north window of the north-east chapel off the north transept, where the arcs used to form the head of a two-light window (the maximum size possible) are actually the same in radius as those of the five-light windows in the aisles (Pl. II). As a result, the springing-points can be the same in all the windows and the apex of the two-light windows is not noticeably

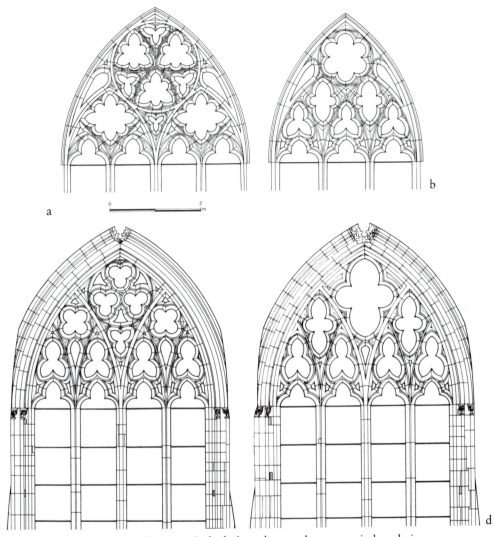

FIG. 1   a, b, c, d Exeter Cathedral presbytery clerestory window designs
Courtesy J. P. Allan and B. Jupp, Exeter Museums Archaeological Field Unit

much lower than that of the wider windows. Another example of this creative 'cheating' is to compare a four-light clerestory window with, for example, the three-light clerestory window in the seventh bay from the crossing where the available width for a window is restricted (Fig. 1a and b); the arcs of the four-light windows, whose radii are equal to four light-widths, are repeated to create a three-light window whose height nearly matches its neighbour; this produces an 'equilateral' arch over one and an acute arch over the other.[5] The average viewer does not notice this discrepancy in width for two reasons: first, because the three crucial levels of apex, springing-point and sill are effectively identical throughout the clerestory windows which, furthermore, all have identical light-widths of 770 mm, and secondly because the design of the three-light window is an adaptation of one already used twice in the clerestory for four-light windows. Such a stratagem would have been impossible if 'Westminster'-type tracery had been used.

2. THE OVERALL SCHEME OF THE WINDOW TRACERY: REPETITION OF DESIGN FORMS

The overall impression given by the clerestory windows is one of tremendous variety, yet it can be demonstrated that only three designs are used in the seven windows of the choir clerestory. Beginning from either end, the designs are organised A–B–C–A–B–C–A; (see Figs 1a, b and c). Design 'A', in the first and fourth bays from the crossing, employs a 'Y'-version of Intersecting Arch Tracery, unusually in two planes, with the topmost intersections omitted to leave room for a small oculus which contains three trefoils.[6] Design 'B', in the second and fifth bays from the crossing, contains two pairs of equilaterally-arched minor lights, each pair under an 'equilateral' major arch, with an oculus at the top to fill the remaining space below the obtuse two-centred arch of the window-head. Design 'C', in the third and sixth bays from the crossing is similar to design 'A' in general layout, but the impression it gives is quite different. This is because larger units of glazing are used to fill the space above the central 'Y' (formed by the major arches and the spaces between the heads of the main lights). These large quatrefoils are taller than they are wide; they lack the perfect symmetry of the original units, and they are important because they represent the first step towards curvilinear tracery.

In the presbytery aisles, many of the designs are broadly similar to ones used in the clerestory, merely translated into five-light versions. In fact, the tracery in the third aisle bay from the crossing is fundamentally the same as Design 'B' in the clerestory, and this version is repeated in the western bay of the Lady-Chapel. The aisles, however, lack the rhythm of repeated patterns which is a feature of the clerestory, though they achieve their own unity from a repeated grouping of the five main lights of each window into groups of 2 + 2 + 2, and from a preference for forms from the Intersecting Arch Tracery repertoire. The general effect is paradoxical, one simultaneously of unity and of variety.

3. THE HIGH EAST WINDOW

So much for window designs which have survived in their original form. My third topic is the high-level presbytery east window, whose original design completed the series in the choir aisles and clerestory. It is situated above the high altar and now contains Perpendicular tracery presumably coeval with its stained glass of 1391 (Pl. IV).[7] An examination of this part of the building reveals that enough of the original fabric survives to suggest a reconstruction. The jambs and rere-arch of the east window and of the north and south clerestory windows which flank it (Pl. XVc) show no sign of disturbance, and the capitals of all three are similar in style. The conclusion is that the size and shape of the window-head, which follows closely the curve of the vault, is as was originally intended by the designer of this part of the building. Such a shape might appear ungainly, but the policy of filling all available wall-space matches that of the north and south windows of the east end examined above. Furthermore, on the sill of the high east window behind the later quatrefoil parapet, the original mullion-bottoms can be seen, situated well below the level of the glass and coursed in with the rest of the sill, which I believe must be original (Pl. XVc).[8] These mullion-bottoms and the matching mullions above them are identical in form to those of the

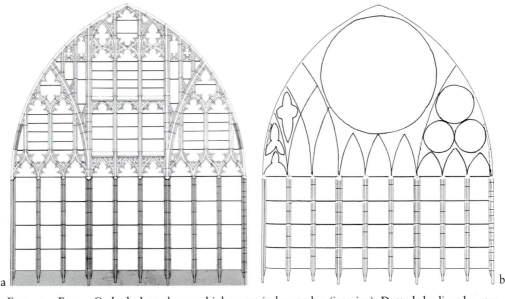

a   b

FIG. 2a.   Exeter Cathedral presbytery, high east window today (interior). Dotted shading denotes
primary Salcombe stone
Courtesy J. P. Allan and B. Jupp, Exeter Museums Archaeological Field Unit

FIG. 2b.   Exeter Cathedral presbytery, high east window, hypothetical reconstructions of
Decorated tracery (right, original intention; left, as constructed). Extant mouldings drawn in full.

windows at both clerestory and aisle level, apart from the first group of three pairs of
windows in the retrochoir area analysed above. Finally, close scrutiny of the eight mullions
themselves reveals that a change in mouldings take place at the level of their capitals; below,
the profile is similar to that of the north and south clerestory windows, while above it is
typically Perpendicular. The mullions of the north and south clerestory windows do not
have capitals with which those of the east window can be compared. Nor do these capitals
resemble those of the rere-arches of the Decorated windows in that they have no foliage. In
fact these capitals are later inserts, 'half-soled' on the inside only of the mullions and jambs
(Pl. XVc).[9] From the exterior it is clear that the Perpendicular tracery is an insert, since the
'frame' of stone from which the tracery springs is not quite properly set into the window
arch (Pl. XVb). Though the shape of the new tracery matches the old window-arch
correctly, it seems that the masons failed to push the new stonework fully into place when it
was offered-up to the arch. The tracery therefore leans out (eastwards) about 60 mm at the
top. Presumably the late 14th-century masons first took out the equivalent Decorated
moulding from which the original tracery sprang in order to provide a smooth arch which
would accept their new tracery, with the possible exception of two sections of the frame
which may have been reused in new positions (see Fig. 2a).

In conclusion, far from being a 'lost' window, the nine-light Decorated high east window
of Exeter Cathedral survives, with exception of its tracery head. Even the outlines of this can
be reconstructed from the evidence of the surviving fabric. The first clue is provided by the
shape of the head, for, like the vault which it parallels, it is two-centred in shape. This makes

Intersecting Arch Tracery highly probable — the arcs in this case being equal to two-thirds of the width of the window. This is what one would expect with a three-light window, though we know from the surviving mullions that the original window (like both today's and the nave west window) had nine. The explanation is provided by the mullions; instead of being of equal size, the third and sixth are larger and more complex than the others. In other words, there was a hierarchy of mouldings following a preliminary division of the window area into three major 'lights' with matching major arches above. Each of these major lights was sub-divided into three minor lights, in order to give the width of light that could be handled by the glazier and that accorded with the other windows of the clerestory. Precedents for such subdivisions of Intersecting Arch Tracery (rare in itself) can be found in the north window of the Nine Altars at Durham and the west nave window at Newstead Abbey, which probably mirrors Lincoln Cathedral's lost west window.[10] In both these cases it is interesting that the designer used 'Westminster' tracery to form the subdivisions, and this precedent may well have been followed in the design of the 1270s at Exeter. It is also possible that the details were modified by the designer of the clerestory windows. Unfortunately we shall never know, nor can we tell in detail how the upper part of the tracery head was designed. It is possible, for instance, that the central major arch was omitted in order to leave space for a large oculus in the manner of the oculus at Bristol Cathedral Lady Chapel or alternatively an oculus of the more usual wheel form (see Fig. 2b).[11]

The nave west window at Exeter may (for all that we know) in fact be a sophisticated echo of the original high east window. The west window is more successful visually than the latter can have ever been, largely because the designer adopted the expedient of dropping the head of tracery well below the springing-point of the window-head. This gave him a better shape to work in, for the tracery area approximates to equilaterally-arched triangle instead of the flattened shape of the tracery head of the high east window. It is possible that the design of the east window of the Lady Chapel (see pl. I), which is closer in date to the Decorated high east window, may give a closer indication of the 'lost' design. It consists of seven foiled lights arranged 3 + 1 + 3, with a small cinquefoiled oculus over each group of three and three trefoils in the major oculus above. One should take into account however the possibility that the Lady Chapel window was, like the nave west window, probably more sophisticated in effect since it too has an almost equilaterally-arched head, for which space is allowed by the more acutely-arched cross-section of the vaulting in this part of the building. Furthermore, the Lady Chapel would seem to be the product of a later campaign (see Jansen above, p. 43) in a building where ideas seem to have matured in a matter of years rather than decades, as is more usually the case. Given the way in which the major features of the original high east window are dictated by the proportions of the presbytery (which must have been decided on from the very beginning), it is tempting to see the general layout at least of this 'lost' window as a product of the original designer, who would also have been responsible for the three pairs of windows in the retrochoir area, above which the high east window is situated. Lack of evidence precludes certainty, especially as one would expect the tracery to have been put in at the same time as the other clerestory windows, which, as I argue above, conform to a scheme of repeated designs which were obviously conceived as a single group.

4. THE PLACE OF EXETER'S FENESTRATION IN THE CONTEXT OF ITS PERIOD

Though tracery (predominantly of the 'plate' variety) appeared in England many decades before 1250, the first major building to make an important feature of it in its windows was Westminster Abbey.[12] There, apart from the large transept windows, a single design is used for both aisle and clerestory windows throughout the entire mid 13th-century *chevet*, and another in the gallery windows, for which the first design would have been unsuitable due to the shape of the wall space. This could have been said to be in the French tradition, which was also followed some 50 years later in the nave of York Minster, where there is a single three-light design in the aisles and a four-light design in the clerestory. The early 14th-century clerestory over the nave of Malmesbury Abbey carries on this tradition by having only one design of window tracery, and there are of course many other examples. But in complete contrast, a group of buildings can be isolated whose designers obviously favoured variety in window tracery. Perhaps the earliest extant of these is Exeter. This demonstrates true variety in the sense that, in a given part of the building, each pair of windows is different from all its neighbours. This applies to the windows of the presbytery aisles, to all the windows of the nave, and to a sequence of three designs in the presbytery clerestory,which, I suspect, were meant to be 'read' as true variety. Another example of this is Wells, which has an alternation of two designs in the presbytery aisles and eastern transepts (even alternating north-south in the western half of the aisles), with extra designs for 'façade' windows in this part of the building, and a further design for the Lady Chapel. There are also indications that true variety was aimed at in the windows of the presbytery clerestory, but this seems to have faltered towards the crossing. Other examples of this group are Merton College Chapel, Oxford, and the hall-church east end of St Augustine's Bristol. The latter is slightly more restrained; it has two four-light designs alternating in the north and south windows of the Lady Chapel and aisles except in the easternmost bay of the former, where there is only room for a three-light window, while another design is used for the eastern 'façade' windows of the aisles. As for the Lady Chapel at St Alban's Cathedral, it takes variety to surprising lengths, for the windows in each of the three bays are not only different from each other but different north to south as well.[13] Such total variety is most unusual, however; even with true variety of design the designs are usually paired north-south.

Buildings with such diversity of window design are comparatively rare in the first half of the Decorated period; it was not until curvilinear window tracery was in vogue that we find variety in tracery more widespread, for instance at Sleaford in Lincolnshire, St Mary's Beverley, and Tilty in Essex. Exeter Cathedral has perhaps not been given due credit for the dissemination of the principle of variety — a particularly English feature in medieval architecture.

ACKNOWLEDGEMENTS

I should like to record my thanks for the co-operation of J. P. Allan and Barbara Jupp of Exeter Museums Archaeological Field Unit, who, unbeknownst to me, were working independently on a survey of the clerestory windows in the presbytery and on a reconstruction of the lost east window. Our conclusions were very similar.

APPENDIX: THE MASONRY OF THE EAST WINDOW
By John Allan

Whilst scaffolding was erected in the presbytery in 1982 the writer and Miss Barbara Jupp undertook a study of the masonry of the east window; this was carried out concurrently with the study of the window glass by Brooks and Evans. Our initial intentions were first to make an accurate line drawing of the window (Fig. 2), since none existed, and second to see whether there was any evidence for the existence of the six-light window of *c.* 1300 postulated by earlier writers. Upon inspection, however, it was apparent that there survives substantial evidence of an original window of nine lights rather than six, only the head of which had been replaced in 1390–1.

G

The evidence that all the main lights of the window belong to the original construction of the presbytery of *c.* 1300 is overwhelming. First, the masonry forming the frame to the present large window is clearly part of the primary build. Examination of the Salcombe stone jambs of the window shows that their coursing is continuous with that of the stair turrets, and with the eastern shafts supporting the presbytery vault on the interior. There is no sign that these jambs have been cut back or re-set. Similarly the broad sloping internal sill of the window stretches in one uninterrupted chamfer across the full width of the nine lights; clearly this would not be the case had the window been enlarged. The long sloping sill is in fact the equivalent of those which formerly ran from the top of the presbytery arcades to the bases of its clerestory windows, which were largely buried in the wall thickness when the triforium was added to the presbytery bays in 1317–18.

Likewise the window mullions of the primary build survive, although their external faces have largely been replaced in Doulting stone, a stone much favoured in repairs at the end of the last century and the early years of the present one. The profiles of the common mullions, simply chamfered externally and with chamfers and a central roll moulding internally, are identical to those used in the presbytery clerestory. Not only are their dimensions identical, but so is the spacing of the mullions, with lights of 77 cms between them. Again, the spacing of the lower saddle bars in the east window is identical to that in the clerestory, although the higher bars of the east window are rather more widely spaced. Finally, the geology of the mullions, internal sill and jambs is entirely consonant with that in the rest of the presbytery. The mouldings and vaulting ribs of this phase of construction are almost exclusively of Salcombe stone. As work progressed westward there was a gradual change to the employment of Beer stone in all these elements. By the time that the nave was constructed Beer stone was being used for all vaulting ribs, all bosses, most tracery and even for voussoirs in the arcades. By the mid and late 14th century Beer stone seems to have been used exclusively for all these functions. One might note here that the accounts of 1391 specify that the stone removed from the east window was Beer stone. If so, this was the only example of its use on a large scale in the eastern arm of the church. This is not impossible but it is perhaps more likely that the writer of the accounts could not distinguish between these two types of stone.

At the top of the mullions there is an obvious building break. Above this level virtually the entire tracery of the original window has been removed. At this point there is a change in the form of the mouldings, with concave mouldings of the head sitting uncomfortably on the plain chamfers of the mullions. The geology of the window head is also completely different, being entirely of Beer stone. Like those of all the other windows of the presbytery, the mullions of the original east window lacked capitals. Small capitals of Beer stone were therefore cut into the tops of the original mullions. Of the window head two small portions of the original remain; the sections of the main arch on each side (Fig. 2), both in Salcombe stone. One can, however, go some way to reconstructing the primary form of the tracery. The original form of the cusps of lights 1–3 and 6–9 is known; they were identical to those used elsewhere in the clerestory of the presbytery and choir.[14] Mullions 3 and 6 are principal mullions, more massive than the others and with additional mouldings. Given the Geometric Decorated form of the window, sub-arches must have run from these to strike the outer frame, just as they do in the Perpendicular tracery which followed. Since no cusps project from the surviving stones of the frame (Fig. 2a), these lights seem to have differed from all those used in equivalent positions in the other windows of the choir and presbytery, which are all cusped. No structural element survives from the centre of the window, but a circle drawn from point u fits perfectly in the centre of this space. One might therefore-suggest that the centrepiece of the tracery was a circular motif of ambitious proportions. Central circular motifs are, of course, the most common element in the tracery of the eastern arm of the cathedral, and there are also large ones in the transepts and west window. However, as Bridget Cherry has suggested to the writer, this does not make a particularly elegant design, and this suggestion should be regarded as tentative; there are other possible solutions.

One further problem arises. Where could the group of three early 14th-century figures (Isaiah, Moses and Abraham: Brooks and Evans lights 2E, 2F, 2G) best fit in this reconstruction? These would require much larger lights than any in the surviving tracery of the cathedral's eastern arm, and this writer is inclined to favour the possibility that they come from the main lights of a different window rather than the central element of the east window.

REFERENCES

1. Malcolm Thurlby (oral communication); no evidence survives at all.
2. See Malcolm Thurlby, above, p. 20 fig. 2 (Radford's plan shows surviving Romanesque masonry above ground level).
3. The decision to retain the core of the Romanesque fabric in the main vessel in the first two bays east of the crossing (Malcolm Thurlby, p. 19) may have been taken at this point. Incidentally, the change to a three-storey elevation, which must have detracted from the visual impact of the windows, may in fact reflect the original wishes of the Dean and Chapter who may, to begin with, have been overborne by the first Master Mason, but who reasserted their preference for a more traditional elevation at the time his successor was appointed. (The same happened at St Peter's in Rome, where Michelangelo persuaded the Curia to adopt a central plan against its better judgement, which later reasserted itself [Prof John Shearman, lectures at Courtauld Institute, University of London, 1971]).
4. Lichfield Cathedral west window is an exception, but building evidence suggests a major change of plan between designing the nave and constructing the west front.
5. The stair-turret at the angle of the clerestory impinges on the bay adjacent more than an average buttress would.
6. This design is also used in the east bay of the Lady Chapel.
7. Brooks and Evans (1988).
8. The original sloping sills (together with their mullion bases) are still to be seen behind the quatrefoil parapets of the three eastern clerestory windows; the whole eastern arm must originally have resembled the east wall of Aquablanca's earlier transept at Hereford. There is some disturbance to the exterior of the top course of the high east window sill, but this was probably associated with repairs or modifications to the retrochoir roof.
9. I am indebted to Mr Peter Dare, a former Master Mason of the Cathedral, for this technical observation. See also Henderson and Blaylock (1987), 26 and fig. 21.
10. Russell (1980), 87–9, and Russell (1986), 83–9.
11. Brooks and Evans (1988).
12. The sole exceptions to this are the south window and the south-east chapel of the south transept and the south window of the muniment room.
13. Their authenticity is vouched for by Carter's engravings (Carter (1813), pls iv and v).
14. Brooks and Evans (1988).

The West Front: I

The Structural History of the West Front

By J. P. Allan and S. R. Blaylock

In the wake of the programme of conservation and restoration on the west front of Wells Cathedral, the Dean and Chapter of Exeter decided in 1978 to carry out a scheme of similar scope on the western image screen of their own cathedral. Work began in the following year and continued until 1985.[1] In the early years quite extensive restoration, including the replacement of the most seriously decayed figure sculptures, was contemplated, but following the replacement of several canopies and shafts on the southern portion of the screen in 1980–1 (Pl. B) a progressively more conservative approach was adopted; in subsequent years only small projecting mouldings were replaced (Pl. B). In 1982 the writers were invited by the Dean and Chapter to join the team of masons and conservators to provide a detailed record of the screen and if possible to establish its structural history. It was by that stage clear that the front had been subject to a series of restoration programmes. The most recent were readily identifiable but the extent and sequence of those dating before 1892 were matters of considerable uncertainty.

In the absence of detailed, accurate drawings,[2] new large-scale (1:10) elevations of the entire image screen have been prepared (Fig. 1) and an archive, recording in line drawings, photographs and written descriptions the extent of decayed stonework, previous repairs, repairs of 1979 to 1985, details of construction, etc., has been built up.[3]

Previous records

The most important records of the image screen are those made by John Carter, who made a series of pencil drawings of each west front sculpture in or shortly before 1794,[4] publishing pen-and-ink drawings of the two lower registers (angels and kings), evidently copied from the pencil drawings, in his *Specimens of Ancient Sculpture and Painting* in 1794.[5] His grand folio volume, published for the Society of Antiquaries in 1797,[6] includes one engraving by James Basire showing the entire image screen, based on two annotated sketches by Carter also surviving in the British Library.[7] Whilst the published drawings and engravings are not without their faults, recourse to the original pencil drawings allows one to distinguish between those details which were carefully portrayed and those which were hurriedly treated on site.[8] Carter's drawings are the only record of many details destroyed by restoration or decay during the 19th century.

Surprisingly, and perhaps because Carter's engraving was so well known, the front did not receive more thoroughgoing recording in the last century, and it was only towards the end of the major restoration of 1892 to 1913 that Miss Edith Prideaux, recognising the alarming acceleration of decay, compiled the second major record of the west front: her valuable series of photographs of each sculpture, accompanied by a commentary and discussion.[9] Miss Prideaux's numeration of the figures will be followed here.[10] In the period between these two major records fall at least seventeen engravings, most of them of limited value,[11] and a quite extensive collection of photographs, useful in showing elements of both medieval work and restoration removed between 1892 and 1913. Detailed drawings of the

19th century seem surprisingly rare: those of the north and south sectors by Edward Ashworth[12] are the most informative known to the writers.

MEDIEVAL STRUCTURAL DEVELOPMENT

1. The design of c. 1328–42

Contrary to our initial expectations, and to the views of a number of writers,[13] we believe that none of the west front fabric now visible is earlier than the reconstruction of the nave under Bishop Grandisson, datable to the years *c.* 1329 to 1342 (below). The primary design, attributable to Thomas Witney, formerly displayed a series of large arches running across the main vessel of the church (Fig. 2, B), now partially obscured by the later image screen. Its upper portions, extending to the full height of the front, remain largely undisturbed. At least three stages of construction can be distinguished within this phase of work (Fig. 2, A.)

The earliest stage is the construction of the doorways and the lowest 5 m of the nave and aisle walls. On the interior this work is characterised by the use of plain Salcombe stone ashlar, most of it similar in size to the Romanesque masonry. This has been claimed as Romanesque work, but examination of the relationship of the doorways to the plain ashlar shows, in our view decisively, that they are contemporary.[14] The masonry of the doorways consists of very large Beer stones which could not always be coursed neatly with the adjacent work, but at several levels their coursing is continuous.[15]

The external face of this stage of work is now partially concealed and somewhat disturbed by the construction of the image screen; only the inner orders of the central doorway, with their high bases and foliage scroll, were retained when the image screen was added. The straight joint between this work and the image screen added to it is clearly evident on each side of the doorway (Pl. XIIIA). At the south doorway the junction of the two phases of work is equally evident. Here the entire head and the base of the doorway were retained, but the intervening jambs were removed and replaced by masonry forming part of the south porch of the image screen. The roll moulding and tablet flowers of the head come to an abrupt and untidy end. In the north porch the inner mouldings of Witney's north aisle doorway can be seen receding behind the line of the porch walls. Mouldings which may represent the outer order of the arch were found when stones were removed from the southern wall of the porch in the 1890s.[16]

Between the central and south doorways, and now forming the east wall of the Grandisson chapel, stands a blind archway, the high bases, leaf ornament and mouldings of which are comparable to those of the central doorway. The outer mouldings were likewise cut back when the chapel was built. The chapel piscina cuts awkwardly into the mouldings. Clearly this arch forms part of Witney's front. If the arrangement of the front was symmetrical,[17] a corresponding arch lies on the north side of the central doorway, now concealed behind the image screen (Fig. 2, B).

This stage is usefully documented in the fabric rolls. Work on the west end can hardly have begun before the translation of the clergy from the nave to their new choir, an event which presumably took place at the dedication of the high altar in December 1328.[18] By 1330 payment was made for 123 feet of Silverton[19] stone for gutters for the porch between the gables (*pugnones*) outside the west part, and for 31 Silverton stones called 'schywes'[20] containing 48 feet, also for the porch. By 1330–1 payments were made for the ironwork of the great (i.e. nave) door. In 1332 final settlement was made for the nave piers including those embedded in the west front.[21]

The payment for porches indicates that Witney's design included gabled elements, presumably in front of the western doorways, which no longer survive. One element of

G*

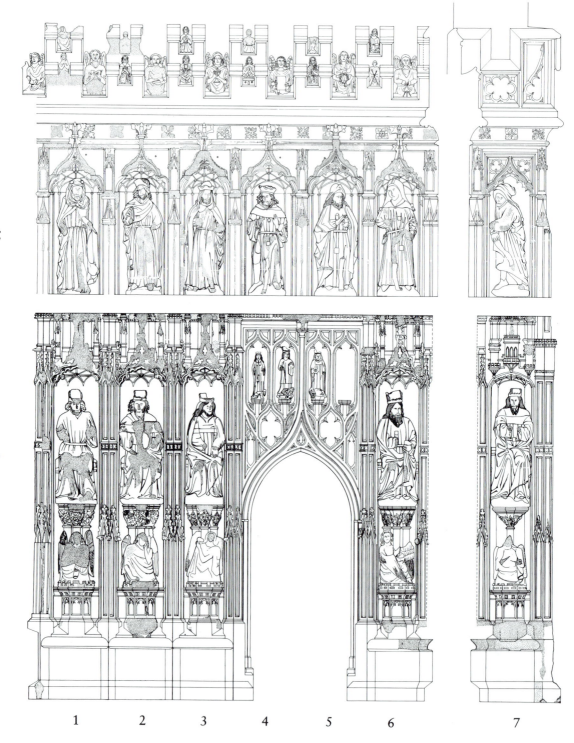

C

B

A

1   2   3   4   5   6   7

reused jamb which probably came from the porches survives incorporated above the doorway of Grandisson's chapel.[22]

Above the doorways there is a distinct change in the character of the ashlar at 5–6 m above floor level. The masonry above this break extends in small, neat courses around the nave and aisle windows,[23] rising to fill the spandrels above the great west window. Its construction marks the closure of the main vessel of the church. This work is characterised by a random mixture of Salcombe, Beer, Caen and Portland blocks (Fig. 2, A.II; Pl. A), contrasting with the virtual uniformity of geology in the preceding stage.

At the south-west corner of the nave is a buttress ornamented with quatrefoils below a course of crenellation (Fig. 2, B). In 1979 the decayed canopy and rear wall of the adjacent niche of the image screen (C35) were removed, followed by the canopy of the figure below (B35). This work exposed the junction of the south- and west-facing buttresses. The crenellated course could be seen extending onto the west buttress, with a sunken quatrefoil in the internal angle (Pl. XXIIA). The projecting chamfered course visible on the south buttress could also be seen turning westward, but had been cut back when the canopy B35 had been inserted; a small diagonal chamfer bridged the internal angle (Pl. XXIIB). Below the chamfer the masonry of both buttresses could be seen running tidily round a small slit window lighting the south-west stair. At the base of the buttress a further string-course was exposed on the removal of shaft A34/35 in 1979 (Pl. XXIIC; Fig. 2, B). These features are all of a piece and clearly precede the image screen. Since the sunken quatrefoil at the internal angle is strongly reminiscent of the west front of Wells, and since the south buttress is broader than the other nave buttresses and differently ornamented, it initially appeared likely that this represents a fragment of an early 13th-century front. However we now consider that this is part of Witney's design, its crenellations continuing a theme popular in the nave.[24] The crucial relationship here is with the adjoining stair turret which serves the 14th-century elevation and must surely be Witney's. Interpretation of the relationship is made difficult by some repairs and by modern ribbon pointing, but sufficient courses do correspond to suggest that the stair and buttresses are contemporary. Both use ashlar of mixed geology like stage II of the nave (Fig. 2, A), but with an admixture of massive blocks of coarse Salcombe stone. Moreover there are no signs of seams indicating that the staircase slit window onto the front was cut into the buttress.

This kind of masonry can also be seen on the west face of St Edmund's chapel. Between the chapel and the north aisle is a buttress which clearly displays two phases of construction. The primary phase courses consistently both with St Edmund's chapel to the north and with the ashlar of the north aisle which, in turn, courses with the aisle window. The west (and north) walls of the chapel must therefore be contemporary with the construction of the aisle, so cannot be associated with the reference of 1279 referring to a window opposite St Edmund's altar.[25] The chapel is the obvious candidate for the new chapel beside the well-house mentioned in 1330.[26]

On the south side of the front progress on the masonry between the great west window and the aisle window evidently preceded that on the south-west corner. The junction between the two pieces of work above the aisle window is marked by blocks on the south side cut into those of the central portion (Pl. A). It is possible that a further stage in the construction of Witney's front can be discerned: the neat ashlar disappears in the highest portions of the front (Fig. 2, A.III). Face-bedded Beer stone slabs were used for the series of ascending niches above each aisle. The change to this kind of masonry could simply be functional: Beer stone, being soft and fine, is more easily carved. However, the plain medieval masonry of the high gable is also quite different; this is poor indeed, in places using miscellaneous small blocks to fill the space between window and coping.

One indication that there may have been some change in design in the upper stages is the curious termination of the pilaster buttresses flanking the central window. The frame of the spandrels of the window sits uncomfortably on the centre of each buttress (Fig. 2, B). The pilasters are very similar in form to those between the nave windows, which were met by flying buttresses. Might there perhaps have been an intention to provide similar flying buttresses on the front?

Witney's front must have been finished by about 1342, the year in which the figure of St Peter in the high gable was painted, and the last year for which he is known to have been master mason at Exeter.[27] Whether during his time or shortly afterwards, one further change to his front may be noted: the outer pair of west-facing buttresses was remodelled. The primary builds of the buttresses are of Salcombe stone. Both were extended westward using Beer stone; that on the north also employs mauve volcanic trap, a stone hardly ever used for facework on the cathedral. The low flying buttresses flanking the central window are also composed of Beer stone and may also have been added at this time. At the junction of the arches with the pilaster buttresses of the west front (now much repaired), the stones of the arches appear to be cut into those of the buttresses.[28]

II.   *The addition of the image screen*

In the course of recent repairs it was possible to see a number of constructional features in the image screen. In 1985 new iron gates were installed at the entrance to each porch. In the north porch two mortared wall footings at right-angles to the front were encountered immediately below the paving slabs; they may relate to the screen but, perhaps more likely, to Witney's porches or to some earlier design (the position of the footings is indicated by shading, Fig. 2, B and C). At the central doorway, however, the image screen sat on no foundation at all; immediately below the south jamb loose mortar layers could be seen tipping westward, incorporating the broken fragments of the stepped base of a Purbeck marble grave cover.

Turning to the superstructure, all the medieval figures and facing blocks are of Beer stone. Many of the shafts and canopies and most (perhaps all) of the figures are either face- or joint-bedded; this has encouraged their disintegration. In the few places where the core was observed it lay between 0.12 and 0.3 m behind the wall surface at the back of the B-register niches and consisted of undressed veined volcanic ('Pocombe'), Salcombe and Beer stone rubble. Some elements of the niches were made in standard units. For example, the canopies B1–3, 6, 11–14 and 19–22 are each composed of two principal blocks, the upper one 0.34 m and the lower one 0.62 m high (Fig. 3, a). In some instances (canopies B1, B3, B6) the lower block is a composite of three stones, with very tight vertical joints running through the small circular attached shafts. When the shafts B30/1 to 34/5 were dismantled in 1979–80, grooves of V-shaped profile were found channelled into the horizontal faces of the blocks.[29] These presumably functioned to bed the mortar more securely. When shaft B11/12 was removed during conservation in 1984 it was possible to see the manner in which adjacent canopies were jointed to intervening shafts (Fig. 3, a; Pl. XXIIG). In this case the shaft was held in place by a horizontal iron cramp, the vertical joint being masked by the attached shaft.

Whilst the angel sculptures were cut from the same block as their architectural surrounds, and were therefore installed as part of the structure, the B-register figures are independent. The placing of these figures in their niches evidently occasioned some problems. Several of the mouldings of the niches and some of the figures show signs of rough trimming where a large figure did not readily fit the space available: this is evident, for example, on the seat of

FIG. 2.   Medieval structural development of the front

B2, a sleeve of B7 and the beaded surround of B19. This last figure seems to have been a particular headache, being an unusually large figure fitted into a niche which was narrower than most.

There are a number of other instances where things evidently went wrong. The paired gablets running up the internal angle between the buttresses and the front are one instance. On the north buttress (B10/11) they run neatly upward. On the north side of the south buttress a crenellated shaft is paired awkwardly with a motif from the more elaborate gablets of the shafts of the south end (27–33); this is the only instance of this type of gablet in the central and northern sections (Pl. XXIID). More untidy are the inconsistencies of the south porch, where the vertical bands of birds and flowers show many irregularities and where the shafts between the sculptures come to an abrupt halt, perhaps reflecting a change in the layout of the vault. Similar peculiarities can be seen within the Grandisson chapel. The mouldings of the rere-arches of the window-heads do not correspond to the mouldings of the jambs below; likewise the foliage carving on the inside faces of the jamb is of a slightly different character from that in the equivalent position on the soffits of the window-heads. On the frontage the beads on the inner mouldings of the shafts are omitted periodically (shafts 27/8, 30/1, on one occasion being pieced later into individually drilled holes (shaft A27). The beads are replaced in part by small fleurons on the shafts of B21 and A30.

Finally, there are further infelicities in the arrangement of the two pairs of angels in the spandrels of the central doorway (Fig. 4). These are particularly apparent on the south side, where the upper angel does not fill the space provided and a triangular gap above it has been filled with miscellaneous fragments of foliage carving. The tips of the feathers of this angel's lower wing and the lower left edge of the block have been trimmed, while the upper wing is separated from the body by a sprig of foliage (Pl. XIXB). The failure of this block to fit the allotted space can be explained by a comparison of the two spandrels. In the northern spandrel the distance between the outer corner and the edge of the wing at the inner corner is 0.71 m; the upper edge of the panel bearing the angel fits snugly into this space. On the southern side, however, the equivalent gap is less, 0.66 m; it may be suggested that the two panels were cut to the same size based on measurement of the northern spandrel. When the southern panel came to be positioned it would have been necessary to trim one or more of the edges in order to fit it into the smaller space. To have trimmed the left-hand edge would have entailed the loss of prominent detail of the reclining figure, so a less radical solution was adopted whereby the lower edges of this panel and the upper edge of the carving beneath (removing a sliver of the right arm and face of the angel) were trimmed. This resulted in the narrow triangular gap above the top edge of the upper panel.

Whilst conservation was in progress it was possible to examine the spandrels closely to consider the possibility that the angels are not *in situ*. It is apparent that the inner wing of each of the upper angels (beside the apex of the arch) is cut from the same structural block as the mouldings of the doorway. However in the remainder of each spandrel the structural masonry is recessed to a depth of *c.* 0.08 m and the angel sculptures are carved on shallow panels. During conservation the removal of recent cement exposed small areas of the plain facework at the rear of the angel panels. This was smooth and carefully dressed; it seems very unlikely that any earlier design had been removed. Some of the joints between the structural blocks at the rear could be seen (Fig. 4). These would have cut across the angel figures, had not separate panels been cut to take the figures. The wings on the structural blocks (Fig. 4) are very similar to one another but quite different from those of the detached panels. They appear to have been carved by a different hand. The failure of the south angel's wings to fit properly onto the body seems simply to reflect a failure of two carvers to marry their work together. We therefore reject the possibility that the angels are re-set.[30]

In its present form the 14th-century screen survives to a lower level at the central doorway than in the rest of the screen (Fig. 2, C). This can hardly have been the original design and it is reasonable to envisage some form of central emphasis: perhaps a central gable.

The highly animated sculptures with complex tubular-fold drapery must be contemporary with the structure of the screen, matching in style the angels which are structurally part of it (Pls XVIB, XVII, XXD; details of costume of figures B19, B12 and B27 appear in Pl. XXA–C). It is noticeable that these fill the most prominent niches: B11–14, 19–20 and

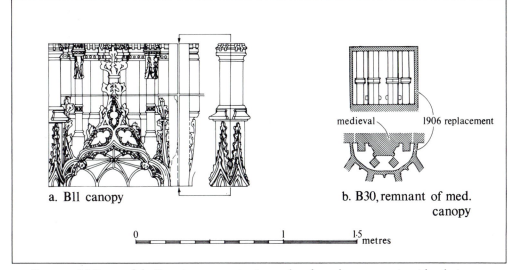

FIG. 3. (a) Form of the B-register canopies (central and northern sectors), with relation to adjacent shafts; (b) remnant of medieval canopies of B27 and 30, preserved within hollow upper blocks of replacements (cf. Pl. XVIB)

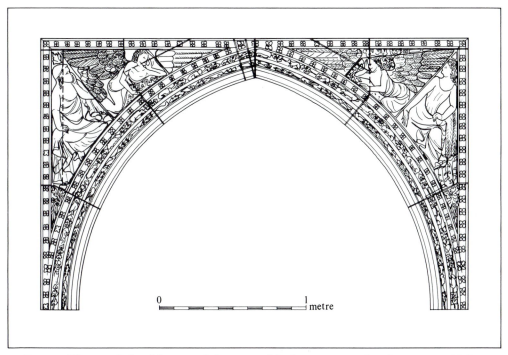

FIG. 4. The spandrels of the central doorway of the image screen, showing structural joints behind the angel panels, partially visible during conservation (Shown as dashed lines)

27–32 (and formerly B10). The scenes of the Annunciation and Adoration of the Magi on the south and north sides of the south porch also belong to this group (Pl. XVII). The presence of later sculptures (discussed below) in the less prominent positions surely indicates that the initial scheme was never completed. Two figures in the upper register, in the same style but differing in subject (C10 and 28) must have come from elements now removed; perhaps they flanked the central gable conjectured above. Both figures are standing (all of the surviving B-register figures of this phase are seated) and have the same curved pose, with the weight shifted to one hip. Carter's drawing of the figure C10, the surface of which is almost all weathered away (one fold of typical tubular drapery survives), shows details which are remarkably similar to those of C28 (Pl. XVIIIA, B, C) such as the tightly curled locks of hair in two central 'braids' of the beard, the elongated face, etc. (see Henry, 'Iconography' below pp. 136–7).

   The date of this part of the image screen has been the subject of much consideration, with dates suggested between c. 1330[31] and c. 1350–65.[32] Arguments in favour of the earlier date rested in part on the payments of 1329–31 for work on the central doorways, discussed above. Two other references were believed to support the case:

(i)   Bishop and Prideaux,[33] followed by several later writers, believed that the new bread house for which payments were made in 1331–2 lay within the cavity between the image screen and west front, to the north of the central doorway. It would then have been paired with the Grandisson chapel on the south side. Since, however, no medieval doorway gave access to this space, which is unlit, and since the accounts give no location for the bread house, this was clearly a mistake.

(ii)   Hope and Lloyd[34] identified the payments for two windows in the new chapel next to the well-house in 1330[35] as references to the Grandisson chapel. However since the well-house was outside St Edmund's chapel[36] and the quantity of iron recorded (five quintans valued at 16s. 8d.) was far greater than would be needed for two tiny windows in the Grandisson chapel, their argument can be discounted.

In fact the details of the screen are so different from those of Thomas Witney's work in the nave that it would be surprising if it were started while he was master mason (i.e. before 1342). There is no sign of work in progress on the image screen in the accounts of 1340–2. By the time of the next surviving fabric account in 1346–7 work on the porches was the only substantial building activity at the cathedral. William Joy was paid a fee of 20s. in this year for work in the two previous terms, a reference interpreted by Erskine as a consultancy fee.[37] In the absence of other projects this must surely record his work on the west porches. The activities listed in the account of work on the porches in this year include the purchase of 122½ tontight of Beer stone and payments for carving the 'tablatur'.[38] The following half-yearly account of 1347 records the bishop's gift of £10 for the porches, a gift which followed one of £20 in 1346–7, the purpose of which is not specified.[39] In the same period a further 212 tontight of Beer stone were purchased and William Joy once again received a fee.[40] These considerable purchases suggest that work was proceeding apace before the Black Death. Recent work by Harold Fox[41] indicates that the South-West was afflicted at an earlier date than previously recognised, and its effects were more serious. The accounts of 1348 to 1353 are full of detail, but there is no sign of masonry under construction anywhere on the cathedral. William Joy vanishes from the record. The only possible indication of work at the front is the payment of 14s. to a glazier for setting of glass in St Radegund's chapel, sometimes identified with the Grandisson Chapel.[42] Given the incompleteness of the original scheme of sculptures it seems likely that the plague brought construction to a halt in 1347. By 1352–3 Richard Farleigh was master.[43] In our view, therefore, the image screen and its earliest sculptures, including that in Grandisson's chapel, should be dated c. 1342–7. Nevertheless, Lawrence Stone's alternative of a later date of c. 1350–65[44] deserves brief consideration. This rested principally on the clear stylistic links[45] between the early image screen sculptures and some of the bosses of the nave high vault. The vault had been identified as the *novum opus* recorded in the fabric roll of 1352–3[46] so was dated *c.* 1353–60. However, as Mrs Erskine has now shown convincingly,[47] the new work cannot be the nave vault, which in all likelihood was built in the mid- and late 1330s and early 1340s. One might add that a date in the 1340s fits better with Stone's observation that elsewhere in Britain the highly animated style characteristic of these figures perished around 1350.[48]

III.   *The north sector*

As Harvey[49] has shown, the north porch displays precise parallels to the Gloucester cloisters, falling between the east walk (complete by *c.* 1377) and the other three walks (begun after 1381) and is attributable to Robert Lesyngham, master mason at Exeter from 1377 following his employment at Gloucester,[50] although no Exeter fabric roll associates him with this particular job. It seems more likely that the porch had remained unbuilt than that he replaced an earlier structure. In our survey, however, we have been unable to detect any joints which indicate the edges of the inserted work. The porch masonry courses through so neatly with the adjacent niches that the two look as if they were built together. Minor differences between the ornament of the north sector and the rest of the screen include foliage of slightly variant style on the capitals of the A-register and the omission of the bead ornament in the inner orders of the shafts (Fig. 1). One (rather desperate) solution might be that although the adjacent canopies were carved they were not put in place until Lesyngham's time.

The sculptures of kings in the middle register at the north end (B1–3, 6–7) have long been recognised as later than those of the centre and south, and have been attributed to the late 14th or early 15th century (Pl. XVIA). Quiet, more static, poses with horizontal bands of drapery across the chest, a central fold of the garment between the knees, long gently flowing hair and taller crowns (Pl. XXIH) characterise this group. Examples of a typical earlier crown of the B-register (B12) and the one late 15th-century crown (C17) are shown for comparison in Plate XXIG and I. Further examples in the same style are seen in obscure positions in the southern sector: B26 and 34. These seven figures are strong candidates for the work of the figure sculptor ('imaginator') John Pratt, who worked on the front in 1375.[51] During conservation it was apparent that B1–3 and 6–7 are each composed of two blocks (Pls B and XXIIE), unlike the earlier sculptures which are monolithic. When the joint in the head of B2 was dismantled a crumbly red compound which we suspect was some form of resin was found to be the bonding agent.[52] The B-register contains one further distinctive group of sculptures: standing figures with box-fold drapery matching in style the figures of the upper register (B23, 33 and 35). These are in the most obscure positions and indicate that their niches were not filled until the upper figures were put in place in the late 15th century (below). Finally the series of four figures on the projecting buttresses (B8–9, 24–5, believed to be the Four Doctors of the Church see Henry, 'Iconography', below p. 137), form a group which lacks distinctive traits. They might belong to the 15th century or late 14th century groups.

IV.   *The addition of the C-register*

At the top of the canopies of the B-register a clear horizontal break running the entire width of the front is readily discernible (cf. Figs 1 and 2, C). Above this line the profiles of the shafts, the designs of the canopies and niches, and the foliage and figure sculpture are all quite different. The figures of the upper register sit awkwardly on the tops of the B-register canopies; some look quite precarious (e.g. C7, C21).[53] The C-register is clearly an addition.

The niches of this register fall into two groups, the southern portion (C27–34) differing from the central and northern sectors. We have no evidence of whether this distinction has any chronological significance. With the exception of the two re-used sculptures (C10 and 28), all the figures belong to a single group, characterised by the sharply angular folds of their draperies (Pl. XXE, F) and a variety of elaborate headgear. One (C6) carries a belt from which is suspended a purse with a broad purse-bar (Pl. XXID), a feature which is believed to have come into use in England c. 1460.[54] The crown of the figure of Christ (Pl. XXII) is of the tall 'open crown' type which dates after the mid-15th century (John Steane, pers. comm.). The other headgear is broadly mid- to late 15th-century in character (see Henry 'Iconography' below n. 112) (Pl. XXG, H, I). On the other hand the shoes worn by many of the figures in the northern and southern sectors are not likely to be later than the 1480s (Pl. XXIC).[55] The figures therefore seem to belong to the years c. 1460–80 (with a preference, if anything, for the earlier end of this date-range).[56] We cannot prove that the figures and architectural surrounds are contemporary; if they are, the screen was heightened in the episcopate of Bishop Neville (1456–65), Bothe (1465–78) or Courtenay (1478–87).

Over the central doorway, under the seated figures of Christ (C17) and the Georgian replacement for the Virgin Mary (C16), is a pair of shields. Doubts had been expressed about whether these were part of the primary design of their niches and whether they had been re-carved or were modern restorations; the arms below C16, long regarded as those of Richard II, have been the subject of varying explanation. Upon inspection it was apparent that these shields are integral to their niches and have not been re-carved in the post-medieval period; they retain traces of polychromy, such as the blue field of the lys of the arms of France (Pl. XIXA). As Stone noted[57] the shield under C16 does in fact show the Royal Arms of England after 1408 impaling those of Edward the Confessor. Taken with that under C17, of Athelstan impaling the See of Exeter Ancient (alluding to Athelstan's refoundation of the minster), shield C16 must surely allude to the foundation of the See at Exeter in 1050.

As in the lower registers, all the medieval fabric is of Beer stone, usually bonded with lime mortar. Some very fine jointing was achieved by the use of a red resinous substance with a waxy feel.[58] The figure sculptures are usually composed of two blocks of stone; the junction of the two was, sometimes at least, filled with a black substance, probably pitch, with an admixture of crushed Beer stone.[59] In one instance the joint was secured with a wooden dowel.[60] When figures were dismantled it could be seen or could be felt that their backs had been hollowed out; most are only c. 0.15–0.30 m thick as was seen on figure C24 when the upper block was removed during conservation in 1984 (Pl. XXIIF).

In the spandrels above the canopies is a series of small (10–15 mm wide) circular holes, most of which retain pegs of oak heartwood in which may be seen traces of smaller (c. 2–3 mm wide) pins, some of them of copper alloy, others of iron. These appear to have secured light metal fixtures: perhaps, for example, rosettes.[61] Single peg-holes were present above each canopy of the northern sector, some to the right, some to the left (Fig. 1; although those in niches C5 and C6 are obscured by the canopies). In the central sector there is a pair above each figure except C13, above which is a group of four, the lower pair inclined upward. Four much more substantial stubs of iron bars set in lead project horizontally from the rear of niches C16 and C17, one to each side of the seats of the figures. Since one bar retains patches of red paint and those in C17 are in positions which are virtually inaccessible with the figure of Christ in its niche, they are presumably 15th century.

The iron bars serve no obvious structural purpose, so these also may have have supported some kind of metal armature or ornament, conceivably connected with the theme of the Coronation of the Virgin.

v. Alterations to the C-register canopies

Only one C-register canopy (C6) survives in its original form (Fig. 5a). All of this canopy (including the spandrels but excepting the highest pair of crockets and the finial, now replaced in Ketton stone) is carved from a single block. The soffits and lowest cusps of canopies C1–5 match those of C6. However their upper parts consist of a separate block carved to a different design (Fig. 5b). There are several pieces of evidence that C1–5 and C10–22 were formerly of the same design as C6, and their upper blocks are later insertions:

(i)   When in 1983 modern cement was removed from the hoods of these canopies, it was clear that the upper blocks of C1–5 did not bond with the plain walling to each side of them, but instead were set only a few centimetres into the wall (Pl. XXIIH). The surrounding masonry had been crudely hacked to accommodate the new canopies, and the joint between the primary and secondary work packed with mortar and Beer stone chippings. Since the primary canopies were rather broader at the base than the later ones, the outlines of the primary design can still be seen in the adjacent walling.

(ii) The mouldings of the cusps of the primary work in canopies C1–5 do not correspond with those in the secondary stones above them (Fig. 5b).

(iii) The curvature of the soffits of canopies C1–5 does not correspond to that of the secondary canopy blocks. In several places the awkward join was masked by a liberal application of lime mortar. In the central foil of each canopy the core of the primary work was exposed. This portion was re-carved, and the cental lierne of the soffit bent upward onto the vertical surface (Pl. XXIIi. C12, although the outer blocks of the canopies of C11–22 are replacements by Rowe (see below), the soffits bear the same alterations as those of C1–5).

It is significant that the one remaining primary canopy is that sheltered by the projecting north buttress, and here the detail is much better preserved than elsewhere. The replaced portions are delicate and exposed to the weather. It seems likely that they were already showing signs of decay before the later medieval period. There is no specific dating evidence for these replacements; the details are simply Perpendicular. The most likely date is perhaps the early 16th century.

POST-MEDIEVAL REPAIRS

The earliest post-medieval activity distinguished during our survey was a programme of repainting of most, probably all, the image screen in a powdery dark red paint (see Sinclair below p. 118). Traces of this layer are most extensively preserved on the northern sector, where this paint could be seen on all three registers, both on the figures and on architectural surrounds.[62] The same layer may also be seen within the north and south porches.[63] No precise dating evidence for this repainting was found. It evidently followed a period of extensive weathering of all elements of the B- and C-registers (for example it covers surfaces weathered to a depth of 8 mm in niches C1–5) and must post-date the insertion of the secondary canopies C1–5, since this paint seals the joint between the internal face of the canopy and the soffit of the vaults of C3–4. On the other hand the paint is not traceable on any of the post-medieval sculptures and must therefore have been applied before 1794, the latest possible date of the earliest replacement (see below).[64] The paint layer also precedes the accumulation of much post-medieval grime.

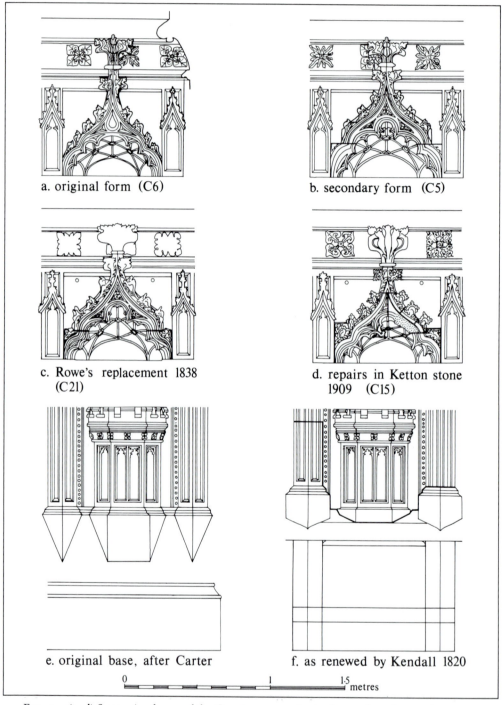

a. original form (C6)

b. secondary form (C5)

c. Rowe's replacement 1838 (C21)

d. repairs in Ketton stone 1909 (C15)

e. original base, after Carter

f. as renewed by Kendall 1820

0   1   1·5
                                                    metres

FIG. 5.   (a–d) Successive forms of the C-register canopies in the north and central sectors.
(e–f) Base of the image screen in its primary form (e) and as remodelled by Kendall (f)

No specific context can be suggested for this repainting. Two possibilities are the Laudian refurbishments of the 1630s and the years which followed the Civil War.

Repairs before c. 1800

That structural repairs were made to the cathedral before 1800 is shown by the evidence in 17th- and 18th-century fabric accounts,[65] but with the exception of the examples quoted below very little routine repair to the west front can be detected. One of the briefs of our survey was to search for repairs to the front preceding those of the 19th century known from documentary evidence. In fact we found very few candidates; a few blocks retain no trace of medieval paint and are not set in a distinctive mortar (e.g. the crude block patching the shoulder of B2, the shaft AO/1) but these could as well be early 19th century. One figure sculpture, the angel A32, was drawn by Carter in 1794[66] so must be earlier than that date. Its highly bizarre pose, and more particularly the curious curling feathers of the wings, differ from all Kendall's figures (see below). The replacement of this figure is not certainly documented.[67] Its pedestal was also replaced; the stub of the original can still be detected at the rear of the niche. It has been suggested that a second figure, that in the high gable, might also be an 18th-century replacement, since a slab resting on its head bore the inscription 'J.. RICE 1723', perhaps a record of its date and sculptor. However, in 1983–4, when scaffolding was erected around this figure, it was possible to see that the slab was merely a re-used gravestone. The very weathered and virtually featureless figure, whose body may have been medieval,[68] disintegrated completely upon removal.

Kendall

John Kendall, the Exeter stonemason, commenced restoration work at the cathedral c. 1803,[69] succeeding his father Edward Kendall who had been executing stonemasonry for the Dean and Chapter since the mid-1760s. Kendall's work is documented by a good, but far from unbroken, series of twice-yearly reports by the Cathedral Surveyor, Robert Cornish, and by a miscellaneous collection of vouchers, masons' worksheets, fabric orders and letters now preserved in the Cathedral Library.[70] After a number of minor repairs in 1803 and 1807 Kendall's first major project at the west front was the renewal of the two pinnacles set above the buttresses of the image screen. The northern pinnacle was renewed in 1809, together with a new figure of King Athelstan;[71] the southern pinnacle and the figure of Edward the Confessor followed in 1810.[72] In 1817 payments were made for three new heads to figures, identifiable as B8, B9 and B25[73] (shown without heads on Carter's drawings), and a new 'Gothic pedestal angel' with carved capital and repairs to the figure above.[74] The only angel on the front carved in Kendall's style is A34 (Pl. XIXc); the capital above this is indeed a replacement, and the figure B34 has a replacement head in the style of Kendall and a new block in its left arm (Pl. B). These appear to be the works described in the fabric bills. In December 1817 a payment was made for 'a statue of Richard the 2nd':[75] the figure in the northern of the two central niches of the upper register (C16), left vacant by the removal of the figure of the Virgin Mary. This group of new figures and repairs displays a distinctive collection of sculptural traits peculiar to the unknown 'carver', to whom payments are recorded in the fabric vouchers for 1817. The most prominent features are the arrangement of the hair in peaks of tightly curled locks, and almond-shaped eyes defined by two concentric incised lines (Pl. XIXc). The figures are carved in inept poses; the draperies are arranged in shallow folds, with no reference to the underlying anatomy. Several of the medieval figures at the south end of the image screen display characteristic features of this

H

style, especially the narrow 'almond' eyes; the carver evidently attempted to improve several figures where facial features were badly weathered. Eyes of this form occur on figures B33, B35 (Pl. XIXE) and C22, accompanied by unusually flat cheeks, a product of the necessary removal of the surface of the weathered stone. The angels A33 and A35 also received some attention from Kendall's 'carver': both bear the distinctive convex vanes of the wings seen on A34 (Pl. XIXC) and the front of the capital of A35 has been cut back and recarved (Pl. XIXD).

In 1820 these repairs to specfic areas and replacement of individual figures gave way to more thoroughgoing restoration of the screen: the Dean and Chapter resolved to replace the crenellated parapets above the north and south sectors of the screen (total estimated price £150 12s.)[76] followed by the 'Base and Lower Range of Pedestals' of the entire screen, up to an average height of four feet, for which the estimated cost was £114 10s. These works were certainly carried out.[77] Kendall's parapets were themselves removed in 1897–1910 (below) with the exception of some fragments of his angels incorporated on the north side[78] and are known largely from 19th-century photographs (Pl. XVIB) and engravings.

At the same time as these repairs were in progress Kendall was engaged on repairs to the masonry above the image screen, inserting a new section of cornice above the great west window and '63 ft of additional ashlar' to the staircase turret on the west front.[79] Also in 1820 the Chapter '. . . ordered the projection containing the pipes at the north-west corner of the church be removed in completion of the repairs and improvements now making in the west front'.[80] This was the crenellated wall forming an enclosure between the northern terminal of the image screen and St Edmund's chapel (Fig. 2, D).[81] Some work may already have been carried out in the area the previous year and the work was completed with payments for repairing a wall at the north corner of the west front[82] and work on 'the returning circular end' in November.[83] Other work on the west end of the church involved repointing.[84] The final touches were made in 1821 with the laying of granite paving and installation of railings.[85]

Kendall's new masonry in the image screen was all of Beer stone.[86] Despite his pleas for imitation 'paying the utmost attention to the peculiarities'[87] and the praise he received at the time for 'correctly imitating corresponding parts'[88] and for 'a scrupulous attention to the . . . style of the surrounding parts',[89] he was not averse to changing the design of the front. Comparison of the medieval plinth with those of Kendall will be seen in Fig. 5 (e–f). William Joy's delicate plinth mouldings and long, elegant socle and shaft bases were replaced by much cruder elements.

Rowe's work

Following Kendall's death masonry repairs were carried out by John Richards (1830–3). Little was done at the west front in these years. In 1833 the Dean and Chapter contracted with a new local mason, Simon Rowe, to carry on the programme of restoration.[90] Rowe's two principal contributions on the image screen were undertaken in 1838–9. First, following storm damage, he provided 26 feet of 'parapet, battlement and coping over the west entrance'.[91] This work can be identified with the remaining pierced crenellations of Bath stone and underlying string course of Portland stone in the central sector which correspond in length to the work described (Pl. B). Second, he provided twelve new canopies and eight 'patrasses', together with the small buttresses and pinnacles over them.[92]

Rowe's work continued in subsequent years with repairs to the masonry above the image screen. These used Bath and Portland stones to a much greater extent than previously (Pl. A). In 1841 the parapet and cornice of St Edmund's chapel were replaced and repairs made to the north turret (that to the north of the gable), and other areas of coping, string courses and ashlar.[93] Detailed accounts for the following years do not survive but the surviving areas of Bath and Portland stone repairs extend to the southern stair turret, the raking parapets above north and south aisles and other areas of coping and weathering (Pl. A).

E. B. Stephens

Following the collapse of the figure B10, the local sculptor Edward Bowring Stephens was commissioned in 1857 to carve new figures of William the Conqueror (B10) and St James the Less (C23).[94] Both figures are in Bath stone.

The programme of 1892–1928

Following the latest work of Rowe, more than forty years were to pass before further masonry repairs were made on any scale. No repairs to the west front were carried out during Scott's restoration of 1870–7. E. L. Luscombe, the surveyor until 1894, made increasingly pessimistic assessments of the state of the external fabric of the cathedral from 1884 onwards, and work seems to have commenced on the great east window in 1888 or 1889. Little was done to the west end of the church until 1892, although the north-western pinnacle of the west front may have been renewed in 1888.[95] The main programme of work began in 1892 and was to last, with interruptions, until 1928. The bulk of the work was guided by the surveyor E. H. Harbottle.[96] Until 1906 all new stonework was in Doulting stone (Pls A and B). The coping on the south side of the gable was renewed in 1892, followed in 1895/6 by the outer face of the high gable window, the arch and jambs of the great west window and the niche and pinnacles of the gable.[97] In the following year a portion of blind arcading and the pilaster buttress to the south of the west window, and repairs to the parapet of the west front (the central portion?) were carried out, followed in 1898 by repairs to the parapet over the west window.[98]

From 1900 to 1903 portions of the south-west return of the image screen were replaced, with three pilaster shafts and four canopies being renewed (Pl. B, B32/3–B34/5) and Kendall's parapet on the southern sector was replaced.[99] The years 1903–4 saw the replacement of the external half of the tracery and mullions of the great west window.[100] No work is recorded in 1905; it resumed in 1906 with the replacement of the six canopies above the kings of the south sector (B26–31), along with the adjacent shafts and cornice in Ketton stone which was used exclusively for repairs hereafter.

Disquiet at the replacement of such extensive areas of medieval fabric initiated a correspondence which was to continue for several months in the autumn of 1906 and bring harsh criticism on the Dean and Chapter.[101] In their defence the Dean and Chapter might have pointed out that much of the fabric being replaced — for example: parapets and finials on the front and the crenellations of the image screen — was not medieval but the work of Kendall and Rowe. They seem curiously uninformed about repairs less than a century old. Parts of the medieval canopies were in fact retained and accommodated within the hollow upper blocks of the Ketton stone canopies (Fig. 3b). The then surviving form of canopies B27–30 is clearly visible on a photograph of the south end of c. 1890 (Pl. XVIb).

Much more ancient work was to be replaced in subsequent years, but none provoked quite such an outcry. Repairs continued to various parts of the screen, including both buttresses and the cornice between them in 1908, repairs to canopies (Fig. 5d) and buttresses and the renewal of the two pinnacles above the buttresses in 1909, along with the north section of the parapet which had been taken down in 1907.[102] In the course of these two years most of the figures of the B and C registers were secured in place by copper bolts tying the block(s) of the figures to the masonry behind.[103] The documentation for the years 1910–14 is imprecise but, by a process of elimination, the work completed by the time that repairs were suspended on the outbreak of war in 1914 can be identified: most of the work of this period concerned repairs to shafts, bases and the plinth of the northern sector, but the jambs of the central and southern doorways were also probably completed by 1914.[104]

Thereafter no records exist until 1922 when a list of works required shows that attention had shifted to the west wall above the screen.[105] By this time repairs to the aisle windows, the remaining portion of the blind arcading on the south aisle wall and various areas of ashlar were under way. The replacement of the mouldings of the frame of the panel around the west window was contemplated at this time and may have been carried out.[106] This work was substantially complete by 1925.[107] Using stone which was foreign to the medieval building, with neat Portland cement joints, this work of 1892–1928 is still unmistakable to the modern observer.

By 1927, although many works were listed as necessary for the following five years[108] the programme of works was nearing an end. Some of the recommended works can be shown to have been done; mainly further repairs to the plinths, buttresses and canopies, but mercifully some items, such as the replacement of the eroded medieval Beer stone blind arcading above the north aisle, were abandoned.[109] This was Harbottle's last year as surveyor, and the final report in the series dealing with this long restoration programme (which extended to every part of the church) was by his son A. C. Harbottle, who took over the post in 1928. In this report he recommends that the cornice to the raking parapet on the north side and the battlement should be repaired, that six figures be stabilised once more, and concludes, 'Beyond the work I have mentioned . . . I do not recommend that any further restoration work should be done to the west front'.[110]

The years since 1928 have seen three programmes of cleaning the image screen: in 1937,[111] in 1954–8,[112] and in 1972. The last was accompanied by the insertion of some new stone to the parapet and turrets above the great west window (Pl. A).[113] All three of these cleaning operations included minor repairs to the figures and surrounds of the image screen, mainly in cement, but occasional blocks of stone were inserted.[114] Much applauded at the time, these exercises must certainly have unwittingly removed many areas of surviving paint.

ACKNOWLEDGEMENTS

We owe a particular debt to the Dean and Chapter of Exeter for making financial provision which allowed the archaeological programme to proceed, and for taking a lively interest in our work. We are grateful to Mr Peter Gundry, surveyor throughout the conservation programme, who kindly gave us access to the photogrammetric survey of the front and gave other practical help. We benefited greatly from the experience and knowledge of Peter Dare, chief mason of the cathedral during the programme. The recording of the image screen was completed with the aid of grants from Exeter City Council (our employers), Devon County Council's Amenities and Countryside Committee, the Devonshire Association and the Society of Antiquaries of London. The project also owed much to the Cathedrals Advisory Commission, whose staff argued the case for the provision of a full archaeological record. In particular Dr Richard Gem took a close interest in our work and provided us with valuable advice, discussion and encouragement. We also profited from discussions with many visitors and colleagues. Finally, Barbara Jupp produced the 1:20 base drawing of the image screen from our large-scale originals and undertook some of the site recording. Pam Wakeham typed the text and David Garner, Tony Ives and Gary Young processed the plates. All are (or were) members of the Exeter Museums Archaeological Field Unit.

REFERENCES

1. The programme was conducted under the surveyorship of Mr P. Gundry. For an account of this work see Erskine *et al.* (1988), 94–6.

2. A photogrammetric survey of the entire front at a scale of 1:20 was carried out at an early stage in the programme. After considerable amendment this provided adequate coverage of plain masonry and the simpler elements of the front but was quite inadequate as a record of the complex, worn detail of the image screen. See also note (note to Plate A) below.

3. These records are now housed in Exeter Museums, where they are available for examination. A duplicate set of the records is to be lodged in Exeter Cathedral Library.

4. BL Add MS 29931, ff. 45–6, 70–86; 29943, f. 82.

5. Carter (1794), 65, 69, 70.

6. Carter (1797b).

7. Ibid., Pl. VII, cf. BL Add. MS 29931, ff. 45–6 and 29943, f. 82.

8. Carter's drawings of the figures are mostly very carefully made; for example his drawing of the figure C10 (BL Add. MS 29931, f. 72), one of the two early figures in the register (below p. 102), shows details of remarkable clarity, including the hair of the beard which is very similar to that which survives on the second early figure, C28 (cf. Pl. XVIIIA, C). The figure C10 is now thoroughly weathered and none of this detail survives. In other cases Carter's drawing has enabled an identification to be made. The detail shown on the drawing of C33 for instance (BL Add. MS 29931, f. 76) shows an armoured figure with a shield, with a dragon beneath his feet (Pl. XVIIIE) and is thus probably St Michael (Henry 'Iconography' below p. 140). This figure, in the most exposed position on the screen, has now lost all surface detail and is very severely cracked (Pl. XVIIIF after stripping and before repairs in 1985). By contrast some of the architectural detail such as the canopies to the niches can be seen to have been sketched very lightly on site and worked up from a specimen sketch of a single canopy. Likewise Carter's depiction of only four small figures on the jambs of the central doorway (evidence that there were six still survives) can be attributed to hasty drawing.

9. Prideaux 1912a. The originals of the plates published in Miss Prideaux's paper survive in Exeter Cathedral Library (D&C MS Ph./Coll. 2). The published plates were much cropped, so the originals provide extra details.

10. Her letters A, B and C refer respectively to the lowest (angel), middle (king) and upper registers of figures. Her numbers 1–35 refer to each niche, starting with the most northerly.

11. A full list will be found in Somers Cocks (1977), 65–71. Some copy details shown by Carter long after they had been removed. For a commentary on the worth of those recorded by 1922 see H. Stone in Bishop and Prideaux (1922), 166–70.

12. Devon and Exeter Institution Library, no numbers. They probably date from *c.* 1855–75.

13. Lethaby (1903), 168; Bishop and Prideaux (1922), 66 and plan facing p. 24; Radford (1960), 28–36.

14. For further discussion see McAleer (1984), 76 who notes that the west wall ought to be later than the Norman nave walls, in which the mortar is brownish. White mortar of the kind visible in the west wall was, however, used on the south tower, at least on its upper half (i.e. *c.* 1160+).

15. The contemporary Purbeck marble half-piers do not course with any surrounding masonry, perhaps because they were dressed separately in William Canon's workshop.

16. At the time these were interpreted as late Romanesque work: Edmonds (1897), 16; Bishop and Prideaux (1922), 66.

17. Excepting the adjunct of St Edmund's chapel.

18. See, for example, Everett and Hope (1968), 180–5.

19. I.e. vesicular volcanic trap.

20. FR 1329–30; Erskine (1983), 232. For 'schywes' see Salzman (1952), 101, 104, 110. These were cut on an angle for use in gables.

21. FR 1331–2; Erskine (1983), 250–1.

22. This point was first observed by Richard Gem during the BAA Conference in 1985.

23. The relationship of this masonry with the great west window has largely been destroyed by the replacement of window mouldings in 1895–6. However, in several surviving instances, its courses correspond with the large blocks of the aisle windows, with which it appears contemporary (Pl. A).

24. This buttress seems to have formed one end of a wall enclosing the west side of the cloister. Three late 16th- and early 17th-century drawings: Hogenberg's view of Exeter, issued in 1587; Hooker's *plat* of the Close (Exeter Cathedral Library, D&C 3530, between ff. 59 and 60) and one anonymous early 17th-cenury map datable to *c.* 1621–6 (Devon Record Office, Letter book G, 618), record the former existence of a crenellated wall in this position. One 18th-century engraving (*A west view of the Cathedral Church of St Peter in Exeter*, drawn by W. Davey, engraved by F. Jukes, published 1791; see also Carter 1797b, Pl. III)

and one drawing show a portion of this surviving attached to the buttress. At the south-west corner of the cloister a further fragment, also displaying a sunken quatrefoil, survives.

25. FR 1279–87; Erskine (1981), 3.
26. FR 1329–30; Erskine (1983), 229.
27. FR 1341-2; Erskine (1983), 270.
28. It may be noted that the arches do not align precisely with the pilaster buttresses; the northern one is set some 50 mm further to the north and the southern one 40 mm to the south. The discrepancy of axis is continued with the buttresses to the west, the total difference between the axis of the pilaster and the pinnacle of the buttess on the north side being 130 mm; that on the south side 110 mm.
29. We were not present when these were found in 1979–80 and are grateful to Peter Dare for descriptions.
30. It was also suggested that the angels' faces may have been re-carved, since they have a somewhat neo-classical look. We were unable to detect any re-cutting.
31. That was the starting date suggested by Prior and Gardner (1912), 351; Bishop and Prideaux (1922), 66–73. Pevsner (1953), 30–2 dated the Christ in the vault of the Grandisson chapel *c.* 1330 and the kings of the image screen *c.* 1330–40. In B/E (1952), 138 he suggested 1330–50 and 1340–50 for the kings.
32. Stone (1955), 175 and Pl. 138.
33. Bishop and Prideaux (1922), 67–70.
34. Hope and Lloyd (1973), 20.
35. FR 1329–30; Erskine (1983), 229.
36. Its position is recorded on Hooker's *plat* (above, n. 24). Excavation outside the west front in 1976 confirmed that it was not there.
37. Erskine (1983), 274, xxi.
38. Ibid., 273–4.
39. Ibid., 275.
40. Ibid., 276.
41. We are grateful to Dr Harold Fox for advice on this point.
42. For discussions of the problem see Orme (1986), 113; Erskine (1983), xxxiv.
43. FR 1352–3; Erskine (1983), 270.
44. Stone (1955), 175 and Pl. 138.
45. First pointed out by Pevsner, B/E (1952), 138; (1953), 30–2.
46. Following Bishop and Prideaux (1922), 81.
47. Erskine (1983), xxxiii, xxxv.
48. Stone (1955), 175. It also seems to fit better the stylistic dating of the armour of figures B19 and 31. The cyclas worn by B19 (Pl. XXIA) is of a short-lived transitional type, short at the front and long at the back datable to *c.* 1325/45–45/50 (e.g. Prior and Gardner (1912), 352; Stone (1955), 175; Blair (1972), 47). See also note 55.
49. Harvey (1978), 92.
50. We are grateful to Dr R. K. Morris, who informs us that the mouldings of the two works match very closely. Walter Leedy (1980), 163–4 draws attention to a number of fine distinctions between the two works but they do not seem sufficiently substantial to undermine the case for Lesyngham's authorship.
51. FR 1375–6, D&C MS 2638; Bishop and Prideaux (1922), 90.
52. We are grateful to Mr J. Sampson for showing us similar resinous bonding agents in the sculptures of the west front of Wells. At Wells some adjacent stone surfaces showed signs of discoloration, believed to result from heating before application of the resin. No such discoloration was noted at Exeter.
53. The remains of the original canopies of B27–30 look particularly unstable in the photograph of *c.* 1890 (Pl. XVIB). The upper blocks of plain stone in the two central canopies of this series (B28, 29) were probably post-medieval insertions to support the C-register figures above. The blocks are preserved within the replaced canopies of Ketton stone of 1906.
54. *London Museum Medieval Catalogue* (1954), 162–74. Comparative details of other C-register purses are shewn in Pl. XXIE (C4) and XXIF (C20).
55. We are grateful to Miss June Swann, formerly Keeper of the Boot and Shoe Collection, Northampton Museums and Art Gallery, for the following comments on the date of shoes worn by both B- and C-register figures:

> Figure B12 wears high-cut shoes, with a rather short, pointed toe, which if you are offering 1330s–60s, should put them before the exaggeration of the toe starts in 1350. The shoe has cut-outs on the front, but I cannot see enough detail to work out the pattern; the top section may in fact be the 'bar', which fastens the shoe with toggle or buckle at the outside. Both cut-outs and bar would be acceptable for the second quarter of the 14th century.
>   The shoes of C2, C4 and C7 are acceptable for 15th century, C7 (Pl. XXIc) showing the typical V-dip at the sides, which lasts through to the 1480s. This type is usually laced centre front, possibly to be seen on

C7, but otherwise I can't be certain. The toe shape on C2 is quite a modest point, which was elongated in the 1460s, and may be depicted even on holy figures. I would therefore prefer to place these in the 1450s, rather than after the extravagant toes had passed *c.* 1480–5. They are unlikely to date from the 1460s, and probably not from the 1470s when the poulaine was modified into an uglier long point. C7 looks a particularly typical example of this period.

56. It was, we believe, William St John Hope who, during the meeting of the Royal Archaeological Institute at Exeter in 1913, first pointed out that the figures are of this date. See *Archaeological Journal* 70, 513.

57. Stone (1955), 223.

58. E.g. in gablet C8–9, but only used for very fine jointing of small blocks (piecing-in).

59. This was noted in the central joints of C15 (St Peter) and C11 (St Bartholomew).

60. The sloping joint running through the head of C25.

61. Perhaps like those recovered from excavations at Clarendon Palace, Wiltshire (Salisbury Museum, Accession No. 47/57) or Rest Park, Yorkshire (Le Patourel (1973), Fig. 35, nos 14–15).

62. It was, for example, noted on the rear walls of niches B1–3, in the vaults of canopies B1–2 and C3–4, on the underside of the crenellations of canopy B1 and on the shafts rising from angel to capital A1.

63. For example, it fills graffiti in the north wall of the north porch.

64. The layer is demonstrably earlier than Kendall's work: e.g. Kendall filled the panels on the north and south sides of pedestals A19–21 with mortar. Recent partial removal of this mortar has exposed powdery red paint which we take to be this layer.

65. Collation of information from the Chapter Act Books, the volumes of 'Fabric Solutions' (D&C/3776/1–12), and, for the period after 1800, various other sources, enables a provisional list of the holders of the post of Surveyor to the Dean and Chapter to be constructed. The earliest named individual in the post-medieval accounts is George White, paid as 'overseer of the worke' from 1685 to 1688. He was followed by Thomas Whitheare (1688–95), P. Passmore (1695–1707), and Robert Burrington (1707–30). John Weston (1730–42) is the first to be termed 'Surveyor of the works' (on Weston's career as a monumental mason see Gunnis (1968), 429–30; B/E *Devon* (1989) 88, and entries cited on p. 946). Arthur Bradley was 'Surveyor' 1742–59, being relieved of his office as a result of scandalous behaviour (Chapter Act Book, Dec. 1759: D&C/3569, pp. 400–1, 409), and was replaced by John Tothill (1759–99). It is noteworthy that from the first named holder to the death of Tothill in 1799 the office of Surveyor carried the same quarterly remuneration of £2 10s. On the succession of Robert Cornish sen. (1799–1838) the salary was increased to £31 10s. per year (Colvin (1978), 233–4). Robert Cornish jun. succeeded his father (1838–70) and was followed by Edwin L. Luscombe (1871–94). Thereafter another father-and-son team held the post: E. H. Harbottle (1894–1927) and A. C. Harbottle (1927–39).

A similar sequence, although shorter, can be formed for the stonemasons who carried out the work of restoration and maintenance. Edward Kendall (*c.* 1767–99); John Kendall (1799–1829); John Richards (1830–3); Simon Rowe (1833–57; although Rowe died in 1850, payments continued to his widow, Mary, until 1857); George Marley (1858–63); Luscombe & Son (1864–1916); and Stephens & Son (1917–35). From 1935 stonemasons and other craftsmen were employed as direct labour by the Dean and Chapter.

66. BL Add MS 29931, f. 83.

67. The style of the sculpture is clearly not medieval, *contra* Prior and Gardner (1912), 353 who dated it *c.* 1345. It might be the figure inserted in 1755 if the Chapter Act Book record of 1755 recording that 'a statue lately fallen down from the W end of the church' should be replaced was ever carried out. We owe this reference to Mrs Erskine.

68. Photographs taken at the time of the restoration of the high gable in 1894/6 show a figure with a modern head but very decayed body (e.g. D&C Ph. Coll./2 p. 39). Carter's drawing too, hints that the head was an addition: a faint line is drawn on the neck suggestive of a joint (BL Add. MS 29931, f. 70).

69. And probably a little earlier; 1803 is simply the date of the earliest surviving fabric voucher. John Kendall received occasional payments for work in his own right in the late 1790s whilst Edward was still alive. The surveyor's report of March 1812 (D&C/7003/1812) records repairs to the upper gable window of the west front 'about thirteen years since' but the name of the mason who carried out the work is not stated.

70. For Kendall see Colvin (1978) 488–9; Gunnis (1968), 225. For an ample account of his extensive work on the cathedral see Erskine *et al.* (1988) 77–80. In this section we are particularly indebted to Mrs Erskine, and have drawn on her 'Summary Extracts from the Records' (1979).

71. D&C/7001/1809. The pinnacle cost £45, the figure with the arms and pedestal below cost £11.

72. Ibid. (1810). The figure cost £10. Drawings of the medieval figures on the pinnacles were made by Carter, see Henry 'Iconography' below n. 57.

73. Ibid. (1817). Cost £3 3s. 0d.

74. Ibid. Total cost £12.

75. Ibid (1817). The figure cost £5 5s. 0d. Richard II was assumed to be the figure missing from the niche as a result of mis-reading the arms at the base of the niche (Pl. XIXA), see above p. 104 and below p. 141.

76. D&C Fabric Order Book 3776/C (1820). In fact the Surveyor had asked for approval for this work as early as 1814.

77. Payments of £114 and £125 12s. od. were made for 'repairing base' and battlements respectively in September 1820. The lower figure for the battlements was caused by the re-use of more medieval stone than had been anticipated, £25 being deducted 'for leaving the small figure in the centre of each Buttress', Chapter Act Book, 22 April 1820, D&C MS 3578.

78. Kendall's estimate, recorded in the order book quoted above, records that medieval sculptures were to be re-set but inspection of these fragments leaves no doubt that they are his. There is no surviving paint on any of them, and the sunken eye-sockets and sharp protruding noses (especially above C1/2 and C2), curling locks and protruding eyelids (especially above C2/3) match Kendall's work. If medieval figures were retained by Kendall they must have been removed in the second restoration of 1907–9.

79. D&C/7001/1820, 9 June 1820. The location of this work is not known; perhaps it was on the south side and subsequently replaced in Doulting and Ketton stone (Pl. A).

80. Chapter Act Book, 5 August 1820.

81. This crenellated wall running north from the north-west return of the image screen and turning to meet the north-west corner of St Edmund's chapel is shown on Hooker's *plat* of the Close (above n. 24) and in several late 18th- and early 19th-century views: Carter's plan (1797b, pl. II) and view of the west front (ibid., pl. III), Storer's engraving (Brewer (n.d.), pl. 4), but not by later engravers, e.g. Britton (1826), pl. 2.

82. D&C/7001/1820, 19 August, 11–23 September.

83. Ibid., 25 November.

84. Chapter Act Book, 29 April 1820 'the west front to be pointed with Roman cement by Mr Read according to his estimate of twenty Pounds'. Read was regularly employed as a mason (not stonemason) and bricklayer at this time.

85. Chapter Act Book, 16 March 1821. This seems to mark the completion of Kendall's work at the west end. Although work continued elsewhere in the cathedral, there is no further mention of the west front until after Kendall's death in 1829.

86. Although Kendall and Cornish recommended Bath and Portland stone and even granite for better durability, we have found no evidence that these stones were employed at the west end of the church until after Kendall's death. D&C/7003/1813; 7003/1825/1.

87. Kendall (1818), 32.

88. Brewer (c. 1820), 0 (pages lettered, not numbered).

89. *Gentleman's Magazine* (1817), part 2, 358.

90. For Simon Rowe see now B/E *Devon* (1989), 101 and works cited on p. 944.

91. D&C/7003/1838/1. The total cost was estimated at £44 10s. od.

92. D&C/7003/1838 headed 'Continuation of reinstating to the W Front', 15 September 1838. At the foot of this entry this note is added: 'Mr Rowe is very desirous of reinstating 2 Figures now wanting in this Front, the cost of which he would engage should not exceed Twelve Pounds'. These are the figures which were eventually replaced by Stephens in 1857 (numbers B10 and C23, see below). This entry provides a terminal date for the loss of the figure B10 (Pl. XVIIID) which is referred to by Prideaux (1912a, 13, note 2). We have been unable to trace any contemporary documentation of the loss of the figure.

    The evidence that the upper portions of the canopies C10–22 are the canopies in question is as follows:

    (i)   None of these retains any trace of paint, nor of the dark pink-red early post-medieval wash. By contrast, the repaired canopies of the same style in the northern sector retain extensive paint, particularly at the junction of the canopy soffit with the rear face of the cusps.

    (ii) The carving style of the leaves is noticeably coarser than in the northern sector.

    (iii) The mortar surrounding the upper canopy block is sometimes pink in colour (?Roman cement) and unlike any medieval mortar. Other joints contain powdery lime mortar without the fine stone inclusions usually seen in medieval mortar.

    (iv) The joint between the upper surface of the projecting canopy and the adjacent spandrels is commonly sealed with lead. This feature is not seen on any medieval work on the front.

    (v)   The medieval replacements of the canopy hoods of C1–5 had left an awkward junction between the two different series of mouldings. By contrast, Rowe's new canopies married together the discordant elements of the cusp mouldings (Fig. 5c).

93. D&C/7001/1841. A very detailed account: the areas in question were 'embrasures to W Front', 'repairing coping to W Front', '7' 10" run of new Portland stone coping to the west front': this is at the base of the blind arcades on the south aisle, and repairs to 'weatherings' and battlements of the 'west plot'.

94. D&C/3776/5 (Fabric Solutions 1822–61) 1857, 'New figures to West Front of Cathedral:

    E. B. Stephens for a statue of William the Conqueror and one of St James the Less £73. 10. 0.
    Railway company for carriage of same from London £2. 10. 5.

For Stephens' career see Gunnis (*c.* 1964), 371; Pycroft (1882), 306–9; neither source mentions his west front figures in lists of his work. It should be noted that the date of 1865 given for these figures by Prideaux (1912a), 13 and followed by all later writers is incorrect.

95. D&C/7003/1888. 'Take down and renew the pinnacle on the north-western turret of west end.' This pinnacle, in Doulting stone, receives no further mention in summaries of repair work and it is possible that it was erected in this year.

96. A list of work summarising the repairs to 1907 was given by Harbottle in D&C/7003/1907/6; however, the entries listed for the years before 1896 do not tally with evidence elsewhere in the accounts, and some fairly major works are omitted.

97. D&C/7003/1896/2.

98. Ibid., 1897/2, 1898.

99. Ibid., 1907/6. The list does not include the parapet but this must have been completed before 1906 when the change to Ketton stone took place.

100. Ibid.

101. Thackray Turner, the secretary of the SPAB, wrote (*The Times* of 16 October 1906): '... the iconoclasts were at work ... The shock of this work is almost more disturbing than any example of "restoration" I have ever seen ... the old images in such a setting are absurd ... it is quite certain that the medieval art treasures of England cannot be of modern carved stonework and it is time to ask whether a modern Cathedral or an ancient one is required.' Turner rounded it off by calling the work an 'evil deed'.

Dean Malborough in reply (*The Times*, 19 October 1906) commented on 'the questionable amusement of calling other people by offensive names and by bringing public accusations against them ...'. On the west window he wrote: 'The work was undertaken after grave deliberation and under the best advice and not one single inch of old work that was capable of preservation was not preserved .. Our duty is not to provide an interesting ruin for Mr Turner's society but so to arrest decay and to prevent ruin as to leave behind us a glorious building which shall be ... at once a faithful witness of the architecture of the past and the sanctuary ... fit for the service of Christian men.'

Further opinions were contributed as the controversy continued. W. R. Lethaby wrote: 'The whole front is well on the way to become as up to date as money, enthusiasm and good intentions can make it.' (Lethaby (1906), 859).

Harbottle was at pains to make clear that the work had been carried out competently and accurate replacements had been made; various of his writings in the succeeding year throw light on the restoration work of 1906. In his surveyor's report for 1907 Harbottle stated 'careful plaster casts, measured drawings or photographs have been made ... to produce a record of the ancient features' (D&C/7003/1907/3). Unfortunately, if these were ever made, they have not survived. Later in the year he listed the credentials of the carvers: 'The carving is done by experts who have been engaged at Lichfield Cathedral, Westminster Abbey, Canterbury, Bristol and Truro Cathedrals, Beverley Minster ... Westminster Roman Catholic Cathedral and other important buildings' (ibid., 1907/5).

102. D&C/7003/1909/1; 1909/8.

103. Ibid., 1908/2; 1909/1. The bolts remain in position (Fig. 1). Where the figure is of a single block one bolt was used; for two blocks of near-equal size a bolt apiece was inserted. The heads of the bolts were drilled back and masked by mortar in the conservation programme of 1981–5.

104. Ibid., 1910/3; 1911/10.

105. Ibid., 1922/1a.

106. Ibid., since there is no further reference to this section and it was replaced in Ketton stone (cf. Pl. A).

107. Ibid., 1925/2a.

108. Ibid., 1927/4.

109. Ibid., 1927/5, in a letter to the Chapter clerk Harbottle elected not to carry out many of the suggested replacements: 'So far as the structure of the fabric is concerned, I do not consider the fact of some of the moulding stones being in such a state of decay that portions falling will seriously affect the stability of the fabric.' He concluded: '... the coping and parapet of the NW turret, I think this should be done to preserve the main wall, but I recommend as little of the old work as possible be interfered with.'

110. Ibid., 1928/1a.

111. Ibid., 1937/3.

112. Drury (1957); Drury (1958).

113. Gundry (1972).

114. For example, repairs to the traceried panels and corner shafts of the buttresses were made in 1954–58.

* Note to Pl. A. The lowest 10.5 m of the elevation in Pl. A was measured by hand, as was most of the upper gable. The intervening masonry is based on the photogrammetric survey (see n. 2 above) which contained some errors and omissions, not all of which we were able to correct. The geological identifications of the inaccessible parts of the upper stages were made from the ground with the use of binoculars and may include some errors.

The West Front: II
The West Front Polychromy

By Eddie Sinclair

Exeter Cathedral's west front, like most medieval sculpture, has lost the colour which formed an integral part of the artist's work. No mere embellishment, it also protected the stone from the wet climate of the south-west of England, and its loss 'irreparably distorts our vision of mediaeval art'.[1] However, sufficient scraps, usually a few millimetres or less (though measuring some centimetres in protected corners of the south porch) still act as the fragile repository of much exciting information about the original appearance of the image screen.

Conservation work on the west front ran concurrently with that of the interior high vault; this writer had the unique opportunity of assisting with both. The bosses are only slightly earlier than the west front and their polychromy has the rare distinction of being well preserved and well documented in the cathedral's fabric rolls, in which entries for the west front are much scarcer. For the image screen, therefore, the evidence lies within the minute fragments of colour collected to form an archive, on which study began in 1985.[2]

The Vicissitudes of the West Front

Exeter's west front is low and has suffered from its accessibility. In spite of salt-laden south-west winds from the sea only twelve miles away, and intense heat from 5 November bonfires[3] which made the stone too hot to touch, not to mention generations of roosting, defecating pigeons, early photographs show that in the mid-19th century it was still reasonably clean and well-preserved. Although Exeter has no heavy industry, deterioration of the west front must have accelerated with the increased use of coal for domestic fires, for by the 1950s the stone was completely encrusted with hardened deposits of soot.[4] The image screen was hosed with powerful jets in 1935,[5] and water-washing, a particular enemy of paint, has been used in three other cleaning operations since then, together with a lime poultice in the most recent.[6]

Polychromy

The bare creamy white stone of the west front was, of course, never meant to be seen. The richly carved ornate exterior would have reflected the glorious colour of the interior, with its painted sculpture, glass and wall-paintings and its polished, dark grey Purbeck columns. The hills outlying the city of Exeter would have enabled the painted west front to be seen from great distances.

As Audrey Erskine has observed, the impetus of the Cathedral building work was slackening off, even before the Black Death[7] with income receipts greatly reduced. In addition, it is demonstrable that Bishop Stapledon was undoubtedly wealthier than Bishop Grandisson. A brief survey of the two polychromies on the nave bosses underlines the differences with, for example, Grandisson's greater use of red earth instead of red lead for backgrounds, the use in places of glazed silver leaf to imitate gold, and the restricted use of blue, the most costly colour.[8] Grandisson, in building his own chapel within the walls of the west front, obviously felt that the image screen was the crowning achievement of his episcopate and perhaps here he was able to lavish the same attention as Stapledon had been able to do elsewhere. The magnificent painted portal of Lausanne Cathedral[9] may well have been known to Grandisson as his family came from Switzerland, and similar sources from nearer home, such as the Wells west front, perhaps inspired him to create an image screen to rival in splendour Stapledon's magnificent altar screen.[10]

The colour can be found, as one would expect, in sheltered corners of the carving on both sculpture and architecture alike, mainly on the middle and top register. The south end of the screen (Pl. XVIB) which is the most exposed retains very little paint, whilst the most extensive traces are found at the north end (Pl. XVIA) which has been sheltered by the north-west buttress. The fragments of paint on the figures, surviving for the most part in the corners, provide information therefore for no more than the shadows in the deep recesses of the draperies. The only evidence of any colour elsewhere on the drapery folds are compacted areas of paint which are impossible to sample and which no longer appear to retain any interpretable information.

It was hoped that a detailed examination[11] of the paint would help to answer some of the questions arising out of the archaeological survey of the west front.[12] As the sculptures fall into definite stylistic groups, covering possibly as long a time span as 140 years, there was a possibility that analysis of the paint would provide further links. However a comparison of the polychromy of two groups of middle-register figures, that is B11–14, 19 and 20 and 27–32 (from the earliest building period of the image screen c. 1342–7) and B1–3, 6 and 7 (believed to be carved by John Pratt, 'imaginator', in 1375) with the paint from the later upper-register figures (1460–80) reveals no obvious links with one group or differences one from another. Other groups of figures which it may have been helpful to try and link through paint, such as B27, B32, C10 and C28 which belong with the earlier group are on the most exposed parts of the building and unfortunately retain no samples.

Most of the surviving paint comes from the upper register, added to the image screen between 1460 and 1480.[13] Although the earlier sculpture of the period 1342 to 1347[14] may well have been painted it is impossible now to identify previous colour.

Documentation

The fabric rolls, though helpful in building up a picture of the interior polychromy[15] are missing for the last decade of Grandisson's episcopate and entries relevant to the west front are almost non-existent.

Carter's drawings of the lower two registers of the west front sculpture[16] with their short written descriptions make no reference to colour but they are of great value, with some allowance for artistic licence, as details are there recorded which no longer exist.

The photographic archive compiled by Edith Prideaux in 1912,[17] includes each sculpture on the figure screen; it is also an invaluable source of reference. The numbering system devised by Prideaux has been retained for identification of the west front sculptures: the lower tier of demi-angels is 'A'; the middle tier of seated figures is 'B'; and the top tier of standing figures is 'C'; the numbering goes from north to south (see Fig. 1 in Allan & Blaylock).

When Prideaux wrote in 1912 that there were no traces of colour remaining on the west front it has to be remembered that the stone still bore the deposits of centuries of dirt. However, Lethaby writing in 1906[18] comments that 'Here and there a trace of colour can be seen', whilst in 1932 the trained eye of Professor Tristram noted that 'there is ample evidence to show that gold and colour was not confined to the interior. The west front was a blaze of colour ...'.[19]

The Survey

The conservation programme which took place in the summer months of 1979 to 1983 did not involve treatment of the polychromy. However surviving colour was documented by plotting the traces of paint onto photographs and archaeologists' drawings.[20] The combination of awkwardly-positioned scaffolding and obstructing poles, together with gale-force winds and occasionally the conservation programme itself (since there was never enough time to study a newly-scaffolded section before work began) has meant that the archive, though consisting of 560 samples, taken over five years, has gaps that can never now be filled. The decision to conserve the west front with a limewash shelter-coat,[21] and the fragile state of many of the paint fragments, made it imperative to create an archive of paint samples for study at a later date.

Samples were numbered as they were taken, with the earliest using a slightly different system whereby they were numbered according to the figure they had come from. For example, C22/1 was the first sample to be taken from figure C22 and this was mapped on the drawing. Later, when the scale of the work became apparent, samples were merely numbered from 1–560. These vary in size from minute specks of indigo to thick multi-layered specimens of 4.5 mm in length. The thicker samples tend to be those from the upper surface of the carving where the paint accumulates, for example the top ledges of the crockets.

ANALYSIS

The Layer Structure

The careful preparation of the stone with appropriate sealant, primer, and ground has contributed to the survival of the colour layers; most samples are well-bound but loss of medium and migrating salts cause some to delaminate. These damaged samples can still be studied by careful comparison with others. Once a 'marker' layer, common to all samples, has been identified (at Exeter the pink primer) it becomes possible to determine where elements are missing.

A typical sample from the west front has (on top of an invisible sealant) a red earth primer, followed by a pale pink primer, and a white lead undercoat carrying the colour layer, sometimes with a glaze. Where colours meet in a corner there may be an overlap of repeated layers. Repaintings, not always exhibiting multiple strata, can be hard to identify as parts of the earlier painting may already have been lost. In the niches a layer of limewash, or thin lime plaster, lies over the reddish primer. Figure 1 shows the range of cross-sections found in one area.

Much red primer, and also limewash, is found in weathered holes and scratches, indicating that the stone had received some wear before it was painted. A further thick, dark coat of iron-oxide red seems to have been applied to tidy up all three tiers of the image screen, sculpture and architecture alike, some time before the extensive restoration which commenced in 1794;[22] further post-medieval grime lies over it. We cannot determine how long the west front was covered in this deadening expanse of thick red limewash. Later there seems to have been some further redecoration with coloured limewashes (found in the south porch over the soot deposits). Some samples, on both drapery and architecture, have a resinous layer, probably an original varnish; sample 64 (Pl. F. b) has two such layers — the lower conceivably a sealant for a repainting and the upper a varnish for azurite, with red iron-oxide over it. Surviving paint that is not in protected corners, but exposed to the rain, seems to have absorbed calcium from the Beer stone and formed a compressed fresco-like polished surface no longer displaying a layer strucure.

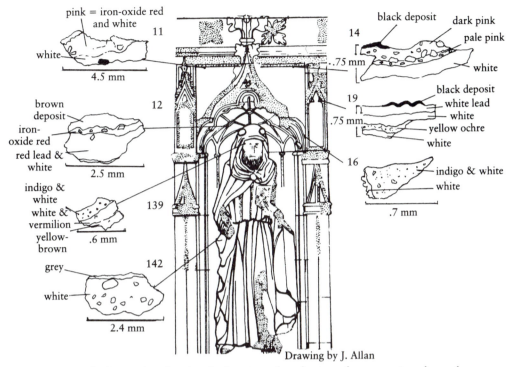

FIG. 1. Sculpture C1, showing the location of a selection of cross-sectioned samples

Surface Preparations

1. Sealant

As stone is such a porous carrier for paint, the surface needs to be sealed before priming and painting. There is very little information available as to the types of sealants used on stone in the past. Eraclius,[23] writing at an unknown date between the 10th and 12th cenuries, in *De Coloribus et Artibus Romanorum* talks about preparing stone with finely ground white lead and oil, whilst in 14th-century Italy, at around the time when the lower two tiers of the west front were being built, Cennino Cennini[24] describes only the use of animal glue prior to gilding stone. Nearer to home, in 1604 the front of Exeter Guildhall was, according to the Chamber Act Book,[25] to be 'white ledded and beautified'. Though this could refer to a new white undercoat, it may well relate to the method already described by Eraclius and found again in the *Livre des Metiers* of 1268,[26] where impregnation with some kind of linseed oil with a white lead undercoat is described. Analyses carried out at other European cathedrals[27] reveals in most cases a preparation of the stone with white lead, mixed largely with oil, but at Lausanne and Bourges with a protein (on all portals except the southern one). Small amounts of animal glue are mixed at times with the oil, in the south porch at Bourges, at Strasburg and in places at Ferrara. In the Exeter Cathedral fabric rolls purchases of large quantities of oil are recorded which were probably used as a sealant for the vault bosses.[28] Beer stone, out of which most of the west front is carved, is particularly porous and would absorb a lot of oil. Tests carried out on the effigies of William Fitzalan and Joan Nevill in the Fitzalan Chapel at Arundel[29] have identified a sealant of linseed oil with a little protein, probably egg. These figures are, of all the examples cited here, the most nearly contemporary with the later phase of the west front, dating probably from shortly after the death of Joan Nevill in 1462, which is approximately the time when the top tier of the west front was added.

An attempt was made to compensate for the lack of records relevant to the west front by using staining tests to identify a sealant, but these were inconclusive either because the binder had broken down or because it had been affected by further treatments to the stone. The results showed a predominantly oil based medium in the lowest layer of the majority of samples, though significant results for protein were also obtained, suggesting that, as on the many boss samples, an emulsion was used to seal the stone (Pl. F. c.). No paint has an obvious sealant layer, perhaps because the sealed surface seems to have peeled away where the stone is expoliating.

11. *Priming*

The grain of the sealed stone was filled with a primer to form a surface on which to paint. The smoothness of Exeter's dark brownish-red ground, doubtless made from the local red earth, recalls the polishing of the costlier white lead primer described by Eraclius.[30] The red primer that survives at Exeter on wide areas where the paint itself is lost now highlights toolmarks and delicate carved detail, such as angel feathers and links of mail (on figure B19) and the decorative clasps on the up-turned cuff of the early figure B11, and on the cloak of B30. This dark red ground exists all over the figure screen, surviving particularly extensively at the north end, on both architecture and sculpture. After its application it seems likely that the stone remained like this for some time, exposed out of doors whilst awaiting erection or placed *in situ* without further painting, as successive layers can be found in weathered holes. If this was the case perhaps it explains why the future polychromy adheres to the stone but does not bond as one unit with it. This dark red layer is almost never shown on the bottom of a paint section; it remains firmly attached to the stone whilst the layers above remain bound together. Perhaps this is because the subsequent layers were largely part of one scheme and each colour was laid down whilst the previous one was still relatively fresh.

The first layer to be seen in most cross-sections is a pale pink primer that is comprised of iron-oxide red, chalk and white and red lead, all in varying proportions. Traces of dirt on the bottom edge of this pink layer confirm that it was applied after the stone had been exposed for some time; the absence of dirt between the pale pink primer and the white lead undercoat that follows it suggests that they were presumably part of the same painting. The function of the white lead layer was both to improve the quality of the ground and to provide an opaque undercoat for the more expensive, sometimes translucent topcoat.

The treatment of the sculpture and the architecture would not necessarily be the same. The primer extends around the backs of the sculptures and must therefore have been applied in the workshop, as the protruding architectural features would not allow access here. An examination of the bosses in the cathedral vault shows that they were primed (and partially painted) in the workshop, as the red lead backgrounds continue inside the masonry joints.[31] It would be most practicable to prime the architectural elements *in situ*, after erection and prior to the insertion of the sculpture. There are plenty of traces of primer to be found covering the masonry joints, for example in the backs of the niches, to show that on the west front at Exeter this was the case. The backs of the niches, now bare of all but the later red iron oxide, may have been limewashed: one sample from behind figure C28 is unique in having no white lead in its ground (Pl. XVIIIc).

On the internal vault bosses, where there are three known phases of building work, the differences in primings are slight; variations in colour or texture are perhaps on the whole no more than the result of a dirty brush. One difference however, probably the result of economic necessity, between the primer of Stapledon era bosses and that of his successor Grandisson, is a greater proportion of the tougher lead (both white and red) pigments, with less chalk, providing a durable ground, resistant to moisture, on the earlier bosses. On the navé bosses (from which, unfortunately, not much sampling could be done), Bishop Grandisson's painter had to use greater proportions of iron-oxide red and chalk, though with some red and white lead, resulting in a more readily soluble primer. Whilst this should not cause too many problems in the relatively stable environment of the vault, the west front paint has had to withstand exposure to weather, movements of salts, and the effects of pollution and human intervention. Perhaps Grandisson was saving his best for the image screen, for given these factors if his materials had been so inferior no paint would survive at all today.

Pigments

A wide range of pigments has been found on the west front figure screen, both on the architecture and on the sculptures, indicating that the whole façade was one integral sculptural form. The pigments, all typical of the medieval palette,[32] are of mineral, vegetable and synthetic origins. Mineral colours include the exotic, imported (and therefore expensive) pigments such as azurite, vermilion and orpiment, as well as the more common earth colours, the iron-oxide reds and ochres. As well as occurring naturally, both vermilion and orpiment were also manufactured synthetically and it is most likely the synthetic form that is in use at this date. Synthetic colours also include the copper green, verdigris, and red and white lead. In the final category of vegetable dyes, is indigo or woad. The lake pigments, which are not easily identified, originate from either a vegetable or an insect. Of the pigments still surviving the extensive traces of exotic colours such as vermilion, azurite and orpiment suggest an expensive polychromy. Though often used in a pure form, the pigments frequently appear in complex mixtures within one layer. Theophilus in the early 12th century[33] actually gives these compound mixtures names, veneda for grey, exudra for brown, etc., so they were considered as much part of the palette as the individual elements.

Many of the pigments are very coarsely ground, which in some cases at least was a deliberate exploitation of the pigments' characteristics. For example azurite actually loses its brilliant reflective quality the finer it is ground, becoming increasingly paler. In contrast Cennini tells us that with vermilion 'if you were to grind it every day for twenty years, it would still be better and more perfect'.[34] However, whilst vermilion occurs finely ground in flesh tints, it appears on draperies very coarsely ground, particularly on the central figure, C17.

Whites

On the whole, the most common white to be found is white lead (basic lead carbonate), used as an undercoat, and in mixtures with most other colours, particularly frequently with vermilion for flesh tones and with iron-oxide red and a little red lead for the priming. Calcium carbonate white is also present in significant quantities in the form of chalk in the primers, and traces of a pure calcium carbonate white layer have been found in the niches.

Reds

Three different reds have been found extensively, iron-oxide red earth, vermilion (mercuric sulphide, occurring naturally as cinnabar, or made synthetically) and red lead (minium). The iron-oxide red ochre was used as a primer, as an additive to the primer-ground, giving it its pink colour, and later as a general weather-proofer. It is found in many different mixtures, possibly because a dirty brush was used. However, as the rich red Devon soil makes this pigment readily available in unlimited quantities, it seems likely that it was used wherever it would serve the purpose.

The costly vermilion is found both on the architecture and on the sculpture, particularly over the north and central porches. It is used, usually alone, on the garments of the figures, as well as on the parapets, occurring as a mixture of extremely coarse and finely ground particles (Pl. F.e). With an admixture of white lead it is used in its finely-ground form for the flesh colour. Whilst some samples display a surface darkening, on the whole the vermilion has remained remarkably bright despite its exposure to light.

Red lead occurs in small amounts in the pink priming. There are several places where red lead occurs in an almost pure form, with a dense, brittle feel, notably in weathered holes on the pilasters (Pl. F.c). A suggestion that this is possibly a putty or an undercoat is discussed under the heading 'Use of Colour' below.

Traces have also been found of a red lake pigment, largely on the architecture. In a sample from the canopy of B13 there are residual fragments of a crimson. These can no longer be put into the context of a layer as they appear to have leached into the body of the primer, and some repainting is also in evidence, but not easily deciphered here. Similar particles were found on samples from the draperies of B19 and C22 but in such small occurrences that they remain elusive. The sample taken from the pilaster of B3 comes from an area where a glaze is often used in medieval polychromy to provide a shadow for a moulding, such as can be seen on the stone screen of the chapel of St Gabriel inside the cathedral. However some samples from the bosses which were thought to be lakes proved instead to be a fine iron-oxide red, and some of these exterior samples where the red has lost its body and become a translucent non-particulate stain may turn out similarly. It is to be expected that if a lake was used it would fade in an external environment, in the words of Cennini, '. . . the air is its undoing'.[35] In samples from the painted portal at Lausanne Cathedral[36] particles of what could be a lake have been observed, occurring mainly in the complex bole layers for the gilding. On Wells west front[37] the only lake to have been tentatively identified is a possible yellow lake.

Greens

The next most common colour to be found on the west front is green, probably verdigris, a copper acetate, which has survived extensively in corners and crevices from ground level to parapet. It occurs mixed usually with white lead, often as a thick opaque layer with the character of an undercoat. Although this green varies greatly in tone and hue (sometimes closer to a blue than a green), all of it appears to be copper acetate. At times no distinct particles can be seen, and it has the appearance of a dye in a body of white lead, but no other pigment has been detected. Verdigris can be seen on all foliage, that is on the crockets, the capitals and the paterae, and on the 'hillocks' upon which the figures stand. This green is the thickest of all pigments on the west front; its use on some of the smaller carved details must have clogged the carving considerably, for example on the tiny crockets of the B-register canopy shafts.

Many fragments survive of a thin translucent green glaze which is made up of verdigris mixed with resin to form copper resinate, and applied over an opaque white layer.

Sometimes this glaze is found crushed and mixed with the verdigris and white and this occurs frequently on the architectural features (Pl. F.g). Copper resinate turns brown upon long exposure to light and in places it has done so at Exeter, but in some samples it remains a vivid, fresh green. It is found on the draperies of B- and C-register figures and on some of the architecture, and traces are found in the wings of angels in the spandrels of the central porch and supporting coat of arms.

The green has been re-applied at some stage and, for example on sample 459 (Pl. F.a) taken from the north spandrel of the central porch, it can be seen extending over a discoloured, cracked glaze.

Blues

Blues were among the most expensive ingredients of the medieval palette; there is very little blue either in Grandisson's part of the nave or on the west front. The most frequently encountered blue on the west front is the vegetable dye indigo, which was made either from imported indigo or from native woad.[38] Fragments can be seen at ground level in many corners of the sheltered south porch. Minute traces survive mixed with lead white on architectural elements such as the vaults of the canopies and on pilasters, but some has also been found on the head-dress lining of C1, the beard of B12[39] and on the wings of a small angel in the south porch. Indigo also is used as an undercoat for azurite on the coats of arms. Azurite, which is basic copper carbonate in mineral form, is the only other blue found on the figure screen. The two ways in which it appears to be used could date from different periods. Firstly, thickly applied and still brilliant in spite of its exposed location, it is found on the wings of supporter angels below the two central figures C16 and C17, and in weathered holes on shields (Pl. XIXA) where a blue field is to be expected. The blue stylised cloud upon which the shields rest is painted with a mixture of azurite and lead white. Secondly, at the north end of the screen two samples from the architecture represent a different technique. On both samples 55 and 64 (Pl. F.b for the latter), from architectural elements of the upper register, the azurite was mixed with white lead and a little yellow to make a blue-green colour. On sample 64 it overlays an earlier mix of indigo and white. Azurite has also been observed in a thin layer of red and white lead on the hair of C15, and this probably ties in with the similar use of indigo on the beard of B12 not far away.

Yellows

Three yellow pigments with very different qualities have been found on the screen, orpiment, lead-tin yellow and yellow ochre. Orpiment, trisulphide of arsenic, occurs both in mineral and artificial form. The costly orpiment[40] ('gold-pigment') was used because its mica-like sparkle made it resemble gold. It had good covering power but because by its nature it is highly poisonous and incompatible with so many other pigments, it was not often used. In fact cross-sections show that it was not applied on a lead white undercoat as other colours were, presumably because it was known that they were incompatible.[41] On the west front it is found on crowns and hats on the middle and top registers, mostly at the north end, though one sample was found on the crown of B14 in the central section. It is usually applied pure and thinly (Pl. F.f) but there is one example, sample 451, where it was applied more thickly with yellow ochre.

Minute traces of the lead-tin yellow (synthetic lead stannate), have been found, on the wing of a supporter angel for C17, and on a rosette on the armour of the knight B19, whilst the merest speck was also observed on a moulding on the north-west return of the screen. A

paler, more lemon yellow than orpiment, it frequently occurs on roodscreens. Yellow ochre, the easily obtainable iron-oxide earth, is found in deep recesses of hair and beards, with modelling in other contrasting colours. On drapery traces are found on the small kneeling figure below B4/1, and in a single problematic layer from C14. Yellow ochre being a hydrated iron oxide is very susceptible to salt damage and little survives on the architecture. An example is the trefoil of C7 and possibly the deep golden yellow on the parapet above C8.

Blacks and Related Colours

The chief use of black, invariably a carbon pigment, often used in mixtures, is on hair and beards. Particles of charcoal can be found in some primers. A very fine black pigment, probably made from soot, is found in locations all over the screen, on a white lead primer. Although samples have mostly survived on the heads of figures, some have been noted elsewhere, on drapery or shoes, and even on the architectural elements such as pilasters and on a little carved head on a B-register canopy. A coarser black, with angular particles, possibly bone or coal, is used in mixtures, with white and iron-oxide red to give a grey paint, and with finely ground vermilion and iron oxide to give a rich brown. Both mixes are found for the hair colour.

Several grey samples have been collected. Two layers of grey, a light coat applied over a dark coat with a white lead layer between them, were found on the drapes of the armour of the knight B19. The basic grey is made up of large lumps of white lead and a little red iron-oxide with a very pale grey-looking black that has no density; perhaps made from a material like slate. A similar grey was also observed on the neighbouring figure of B20. Here a very thin layer of a different pale grey, consisting of lead white with a scattering of fine black, was found in corners of the draperies. As it is more likely that the draperies were white than grey these fragments are presumably the remains of painted modelling emphasising the relief of the carving.

Metal Leaf

Whilst gold and silver are recorded in the fabric Accounts of 1341–2[42] as having been purchased for the painting of St Peter in the gable of the west front, no traces of metal leaf have been detected during this research. It may be that for economic reasons they were confined to the crowning figure at the apex of the west front. Where metal leaf survives in good condition, as on bosses and roodscreens, it seldom extends into crevices. Not only is it difficult to apply in the very places where paint survives on Exeter west front, but often no attempt was made to extend such expensive materials beyond the most prominent parts of the carving whence all traces of the original surface have long since disappeared at Exeter. In view of the discovery of orpiment, 'gold-pigment', on the image screen it seems that this was employed in the place of gold as it is found in all those places where gold would be expected.

Media

Paint consists of pigment and binder, along with various fillers and extenders, but the medium may leach out, especially when exposed to weathering, resulting in loss of adhesion and a powdery surface. Analyses at various European cathedrals[43] have revealed both oil and protein used as binding agents in the Middle Ages; at Exeter linseed oil and egg tempera were identified (Pls IIIc and Fc, d) either in separate layers or, as in the white lead undercoat and most colours except green glazes, usually forming an emulsion.[44] Tests showed that the pink primer was largely proteinaceous. The thickness of many colour layers at Exeter makes the use of egg alone unlikely, where egg tempera is known to have been used, as on Wells west front,[45] the layers were thin, with little body and a totally different character from these thick Exeter examples, which included azurite. This vibrant blue is spoiled when mixed with oil but retains its brilliance in glue size, found for example on 15th-century Utrecht sculptures[46] and, evidently damaged by the damp atmosphere, on countless Devon roodscreens.[47] If a water-soluble glue size were used on the west front, even if varnished (see 'Layer Structure' above) this would account for the scarcity of azurite.

Several interesting pigments, including azurite and orpiment, are represented in samples too small for successful medium analysis.[48]

Repainting

The very complex layer structure of some samples indicates at least one repainting. The eight layers of sample 459 (Pl. F.a), from the north spandrel of the central doorway, include red overlying green, which in turn lies on a green glaze already deteriorated when overpainted. Other repaintings may not be obvious, as the earlier surface they replaced may have altogether weathered away; azurite and other colours on the two coats of arms could be such a case.

Perhaps the whole central section was repainted, being the important focal point of the screen and the main entry into the cathedral. The evidence certainly suggests that this was the case. The upper tier of figures dating to c. 1460–80 was less than a century old at the time of the Reformation when such practices can be taken to have lapsed. However, as the west front iconography has frequently been misinterpreted as secular, depicting kings of England,[49] perhaps a retouching was permissible at a later date than would otherwise have been allowed. Certainly heraldry was regarded in a different light from figure sculpture and may have been repainted later than other elements. (The painting of heraldic roundels on the walls of the nave in the 1630s is proof of this).[50] Traces of brilliant, unmixed azurite are found only here, in weathered holes on the coats of arms (Pl. XIXA). Under the azurite on the blue stylised clouds beneath the shields are two layers of red earth priming, one of which could belong to an earlier painting.

The vaults of the canopies of the upper-register figures in this section retain the most extensive traces of colour to be found on the front. Interestingly all are green, both in their original painting and in their later repainting, with the colour extending over both webbing and ribs. On the north end of the image screen a single speck of green was found, together with traces of indigo, which in one case was overpainted with azurite (Pl. F.b), indicating that the soffits were painted and repainted blue. The latter pigment is rare on the west front but this sample corresponds exactly with azurite on the string course of the 15th-century north return of the screen. In some instances, such as the black found on the pilaster between C16 and C17, dirt traces separate the original from the new colour.

There is evidence that the carved detail of the hair became clogged with primer when repainted, but definition would have been restored with further colouring. Two different structures suggestive of retouching were found on the hair of C9. Various types of black on both hair and beards, although not on the same cross-section, could represent repaintings.

In the south porch is evidence of both repainting and various later coloured limewashes, but the powdery condition of the intervening layers of priming causes cross-sections to de-laminate. Some green repainting (over thick pink primer) resembles that on the canopies of the central section of the west front. There is also yellow-wash, which since it lies on top of soot deposits is probably later than the yellow-wash with which the interior was decorated in 1780.

Fourteenth-Century Workshop Practice at Exeter

An early quest in this research was the identification of an additional colour layer on the lower two registers, which would indicate that they could have been painted before the erection of the upper tier. Evidence of 15th-century repair to the weathered colour of 14th-century statues, carried out when the upper tier was added, may not show if it was only a retouching; the corners where paint now survives may never have received a complete fresh coat of paint. The techniques of polychromy are remarkably uniform on the sculptures of different periods; the greatest evidence of retouching is on the later top tier. Comparison with the evidence found at Bourges Cathedral in France[51] indicates the priority given to colouring even a temporary entrance. There, 12th-century carvings, unpainted until incorporated into the south portal in 1225, were then polychromed *in situ*, forming a temporary main entrance whilst other portals were under construction. The appearance of the lower two tiers at Exeter before the addition of the top one in the 15th century may well be illustrated by the illumination of *The Building of Solomon's Temple*, painted by Jean Fouquet in 1470, which shows the finished lower portion of the Temple's west front already gilded whilst the top newly-built portion is still unpainted.[52]

The single surviving fabric roll entry for the west front polychromy, namely the purchase at Christmas 1341[53] of 'gold, silver and various colours for painting the image of the blessed Peter', may profitably be compared to that of Midsummer 1302[54] in which the same fragile and expensive metal leafs are purchased for the presbytery bosses. We know that while colours such as the white lead ground and red lead background were applied to the bosses at floor level, the final touches were applied *in situ*.[55] Certainly one would pity any gilder given the task of applying expensive leaf high on the west front in the Christmastide winds, but the document for the actual painting of the bishop in the gable (*in pictura episcopi in gabl*) appears at Easter[56] when the weather was better. Perhaps, like the bosses, most of the painting was done at ground level and only the metal leaf applied after the statue had been hoisted to this, the most inaccessible, niche of the west front. In the days of wooden scaffolding the builders would have sought to avoid providing access to the gable for a second time.

Surviving colour is sparse on the middle register, and almost absent on the lowest. The evidence for various repaintings discovered around the central doorway may emphasise the importance of the ceremonial entrance as mentioned above. How far the procedure at Bourges,[57] where early sculptures were left unpainted for fifty years, was paralleled at Exeter we can only guess, but as Allan and Blaylock observe[58] some of the sculptures in the middle register belong to the later building phase. We can merely speculate how long the niches themselves remained primed and empty.

We have already seen that the architecture was primed, and thus also painted, *in situ*. The priming is found in weathered holes but such weathering need not have occured *in situ* since evidence from contemporary manuscript illustrations[59] shows that structural stones were stock-piled out of doors. How far the procedure for which we have good evidence in the bosses[60] was paralleled in the painting of carved details such as capitals on the west front we cannot now deduce. The angels of the lower register are cut, together with the back walls of their niches, from a single block of stone, awkward to paint in any situation, and the green on the backs of the capitals which they support could have been applied at any date. The tight fit of many of the sculptures at Wells Cathedral and the protruding nature of ornate architectural features provides some indication that they would have been painted in the workshop.[61]

Techniques

The fabric accounts are full of details which allow a glimpse of the painting process as it was carried out on the 14th-century bosses. As methods would be basically the same for the period when the west front was painted, it is interesting to try and build up a brief picture of the procedure. Purchases are made over the years of: candles for the painter,[62] a marble stone on which to grind colours,[63] an iron plate on which to mix them,[64] 12 dishes for storing them in[65] and an interesting purchase of linen cloth for purifying colours.[66] Barrels are made in which to store the oil[67] which is bought in large quantities for priming and painting.[68] Once the painting has started a grinder is employed full time to prepare the pigments for the painter; at times two grinders are necessary as painting is in full swing.[69]

Use of Colour

The red, green and white surviving on the image screen may owe their predominance to the good survival of vermilion, verdigris and lead white, while more fragile colours have perished. The polychromy of later Devon roodscreens, however, is also dominated by these colours. Locked in an oil medium they display little in the way of the problems sometimes attributed to them. The vermilion remains brilliant, the verdigris permanent and the lead white unblackened.[70]

The painters' bold use of vermilion and veridgris was complemented by the mica-like sparkle of orpiment (of which samples are widely distributed) providing a natural counterpoint to the vivid vermilion. Even the minute surviving traces of indigo demonstrate how it provided a rich dark background out of which the carved forms would emerge. Since we have seen that stone was sometimes painted when already weathered, we cannot interpret the presence of dirt at the bottom of the red lead sample B21/2 as certain evidence of repainting and such red lead, when found in weathered holes, could have been a putty[71] and therefore its startling vibrant surface may be an undercoat never intended to be seen. Sadly the survival of strong coloured grounds, where the subtle glazes of medieval polychromy have been lost, have frequently led to misinterpretation of that polychromy as a harsh non-tonal colouring: sample 449, from the north spandrel of the central doorway, has two further layers above this red lead, of lead white followed by a red lead and vermilion mix. Costly vermilion could be eked out in such a mix; where red lead (usually with a very smooth upper surface) is found, one must expect that there would have been a further final layer. The compound mixtures such as greys (already subtly developed by the time Theophilus wrote in 1122)[72] would have been juxtaposed with the vibrant vermilion, copper green, orpiment and indigo, themselves used in more subtle combinations.

Use of Decoration
1. Stencils

There are no traces of painted patterning on the west front, but comparison with surviving interior polychromy at Exeter (notably the cross-legged king on boss 195, dating from Grandisson's episcopate and echoing figure B12, whose crimson robe is sprinkled with fleur-de-lis) and elsewhere, enables us confidently to visualise Exeter's figure sculptures with stencilled or freehand designs upon their draperies and decorative borders along hems and cuffs.[73] On the north end of the screen, for example (Allan and Blaylock, Fig. 3, Pl. XXG, H, I), the exotic and richly coloured headgear of the prophets suggests that the robes which appear to have been white would have probably been embellished further.

Of greatest iconographical importance were the saints and apostles in the centre of the image screen, for the most part bare-headed, whose simple full garments contrast with the ornate B row kings (see below) at the south end. These central figures, devoid of all carved surface ornamentation, must once have been the painter's pride. Large expanses of sculpted cloth lend themselves to all manner of decorative effect, provided perhaps by the inspiration of the cathedral interior, with its fine polychromed effigies, such as that of Bishop Bronescombe. Cennini describes the means to achieve the effects of different cloths, such as velvet, wool, silk and brocade.[74] The Arundel effigies[75] already mentioned are a perfect example of the degree of sophistication possible with such effects, though such detail is not practical or even necessary wholesale on a sculpture the scale of the image screen.

II.   Carved Decoration

Similarly, the splendid carved detail such as the birds and flowers on B27 (Pl. XXC)[76] would have been picked out in colour, especially necessary since some fine cutting would inevitably have become clogged by the priming and ground layers. Elaborate hems, like that on the draperies of the Kings in the Adoration of the Magi in the south porch (Pl. XVII), are carved but must also have been embellished by the painter.

III.   The Images

The facial similarity of some of the figures is not original: they would each have acquired individual personality through naturalistic painting. The whole spectrum of hair colour is represented, from the grey of balding St Paul, C18, to the ginger beard of C3 (Pl. F.h) whose hat and cloak cover his hair. The mixture of red lead, red earth, black and white is identical to that identified on another redhead: a 15th-century head discovered at Winchester,[77] suggesting a common pool of knowledge or even a travelling painter.[78] On one figure alone different cross-sections reveal subtle changes, some shadows being deepened with indigo and azurite. On the hair of the beardless C19 (probably the youthful St John) samples of less than 1 mm reveal both yellow ochre with black and a brown made with vermilion and black. Unique use of vermilion must have given his colouring an appropriately youthful richness. This brown has a lead white undercoat but unfortunately the yellow ochre has become separated. The eyes of the 15th-century Winchester heads[79] match their hair colouring. On Exeter west front unfortunately only the merest speck of paint has been found in the location of the eyes, on the sheltered, hairless figure C6. Here a few crumbs of a rich dark mixture of black, vermilion and white can be seen, found in the outer corner of the lower eyelid, used apparently to outline the eyes. On the other eye a thin grey can be deciphered from the inner corner, suggesting the use of shading in this outline. A small polychromed angel's head (now housed in the Cathedral Library), believed to come from the original west front parapet, shows the sensitivity of touch that the painter applied, regardless of scale. The wings of the angels supporting shields below C16 and C17 (Pl. XIXA), provided samples of azurite, vermilion, copper resinate and lead-tin yellow, which may suggest an alternation of different coloured feathers as on the angels on boss 195 but far more vivid.

Lettering such as the lombardic script recently noted around the west front niches at Wells Cathedral[80] does not survive at Exeter but as in contemporary panel painting some figures would have been identified by texts. Jenkins[81] records the word *Noah* on the scroll of C7 as legible in the early 19th century but this is probably a misreading.[82]

IV. *Architectural Decoration*

The pilasters framing the niches appear to have been white with mouldings picked out in red, and black lines added perhaps to imitate mouldings not actually carved.[83] The polish of marble may have been suggested by an oil-rich medium. Surviving fragments of dark grey and black on the columns of the middle-register canopies (Pl. XXIIg), indicate that they were painted (like the pilasters of the minstrels' gallery), to imitate the polished dark grey Purbeck columns inside the cathedral. The only original section of parapet is on the north buttress, remarkably retaining extensive traces of red and green.

V. *Embellishments*

The spandrels on the fronts of the upper-register canopies are now devoid of all colour beyond a red stain left in the stone, presumably from its priming. A series of small holes still preserving wooden pegs can be seen in these spandrels,[84] containing traces of little pins that may have secured metal fixtures such as rosettes or stars, which may themselves have been painted, and such embellishments can be seen as a continuation of the painted decoration. Similar devices can be seen occasionally on screens in parish churches;[85] Cennini describes how to make such embellishments out of white or gold tin.[86] On the west front figure screen it is now just a question of conjecture as to the appearance of these embellishments. In the niche of C17 the remains of two iron bars projecting horizontally at the height of Christ's chest appear to be original, and were presumably supports for some decorative feature.[87] Devices such as raised putty decoration were also often used, examples of which can be found in the cathedral, though not on the west front. On the pulpitum screen little roundels at the bottom of the supporting pillars can be seen, mostly where the oily putty has peeled away leaving a stain in the stone. The effigy of Sir Henry de Ralegh (died 1303) retains fine putty decoration as mail on his armour, a feature that the two knights of the west front may once have borne. However B19 has such fine carved detail that it seems unlikely that putty would have been used here.

RECONSTRUCTION

Although so much of the evidence is lost, we can visualise, on acquaintance with the paint fragments, the appearance of the west front after completion in the 15th century (Pls D, E).[88] The vertical aspect of the image screen would probably have been picked out with bands of white, red and black, as the mouldings of the lower registers are echoed in the paintwork of the upper tier. The horizontal planes of the three tiers appear to be defined largely in green, which can be found in significant quantities on foliage capitals, crocketed canopies and plinths, thrown into bold relief by deep blue backgrounds and dark grey marbling. The main entry into the cathedral, with its spandrels of green-glazed angels and foliage was outlined in paterae, creating a chequered effect of contrasting red and green. Gilded ornaments like stars would have filled the spandrels on either side of the upper niches which, within a framework of green mouldings would probably have been darker than the figures, with perhaps a painted background pattern, while the soffits were picked out in blue or green. For the niches of the central figures, of greatest iconographical importance, there must have been further, more elaborate decoration, perhaps a diaper pattern, or the use of devices such as stencilled initials to fill the space. The figures within these niches would have drawn the eye with their richly coloured, decorated robes; even today the brilliance of the vermilion on the drapery of Christ, C17, is apparent. Further detail such as painted hems and cuffs would have made these figures yet more majestic and awe-inspiring.

Within the other niches, the lifesize naturalistic figures stood out proudly, some bearing scrolls with texts or carrying familiar attributes. Clad in garments decorated with all manner of devices, the sculptures would have reflected the glorious colour of the surround-ing architecture, as the whole screen was united in one magnificent illumination. The middle-register kings and knights, who have managed to retain their authority despite the erosion, would, with sparkling orpiment crowns and other regalia, have presented a formidable front. We need to remember that all three tiers would have been equally striking. The supporting angels of the lower register, now in places so deformed that they are unnoticed, would have also supported the kings above in appearance. Their beautifully carved wings must have been exquisitely painted, perhaps in contrast to plainer drapery, whilst the instruments they once played would have been depicted naturalistically. The parapet with which the screen is capped must have produced a bold silhouette with its powerful use of vermilion and green, above which the white Beer stone of the west wall of the cathedral would have provided a striking contrast. High above, with the light glinting off the west windows giving a suggestion of richness and promise within, the gilded St Peter must have shone like a beacon.

ACKNOWLEDGEMENTS

I would like to thank the Dean and Chapter for giving me the opportunity to develop this research over the years and for their patience and continued interest. I am especially grateful to Anna Hulbert for her tremendous support and help with all aspects of the work. The drawings used are those of John Allan and Stuart Blaylock. My thanks also go to the following for giving of their time and skill: Dr Avril Henry, Dr Roy and Dr White of the Scientific Department of the National Gallery, Ms J. Darrah of the Scientific Department of the Victoria and Albert Museum, Peter MacTaggart, and Professor J. Murray of Exeter University Geology Department and his entire technical staff. I also would like to thank my family, for whom it has not been easy.

With the financial support of:
The British Academy
Mr J. Michelmore
The Friends of Exeter Cathedral
The Radcliffe Trust
The Francis Coales Charitable Trust (colour plates)

The Ernest Cook Trust
The Pilgrim Trust
The St Andrew's Trust
St Luke's College Foundation
Miss B. Thorold

REFERENCES

1. Stone, (1972), 3.
2. The discoveries of the initial investigation were published in the Friends of Exeter Cathedral, *Annual Report* (1985), with a follow-up interim report in 1987.
3. Prideaux (1912a), 3–4. The 18th- and early 19th-century Exeter custom of having the annual bonfire in front of the image screen must have had a devastating effect on both stone and paint. 'Every morning after the bonfire a large quantity of debris, including particles of the stone of which the figures on the west front are composed, was swept up inside the rails.'
4. Drury (1957) 3–7. This paper reports on the condition of the west front, and describes the cleaning operation carried out. There are also photographs showing the central doorway and upper register figures after cleaning, whilst the surrounding stonework remains blackened.

5. A photograph in the *Western Morning News*, dated 17 September 1935, shows the workmen hosing the north end of the image screen.

6. Cleaning operations have taken place, commencing in 1935, 1956, 1972 and 1979. The latter was carried out largely as conservation, under the consultancy of Mr Robert Baker.

7. Erskine (1983), xxxiv.

8. In carrying out the conservation of the majority of the vault bosses, Anna Hulbert has observed these differences. Research is in progress.

9. Recent conservation work at Lausanne has revealed a remarkably complete polychromy, documented by Furlan and others (1982).

10. Morris (1943, 1944).

11. It is hoped that the technical aspects of this research will also be published shortly.

12. Carried out by the Exeter Museums Archaeological Field Unit. See Allan and Blaylock above.

13. See Allan and Blaylock above.

14. Ibid.

15. See Erskine, above.

16. Carter (1794 and 1797).

17. Published in Prideaux (1912a).

18. Lethaby (1906).

19. Friends of Exeter Cathedral, *Annual Report* (1932). Also the 1935 cleaning of the west front drew attention to colour around the central doorway. *Annual Report* (1935) 35–6.

20. The drawings were produced by the Archaeological Field Unit. See Allan and Blaylock above.

21. The final process in the 1979–84 conservation of the west front involved the application of a lime shelter-coat. This was designed to act as a sacrificial coat, as the paint layer had once done, to be renewed as it started to weather.

22. See Allan and Blaylock above, p. 17.

23. Eraclius, see especially 'How a column is prepared for painting', p. 203.

24. Cennini, 118, 'sweep and clean your figure up nicely; then take some of the usual size, that is, of the strength with which you gesso anconas; and get it boiling hot. And when it is boiling so, put a coat or two of it over this figure, and let it dry out well'.

25. Chamber Act Book 6, 21 January 1604. The paint from the façade of the Guildhall has recently been documented and analysed by the writer, in a private report to Exeter City Council. See also report of S. R. Blaylock and K. A. Westcott, 'Exeter Guildhall: A Survey of the Front Block' (Exeter Museums Archaeological Field Unit, 1986), p. 9.

26. The *Livres des Métiers* written by Etienne Boileau, the Dean of Paris, in 1268 is quoted in Gaborit and referred to again in Aubert (1964) 59 and 62, 'que nulle sculpture de pierre séant à l'église ou ailleurs ne soit faite qu'elle ne soit imprimée'.

27. In recent years analyses carried out during conservation work on several European cathedrals has revealed evidence of materials and techniques hitherto inaccessible. Rossi-Manaresi (1987) brings together all discoveries to date.

28. The fabric roll for Michaelmas 1320 records the purchase of 16 gallons of oil for painting, at a cost of 21s. 6d. Masons at Exeter have continued to use linseed oil. The late Harold Downes of the Cathedral Works staff described to Anna Hulbert how he was taught to seal stone with lots of linseed oil.

29. See Brodrick and Darrah (1986), 65–94. These sculptures are carved out of Caen stone, which has similar properties to Beer stone. It is interesting therefore that whilst a distinct sealant layer was visible on the Caen effigies, none was apparent on the Beer stone. Obviously the history differs in each case and most importantly the Arundel effigies have had a sheltered indoor life.

30. Eraclius, see n. 23.

31. See Anna Hulbert's paper in this volume.

32. For a full description see Thompson (1956).

33. Theophilus (1979). The precise date, which is the subject of debate, is accepted to be somewhere in the early 12th century.

34. Cennini (1933), XL.

35. Cennini (1933), XLIIII.

36. See n. 9 above.

37. Dr Roy of the National Gallery has analysed the Wells paint and found what is possibly yellow lake in the niche of *The Coronation of the Virgin*.

38. Although the fabric accounts of Christmas 1320 actually mention the purchase of indigo of Bagdad, 'inde baudas' for the bosses, both the native form of woad and the more expensive imported indigo were known by this name. This reference of 1320 to indigo is its first appearance in the fabric accounts where it is priced as 18d. per lb at a time when 1 lb of vermilion cost 8d. At this date perhaps such a high cost suggests that it was

the imported indigo that was in use, whilst in 1321–2 indigo is listed as 8*d*. per lb which, even given normal fluctuations in price, suggests a cheaper source, perhaps in the native woad.

39. *The Strasburg Manuscript*, 59, gives detailed directions in the use of indigo for colouring hair, as well as its usefulness in painting shadows.

40. See Erskine (1981), 146 for Michaelmas 1323: reference to 1 ½ lb of *arnamentum* at a cost of 7*s*. 4*d*. Erskine [(1981) 154 n. 3] tentatively translates this as 'black colouring', as an alternative form of *atramentum*, black ink. A. C. Hulbert, who has drawn this to my attention, has pointed out that this item is more expensive than vermilion, whilst black colouring materials, usually of a carbon derivative, are cheap. Although no orpiment has been found to date on the interior of the cathedral it is quite likely that the scribe of the accounts has muddled the more costly *auripigmentum* (orpiment), with *arnamentum*. An example of such confusion can be seen in the Jehan Le Begue manuscript of 1431 as transcribed in Merrifield (1967), I, 298; section 313 begins, 'Orpiment (*atramentum*) is thus made — '. The recipe that follows is for making ink. the medieval author states that he was unaccustomed to such writing, and as Merrifield points out 'the numerous mistakes throughout the manuscript prove that he told the truth'. A glance at the table of synonyms at the front of the manuscript illustrates how easy it would be to get confused, with references to *aurum, auripentum, auripigment, attramentum,* etc. Le Begue considers *arzicon* and *arzica* as synonymous but Merrifield's note explains that according to Eraclius *arzicon* is orpiment. *Arzica*, on the other hand, is weld. *Arzicon* appears as a corruption of *arsenicon*, which Vitruvius says was Greek for *auripigmentum*. Whilst Eastlake translates *arnament* as ink he also points out that Smith, in *Antiquities of Westminster*, explains *arnament* incorrectly as *orpiment*.

41. There is an interesting observation in Plahter *et al.* (1974), that, 'all areas painted with orpiment have suffered severely from losses of pigment . . .'. Used widely in Norway, 'it seems to be a general phenomenon that areas painted with orpiment are all in a poor state of conservation'. This could be because the pigment has a corrosive effect on the binding media (see Thompson (1956) 178 n. 30.)

42. Erskine, 269.

43. See Rossi-Manaresi, (1987).

44. Samples from the bosses, when subjected to stains for purposes of comparison, revealed largely the use of oil, except for the lowest sealant layer which in many cases also contained traces of protein. The cathedral fabric accounts record many purchases of oil for the interior polychromy, both for priming and painting, for example Michaelmas 1320. '16 gallons of oil for priming and painting'. No mention is made of any proteinaceous material in the accounts, but it may not have been recorded as a purchase because it was not of a significant quantity, or the odd egg could be easily acquired as needed with cash. Were the egg content of sufficient significance it would presumably have warranted an entry, as is shown in Bomford and others (1990) Appendix IV, where eggs purchased in 1347 are listed though details such as quantity are left unspecified.

45. Media analysis for Wells Cathedral carried out by Dr White at the National Gallery.

46. Groen (1978).

47. Hulbert (1987).

48. Plahter *et al.* (1974), 95. The main constituent of the binding media is oil, except for areas of blue and orpiment. 'The comparatively minor areas of azurite . . . as well as the orpiment areas, seem to have a medium on the base of egg tempera, containing some oil.'

49. For an updated study of the iconography of the west front, see Dr Henry in this volume.

50. Bishop and Prideaux (1922).

51. Rossi-Manaresi and Tucci (1984).

52. Miniature of *c.* 1470 by Jean Fouquet from *Antiquités Judaïques*, 'The Building of the Temple' in Paris, BN, MS fr. 247, f. 163ʳ. Illustrated in *The Flowering of the Middle Ages* (Thames and Hudson, 1966).

53. Erskine (1953), 269.

54. Erskine (1987), 24.

55. See Anna Hulbert's paper in these Transactions.

56. Erskine (1983), 270

57. See n. 51.

58. Allan and Blaylock's paper in this volume.

59. For example, in *The Duke of Bedford's Book of Hours* (*c.* 1430), there is a representation of the mason's lodge at work in the building of the Tower of Babel, shown in Svanberg, (1983) where cut stone can be seen lying on the ground, awaiting erection.

60. See Anna Hulbert's paper in this volume.

61. I am grateful to Jerry Sampson for discussing this point with me.

62. Erskine (1981), 147.

63. Ibid., 145.

64. Ibid., 104.

65. Ibid., 144.
66. Ibid., 135.
67. Ibid., 78.
68. Ibid., for example, 126.
69. Ibid., 135.
70. Cennini (1933) instructs, LVI, that the verdigris does not last and that it should not be used with white lead 'for they are mortal enemies in every respect'; both instructions are disproven on the west front. For the blackening of white lead see LIX. Similarly with vermilion, XL, he talks of its impermanence when exposed to air.
71. Anna Hulbert has found red lead putty used to fill holes under the Entombment wallpainting of 1508 in the Sylke Chantry in Exeter Cathedral.
72. See n. 33.
73. Tracings by Anna Hulbert of some of the stencil patterns in the cathedral are illustrated in the Friends of Exeter Cathedral *Report* of 1987.
74. Cennini, CXLI–CLIV.
75. See n. 29.
76. Carter (1974) describes the vest worn by B27.
77. Jo Darrah of the Scientific Department at the Victoria and Albert Museum has studied the paint on the Winchester heads and pointed out to me their similarity.
78. We know from the fabric accounts (Erskine (1987), 131) that earlier in the 14th century there were links with Winchester, as in Midsummer 1320 pigments are purchased and transported from there.
79. See n. 77.
80. I am grateful to Jerry Sampson for discussing this feature with me.
81. Jenkins (1806), 34.
82. Dr Henry discusses this point in detail in her paper in these *Transactions*. Carter gives no indication of any lettering in his drawings, and an examination of the scrolls by Anna Hulbert with an ultraviolet lamp failed to reveal any evidence.
83. Red lead, used in its pure form, is found in several places, such as in sample B21/2 from pilaster B21, and sample 416 from pilaster C12/13 has a vermilion layer above the white. One large sample, 413, which was found in a weathered hole from pilaster C16/17, has a continuous black layer with later additions above.
84. For a more detailed archaeological description of this feature see Allan and Blaylock's paper preceding this one.
85. A. Hulbert (1987), for example at Mattishall, Norfolk where the stars were gilded and set on an azurite background, or at Bramfield, Suffolk where vaulting and tracery are strewn with stars and flowers.
86. Cennini (1933) LXXXXV–CI.
87. Conservation work at Wickhamford, Worcs. revealed holes, probably for candle brackets, on either side of the Virgin and Child wallpainting, and also at Great Ellingham, Norfolk and Ampthill, Beds.
88. Plate F has appeared in Swanton (1991), 96 (without analytical discussion). For another such reconstruction, this time of the Wells Cathedral West Front polychromy, see *Country Life*, 6 December 1990, 152–4 ('Gloria in Excelsis', by U. Hall).

The West Front: III

The Iconography of the West Front

By Avril Henry

THE PROBLEM

Iconographical interpretation of the figure screen (Allan and Blaylock Fig. 1) must take account of the fact that the apparent orderliness of the present structure disguises an accretion of figures over centuries. The common assumption that the three registers (A, B and C) form a considered unit ignores the archaeological evidence, and frequently falsifies the witness of the iconography.

Even when post 15th-century figures (A31, parts of A32, A34, B10,[1] C16, C23) are discounted, there is still the risk of misreading the B-register by interpreting it in the light of the C-register which formed no part of the primary, 14th-century scheme.[2] Any hypothesis concerning the meaning of the latter must discount not only the C-register but also figures in niches still empty in the 15th century (B8, B9, B24, B25 on the buttresses, and B23, B33, B35) — all standing figures and unlike those in the rest of the register. The facts are best revealed by concentrating first on the B- and then on the C-register. It must be stated at the outset that no certain form, let alone meaning, of the whole primary scheme is recoverable. Some old conjectures will be rehearsed, and some new ones made.

CONFLICTING AND UNSUPPORTED EARLIER INTERPRETATIONS

Earlier conjectures fall into two main groups: those regarding the seated B-register figures as Saxon and Roman kings,[3] or kings and saints of England (in the tradition of the Wells west front)[4] and those regarding them as kings of Judah.[5] These diverse interpretations show the figures' ambiguity. B2, for example, has been described as Edgar,[6] Alfred,[7] Athelstan,[8] and David;[9] B9 has been described as a bishop,[10] St Gregory,[11] and St Ambrose.[12] Although it is generally agreed that the C-register's northern and southern sections carry prophets, C6, for example, has been called Deborah,[13] Joel,[14] and Daniel.[15] There is no written medieval identification of these figures. Such evidence as we have is in their attributes, primarily as they survive, partly as recorded in early drawings. This evidence must be read in the light of the phasing of the architecture.

THE B-REGISTER

Excluding the later standing figures, the B-register bears seated male figures of high rank. All these are crowned, with the exception of B19 and B31 who are in armour. The majority show the active posture, angular movement and lively carving of the period (c. 1342–7).[16] One king (B13) and one armed figure (B19) once held something, while B31 (an armed figure) still holds the remnants of a long dagger pointing towards his left armpit. The hands of several other kings are well enough preserved to show that either they never grasped anything or they held rods of some kind.[17] The armed figure B19 has a dog between his feet, and the king at B30 has on his gauntleted wrist the remnants of a hawk's tail.[18] At Wells, names may occasionally be found on figures' plinths, but Exeter offers no room for this.

None of the seated figures has any identifying attribute. It is hard to believe that they were ever distinguishable as individuals.[19]

A JESSE TREE?

Basing her view on precedents set by west fronts at Paris, Chartres, Amiens and Reims, Prideaux interprets the crowned figures as kings of England or of Judah, or as the specific kings in the first chapter of Matthew, as in a Jesse Tree.[20] Incorporated in this concept is the belief that B2 is King David,[21] an essential Jesse Tree component. One would expect David to be near the root of the tree, and if one assumed B1 to be Jesse, followed at once by David, the tree might reach a kind of fruition in the *Annunciation* (Pl. XVIIA) and combined *Nativity/Magi* (Pl. XVIIB) within the south porch.[22] Indeed, the great reredos at Christchurch, Hampshire, from the same school as the Exeter kings and south porch sculptures, shows a Jesse Tree culminating in a similar *Nativity/Magi*.[23]

Unfortunately, the supposed outline of the identifying harp which appears in Lethaby's conjectural drawing of B2 was no more than the curve of drapery round a bent arm.[24] Carter shows no harp.[25] Even if a harp were once present, it would not necessarily identify David. In addition, the Jesse Tree's stem framework would have to be visible: without it, a series of high ranking, largely crowned, men is highly ambiguous, as we shall see. One might regard the Tree as implied by the elaborate foliage capitals below the figures, but this is very unlikely: the designer could have indicated a twining stem, as on the Christchurch reredos, and did not. It is also unfortunate for the Jesse Tree theory that the two armed figures are not certainly royal. There is no sign of their bascinets having borne carved coronets such as that on the Black Prince's tomb effigy,[26] and if they ever carried metal coronets, the fixtures left no scars. Most importantly, the primary scheme held no prophets, an integral part of a developed Jesse Tree.[27]

A COURT OF HEAVEN?

Prideaux interprets the Exeter screen as the Heavenly Jerusalem incorporating a Jesse Tree.[28] However, the presence of a Jesse Tree is not really compatible with the hypothesis that in the 14th century we had (and possibly have, if that is what the C-register is intended to complete) a Celestial City or Court of Heaven. The Court of Heaven usually includes not the kings of Judah, but the 24 crowned elders around the throne of God:[29]

and behold, a door was opened in heaven ... And, behold, there was a throne set in heaven, and upon the throne one sitting./And he that sat was to the sight like the jasper and the sardine-stone. And there was a rainbow round about the throne, in sight like unto an emerald./And round about the throne were four and twenty seats; and upon the seats, four and twenty ancients sitting, clothed in white garments, and on their heads were crowns of gold.[30]

In 13th- and 14th-century illustrated Apocalypses,[31] some or all of these 24 crowned figures bear musical instruments, especially harps. There are 27 figure niches on the B-register of the screen, counting those of the demi-figures over the south door, and excluding the two window-niches of the Grandisson chapel, which can hardly have been intended to bear figures. (The four niches on the west faces of the buttresses which now contain the later figures probably representing the Doctors of the Church are likely to have been originally intended for crowned figures.) However, if one excludes the south return — which has no equivalent on the north, and has no 14th-century figures — there are 24 figure niches. Just conceivably the figure-screen's main façade was designed as a unit distinct from the south return, to bear 24 royal figures.

In the traditional image relating to the passage above, we have the Court of Heaven with Christ in Majesty. Enthroned in front of a rainbow and seven lamps, with the four living creatures and the crowned elders round him, he holds an unopened book.[32] The scene appears in the early 14th-century continental Cloisters Apocalypse, based on English models, and known to have belonged to the Grandisson family,[33] though one must not overestimate the significance of this fact, as such books were not uncommon.

It must be said that even if some mark of their royalty has been lost, it is difficult to fit the two armed figures of the screen into any scheme depicting elders: the armed figures' animals are quite out of place in heaven.[34] Could our two figures represent an allegorical aspect of the elders? The elders' crowns have been interpreted as indicating the spiritual victory described by St Paul.[35] Another explanation of the armed figures might just be offered by the later scene in the Apocalypse where Christ is enthroned with the wounded Lamb, surrounded by angels and those protected by the seal — the elders and the blessed, the latter containing representatives of various walks of life.[36] Such modifications of the usual sequence of 24 figures would be very unusual.

What is more certain is that if the B-register bore elders, they probably carried some connotations acquired from scriptural exegesis. They were interpreted as the 12 thrones of the New Testament plus the 12 tribes of the Old Testament; the six-fold perfection of the Church multiplied by the four gospels;[37] the 12 prophets and 12 apostles;[38] the 12 judges of Israel and the 12 apostles who are to judge the 12 tribes;[39] and the 24 doctors in both Testaments.[40] These interpretations might indicate that the C-register later made explicit, in its prophets and apostles, what was implicit in the B-register.

If the primary scheme was a Court of Heaven, perhaps it used a version of yet another scene showing elders. The B-register does not survive to its full height above the central doorway, and an element such as a central gable may once have existed.[41] A group over the central porch might have shown God enthroned, holding the 'book, written within and without, sealed with seven seals' and 'a Lamb standing, as it were slain, having seven horns and seven eyes'.[42]

Two pieces of evidence suggest that the original scheme might have illustrated this passage. Two standing figures, C10 and C28, are not in their original position, and both show the delicately carved drapery of the B-register's earlier phase.[43] The outstretched right hand of C28 shows a draped object suggestive of a covered goblet, or of a hand ceremonially covered to hold such a goblet (Pl. XVIIIc). The left hand holds what could be a squarish divided loaf, or loaves. The venerable features of C28, its posture, gesture and attributes, suggest that this may be Melchisedech offering to Abraham the bread and wine which made him a type of Christ,[44] who was 'a priest after the order of Melchisedech'.[45] C10 has been interpreted as representing Philip holding loaves (Pl. XVIIIA, B):[46] Carter's drawing shows the figure holding roundish objects in a container.[47] It can hardly have been designed as Philip in the 14th century, for the B-register holds no other apostles — but Abraham may hold loaves to represent the battle spoils he tithed to Melchisedech.[48]

If C10 and C28 are from the primary scheme, the absence of other reused figures in the C-register suggests a very limited primary upper register or gable. It is tempting to speculate that C10 and C28 were once part of a scheme in which the B-register was crowned by a central figure or group (an apocalyptic *Lamb*, a *Christ in Majesty*, a *Throne of Grace* or a *Crucifixion*) flanked by the offering of Melchisedech and Abraham to each other: a popular prefiguration of the Eucharist.[49] The primary scheme image would then signify our redemption by Christ's blood, referred to in the Apocalypse verse quoted above.[50] This must remain conjecture. However, such a group would be highly relevant in the context of angelic and high-ranking figures of the A- and B-registers, and to the cathedral entrance, for as the popular 14th-century *Speculum Humanae Salvationis* remarks, Melchisedech, king and priest, prefigures the King of kings, the first priest ever to say mass.[51]

THE NORTHERN PORCH

Three of the four Cardinal Virtues over Lesyngham's north porch survive (Pl. XVIA).[52] Justice carries sharply tilted scales, only one pan of which remains; a clothed Vice lies under her feet. Fortitude bears shield and lance (the presence of Fortitude's arms conveniently precludes the figures' being the Four Daughters of God: Mercy, Truth, Justice and Peace); the Vice is again clothed,[53] showing a sleeve and the neck of a tunic. Prudence holds an indecipherable object;[54] the ribs and navel of the Vice under her feet are visible. Temperance and her conquered Vice are missing.

Piers Plowman's explanation of the Virtues' title — Cardinal because like *cardinales* (hinges) they open the gate to heaven — may be relevant to their position over this doorway.[55] Moreover, they are presented in the context of the power of Peter, and the Kingdom of Heaven, as they may be at Exeter. Langland's Dreamer sees avaricious clergy who have gone to London to make money. 'I fear', he says, 'that there are many whom Christ, in His great Consistory Court, will curse for ever'. Suddenly he understands the awesome dignity and responsibility of the papacy, preserving apostolic succession, and so the power of the priesthood:

Then I understood something of that power which was entrusted to Peter — to 'bind and unbind' as the Scripture puts it. Peter, by our Lord's command, left it in the hands of Love, sharing it out among the four greatest virtues, which are called Cardinal. For these are the hinges on which swing the gates of Christ's kingdom, closing against some, and opening on the bliss of Heaven to others.[56]

THE GABLE

The 'power of St Peter' was represented in the original figure in Exeter's existing topmost gable, installed before the primary screen.[57] No doubt St Peter was there not only as a saint to whom the cathedral was dedicated, but also as the first pope, spiritual lord even over the high-ranking figures of the B-register. He would have had particular meaning for a community who in the conflict between Pope and Antipope must have felt the rock on which the Church was founded shifting, as it were, beneath their feet.[58] If there was a Court of Heaven on the original screen, the people would have seen the First Bishop in the context of 'Christ, in His great Consistory Court', the whole contemporary situation being related, as it was for Langland, to the implied Last Judgement. When the north porch was added, the Cardinal Virtues would have played their punning part. When the C-register was added, St Peter in the topmost gable would have acquired a further emphasis as guardian of the word of God celebrated by the prophets and apostles beneath him.[59]

THE CENTRAL PORCH: FLANKING FIGURES

Six little seated figures flanking the central porch are indecipherable. They seem to have worn crowns. The top one on the south side holds a book or box in its right hand, and in its left what looks like a leafed stem.[60] If Prideaux is right in identifying them as Virtues (though mistaken in referring to four), we have ten Virtues on the screen.[61] However, Stuart Blaylock tells me that he is convinced that the figures were kings, the remains suggesting not only crowns but also beards. If the six figures were kings, they might preclude interpretation of the primary screen in terms of 24 elders.

THE CENTRAL PORCH: THE SPANDRELS AND INTERIOR

The iconography of the spandrels, which are apparently *in situ*, is almost as odd as their construction.[62] The upper angels' sleepy postures are extraordinary in any context, and particularly in the liveliness of adjacent 14th-century work. The figures seem inadequate for the importance of their position on the primary scheme, though they would have made more sense if related to the imagined B-register gable. Perhaps the contrast between the high quality of the best carving on the spandrel figures and their botched fitting is due to interruption of the primary stage by the Black Death, which also resulted in less prominent niches in the screen remaining empty until the 15th century.[63] It is hard to imagine a more eloquent index of disaster.

Inside the central porch, two vacant niches on the north side, opposite the entrance to Grandisson's chapel, bear the scars of sculptures. The two windows looking out of Grandisson's chapel into the figure screen's B-register also carried two reliefs, deep, like the *Annunciation* and *Nativity/Magi* in the south porch: the capital under B22 has been cut back, as if an element of sculpture descended over it. It is tempting to speculate that these four carvings represented part of the apocryphal life of the Virgin, to whom the cathedral was dedicated with St Peter, and for whom Grandisson had great devotion. Their absence may testify to anti-Marian iconoclasm.[64]

THE SOUTHERN PORCH

The deep reliefs in the south porch are an integral part of the primary screen.[65] Their presence in endearing seclusion within the small southern porch is, as we have seen, appropriate if the primary screen bore Jesse Tree kings. It is also appropriate if the screen celebrated Christ enthroned in the Court of Heaven: the *Annunciation* on the south wall (Pl. XVIIA), presents the Word Made Flesh; Gabriel's announcement to the Virgin is above two small scenes showing Moses holding the tables of the Law (the Old Testament to be fulfilled in the New) and Joseph (or possibly Joachim) receiving in his ear the angelic announcement of his wife's miraculous conceiving of a child. In the *Nativity/Magi* opposite (Pl. XVIIB), adoration is offered by wise men (kings by tradition) to the King of kings, at the beginning of his earthly life.

Outside, the surviving lower portion of a seated griffin (lightly sketched by Carter)[66] is visible between the demi-figures over the south door (Pl. XVIB); the remnants of the upper portion were excised in 1982. This creature, half king of beasts and half king of birds, signifies fusion of the divine and human in Christ, so may be related to the Incarnation depicted inside. The immediately visible portion of the animal would have been its eagle's head. Possibly this was intended, with a dualism common in medieval art, to recall St John the Evangelist's eagle as associated with lecterns, for the two demi-figure kings in niches above the porch look as if they are delivering to passers-by a kind of royal pulpit-announcement of the Good News.[67]

THE C-REGISTER

Whatever the B-register represented, it is possible that the designer of the C-register found it sufficiently ambiguous to bear interpretation as the kings of Christ's genealogy, and so added the prophets normally part of a Jesse Tree (as well as the apostles not usually present).[68] It is tempting to imagine one theme thus informing the whole 14th- and

15th-century screen.[69] The Word of God as embodied in Christ, whose genealogy is recorded by Matthew, would be represented by the B-register. The 15th-century elements certainly present exponents of the faith:[70] the Word as written by the four Evangelists appears at the top of the buttresses; it is explained by the four Doctors under them; it is disseminated by the apostles forming the central portion of the C-register. The New Testament is thus presented as woven by God into a pattern in which prophecies from the Old Testament, represented by the prophets on the outer sections of the C-register, are fulfilled in the New, the whole plan being celebrated by angels. On the other hand, it is not impossible that the designer of the C-register perceived the B-register as composed of elders, and added figures to complete a full Court of Heaven.[71]

In any case, C-register and buttresses form a unit. Its iconography is lucid in general terms, though details are obscure. It is clear that twelve apostles (one of whom is Paul) flank the central pair of niches, while the four evangelists are on the buttresses. However, only nine of these figures can be individually identified. The four evangelists in the buttresses are clearly Matthew with his angel (C8, Pl. XVIA), John with his eagle (C9, Pl. XVIA),[72] Luke with his ox (C24, Pl. XVIB) and Mark with his lion (C25, Pl. XVIB).

The group of twelve 'apostles' (Allan and Blaylock, Fig. 1) may be variously made up from the following fourteen: Peter, Andrew, James the Less, John the Divine, Philip, Bartholomew, Thomas, Matthew, James the Greater, Judas-Thaddaeus, Simon, Matthias (replacing Judas Iscariot),[73] as well as Barnabas and Paul. Certain identification is only possible for five of the twelve.

C11:   Bartholomew holds his own skin to signify his flaying (his upside-down face is still just visible on the skin).
C14:   Andrew carries his saltire cross.
C18:   Paul shows his characteristic long, high-foreheaded features, and his laced scabbard.[74] Suspended from his belt in a pouch (shown in Carter's drawing)[75] is a book, its leaves and spine still clear (Pl. XXIB).[76]
C19:   John bears his poisoned cup and serpent.
C20:   James the Greater has his pilgrim's scrip and staff, and his scallop-shell on his hat.

Depending on who was replaced by Paul, the remaining apostle-figures might include Peter, James the Less, Philip, Thomas, Matthew, Judas-Thaddaeus, Simon, Matthias (replacing Judas Iscariot), Barnabas. Unfortunately, their attributes are absent, or ambiguous either in appearance (as when an attribute may be loaves or stones, a miniature palace or a money-box) or in significance (as Bedford observes, carpenter's square, halberd, spear, staff, wool bow and club are given to various apostles).[77] The doubtful figures are as follows.

C15 is almost certainly identified as Peter by his features and his pairing with Paul to flank the central group, but the supposed keys which Prideaux says he 'doubtless once held'[78] are not in Carter's drawing, where both hands are missing as at present.[79] If this is not Peter, it might represent any one of several apostles, depending upon one's interpretation of C10, C12, C13, C15, C21, C22.

Two figures showing objects variously interpreted are C10 and C13.

C10 (Pl. XVIIIA, B), now reduced to an elegant anonymity, appears in Carter's drawing holding a box or tray containing four roundish objects.[80] The figure belonged to the primary scheme, so was not originally an Apostle. The objects might subsequently have been read as loaves signifying Philip,[81] or stones signifying either Philip or Barnabas.[82]
C13 holds an object hitherto interpreted as the miniature building that identifies Thomas, who according to tradition built a palace for the king of the Indies.[83] However, two courses of chain round the object suggest rather a money-box secured by safety-chains;[84] in this case the figure might represent Matthew as customs-officer or tax-collector.[85]

K

Most of the other figures show clear attributes which may, however, indicate various apostles.

C21 holds a spear,[86] and an undoubted wool bow (Pl. XXF).[87] This might be James the Less,[88] who according to legend was killed by a blow from a fuller's club, and became the patron saint of cloth-workers; he came, particularly on the Continent, to bear their symbol the bow, rather than the object by which he was killed.[89]

C22 holds a long club; this might be James the Less,[90] Judas-Thaddaeus,[91] or Simon Zelotes.[92]

One figure shows objects both variously interpreted and variously attributed.

C12 has been identified as Matthew holding an open book.[93] Unfortunately, any of the apostles may bear a book.[94] In addition, the broken staff he holds might have belonged to a long cross, halberd or spear. If the shaft belonged to a halberd, the figure might be Matthew,[95] Matthias,[96] or Judas-Thaddaeus;[97] if the figure held a long cross, the apostle might be Philip;[98] if he held a spear, the figure might be Philip,[99] Thomas,[100] or Simon Zelotes;[101] if he held simply a staff, the figure might be Barnabas, holding the open Gospel of Matthew.[102]

C23 is a modern replacement by Stephens.[103]

Four figures are identified mainly by their position, and their place in the architectural phasing. B8, B9, B24, B25 occupy the west faces of the buttresses in the B-register (Pl. XVIA, B). They are no doubt correctly identified by Prideaux as the four Doctors of the Church: Augustine, Ambrose, Gregory and Jerome (though none of these is individually distinguishable) for they are of the same date as the C-register, and are directly under the four evangelists whose gospels they explained. This relationship is perfectly allegorised in *Piers Plowman*, where the Church's Field of Truth is ploughed by Piers using oxen who are the Evangelists, and then the large clods are broken up with a harrow drawn by draught-beasts (possibly horses) who are the Doctors of the Church. The seed sown is of the four Cardinal Virtues (which are depicted over our north porch).[104]

The now fragmentary 15th-century B23 is a problem. It may once have been a crowned figure, since it still holds the greater part of an orb: a sphere bearing a horizontal band across its centre and wavy lines on its underside indicating the earth, with a small dowel on the top surface which probably carried a cross. Prideaux thought she detected a 'rope or chain' attached to a human figure under the figure's feet, signifying St Radegund, who released prisoners.[105] However, the 'rope or chain' is not visible, and the creature is a quadruped.[106]

Of the sculptures on the flanks over the aisles, only one is highly distinctive: C33 (Pl. XVIIIE, F). Carter's drawing shows a headless, mantled figure, perhaps winged, with a large upside-down head of a dragon stretching up between its feet, the dragon's nose just below a long shield.[107] The figures's right arm is shown raised as if it once held a spear thrust down into the dragon's mouth. Carter refers to it as 'St Michael triumphing over Lucifer',[108] and this is confirmed by the feathered costume covering the archangel's arms and legs.

It has been said that a second figure (C7, Allan and Blaylock, Fig. 1) was once identifiable, by remnants of the name 'Noah' on the scroll.[109] This is unlikely. The builder of the ark is usually represented either with his ship or in narrative context: neither is present here. In any case, at that date his name would read *NOE* or *noe*. If original letters did indeed survive in 1806,[110] it is much more likely that they were part of a prophet's name.[111] That the figures on the north and south sections of the C-register are prophets is suggested by the position flanking the apostles, by their being with two exceptions (C28 and C33, discussed above), shod and hatted,[112] and by their scrolls (Pl. XVIA, B).[113] Prophets in the company of the apostles are ubiquitous: they appear, for example, on numerous late-medieval Devon screens.[114]

The ludicrous, not to say blasphemous, figure of Richard II in C16 is by John Kendall.[115] The absence of the original north figure from the central pair in the C-register probably indicates that a Virgin in an *Enthronement* fell to iconoclasm.[116] In this case, the surviving figure would be Christ. However, an 'empty' niche is inconclusive evidence,[117] and it is not impossible that the central group formed a *Trinity*, the missing figure being Christ, while the surviving one (which is bearded) is the Father (Allan and Blaylock, Fig. 1) the Dove of the Spirit having appeared somewhere in the group.[118] The elaborate crown (Pl. XXI1), and the orb under the foot, might indicate Christ or the Father.

CRENELLATIONS

Of the replacement of the north and south crenellations, the less said the better. In the sentimental idiom of the early 20th century, winged human beings appear as 'angel-souls' (among them St Peter, keys in hand). Basire's engraving shows demi-angels,[119] though the tiny figures in Carter's sketch are unidentifiable.[120] Stored in the cathedral archives is a small head, still bearing original medieval colour (the eyes are painted with considerable delicacy). Tradition says that this head was found in a roof-gutter near the west front.[121] The head's size and quality suggest that it may be the last surviving angel of the crenellations,[122] which merciful decapitation seems to have preserved from the fate that overtook the others. By comparison, its handling by five centuries of weathering has been gentle.

ACKNOWLEDGEMENTS

This paper draws extensively on the re-examination of the attributes of the figures made by Allan and Blaylock in 1982–6. Both have generously shared their knowledge and time, and given me access to their detailed records, drawings and photographs, now housed in Exeter Museum Archaeological Field Unit.

REFERENCES

1. Carter's drawing shows that the original figure had folded arms (British Library Add. MS 29931, f. 78; Pl. XVIIID); sometime before 1838 it fell, by popular repute killing a man who attempted to climb it (Prideaux (1912 b) 13 n. 2; Allan and Blaylock, n. 92).

2. I use 'primary scheme' to refer only to the first design of the figure screen (Allan and Blaylock, Fig. 2c) — not to the first design of the west front by Witney, concealed by the screen (Allan and Blaylock, Fig. 2b).

3. The unnamed 'Lieutenant from Norwich' who in 1635 described his impressions of the cathedral (cited by Erskine [1988] 56).

4. Cockerell (1851) 28 calls them 'five Saxon kings and special benefactors of Exeter, and the Norman and Plantagenet kings from the Conqueror down to Henry VI' and identifies the kings by their supposed characters (31–2) — for example, B31 (No. 22 in his numbering) is Henry V, in which 'the quiet wit and intensity of the quondam madcap, come before us'. For the iconography of the west front of Wells see Tudor-Craig (1976).

5. Gardner (1935), 268.

6. Carter (1794).

7. Lethaby (1906), cited by Bishop and Prideaux (1922), 88.

8. Cockerell (1851), opposite 28.

9. Lethaby (1903), 118, followed by Prideaux (1912b), 10. Prideaux's original photographs, held in the NBR, show more detail than appears in the book.

10. Carter (1797b), 21. Pl. VII in his book is Basire's engraving of the whole figure screen. Carter (1794) contains large individual engravings of figures from the B-register, excluding the A32–5 and B32–5. Plates from it are tipped into the copy of the later book which is in Exeter Cathedral Library. Both must be distinguished from Carter's original drawings (British Library, Add.MSS 29925, ff. 7–12; 29931. ff. 38–142; 29943, ff. 75–100). The date '1770' is found on f. 7ʳ of British Library Add.MS 29925, which has

Carter drawings of Exeter Cathedral on ff. 7–12, though it does not contain screen figure drawings. The latter, in British Library Add.MS 29931, might be dated in the earlier 1790s, since the commission for the 1794 Carter book must have been received some years before it was published.

11. Cockerell (1851), 28.
12. Prideaux (1912b), 12.
13. Davey, cited by Cockerell (1851), 29.
14. Cockerell (1851), opposite 28.
15. Prideaux (1912b), 31.
16. See Allan and Blaylock above, p. 102 for the date. Among the clearest evidence of similarity in style between the nave vault and the early figures of the B-register is the relationship between boss 195 and B27 (Cave (1953) pl. 50, and Prideaux (1912b) pl. X, respectively).
17. Prideaux (1912b), 9, believed that most of the kings would have held small staffs emblematic of the Tree of Jesse.
18. Carter's drawing (British Library Add.MS 29931, f. 82) shows the body of the bird surviving at that time.
19. The same is true of the slightly later row of kings on the west front of Lincoln Cathedral; Stone (1972), pl. 13BB shows one of them.
20. Prideaux (1912b), 9, 37–8. Stone (1972, n. 74), observes that the screen seems to be 'witness of the extreme popularity of the theme of the Tree of Jesse'. The standard account of the Jesse Tree is still Watson's (1934), though the book does not cover the 14th- and 15th-century examples which Watson listed in a typescript held at the Courtauld Institute. See Woodforde (1937) for an account of English examples in stained glass of 1330–50, made by one hand for churches in the mid-west.
21. Lethaby (1903), 118.
22. The 'fruit' of a Jesse Tree may, of course, be many things, including Mary, the Infant Jesus, the Virgin and Child, the Virgin Enthroned, Christ Crucified, or Christ Enthroned with the Gifts of the Spirit.
23. Lethaby (1903, 119), notes the similarity; see also Gardner (1935), fig. 328, Stone (1972), pls 132B, 134A. Gardner (1935, 268–9) notes similarities in attitudes, head shapes, beards, high cheekbones, and pearl beading on architectural details; Stone (1972, 176) also notes how they show the same ogee canopies to niches, and the same 'damp, clinging draperies', and dates the reredos c. 1350–60. It is a great pity that surrounding reredos figures, which might have thrown light on Exeter, are missing. Stone (1972, 176), observes that they have 'long since fallen victims to human cupidity' possibly because they were 'of wood covered with silver plate'.
24. Lethaby (1903), 118.
25. Carter (1794).
26. Stone (1972), pl. 143.
27. Moses, often treated as prophet in Jesse Trees, does appear as part of the *Annunciation* in the south porch.
28. So too Bishop and Prideaux (1922) 89; Prideaux claims (1912a: Appendix) that the very form of the architectural structure echoes

> the usual mediaeval mode of representing the Celestial City, the pinnacles of the buttresses serving for the turrets, which, with the battlemented parapet cresting the walls, were salient features in the type adopted … That the enthroned Saviour and Virgin, as King and Queen of Heaven (the Virgin thus enthroned, symbolising the Church triumphant), should occupy the central position, would be a natural and suitable arrangement in this conception.'

> She goes on: 'That the royal line of their earthly ancestry should appear ranged beneath them in this heavenly assembly would … be … appropriate; and the angel supporters to this lower tier of persons would indicate their translation to the celestial city.

Here Prideaux either reads the B- and C-registers as one design, or assumes that a *Coronation of the Virgin* was part of the primary scheme. Lethaby (1903, 120) compares the screen to the original west front of Lichfield, and to the west door of Rochester: 'sculptured Heavens where the saints stand tier on tier beneath the throne of Christ'.

29. For example, the elders appear with angels in the archivolts of the tympanum of Chartres's Royal Portal.
30. Apocalypse iv.1–4. Biblical quotations are from the modernised versions of the Douay-Rheims translation of the Vulgate.
31. See Douce Apocalypse, Dyson-Perrins Apocalypse and Trinity College Apocalypse in the references.
32. Deuchler (1971), Vol. 1, f. 5ᵛ.
33. Nickel (1972) presents the heraldic evidence, and suggests that this was one of the books mentioned in Bishop Grandisson's letter to the Bishop of Lausanne in 1328.
34. One should not forget the 13th-century angel improbably bearing a hawk on its wrist: Lincoln Cathedral Angel Choir, Bay 4 (containing St Hugh's shrine) No. S11; Glenn (1986: 103) observes that this figure 'engaged on such a [worldly], even frivolous pursuit defies explanation'.

35. 'Labour as a good soldier of Christ Jesus./No man, being a soldier to God, entangleth himself with secular businesses, that he many please him to whom he hath engaged himself./For he also that striveth for the master is not crowned, except he strive lawfully' (2 Timothy ii.3–5, cited by Bruno Signiensis in *Patrologia Latina*, CLXV, 627). *Patrologia Latina* is hereafter referred to as *PL*.

36. Apocalypse vii.9–17: see Deuchler (1971) Vol. 1, 11ʳ.

37. By the author (unknown, according to Glorieux [1952]) of the commentary on the Apocalypse formerly attributed to Alcuin, *PL*, C, 1117.

38. *Glossa Ordinaria*, *PL*, CXIV, 718.

39. Rupert of Deutz, *PL*, CLXIX, 922, referring to Matthew xix. 28.

40. An anonymous early 13th-century writer, *PL*, CLXII, 1517; the attribution is Glorieux's.

41. Allan and Blaylock, 10.

42. Apocalypse v.1–6; this is followed shortly by an account of how the heavenly host

> sung a new canticle, saying: thou art worthy, O Lord, to take the book and to open the seals thereof; because thou wast slain and hast redeemed us to God, in thy blood, out of every tribe and tongue and people and nation;/And hast made us to our God a kingdom and priests; and we shall reign on the earth./And I beheld, and I heard the voice of many angels round about the throne and the living creatures and the ancients (and the number of them was thousands of thousands),/Saying with a loud voice: The Lamb that was slain is worthy to receive power and divinity and wisdom and strength and honour and glory and benediction.

This would account neatly for the presence of the A-register angels — though of course the presence of angels never needs much justification.

43. This is precisely the kind of vital evidence which would be lost if eloquently worn figures such as C10 were discarded. Allan and Blaylock (10) observe that these figures might have flanked the imagined gable.

44. Genesis xiv 14–20. The great popularity of the Type is attested by its presence in *Biblia Pauperum* (sig. *s* in the first alphabet: see Henry (1987) 81, 83).

45. Psalm 110.4–5, quoted in Heb.v.5–10, vi.20–vii.21.

46. Cockerell (1851), opposite 28, referring to John vi.7.

47. British Library Add.MS 29931, f. 72ʳ.

48. For example in Eton MS 177, where the scene is unusual in prefiguring *The Presentation* (see Henry [1990] f. 3ᵛ).

49. See Cyprian *PL*, IV, 387–8 and (to choose two of the Doctors represented on the buttresses) Augustine *PL*, XLI, 500, Jerome *PL*, XXVI, 173. In the blockbook *Biblia Pauperum*, whose manuscript origins are 13th century if not earlier, one prefiguration of the *Last Supper* is *Melchisedech Offers Bread and Wine to Abraham*, the caption meaning 'The holy things which Melchisedech gave him denote Christ'. Melchisedech appears in art as a type of Christ from the sixth century, for example at St Vitale, Ravenna (*RDK*, VI, 174).

50. John Allan has drawn my attention to the fact that the composition might have resembled that on the Percy tomb (dating from the 1340s) in Beverley Minster: small figure-bearing pedestals flank the apex of the ogee arch (Stone [1972], pl. 132A).

51. *Speculum Humanae Salvationis*, ch. xvi; the *Speculum* survives in English manuscripts, and in one Middle English version, *The Mirour of Mans Saluacioune*. See Henry (1986).

52. See Allan and Blaylock above, p. 103, for the building of the porch.

53. *Contra* Prideaux (1912b), 11.

54. Not the hart suggested by Carter (1797b, 21); he identifies the virtue as Discipline — though his sketch (British Library Add.MS 29931, f. 77ʳ) seem to show a heart. A heart is also mentioned by Cockerell (1851, 26); he calls the third virtue Discipline, though on 29 he refers to her as Temperance (and the fourth, unaccountably, as Charity).

55. Langland, a cleric in Minor Orders, and almost contemporary with our primary figure screen (1342–53), completed the A-text of his poem in about 1370; the B-text, the first to contain this passage, was written between 1377 and 1379.

56. He then refers cryptically and nervously to the ultimate clerical corruption manifested in the Schism of 1378:

> But as to those other Cardinals at Rome who have assumed the same name, taking upon themselves the appointment of a Pope to possess the power of St Peter, I will not call them in question. The election of a Pope requires both love and learning. There is much more I could say about the Papal Court, but it is not for me to say it.
>
> (Goodridge's translation [1959], 65–6.)

57. The fabric roll for 1341–2, Christmas week 12, refers to silver and colours for painting the image of the Blessed Peter (*pro ymagine beati Petri*), an entry probably related to that in Easter week 6 recording

payment of 18*d.* for painting 'the bishop' in the gable (*in pictura episcopi in gabl'*): see Erskine (1983), 269 and 270. Carter's very sketchy drawing of a figure 'in top pediment' (British Library Add. MS 29931, f. 70ʳ) suggests an eroded standing figure holding a rod which was presumably the shaft of a crook or crosier. On the same folio, under the heading 'statues on the west front . . . The 3 f[igs] on the outside' Carter also lightly sketched a headless standing figure 'in buttress on left hand' holding something in its right hand, with a small figure leaning against its left side, and a standing figure 'in buttress on right hand,' marking these two 'both above the screen'.

58. The papal court was at Avignon 1309–77: Grandisson himself was consecrated there by Pope John XXII.

59. It has to be said that the present naked figure of the saint by Simon Verity, inserted in 1985, however effective as a symbol of man's courageous vulnerability, fails to take its place as a crowning episcopal symbol.

60. Basire's engraving (Carter [1797b], pl. VII) shows only four, following some of Carter's drawings which show two pairs, the first labelled 'two statues on L side of middle porch', the second 'on the right' (British Library Add.MS 29931, f. 80). Carter's published statement (1797b, 21) is that 'in four small niches on the side of the architrave are four small statues of royal personages seated.' This error persisted: Lethaby (1903: 119) refers to 'the four little crowned figures on the jambs of the great door.' Oddly, even Prideaux seems to imply four in this position (the other four to which she refers presumably being those over the north porch): 'about the doorways the eight small crowned figures representing the principal virtues [*sic*] would have special significance as typifying the Christian attainments needful for the *entrance* into the Heavenly City' (Prideaux, 1912a Appendix). However, Carter's faint sketches on f. 45 of British Library Add.MS 29931 appear to show the north side of the architrave correctly bearing three niches, not two.

61. There are at least two series where ten Virtues are related to the Ten Commandments. They occur on all but the first two pages of the Eton Roundels cited above at n.48, and, according to Katzenellenbogen (1964, 48, n. 6 from the previous page), were found on the sides of the roof in the Shrine of St Gislenus, in the Church of St Ghislain near Mons, where ten demi-figures of Virtues (of which five survive) carried books and embodied the moral content of the Commandments. However, it cannot be shown that the six figures round the Exeter door are female, let alone Virtues.

62. See Allan and Blaylock p. 100.

63. See Allan and Blaylock p. 104.

64. Although one might expect them to be a thematic part of the screen, the bosses in the porch (362A–368A) do not appear to relate to it. The only ones not foliage are: 363, a *Crucifixion* with The Virgin and St John; 364A, a *Vine* with a tiny quadruped in it; 364, a *Lion mask* or *Green Man* wearing a cap; 366, possibly a *Face* in a vine — possibly a broken *Lion mask*; 368a, *Foliage* with two sleeping cats, each with a bird spread out over its back.

65. Bosses in the south porch (370A–374A) carry only foliage and animals.

66. British Library Add. MS 29931 f.82ʳ. Cockerell (1851: 29) insisted that this is 'not a griffon' but a double-necked swan, symbol of Edward III and Richard II, whom he thought to be represented by the demi-figures above.

67. Two contemporary, local eagle-lecterns survive: the fine, unrestored example which belonged to the Cathedral and is now in St Thomas's, Exeter, and the sadly repainted example, deserving more sympathetic conservation, which is still at Ottery St Mary.

68. One wonders if the metal fixtures once mounted over the canopy spandrels (Allan and Blaylock 15, 16) might have represented a tree stem.

69. The Jesse Tree was in the mind of at least one designer working for Grandisson (1327–1369): it occurs in reduced form on Corbel P (the second great pier from the West on the south side of the nave), reproduced in Stone (1972) pl. 129. Prideaux (1912b; 205) interpreted the recumbent figure under the Virgin and Child which forms the lower tier as 'the "old Adam" fallen to rise no more and crushed under foot', but the stem of the foliage surrounding the Virgin and Child clearly rises from him, and his posture is of slumber, not defeat. Although prophets and kings are absent, the recumbent figure, tree, Virgin and Child and Coronation of the Virgin filling the upper tier of the corbel reveal a minimal but undoubted Jesse Tree.

70. The same gathering of the exponents of the faith — Prophets, Apostles, Evangelists and Doctors — appears in the eight sixteenth-century westernmost windows in the north and south walls in Fairford, Gloucestershire (see Wayment [1984]).

71. The effect is curiously like St Ambrose's description, with reference to Is. i.2, of a 'tower' of apostles, prophets and doctors, whose duty is to keep peace for the Church, its ramparts guarded by angels *Hexameron* 3.12 (*PL* XIV 189).

72. Carter's drawing (British Library Add.MS 29931 f. 72) shows the now broken object in the figure's left hand as something resembling a martyr's palm (or possibly an outsize quill-pen, one of St John the Evangelist's usual attributes).

73. Matthew x.2, Luke xxii.14, Acts i.2.

74. The scabbard seems to have been mistaken for a fold of drapery by Carter: it does not appear in his drawing (British Library Add.MS 29931, f. 73^r).
75. British Library Add.MS 29931 f. 73^r.
76. Prideaux (1912b; 28) thought she detected a scrip or purse. The difference is noted by Blaylock and Allan, 'Second Interim Report' 6.
77. Bedford (1911), 37.
78. Prideaux (1912b), 25.
79. British Library Add.MS 29931, f. 73^r.
80. British Library Add.MS 29931, f. 72^r.
81. Bond (1914) 61, referring to John vi.7.
82. For Philip see Kirschbaum (1968–1976), Vol. 8, 200; for Barnabas see Milburn (1949), 32.
83. Bedford (1911), 49, Prideaux (1912b), 25, Bond (1914), 57.
84. The chains were noted by Blaylock and Allan 'Second Interim Report' 6. Kirschbaum (1968–1976), Vol. 7, 590 mentions the *geldbeutel* or money-bag; Milburn (1949), 178 mentions a money-box.
85. Matthew ix.9.
86. This is clear in an early photograph in the Conway Library. Bedford (1911), 38 suggests that the spear reflects the saint's name, citing *The Golden Legend*'s derivation of *James* from *jaculo* 'a darte'.
87. Not a saw, *pace* Prideaux (1912b), 29; see Bedford (1911), chap. IV 'The Bow', for a well illustrated and documented account of this tool for clearing or 'whipping' wool by vibrating the bowstring in the pile of fibres to be cleaned and felted. His fig. 24 shows a 16th-century enamelled (possibly Limoges) copper medallion in the Victoria and Albert Museum, with a bow of the same design as that in C21, carried by a figure captioned *SANCTE IACOBE MINORE*. Carter's drawing is inscribed 'Fullers club or Wooll bow' (British Library Add.MS 29931 f. 74^r).
88. Bedford (1911), 27, 49.
89. However, the copy of Bedford's book in the University of Exeter Library once enclosed a letter of his (now regrettably lost) written in 1936 to Rushforth, qualifying the book's confident statement that the Exeter figure is James. The latter is also found with the fuller's club (Bedford [1911], 12–20) as well as with other objects not found on the figure screen (Bedford [1911], 15, 35, 37, 38).
90. Bond (1914), 60; Bedford (1911), 12–20.
91. Milburn (1949), 149, but without evidence.
92. Bedford (1911), 50.
93. Cockerell (1851), opposite 28; Milburn (1949), 178, but without evidence.
94. For example, James the Less (Kirschbaum [1968–76], Vol. 7, 48), Judas-Thaddaeus (Kirschbaum, Vol. 8, 426); Simon Zelotes (Kirschbaum [1968–76], Vol. 8, 369–70); Matthias (Kirschbaum [1968–76], Vol. 7, 604).
95. Bedford (1911), 38, Kirschbaum (1968–76), Vol. 7, 590.
96. Bedford (1911), 38; Kirschbaum (1968–76), Vol. 7, 605.
97. Kirschbaum (1968–76), Vol. 8, 426.
98. Bedford (1911), 38, Milburn (1949), 212, Kirschbaum [1968–76], Vol. 8, 200.
99. Kirschbaum (1968–76), Vol. 8, 200.
100. Bond (1914), 56; Kirschbaum (1968–76), Vol. 8, 471.
101. Kirschbaum (1968–76), Vol. 8, 370.
102. According to Prideaux (1912b) 25, but she gives no evidence.
103. See Allan and Blaylock p. 109. Carter's drawing (British Library Add.MS 29931 f. 74^r) shows the lowest quarter of a fragmentary figure — unfortunately no attribute is visible.
104. Langland (1978), Passus 19, ll. 259–309.
105. Prideaux (1912b), 16–7.
106. Even on Basire's engraving it is clearly a quadruped, though the head is missing (Carter [1794], 69). The orb and lion might signify Solomon as a type of Christ, in the light of Psalm 90.13: 'Thou shalt walk upon the asp and the basilisk; and thou shalt trample under foot the lion and the dragon.' Ostoia (1972), fig. 16 shows a Mosan gilt bronze clasp *c.* 1200 (Metropolitan Museum of Art, NY, Acc.No.47.101.48) composed of a woman with her feet on a basilisk, and a crowned man holding an undifferentiated sphere, his feet on a lion. The suggestion is that these are Sheba and Solomon, probably prefiguring The Church and Christ. Ostoia's n.2 quotes Rorimer's citation of the Psalm in the context of Solomon.
107. British Library MS Add.MS 29931 f. 76^r. It is not a 'shield at his feet' (*pace* Prideaux [1912b], on her key to the statues).
108. Carter (1797) 21. Cockerell ([1851], 30) thought this was St George.
109. Jenkins (1806), 34. For some idea of the wealth of colour which must have helped to clarify the iconography of the figure screen it is helpful to consider the surviving polychrome at Lausanne: see Furlan and Pancella (1981).

110. None appears on Carter's drawing (British Library Add.MS 29931, f. 72^r).

111. For example, *nah[um]* or *[sopho]nia[s]* or *[da]nie[l]* or *[a]mo[s]* or some abbreviation or these. In lower case lettering, at least, it would be easy to misread such abbreviated or flourished fragmentary words as *noe, noa* or *noah*.

112. Some of their hats closely resemble those worn by prophets in the 40-page blockbook *Biblia Pauperum* of *c.* 1460 (where they mostly serve to identify their owners); see Henry (1987), Appendix B, 'The Prophets' Hats' (177–8). The closest resemblances are between the hats worn in the blockbook by Isaias (48, where he is not wearing his usual hat) and the author of Numbers ('Balaam' on 52) and C4; by Sacharias (53, 72, 73, 76, 80, 97) and C5 (pl. 8(i)); by Amos (76, 89, 97) and C6; by Micheas (49, 84, 105, 113) and C29 (pl. 8(g)); and by David as author of Psalms (47, 53, 56, 60, etc.) and C30. The blockbook was probably produced in Utrecht.

113. Unfortunately, no lettering can now be detected on the scrolls even with the help of ultra-violet light to reveal any traces of colour, or 1,000-watt illumination to reveal any traces of incision or relief.

114. Chudleigh, Kenton, Bovey Tracey, Ipplepen, Stoke Gabriel, Bradninch (Bond and Camm [1909], 230).

115. See Allan and Blaylock p. 107. Lethaby ([1903], 118) called it 'mean and silly'. One could wish the figure removed were it not for the fact that it might be replaced by a Virgin, with consequent destruction of the open-ended function of the empty niche which is all we should countenance in the present state of our knowledge.

116. The niche is empty in Basire's engraving (Carter [1797], pl. VII). The gesture of the remaining figure precludes a formal *Coronation of the Virgin* such as survives in mutilated form on the west front of Wells. The distinction between the two moments is nicely illustrated in the 40-page blockbook *Biblia Pauperum* page showing *The Coronation of the Virgin* in the centre, with one of its prefigurations, *The Enthronement of Bethsabee*, on the left (Henry [1987], 116, 119).

117. In her valuable revision of Hope and Lloyd's original account of the cathedral, Mrs Erskine ([1988], 154, n. 21) points out that the 'evidence' taken from a reference in the will of John Langelegh in 1404 to 'the image of the Blessed Virgin outside the west door' (Bishop and Prideaux, 88) relates in fact to the church of Ottery St Mary.

118. Allan and Blaylock found four contemporary iron bars, one bearing traces of red paint, which they thought likely to have held some kind of fixtures (see p. 104 above). Carter's drawing (British Library Add.MS 29931 f. 73^r) shows the figure's right hand holding a rod-like object that might be part of a sceptre or simply a dowel, the left hand supporting a closed book standing on his knee.

119. Carter (1797b), pl. VII. Cockerell's reference ([1851], 28) to 'a choir of angels sounding the trump, the cymbal, and all manner of music' must be to Kendall's replacements; strangely, Cockerell seems to have thought them original.

120. British Library Add.MS 29943 f. 82.

121. The cement holding it to its little mounting has 'West Front Note Colour' written on it in pencil.

122. The suggestion, and identification of medieval colour, were made orally by Anna Hulbert.

The Problem(s) of the St Edmund's Chapel at Exeter Cathedral

By J. Philip McAleer

INTRODUCTION

Because of its modest size and rather plain character, the chapel of St Edmund, which opens off the westernmost bay of the north aisle of the cathedral, seems rather unremarkable and of no particular interest (Pl. XXIIIA, B).[1] It is not part of a balanced layout for there is not, nor has there ever been, a chapel in the corresponding position in the south aisle. Despite its contributing an obvious asymmetrical element to the west front (Pl. A), the chapel appears to have been built with the west end of the nave. From the exterior (Pl. XXIIIA, B), its details match the north elevation. The most immediate and obvious feature is the large, five-light, north window, similar in its tracery to the others of the aisle. As a result, the north window looks like one of the aisle windows simply pushed further out. It rises above the same splayed set-offs as are found under the aisle windows, two courses of which form a continuous band across the width of the chapel's north wall. The top of the wall ends with a crenellated parapet that rises above a pronounced string-course, consisting of a hollow and a roll, enriched with small carved heads at regular intervals: these details again are all continuous from the aisle wall.

On the interior, the shafts of its entrance arch, and those in the angles of the chapel, match the design of the responds against the north aisle wall. There are no significant differences in base profiles or capital types. The tracery pattern of the north window echoes the window at the west end of the south aisle, over the doorway to the former cloister, in the manner typical of Exeter in which the tracery patterns change from bay to bay, and differ between the aisle and clerestory levels, but are identical across the bay. The pattern of the vault is essentially a miniature version of the nave aisle vaults which have ridge ribs and pairs of tiercerons. It is not identical, as liernes form a transversely placed diamond pattern in the centre, simultaneously deflecting the diagonal ribs and terminating the ridge ribs (Pl. XXIIID).[2]

Yet, a careful inspection reveals a series of 'irregularities' in the design of the chapel, more than one might expect or consider appropriate for such a small structure, that cumulatively become increasingly curious, and which seem to require particular explanation.

DESCRIPTION OF THE EXISTING FABRIC

Of these irregularities, the one that may first register is the nature of the vault. The rectangle of the chapel is covered by a single unit of vaulting. The major ribs of the vault spring from single shafts placed in the angles of the chapel room, *except* at the south-east corner where the shaft is only a short one corbelled onto the wall, overlapping a shaft of the entrance arch (Pl. XXIIIC). This draws attention to two other similar short shafts which, however, are not used for rib springers or for any other function: one is corbelled onto the shaft at the west side of the entrance arch (Pl. XXIIIC); the other is on the north wall, immediately west of the window jamb (Pl. XXIIID). Their positions make it clear that it was the original intention to vault the chapel in two bays: a large one, with its north-south axis centred with the apexes of the entrance and window arches, and of the aisle vault;[3] and a very narrow one at the west.[4] This was a logical solution, because the chapel space, larger than the adjoining aisle bay, was not centred on the axis of the aisle bay. At the same time, it also seems unnecessarily complicated to have such a small space divided so unevenly and awkwardly. That the builders also eventually arrived at a similar judgement is borne out by the fact that they abandoned the initial idea, and covered the entire space of the chapel with one unit. Even so, it is curious that the builders did not make provision for a full-length shaft in the south-east angle.

Turning from the vaults to the windows, three different sizes of windows are encountered where only two might be expected: the major and widest showpiece, the north window, and the necessarily smaller, narrower ones to east and west of differing dimensions. Because its jambs are very deep and the embrasures descend past its sill, the single-light east window appears as if set in a deep niche, in contrast to the north window which is set nearly flush with the inner wall plane. The heavy rear arch of the narrow niche is broadly pointed and chamfered, rib-like in effect (Pl. XXIIIc). Consequently, the east wall appears much thicker than the north one.[5] Presumably, this window was initially of some importance, as one might expect that the altar — now under the north window — originally was placed against the east wall. This might explain why the sill of the east window is so much higher than those of the other two (cf. Pl. XXIIIA, B).[6] The tracery of the single light window is relatively simple: a pointed trefoil above a trefoil-headed arch. Last of all, attention may be drawn to the west window. Like the east one, it is narrow. Unexpectedly, it is the larger, being of two lights, and is not set in a niche, although its jambs are much deeper and more widely splayed than those of the northern window (Pl. XXIIID). And its tracery is quite different — a simple uncusped 'Y' pattern. A string-course, composed of a split half-roll above a thinner roll, circles the chapel below the window sills.

The east window, like the west window, when viewed from the interior of the chapel, is off-axis to the north — less so than the west one. If it had been on the interior axis, it would have been nearly in the corner on the exterior and therefore received even less light than it does. Similarly, the west window has been moved away from the angle of the buttress (and screen) of the west front. The east-west ridge rib crosses the chapel on a slight diagonal in order to coincide with the apex of the east window; its deflection is obscured due to its interruption by the liernes.

Returning to the exterior of the chapel, it may be noted that the double set-offs under the north window do not continue on to the east face of the chapel (Pl. XXIIIB), but do run along the west face to stop against the north-east buttress of the west front (Pl. XXIIIA). The jambs of the three chapel windows are all similar, consisting of a thin shaft with moulded bases and capitals, a simple moulded arch — roll/hollow, with a fillet on the roll, and a label of a split roll with hood-stops, all details like those of the adjacent bays of the north aisle. The shaft bases are set on round plinths which match those of the western bays of the nave, as opposed to the polygonal ones found in the Lady Chapel (but not the flanking east chapels), the choir aisles, and the eastern bay of the nave aisles.[7] The profile of the tracery — a roll set against a double chamfer — also matches that of the nave aisle windows. It is apparent that the tracery of the east window is set in a plane more deeply recessed than in the case of either the north or west windows. None the less, the chapel gives the general impression of being stylistically consistent, consistent with the construction of the western end of the nave, and of one build. Only the Y-tracery of the west window suggests a date earlier than the third decade of the 14th century, as it is of a type that is usually dated much earlier, perhaps 45 to 50 years earlier, c. 1280.[8] This tracery is, indeed, the single feature which has been responsible for the construction of a building history for the chapel of St Edmund that at times seems to rival that of the entire cathedral in its complexity.

THEORIES OF BUILDING HISTORY

When exactly was the chapel built, and does it all belong to one phase? These are the two
essential questions that have been raised. Several writers have suggested that the chapel was
first built either around 1200 or shortly before 1279/80, and that about or soon.after 1325
the chapel was greatly rebuilt when the west end of the nave was reconstructed.[9] Accordingly, all that remains from the theoretical chapel of 1280 is the west wall and its window,
and, possibly, parts of the north wall. Everything else is later: the east wall, the entrance
arch, the north window, the vault shafts, the tierceron-lierne vault are all generally agreed to
belong to c. 1325–50. Additionally, there was a tradition that there had been an earlier
chapel on the site dating to the Romanesque period.[10] Thus, in this theory, the 12th-century
chapel is supposed to have been either replaced or rebuilt in the later 13th century and it was
that possibly hybrid structure which was considerably altered in the 14th century by (at
least) the insertion of the north window, the reconstruction of the east wall, and the addition
of the vault.

One of the most complicated and complex sequences, that encompasses almost all aspects
of every other interpretation, earlier or later, was written out by the late V. Hope.[11] In his
reconstruction of the chapel's building history he:

1.   accepted the earlier assumption that the chapel was built originally about the time of the
     completion of the 'Norman' church, and that it had been separate;[12]

2.   interpreted the mention of a 'Capella Sancti Edmundi supra Ossilegium in Cimeterio' in a lost
     Inventory of 1507 to mean that the 12th-century structure had been a 'bone-hole';[13]

3.   assumed the east wall was 'Norman' because of its thickness;

4.   accepted the Y-tracery west window as identical with a window mentioned in the fabric rolls in
     1280;

5.   placed the altar slab at the level of the east window sill, that is, 4 ft 6 in. above the present chapel
     floor or 5 ft 10 in. above the north aisle floor and, as a result, deduced that the original
     13th-century floor was 3 ft 4 in. above the aisle floor (he assumed that the Romanesque aisle level
     was equal to the present one); thus he concluded that the 13th-century chapel had been accessible
     only by means of a portal in its north wall;

6.   proposed that in 1328–50, an arch was opened into the chapel from the aisle, the north wall
     (re)built with a window, the tracery of the 13th-century window in the 12th-century east wall
     altered, and the chapel vaulted.[14]

I suspect that, if it were not for the presence of the Y-tracery, none of these various
building phases would have been proposed. For example, with regard to Hope's and others'
theoretical histories, the following scenario would have to be envisioned. At the time that
work on the new cathedral was concentrated east of the present transeptal towers and
crossing, a small chapel was either rebuilt or newly opened off the west end of the
Romanesque north aisle. Fifty years later, when the west end of the Romanesque church
was being completely demolished and rebuilt, this small chapel was spared in order to be
drastically altered: a new window was put in its north wall (which may have been rebuilt);
the east wall was (perhaps) rebuilt further west or the window alone was remodelled; angle
shafts were inserted; a new entrance arch from the aisle was built; and the chapel
(re)vaulted. Considering the extent of these suggested renovations, it might be asked why
everything was torn down or altered except the west wall and its old-fashioned window,
about which there seems nothing special. Is it more implausible to propose they kept a
window already 50 years old, than to assume it is a late example of its type?

Certainly, the absence of the expected joints in the fabric does not help to corroborate any
of the theoretical building histories. The area of the chapel has never been explored by

proper archaeological methods, although on at least two occasions there have been excavations which did not produce supporting evidence for the theories. Most of the proposals about the history of the chapel actually are based on documentary sources, rather than upon any firm archaeological evidence.

ARCHAEOLOGICAL EVIDENCE
Fabric

A careful examination of the existing fabric of the chapel, and of its architectural details, does not reveal any evidence of successive building phases, alterations of an earlier fabric, or insertion of elements at later dates.

First, the exterior (Pl. XXIIIA, B). The chapel is built out of smallish blocks of stone whose geology is rather varied. Caen, Salcombe, Portland, and Beer stone are all present in a random mix. The west and east corners of the chapel are built out of large, quoin-like blocks of Salcombe, as are the set-offs, which contrast in size with the small blocks forming the main body of the walls. The east, north, and west walls are built out of a mixture of Salcombe, Caen, and Portland stones, with a good deal of Beer appearing in the upper half. On the interior, where the surfaces of the wall are less visible, and the extent of restoration less certain, Salcombe appears to be the primary material below the string-course on all three walls. Above the string-course, the east wall appears to be mostly of Beer, as is true of the interior jambs and arch of the west window. Salcombe is also found above the level of the string, in the segments of wall west of the north window and south of the west window. The geology of the stone used in the walls, therefore, does not confirm the theory advocating two building phases, as the distribution pattern is similar in all three walls and there are no clear divisions, especially vertically, between the use of the various types or sizes of stone.

Although Beer stone has been identified as forming the major building material of the cathedral during the 14th and 15th centuries, and a combination of Salcombe, Caen, and Portland has been considered typical of 13th-century work, in fact the line between their use is not clearly drawn. Most notably and significantly, more than a little Salcombe appears in the west end of the nave, indeed, in all of the nave, particularly in the spandrels of the nave arcade, and the spandrels and back wall of the triforium. Consequently, the presence of a great deal of Salcombe in the chapel cannot be used to support a late 13th-century date as opposed to one in the second quarter of the 14th.[15] On the other hand, the use of Beer stone suggests a later rather than earlier date for the chapel.

The east wall of the chapel, which lacks the sloping set-offs,[16] does not bond into the north aisle wall below the level of the Gothic window sill (Pl. XXIVB). This portion of the aisle wall belongs to the Romanesque church and can be traced for the full length of the aisle. It is marked by a chamfered offset forming a low base plinth, and broad shallow buttresses. Judging from the exterior of the aisle wall in the bay adjacent to the chapel, the east wall of the chapel could never have been further east. The work below the window sill splay appears to be completely Romanesque up to the angle with the east wall of the chapel.[17] Above the level of the sill, the chapel east wall bonds in with the west jamb of the north aisle window (Pl. XXIVC). Considering the substantial thickness of the east wall, it is surprising that it was not made thinner in order to avoid overlapping the west jamb of the north aisle window; instead, the chapel wall is angled back to avoid any reduction in the width of the westernmost light of the window.[18] As remarked before, the crenellated parapet and the decorated hollow moulding immediately below it are continuous from the aisle wall on to the chapel's east wall.

As has also been mentioned, the base moulding of the north aisle wall is formed by a double set-off which does not continue on to the chapel's east wall where there is, instead, a simpler form at a lower level (Pls XXIIIB, XXIVB). Engravings show that until the early 19th century, the north wall of the chapel was in the same plane as a wall which enclosed the entire area, identified as the 'Plumbery', between the chapel and the north porch (Pl. III).[19] This wall was capped by a broadly-sloping weathering which was continued from the base set-offs of the chapel. It is, therefore, not surprising to find the mouldings from the east to the north wall discontinuous.

The north wall of the chapel does not reveal any break in work to either side of its window. The same may be said of the west wall, which bonds in with the rear portion of the north-west buttress of the façade for its full height; it has already been noted that the set-offs continue on to the west wall from the north face. It is impossible to be sure this is an early form because the earliest (18th-century) views reveal there was a small enclosure built against the west face of the chapel.[20]

The frames and shafts of the three windows, much restored in places, appear to be identical and to match those of the aisle windows (Pl. XXIVC). Their form of thin colonnettes, with round bases of a flaring hollow and roll-moulding profile and moulded capitals, and the arch heads of split rolls and thin hollows are all consistent. There is no sign of any disturbance or other irregularities that would indicate that any of them had been inserted into a pre-existing wall, whether of 12th- or 13-century date.

In a similar fashion, the exposed surfaces of the interior of the chapel do not reveal any seams or breaks which would support the suggestion that the north window was inserted into an earlier, late 13th-century wall, replacing an earlier window or entrance portal.[21] Again, evidence is lacking to support the idea that the east wall was built last, as a result of shortening the eastern extent of a 13th-century chapel, presumably in order to avoid overlapping the (new) aisle window.[22] There is also no visible evidence that the corner shafts relating to the vault ribs were added or, especially, that the short, corbelled shaft on the north wall was inserted into the wall rather than constructed as part of the wall. Similarly, the south entrance wall does not in any way suggest a Romanesque wall with a later arch inserted into it (Pl. XXIIIC).

Above the vault of the chapel there is, once again, no evidence for more than one building period. At this level, however, yet one more peculiarity may be observed. The top of the pier buttress with its pinnacle for the westernmost flying buttress of the nave is deflected to the east (Pl. XXVC).[23] Here one realises that the heavy east wall of the chapel — the thickest of the three walls — is, in effect, a pier buttress, as the flyer lands on top of it and the visible part of the pier buttress sits on it. The thickness of the chapel wall is such that there is room on its top for the pier buttress to have continued in a straight plane from the base of the flyer, although this would have placed it on the inner (western) half of the chapel east wall. The buttress may have been deflected to land on the east half of the wall in order to avoid creating an awkwardly narrow gap between the east face of the flyer and the west side of the parapet on the top of the chapel wall: now the two are fused, so a hard-to-maintain area has been eliminated.

Excavations

The earlier of the excavations, in 1896, as reported by Bishop Edmonds,[24] was necessitated by the appearance of a crack in a wall, and the consequent desire to examine the foundations, to see if repairs were necessary. Digging produced a number of Romanesque pieces — voussoirs, corbels, capitals, etc., all of which have apparently been lost without any record of their exact appearance. It was also mentioned that the foundations of the chapel contained much re-used 12th-century material. As reported, it is not specifically stated where exactly the digging took place, inside the chapel or without, or which wall had the fracture. It has generally been assumed, from the nature of Bishop Edmonds' phrasing and narrative, that digging took place inside the chapel, but the only evidence of a crack large enough to have caused concern about the foundations is in the bay of the aisle immediately preceding the chapel. There, both inside and out, a large fracture is quite visible below the Gothic window sill, in the area of the Romanesque masonry beneath the second light from the east. Thus, it was probably outside this bay that digging occurred in 1896.

The second occasion was when the chapel was refitted by E. Guy Dawber to serve as a memorial chapel for the Devonshire Regiment in 1936. At that time, a partial excavation under the floor was made. It was not for archaeological purposes and was not supervised. Two photographs, a plan, three sections, and a brief description by Percy Morris serve as not totally satisfactory records.[25] The digging took place inside the chapel along the foot of the west wall, to a depth of about 6 feet and was extended for a short distance along the north wall, but only to a depth of 18 to 5 inches, thus forming an 'L'-shaped trench (Pl. XXIVA). A roughly built stepped foundation was revealed under the west wall (Pl. XXVA, B). Exposed for a length of 8 feet, it included very little Romanesque material, only two sections of a chamfered plinth, 2 ft 4 in. and 3 ft in length. They were obviously not *in situ*. The short stretch of foundation under the north wall seems to have had a vertical inner face, and was even more roughly built, lacking either regular coursing or a regular shape to the stones (Pl. XXVA). Unfortunately, Morris gave no description of it. The western foundation was the more substantial, but both appeared rather scrappy.[26] Morris's notes indicate that a short section of a wall built of trap rock was revealed at the south end of the west trench, under the entrance arch respond. He identified it as the foundation of the north aisle wall of the Romanesque cathedral, and stated that it over lay the lowest courses of the west foundation.[27] Its character is not clearly visible in the photograph (Pl. XXVB), as the south end of the trench looks more like a section through the rubble fill under the chapel floor, than a foundation. No report of any finds was made.[28]

The meagre archaeological evidence provided by these two excavations suggests that there was never a Romanesque chapel on the site.[29] In this regard, it should be noted that T. B. Worth, writing initially in 1878,[30] at the time of a general restoration of the cathedral, remarked that because it had been 'long suspected that there was a crypt beneath the chapel', there was a 'careful search' but 'no trace' was found. This suggests that the *interior* of the chapel was dug up in 1878 and that, therefore, the Romanesque fragments reported by Edmonds, as lying in the trench 'almost in the order in which once, in higher dignity, they had stood above ground',[31] must have been in the bay before, and could not have been underneath the chapel. The corbels, capitals and voussoirs reported in 1896 probably came from the upper levels of the penultimate west bay of the Romanesque north aisle — it is grievous that they have been lost. It should not pass unnoted that the repair work of 1896 did not produce any post-Romanesque material. The re-used chamfered stones revealed in 1936 probably came from the north wall of the west bay of the aisle, as they match those still surviving *in situ* to the east of the chapel. The lack of any reported or visible debris from the later 13th century also suggests that the foundations exposed in 1936 were made for the existing superstructure, even though they appear surprisingly shabby and makeshift. One would have expected better of the 14th century, but, obviously, they have served the purpose. On the basis of the, admittedly scant, archaeological evidence, it is appropriate to conclude that there was never any earlier structure on the site.

DOCUMENTARY EVIDENCE

In the face of the apparent lack of any conventional signs of more than one simple integral period of construction for the chapel, the various elaborate building histories that have been put forth primarily rest on one factor: the Y-tracery of the west window which, typologically, has been considered too early for the *c.* 1325 + date of the rest of the chapel and west end of the nave. Furthermore, because of its Y-tracery, this window has been associated with a reference in the fabric rolls.[32] The entry is for 30 March 1280 and refers to the glazing of a window: '*Vitrario pro locatione j fenestre . . . . . . Edmund*'' (To a glazier for placing one window . . . . . . Edmund).[33] Unfortunately, the crucial words immediately before the saint's name are illegible in the manuscript, but have been taken to be *contra altari* rather than *contra capelle*.[34] This reference has been linked to another made almost six months earlier, under 30 September 1279, to windows in the chapel of St James: '*pro iij fenestris ad capellam beati Jacobi ex precepto senescalli*' (For 3 windows for the chapel of St James by order of the steward).[35] As it happens, a 19th-century engraving shows that the windows in the double chapel on the south side of the choir, with altars dedicated to St James and St Thomas, formerly had intersecting Y-tracery in three lights (Pl. XXVD).[36] The Y-tracery in the present west window of the chapel of St Edmund, therefore, has been directly linked to the Y-tracery formerly present in the existing chapel of St James, due to the references in the fabric rolls and because of their typological similarities, and consequently dated to *c.* 1280.

While it often seems that when documents have survived, the corresponding building has not, and when a building exists, there are no relevant documents, the temptation to identify the two 'automatically' when both seem to exist should be resisted. In this case, as has been seen, dating the west window to the 1280s raises more questions about the constructional history of the chapel than it solves. The possibility that the reference to a window '. . . . . . Edmund'' in the fabric rolls in March, 1280 *should not* be identified with the existing window of the chapel at the west end of the nave north aisle should be seriously considered. The text of the fabric rolls actually makes no mention of the location of the altar — not chapel — of St Edmund. Indeed, the context suggests the altar should have been in the area of the *east* end where all other work was being carried on, especially as all entries in the fabric roll in the period 1279–88 refer to the construction of the choir.[37] Therefore, should it not be assumed that the '[altar'] Edmund'' referred to was at that time, *c.* 1280, located somewhere in the east end of the new building?

Identifying the existing Y-tracery window in the existing chapel of St Edmund as work of *c.* 1280 raises a number of questions about the intentions of the builders and the extent of the rebuilding they envisioned when work on reconstruction began in the later 13th century. Why was a chapel being built at the *west* end of a nave they presumably intended to rebuild? If the construction of the chapel did take place shortly before 1280, does that imply that, at that time, there was no intention to rebuild the entire church, only the east end? As the west wall of chapel bonds in with the north-west buttress of the front for its full height, does that imply a major campaign at the west at the time work was beginning at the east end? If the chapel *is* to be associated with other work at the west end, such as the south-west corner of the nave for which a date *c.* 1280 has also been put forth, does that suggest *only* a new façade was intended and again indicate that there was no intention to rebuild the nave at that time?

The next reference to an altar of St Edmund in the fabric rolls is more specific, but is not until 38 years later. It is in 1318 and again refers to glazing: '*. . . ad ponendum j formam vitri in vestiario ad altar' sancti Edmundi*' (In one glazier placing one forme of glass in the vestry to St. Edmund's altar).[38] The earliest reference to a *chapel* of St Edmund is not until the same year: '*Et j forma capelle sancti Edmundi*' (And one forme in St Edmund's chapel).[39] Like the entries in the fabric rolls of 1279–88, this reference occurs in the larger context of work at the new east end (*novum opus*) and of the last work in the completion of the structure east of the second bay of the nave, specifically in the context of work in the towers. Nor are the references consistent, as they are variously to '*[altar'] Edmund*' ', '*vestiario ad altar' sancti Edmundi*', and '*capelle sancti Edmundi*'.[40] In the latter case, the reference is to one forme of 36 feet which implies a rather small window: one could suggest the east window of the existing chapel if it were not for the fact that window had not yet been built in 1318, as it clearly belongs to the construction of the chapel dating after 1328 and the beginning of work on the nave. In contrast, reference to a payment in 1330 for ironwork for *two* windows in 'the new chapel near the well' (*juxta fontem*) *could* well apply to the existing chapel of St Edmund since a well was located outside the north-west corner of the cathedral.[41]

There are further ambiguities in the fabric roll text. Among the first surviving references are two to work in a location that has been identified as the flanking double chapels now known as St James/St Thomas (on the south) and St Andrew/St Katherine (on the north). The earlier, already cited, refers to the glazing of *three* windows in the chapel of St James where there are now only *two*.[42] The second entry of 9 March 1280 refers to a window *opposite* the altar of St Katherine: '*In positione j fenestre contra alt . . . . . . rine*' (For placing one window opposite the alt[ar of St Kathe]rine).[43] Yet there are *no* windows in the west wall opposite either altar in the chapel. As St Katherine's is the southern altar in the double chapel, even the existing north window is not next to it.

What then of the Y-tracery west window in the existing chapel of St Edmund? Could it actually date from as late as +1325? An answer to that question may be provided by the chamber over the north aisle, behind the minstrel's gallery — a structure that has always been accepted as at least post-1300 — which also has Y-tracery in its west window.[44] It is interesting to observe that the three external walls of this tall chamber are built of the same combination of small ashlar of varied geology and large blocks of (much-weathered) Salcombe as is the chapel of St Edmund. And although the jambs of the west window are built of large blocks, it is clearly not an insertion. Its tracery, like that of the north window of the chamber, is simply chamfered.[45]

CONCLUSION

The focus on the Y-tracery of the west window has detracted from a consideration of other more genuine problems that arise from the numerous irregularities of the chapel structure. These irregularities might be explained by factors other than two or three phases of rebuilding. The major irregularities are actually only two: the variation in the thickness of the walls, and the variation in the placement of the shafts for the vault ribs. The primary problem or question which has been ignored is any consideration of why the chapel was built at the west end of the nave — that is, what are the parallels for chapels in this location and what was its primary purpose?

The fact that the three walls each have a different thickness, need not be taken as evidence of three widely separated building periods. Each wall must be seen as other than simply one of three walls bounding a space. As has been seen, the east wall is, in effect, a pier buttress which explains its mass, 4 ft 9 in. and, perhaps, the narrowness of the east window. The north wall *is* merely a screen and structurally could be, as it is, the thinnest at 2 ft 6 in. The west wall, 3 ft 7 in. thick, is also a buttress, corresponding and responding to the west wall of the nave and aisle.[46] It is thinner than the west wall proper because it receives no thrust in the east-west direction, and also does not receive a flyer.[47]

Why was there no full-length shaft at the south-east corner of the chapel? The east jamb of the entrance arch forms part of the aisle wall respond to the ultimate nave pier. There could have been room for an angle shaft only if there was a short stretch of wall to the east of the entrance arch, as there is at the west. Due to the necessary thickness of the east wall of the chapel, as a result of its function as a pier buttress for a flyer, its inner face directly abuts the inner shafts of the entrance arch. If it had been thinner in order to allow for a stretch of interior wall east of the entrance arch, it might have been too weak to serve as a pier buttress. If the east wall had been placed further east, it would have overlapped the western part of the last aisle window more than it does, perhaps blocking an entire light; that position may also have been too far east for it to have properly served as a pier for the flying buttress. The reason why the axis of the vault does not synchronise with the apexes of window and entrance arches has already been put forward: it was the result of a decision to simplify the vaulting by using one covering unit instead of two very unequal ones — a change in intentions executed in the course of construction and the only evident change in plan.[48]

Among English cathedrals, there are no true or exact parallels for the location of St Edmund's chapel. Chapels opening off the nave aisles are rather rare occurrences at any date. Chichester Cathedral seems to be one of those rare instances. Chapels were added to both its north and south aisles: five on the north, four on the south, dating from various times in the 13th century.[49] From the early 14th century, there is the Jesus Chapel, which may originally have been a chantry chapel, which opens off the penultimate *east* bay of the north aisle of Worcester Cathedral (c. 1317–24?).[50] In the later 14th century, a chapel dedicated to St Anne was opened off the easternmost bay of the south aisle at St Augustine's Abbey, Canterbury (built by Juliana de Leyborne, died 1367); earlier, a charnel chapel, consecrated in 1299, had been built up against bays 7 and 8 of the eleven bay nave.[51] As to parallels specifically for the location of a chapel opening off the west end of an aisle bay, few really similar examples come to mind. Those that do, have a symmetrical arrangement, belong to more grandiose structures, or are much larger. In the 12th century, there were the apsidal chapels which opened off the east side of the west transept at Ely, possibly preceded in date by the apsidal chapels that once paralleled the end walls of the west transept at Bury St Edmunds.[52] In the 13th century, there is the large pair of chapels flanking the nave and west front at Lincoln.[53]

The lack of convincing parallels or of a generally established tradition leads back to the major problem of why the chapel — why *a* chapel — was built in this location, opening off the west bay of the nave aisle. If, as seems to be true, there was not traditionally a chapel in this position at Exeter, why was it added in the 14th century? Was it to accommodate an altar displaced from some place else in the building, or to serve some other purpose?[54] Does the location of the St Edmund's chapel, for instance, relate it to the history of the consistory court? In the 18th and 19th centuries, it actually served as a consistory court.[55] How ancient a tradition was this? Consistory courts were often located at the west end of a nave; examples are: the south chapel at Lincoln;[56] the base of the early 16th-century south façade tower at Chester;[57] the west bay of the north aisle at Winchester;[58] the (destroyed) north tower at Glasgow (14th century; the court was later moved to the south tower);[59] the north-west tower of Dunkeld (15th century);[60] the north-west tower at Wells.[61] Several physical features of the chapel room perhaps encourage speculation in this direction.

The reduced thickness of the west wall accommodates a bench along its interior base. A bench is, at present, also found along the full length of the east wall of the chapel (Pl. XXVE).[62] The line of a tile floor, at a slightly higher level than the present one, can be traced along the base of both benches. It is at a level that would have oversailed what is now a projecting block of the former Romanesque aisle wall, located near the south end of the

L

east bench. Thus, the original floor level was probably only six to eight inches higher than the present one, and, therefore, higher than the existing aisle floor by about two feet,[63] rather effectively separating the chapel from the aisle.[64] In late 1878, according to Worth, 'the remains of an old altar slab', a piscina and a credence table were still evident on the east wall, seeming to establish that an altar was once against this wall.[65] This testimony conflicts with the still visible evidence of the benches along the east as well as the west wall which appear to be original features. No trace of altar slab, piscina or credence now remain, due, no doubt, to the work carried out in 1936; regrettably no visual record of them was ever made.[66] The benches do suggest the chapel may have had another function. Could its use as a consistory court explain the presence of the benches along the east and west, but not north, walls, and might that use give significance or meaning to the niche-like recess in the east wall?[67] These are the aspects of the 'chapel' that deserve further exploration and consideration, now that, I hope, the structure has been firmly placed in the 14th century, contemporary with the construction of the west end of the nave.[68]

ACKNOWLEDGEMENTS

I wish to express my appreciation to Peter W. Thomas, Assistant Cathedral Librarian, and most especially to Audrey M. Erskine, Cathedral Archivist, as well as to the Head Virger, Clive Lloyd, and his staff. A particular debt is owed to John P. Allan for his generosity in sharing his great knowledge of and familiarity with the cathedral fabric, and for spending much time with me in its examination and in debate about the constructional history of St Edmund's chapel. Thanks are also due to Paul D. A. Harvey.

REFERENCES

1. Indeed, the chapel is only briefly mentioned, if at all, in guide books, and then not with reference to its architecture. For instance, *A Guide to the Cathedral Church of Exeter with an Account of Its Antiquities, Monuments &c* (Plymouth-Dock 1818), 19, lists the cathedral's chapels but omits St Edmund's. The current picture guide, *Exeter Cathedral (Pitkin Pictorial Guide*, London 1976), 3, 23, makes only the briefest mention of it.

2. Its plan is not shown correctly in Britton (1826), Pl. III. It is the only lierne vault in the building, except for the tiny ones of the pulpitum (1318–25; Bishop and Prideaux [1922], 62–4).

3. The north-south axis of the existing vault is about 1 ft 6 in. (Hope [c. 1966] 221) to the west of an axis drawn through the apexes of the north window arch, of the entrance arch, and of the corresponding bay of the aisle vault.

4. The narrow bay would have been equal to the depth of the respond forming the west side of the entrance arch and a portion of the thickness of the west façade wall. This draws attention to the fact that the inner face of the west wall of the chapel is not in the same plane as the inner face of the west front; i.e., the west wall of the chapel is thinner than the west façade wall proper. More will be said about this below.

5. It actually is: I will return to this point below.

6. According to Hope (c. 1966), 219, the 'original sill of the window embrasure' was 4 ft 6 in. above the existing floor level which is the result of the remodelling of the chapel in 1936. The string-course now defining the sill of the niche is about 7 ft 3 in. above the present or 1936 floor level: the sill of the window opening is (and always has been) much higher. How Hope determined his measurements is not clear: a memorial plaque covers most of the wall below the string-course, and the small amount of masonry above it is restored. The original (14th-century) floor level may have been half a foot higher than the present level (the evidence for this will be discussed at the end of this paper), so even if the niche was originally longer, a sill 4 ft above the floor would still have cleared an altar slab.

7. Admittedly, many of the shaft bases of chapel and aisle windows have been restored but this seems to be the pattern so far as the few worn originals suggest. The fifth bay from the east in the nave aisle has been — incorrectly, I believe — restored with polygonal bases. The change from polygonal to round bases also occurs

on the interior jambs, after a bay and a half on the north side, after one bay on the south. This shift also was noted by Everett and Hope (1968), 183.

8. Interestingly enough, Pevsner in Pevsner and Metcalf (1985), 114, identified the Y-tracery as 'early for 1279', and described the tracery of the east window as 'plate tracery (late for 1279)'.

9. Hewett (1848), 24 ('exhibiting earlier characteristics than the nave'); Freeman (1873/1888), 6–7/9–10, ascribed the chapel to the time of Bishop Marshall (1194–1206); Worth (1880), 12, repeated the attribution of a portion of the chapel to Marshall; Addleshaw (1899), 61, thought the chapel belonged 'to an earlier period than the nave — showing, indeed, traces of Marshall's work'. Bishop and Prideaux (1922), 86, considered the present structure the result of a building, 'or, more probably, a rebuilding' carried out before the completion of the nave 'transformation'; to them, the 'style of its vault and carvings indicate[d] the later years of Grandisson's episcopate as the time of their execution'.

10. Bishop and Prideaux (1922), 28: 'It has generally been believed that the Chapel of St. Edmund ... was originally built about the time of the completion of the Norman Church, but that it was separate, and did not form part of it until later times when the Nave was transformed into its present style'. Orme (1986b), 15, 116, continued this tradition in so far as he assumed the existence of a chapel in the Decorated building presumes one in the same position in the Romanesque one.

11. Hope (c. 1966), 213–22.

12. Hope (c. 1966), 217, quoted Bishop and Prideaux (1922), 28 (as in n. 10 above) at this point. They, however, did not agree with the 'general belief' that the existing chapel was only the 'Norman' one transformed. Because of the 'Norman' stones built into the foundations, they believed that any Norman chapel 'was demolished, and the present fourteenth-century one built in its place, or possibly on its site'.

13. The Inventory is now lost, but it was printed in full in Oliver (1861), 320–76; see especially 375, and also 217. The mention of this chapel in the Inventory may be the origin of the tradition of a separate 12th-century chapel in this location referred to by Bishop and Prideaux (1922), 28. Oliver (1861), 217, had only commented: 'Can there be a crypt there?'

14. Apropos of points 3, 4 and 6, Hope never claimed any Romanesque work was visible in the west and north walls, yet he never explained exactly when it had disappeared. His identification of the east wall as 'Norman' conflicts with those theories that suggest the east wall of a 12th- or 13th-century chapel was rebuilt further west in the 14th century.

15. In connection with the use of building materials, it should be noted that Erskine (1983), p. xxxi, pointed out that the fabric rolls for 1317–32 indicate that Master Thomas of Witney was accumulating materials for the construction of the nave, and, for example, more stone from the *Salcombe* quarry was sent into storage than to the building site. In addition, Hope and Lloyd (1973), 19, stated: 'As early as 1324/5 the Fabric Roll shows that immense quantities of building stone were procured from the quarries of Silverton, Wonford, Whipton, Raddon, Barley, Branscombe, *Salcombe* and Beer in Devonshire, from Hameldon in Somerset and from *Caen* in Normandy'. This was also noted by Oliver (1861), 179; Freeman (1873/1888), 50/70; Bishop and Prideaux (1922), 65. Both these extracts suggest that Beer stone was not used exclusively in 14th-century work; that Salcombe and Caen stone were still available; and that a mixture of stone could well have been used for a small job like the chapel of St Edmund in the period after 1328 — small pieces left over from larger works.

16. In place of the broad sloping set-offs, there is a base moulding consisting of a broad chamfered course set one course higher than the narrower (Romanesque) chamfer of the north aisle wall.

17. If this section of the aisle wall is a 14th-century restoration, it is a good imitation of 12th-century ashlar. However, on the interior, the Romanesque masonry does come to an end about 5 ft 1½ in. east of the 14th-century responds to the entrance arch of the chapel. The Romanesque bay is usually restored on a width of 18 ft 3 in. (Hellins [1890], 120–5, first described the evidence of Romanesque work in the aisle walls), so there should have been a buttress at about the point where the chapel's east wall abuts the aisle wall, of which there is now but slight trace. In any case, the condition of the masonry does not substantiate the suggestion that the chapel's east wall was originally built with reference to the Romanesque bay and was then moved (rebuilt) westwards.

18. If it had not been angled back, it would have actually abutted the westernmost mullion of the tracery.

19. See most notably, the engravings by James Basire after the drawings of John Carter in Carter (1797b), especially Pl. IV. The wall is shown as capped by a three-course weathering which gives the appearance of having continued the design of the set-offs under the windows and on the buttresses of the two aisle bays east of the north porch. Carter's plan (Pl. II) shows the wall as a thin structure standing equidistant from the faces of the buttresses *and* the north wall of the chapel, but judging from his and other views, this is probably incorrect. The weathering rose over the polygonal (three-sided) arch of the small doorway just east of the westmost buttress; the asymmetry revealed the rising ground level along the north side of the cathedral. The lower two courses of the three of the weathering continued under the north window of the St Edmund's chapel. If this enclosure wall (of the 'Plumbery') dated to the original building period, its presence could explain the absence of the set-offs on the east face of the chapel.

The Plumbery enclosure wall is shown quite clearly in a number of early 19th-century engravings, most notably in the large engraving, 'North West View of the Cathedral Church of St. Peter, Exeter', drawn and etched by J. Buckler, engraved by R. Reeve, published June 1810 by J. Buckler (see also Buckler [1822], unpaged, for a small-scale version, and a similar small unidentified view in the Exeter Cathedral Archives [Archives List, no. 11]). 'Northwest View of Exeter Cathedral', drawn by R. Creighton, engraved by W. Woolnoth, published by C. Greenwood, c. 1828, still shows the Plumbery wall, but it does not appear in either the plan or view of the west front in Britton (1826), Pls I and II respectively, dated 1825; nor does it appear in an engraving ('N.W. View of Exeter Cathedral') drawn by R. Browne, engraved by W. Deeble, published by Robert Jennings, 1 March 1830; nor in the view of the west front drawn by R. Garland, engraved by B. Winkles in Winkles (1838–42), II (1838), facing 101 (Pl. 96). The wall was probably removed in the restoration of 1805–29 by John Kendall.

20. Carter (1797b), Pls II, III, IV (and others). Because the enclosure blocks the view of the base of the chapel, we cannot tell if the west set-offs are a product of 19th-century restoration or not. This small enclosure was slightly less deep than the exising west porches. There was a small doorway with a pointed arch and continuous jambs in its north wall; the west wall, which rose higher than the sill of the chapel's west window, had three crenellations. What was this area for? On Carter's plan (Pl. II), it is marked 'E', identified in the legend simply as 'inclosures or yards'.

In the north prospect of the cathedral set into John Rocque's *Map of Exeter* (1744), a picket fence extending past the chapel blocks any sight of the Plumbery wall but the west enclosure is visible. This enclosure also appears in: an engraving by F. Jukes after W. Davey ('A West View of the Cathedral Church of St Peter in Exeter'), published by Davey, Exeter and Jukes, London, 1791; the engravings of J. Buckler (1810), J. C. Buckler (1822), and Creighton and Woolnoth (see above n. 19); a view by T. Allom and E. Challis ('Exterior of Exeter Cathedral'), from J. Britton and E. W. Brayley, *Devonshire and Cornwall Illustrated* (London 1832), plate facing 81; and a view published by Rock and Co. London (Exeter Cathedral Archives List, no. 14).

Neither the Plumbery enclosure wall nor the small west enclosure appear in the engraving by D. King after R. Newcourt in Dugdale I (1655), facing 220 (1718 edn between 32/3), but it is not very accurate with regard to details; the engraving of the west front (facing 222; 1718 edn facing 32) even omits the chapel of St Edmund altogether.

21. Hope (c. 1966), 219, 222, it will be recalled, thought the north wall had contained the entrance to his putative separate Romanesque 'bone-hole' and to his later, 13th-century, chapel.

22. Once again, Hope (c. 1966), 216, 219, thought the east wall was 12th-century, except for the window. See also n. 17.

23. John Allan brought this to my attention.

24. Edmonds (1898), 32, 35.

25. The original manuscript appears to be lost: a copy of it is preserved in Hope (c. 1966), 216B.

26. Unfortunately, it could be asked, if the west and north walls of the chapel were built at the same time, why were not the foundations identical and continuous: a problem equally for a 13th- as well as 14th-century date for the walls. Equally unfortunately, I do not have an answer.

27. '[F]or a height of 1 foot 10 inches at the bottom it rests on Wall A [the foundation under the west wall of the chapel], which otherwise is not bounded to the return walls'. This is exactly the point at which one would expect a Romanesque angle buttress of some substance — projecting substantially and turning onto the west front, perhaps forming a turret containing a vice.

28. There are no records of the interior appearance before the restoration. One consequence of the work in 1936 seems to have been the lowering of the chapel's floor level to 1 ft 5 in. (my measurement, versus Hope's 1 ft 4 in.) above the aisle, whereas previously it appears to have been about 6–8 in. higher. There is a low bench at the base of both the west and east walls. The wall below the high sill of the east window certainly does not bond in with the jambs of the existing niche-like recess. This may be a product of the 1936 restoration, and also the corresponding section of the bench (as supposed by Hope [c. 1966], 220, who, additionally, attributed the string-course of the east wall to this same period). As the bases and the tall plinths (which match the entrance arch) of the three angle shafts are raised on the benches, the benches would have been part of the original design. What other restoration work was done on this occasion is now difficult to judge, as the furniture installed at that time obscures much of the wall surfaces.

29. Nor that the area outside the north-west bay of the Romanesque cathedral ever served as a 'bone-hole': Hope (c. 1966), 215, 222, expanding upon Oliver (1861), 217. Of course, all evidence of the latter might have been removed, along with, perhaps, any kind of Romanesque sculptural debris like that reported in 1896, when the foundations of the existing chapel were inserted.

That the present chapel is built on the site of a rectangular stairtower giving access to a westwork-like structure occupying the west bay of the nave (in the present plan), as Radford proposed nearly 30 years ago in (1960), 28–36, is equally implausible: see McAleer (1984), 71–5. (If I may make an addenda to that paper, with regard to the re-used material, mentioned on p. 74 and in n. 16. That material seems to be the 'Transitional [jamb] shaft' mentioned by Bishop and Prideaux [1922], 66, and taken by them as evidence that the 'old Norman West-Front ... had been transformed rather than entirely rebuilt'. However, the 'Transitional shaft' is certainly not *in situ*, so there is no evidence that the Romanesque west front was merely 'transformed'.)

Hope (*c.* 1966), 217, had made a similar suggestion, only he proposed the west foundations belonged to the *east* wall of a tower — possibly never built. Recently, a somewhat similar proposal has been made by Orme (1986b), 15, 116, in the face of the lack of any archaeological or documentary evidence. The symmetrically projecting west bays of the north and south aisles appearing in his plan would also have been unparalleled in English Romanesque architecture: they cannot be accepted even 'symbolically', to make a 'liturgical point'.

30. Worth (1878), 49, going back to Oliver (1861), 217: see n. 13 above.
31. Edmonds (1898), 35.
32. Exeter Cathedral Archives, Dean and Chapter Records, Exeter MSS 2600–2704/11 in Erskine (1981) and Erskine (1983).
33. Erskine (1981), 3 (MS 2600/1 [m. 1]).
34. W. St John Hope, in 1915, thought the missing words were *contra(?) altari*: Erskine (1981), 8, n. 3. (Is it unusual for the form not to have been *beati* or *sancti Edmundi*?)
35. Erskine (1981), 2 (MS 2600/1 [m. 1]).
36. Erskine (1983), p. xxviii, n. 1, pointed out that Y-tracery is shown in the chapel's window in the engravings after drawings by H. S. Storer: Kendall (1818), Pl. XIV. The tracery in both the chapel's east windows is now quite different: three rather short lights support a broad central oval flanked by ogee mullions rising from the lateral lights, all without cusping. Just when the Y-tracery disappeared is not certain. The south double chapel was totally destroyed in an air raid in 1942 (Carpenter [1943]); it was rebuilt after the war (Eeles, [1949], 1442–4). A photograph, *c.* 1873 (National Monuments Record, BB86/880; brought to my attention by Virginia Jansen), shows a window with a Y-pattern of only *two* lights in contrast to the three shown in the Kendall engraving. This pattern is referred to by Bishop and Prideaux (1922), 33*: 'The tracery in the eastern windows of St. James' Chapel and the western window in St. Edmund's are essentially the same'.
The tracery pattern now existing in the rebuilt south chapel copies that in the east windows of the north double chapel about which Bishop and Prideaux remarked, 'the head tracery [in St Andrew's Chapel] has been renewed at some *much* later date; but in all probability it was originally the same as that of the St. James' windows'; they suggested (106) a renewal date of *c.* 1657. Of the window tracery in the upper storeys of both these chapels they further noted they are all alike, and commented they 'are of a design very unusual in the thirteenth century'. The two east windows in the north lower chapel, of three lights each, certainly have profiles to their mullions and jambs unlike any others in the cathedral: a hollow chamfer is employed on the mullions, and the jambs have a succession of fine curves and angles; the four two-light windows (one is blind) in the upper chamber, again without cusping and with a circle in the head, have a more usual vocabulary with mullions of a flat-faced double chamfer (rebated on the interior), a hollow surround, and split-roll labels.
A west-east section (facing north) through the three levels of the chapel of St James and a plan of the main chapel and crypt by E. Ashworth, and a section, plan and north elevation of St Andrew's Chapel by W. W. Hitchins appeared in *Building News*, 8 September 1915; unfortunately, the tracery of the east windows of St James' chapel is not shown.
37. Erskine (1983), p. xxvii, pointed out it is the *only* reference in the fabric rolls during the years 1279–88 to work *not* at the east end — the new work of choir, presbytery, Lady Chapel, etc.
38. Erskine (1981), 102 (MS 2614 [m. 2]). Erskine (1983), p. xxviii, n. 2, noted that this entry 'gives the impression that even at this date [1318] a complete chapel had not been made in this corner, but that the altar stood in a *vestibulum* inside the corner by the present north west door'. Consequently, it would seem, if the altar of St Edmund was in a 'corner by the present north west door', then the window referred to in 1280 is not the west window in the existing chapel, because the chapel either a) did not then contain the altar of St Edmund, but another of different dedication, or (more likely) b) had not yet been built. Furthermore, even if it be granted there was a chapel at the west end of the north aisle with an altar dedicated to St Edmund in it *c.* 1280, surely during the years the main body of the nave was in construction, *c.* 1329–47/48 at the shortest, the altar would have been moved out of the chapel, while the chapel was being extensively remodelled.
39. Erskine (1981), 109 (MS 2614 [m. 3d]).
40. Other early references to altars are ambiguous as Erskine (1983), p. xxvii, has pointed out. Erskine (1983), p. xxv, also mentioned, 'while rebuilding was in progress some chapels had not settled to a definite dedication or had not received one at all, and altars were necessarily moved about to enable the work to proceed'; or, again (1983), p. xxvii, 'reference [was made] to a chapel by an altar in or near it as the most convenient means of locating it' — for 'chapel' read 'window'. And, finally, Erskine (1983), p. xxvii, also stressed that the 1280

reference is to an altar, *not* a chapel. All of which suggests that an altar of St Edmund, variously referred to, was *not* in the chapel now at the end of the north aisle.

41. Erskine (1983), 229 (MS 2627 [m. 1d]): *pro ferrament' ij fenestr' in nova capella iuxta fontem*. Erskine (1983), p. xxxii, preferred to identify 'the new chapel near the well' with the one that was to become Bishop Grandisson's mortuary chapel (an identification also made by Freeman [1873/1888], 51/71, where an alternate translation, 'the new chapel near the font', is given; also Hope and Lloyd [1973], 20), because St Edmund's chapel 'might be described as "new" if the suggestions about it made above [pp. xxvii–xxviii] are accepted, but it had a dedication by which it could be referred to'. Aside from the fact that it is more than doubtful that the altar of St Edmund was moved to this chapel before the 1330s, when the chapel was most likely completed, and that it therefore did not have a dedication by which it could be identified, the suggestion that Bishop Grandisson's chapel was begun as early as 1330 is contradicted by Erskine (1983), p. xxxiii, where she pointed out there is no evidence in the fabric rolls for the beginning of the screen, of which the chapel is part, before 1340–2. See also Bishop and Prideaux (1922), 67. Additionally, in Bishop Grandisson's chapel there are three pairs of small windows in a lower row with two slightly larger ones above: it might be expected that the ironwork for these five small windows would have been purchased all at once.

42. Erskine (1981), 2; or is the reference to one window of three lights? Oliver (1861), 205, stated 'The third window, mentioned in the same roll, appears to have been blocked up when the beautiful, but mutilated, mural monument was placed against its south wall'. The south wall of the chapel and the unidentified monument were, of course, totally destroyed in 1942 (see above n. 36). Three photographs in the National Monument Record, London (neg. nos: 2754; without number; B47/3599(a)) do show the monument and wall before destruction. Although there is some resetting or renewal of masonry around the gable of the canopy, its horizontal coursing provides no evidence for the blocked-up arch of a window. The monument, dated on the basis of style, may have been contemporary with the rebuilding of the cathedral: Worth (1878), 45; Bishop and Prideaux (1922), 118, perhaps *c.* 1310; it is depicted on the title page (Pl. I) of Carter (1797b). 18th-century plans such as those of Carter, Pl. II, and Rocque, *Map of Exeter*, show a wing of the Bishop's Palace abutting the full width of the south wall of the chapel of St James.

43. Erskine (1981), 3 (MS 2600/1 [m. 1]).

44. A window apparently mentioned by Freeman (1873/1888), 10/7: 'A two-light lancet window also survives at the top of the North porch stairs'.

45. Nothing seems to have been written about this chamber, as distinct from what may be described as the balustrade of the minstrels' gallery proper.

46. Measurements taken in 1966 by A. W. Everett: Hope (*c.* 1966), 216. My measurements of the thickness of the pier buttress (2 ft 10 in.), and the unoccupied section of the top of the wall (above the vaults, 2 ft 6 in.) produce an even thicker east wall, 5 ft 4 in.

47. I find that Britton (1826), 106, recognised the west and east walls of the chapel were buttresses: 'On the north side, the angular and the next buttresses form the sides of a chapel: but these are cut through by two lateral windows ...'.

48. Pevsner and Metcalf (1985), 114, thought the vault 'must have been the last after thought of all', and, 122, that it was 'late C14'. I do not think the vault can be described as an after thought, as it was clearly intended from the beginning as the angle shafts indicate. Prideaux and Shafto (1910), 179–80, dated the vault to the period of Bishop Grandisson, and considered its six foliage bosses examples of a type ('patternmaking') common in the nave (see 147, 161, 177–9). I cannot detect any significant differences in the profiles of the chapel's ribs from those of the adjacent aisle bay.

49. See Pevsner and Metcalf (1985), 84 (plan), 93.

50. VCH *Worcester*, IV (1924), 400 (plan between 396/7); B/E *Worcestershire* (1968), 296 (plan), 298, 304–5: of the Y-tracery in the lights of the crossing tower, begun 1374, he remarks (p. 304) 'a motif of 1300 rather than 1350'! Also Morris (1978b), 118, 123, 133.

51. Clapham (1955), 23.

52. The south chapel at Ely still survives: VCH *Cambridgeshire*, IV (1953), 53, 54. For Bury see Whittingham (1951), 171, 174, and pl. XXI; B/E *Suffolk* (1974), 133, 135 (plan).

53. B/E *Lincolnshire* (1964), 102–3.

54. There are two references, cited by Hope (*c.* 1966), 213 (and others), to a St Edmund the Confessor which suggest there may have been an altar to a St Edmund in the cathedral during the later 13th century: one is a calendar entry in a missal dating to the second half of the 13th century (D & C Exeter MS 3510: 'IXe XVI Kal. Dec. Sci. Edmundi Epi.[*sic*] et Conf.'); the other is a description of the burial of the murdered precentor, Walter de Lechelade, *before* an altar of St Edmund the Confessor in 1283 (D & C Exeter MS 1930). In the later case, clearly the burial did not take place in the existing chapel; and as Orme [1982], 17, quite rightly [I believe] observed, 'The chantry ... sited at the altar of St. Edmund, the location of which in 1292 is not known ... must not be confused with the present chapel of that name which was not built until the middle of the fourteenth century'; later he seems to have forgotten this conclusion: Orme (1986b), 25. In this later

writing, Orme (pp. 25, 86, 117) suggested the chapel fell into disuse after the Black Death, and that it was very likely altered 'for other purposes'. In addition to D & C Exeter MS 1930, Orme, 84, n. 10, and 116, cited D & C Exeter MS 3672, ff. 339–40, the Testament of Thomas Le Boteler, dated 1263 (in which he expressed a desire to be buried before the altar of St Edmund in the church of St Peter), which firmly establishes that an altar of St Edmund existed by that time somewhere in the old cathedral. Although not giving any indication of location, the requests for burial in front of the altar suggest a space larger than that occupied by the existing chapel.

55. It is so identified on the plan drawn by Jones (1757); on the plan in Winkles (1838–42) II (1838), facing 113; in Britton (1826), 149 and Pl. I; also Oliver (1861), 217; Worth (1878), 49; Orme (1986b), 25.

56. See above, n. 53.

57. *Chester Cathedral* (9th edn, Gloucester 1959), 17–18; B/E *Cheshire* (1971), 141.

58. Jacob (1913), 68–9.

59. Durkan (1970), 46, 73–5.

60. Root (1950), 15.

61. According to Colchester (1987), 93, the chapel under the north-west tower, dedicated to Holy Cross, 'was later and until recently used as the Bishop's consistory court ...'.

62. The bench along the west wall is certainly original. The base of the bench along the east wall also appears original. There is no trace of a bench along the north wall even though the visible masonry seems original and undisturbed. See also n. 28.

63. Not the 3 ft 4 in. proposed by Hope (*c.* 1966), 215. See also n. 28.

64. The existing aisle pavement appears to reflect the original 14th-century) level. As it appears the chapel floor level was always higher than the aisles, the chapel in effect was always isolated. Was this because it was immediately adjacent to the north aisle west portal — or for some other reason? The wooden screen which defines the space of the chapel that projects 4 ft 6 in. into the aisle is possibly late 14th century: see Glasscoe and Swanton (1978), 3–4.

65. Worth (1878), 49: 'Under the east window of this chapel are still to be seen the remains of an old altar slab, on the right side of which is an ancient piscina and a credence table above'.

66. Of them, Bishop and Prideaux (1922), 28–9, remarked: 'In this present [chapel] the very plain piscina with credence certainly appears early work, but as it is entirely devoid of mouldings any conclusive evidence as to its age is lacking'. So there really is no evidence they were original to the 'chapel'.

67. Benches run the full length of the nave aisles: they, therefore, could be considered a stylistic feature in the chapel, although it still might be expected that a bench would occupy the north wall, or only the west wall if there had been an altar against the east wall originally.

68. Even the dedication of the chapel has been considered problematic. Hope (*c.* 1966), 213–14, suggested that the dedication was not to St Edmund King and Martyr, but to St Edmund Rich, the Archbishop of Canterbury who died in 1242 and who was canonised in 1246, that is, St Edmund the Confessor.

Nevertheless, Erskine (1983), p. xxv, n. 2, has cited an ordinal issued by Bishop John de Grandisson in 1337 which mentions, among many others, an altar of St Edmund King and Martyr: *Ordinale Exon.*, I, 277.

The Charnel Chapel of Exeter Cathedral

By Nicholas Orme

The west front of Exeter Cathedral in the later Middle Ages was more hemmed in by buildings than it is today. Opposite the south-west corner, a mere street's width away, stood a group of dwelling houses and behind them the now demolished church of St Mary Major. Opposite the north-west corner were the conduit — a small round building housing the water-supply of the cathedral Close — and the charnel chapel. The chapel's existence has long been known from written records, but its exact location was a mystery until the excavations carried out by P. T. Bidwell and C. G. Henderson on the site of St Mary Major in 1971 (Fig. 1). These showed that the chapel stood about 30 m (107 ft) due west of the north-west corner of the modern west front. It was a free-standing building, oblong in shape, orientated eastwards and measuring at least 12 m (39½ ft) by 6.5 m (21 ft) externally. Beneath the chapel lay a crypt of the same dimensions and about 3 m (9½ ft) deep, entered by a flight of steps at the south end of the west side. The excavations revealed a mass of bones in the crypt, about one metre deep, many of them sorted into groups of arms, legs and skulls.[1] Until the 17th century, the open ground in the Close constituted the chief cemetery of the city of Exeter, and the charnel chapel and crypt owed their existence to this fact.[2]

Charnel chapels, situated close to charnels, seem to have developed in England during the 13th century, and were often simply known as 'charners' or 'charnels' without the addition of 'chapel'.[3] Charnels and chapels can be traced at several cathedrals, both secular foundations like Exeter and St Paul's, and monastic such as Norwich, Worcester and Winchester. Others occur at the abbey of Bury St Edmunds, the collegiate church of Beverley, the hospital of St Mary-without-Bishopsgate (London), and at several parish churches: Bodmin, Holy Trinity (Cambridge), St Michael (Coventry) and St Alphege, Cripplegate (London). The usual site was in the cemetery, north of the church as at St Paul's and St Mary's Abbey (Winchester), or west of it in the case of Exeter, Norwich and Winchester Cathedral. There was no standard patron saint of charnel chapels. We encounter St Anne (Barnstaple), St Edmund of Abingdon and St Mary Magdalene (St Mary-without-Bishopsgate), St Mary the Virgin (St Paul's), St Thomas Becket (Worcester), Holy Trinity (St Mary's, Winchester), and Holy Trinity and Our Lady (High Wycombe). Exeter's chapel, as we shall see, may have been successively dedicated to St Edward, St Edmund and St Mary the Virgin. Many charnel chapels had chantry priests celebrating daily masses inside them, funded by private individuals or by religious guilds. The chapels could also be used to accommodate burials and tombs with effigies, as at St Paul's. Sermons were preached in or near them, as at Exeter and St Mary's-without-Bishopsgate, and legal transactions could be held inside them as at St Augustine's (Canterbury). Worcester's charnel chapel even housed a library for the use of the local clergy. In short, the chapels had a variety of characteristics and uses, rather than uniform ones, and the name 'charnel chapel' appears to refer to their siting rather than their functions. Apart from sanctifying the nearby charnel house by their presence, they seem to have lacked specific roles with regard to funerals, burials or prayers for the dead.

The earliest certain reference to the Exeter charnel chapel comes in 1322. As this is not an act of foundation but merely the first mention, more than one historian has conjectured that the charnel chapel was older and identical with one of the chapels which are known to have

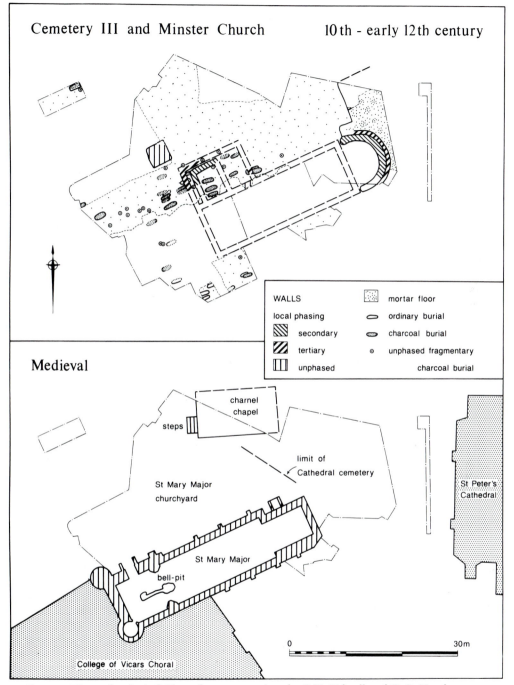

Cemetery III and Minster Church · 10th - early 12th century

WALLS

local phasing

- secondary
- tertiary
- unphased

- mortar floor
- ordinary burial
- charcoal burial
- unphased fragmentary

charcoal burial

Medieval

charnel chapel

steps

limit of Cathedral cemetery

St Mary Major churchyard

St Peter's Cathedral

St Mary Major

bell-pit

0   30m

College of Vicars Choral

FIG. 1. Plans of cathedral Close, from excavations by P. T. Bidwell and C. G. Henderson on the site of St Mary Major in 1971

existed in the cathedral Close in the 13th century. There were eight of these chapels: St Edward, St Mary Minor, St Michael, St Peter Minor and St Simon-and–St Jude, together with St Martin, St Mary Major and St Petrock, which eventually became parish churches.[4] All but the first two can be ruled out immediately, because they occupied known sites different from that of the charnel chapel, and possess distinct and separate histories. So can St Mary Minor, since although its location is not certain, it was united in about 1285 with St Mary Major and thus became part of the parish of that church.[5] The charnel chapel, on the other hand, was under the direct control of the cathedral and lay in the extra-parochial area of the Close. This leaves the chapel of St Edward: a difficult topic in itself. There are only two references to such a chapel, one in about 1214 and one in 1286. Historians have generally assumed that they relate to the same building, but the evidence is worth re-examining.

In about 1214 Peter de Palerna made his well-known grant of 1d. a year to each of 28 named chapels in Exeter. The chapels, as Frances Rose-Troup observed in 1923, are listed in a systematic order which proceeds along the four main streets of the city, 'St Edward' occurring between St John Bow in Fore Street and St Edmund on Exe bridge.[6] Mrs Rose-Troup hypothesised that the compiler of the list committed an aberration after St John Bow and went back the to cathedral Close to include a chapel of St Edward which he had left out. She took this view because she knew that such a chapel was recorded in the Close in 1286, supposed that it already existed in 1214, and therefore sought to find it in Palerna's list.[7] Such a theory is unnecessary, and indeed unwarranted. No evidence exists for the chapel of St Edward in the Close before 1286, although we know a good deal about the topography of that area, and it is highly unlikely that the writer of Palerna's list, who is so careful to proceed systematically, should make such a bad mistake. The suspicion grows to conviction when we find that Palerna's list leaves out the church of St Mary Steps which occupies an ancient site between St John Bow and St Edmund. It is much more logical to suppose that 'St Edward' is an earlier name for the church of St Mary Steps, than for a chapel only known at a later date in another part of the city.[8] The chapel in Palerna's list can therefore be eliminated from the ancestry of the charnel chapel.

The evidence of 1286 is better. On 5 January in that year an inquisition *ad quod damnum* agreed that John de Exonia, treasurer of Exeter Cathedral, might without damage to the king grant a rent in Exeter to a 'chapel of St Edward the King in the cemetery of St Peter of Exeter next to the minster of St Peter' (*capella sancti Edwardi regis in cimiterio beati Petri Exonie juxta monasterium beati Petri*). The rent was to maintain two chaplains in the chapel. On 20 February the crown issued letters patent sanctioning the grant and employing virtually the same terminology.[9] John de Exonia appears to be the alias of John Picot, the treasurer who claimed the deanship of the cathedral and was accused of complicity in the murder of the precentor, Walter Lechlade, in 1283. When Edward I came to Exeter at Christmas 1285 to supervise the trial of the laymen responsible, Picot was handed over to the bishop to be tried as a cleric.[10] It would have been an appropriate punishment to make him build a chapel and endow priests in it, praying for Lechlade's soul. The chapel is more likely to have been new than pre-existing, because there is no previous mention of it and its dedication fits the events of 1285–6 particularly well. 'Edward the King' could refer either to St Edward king and martyr (d. 978) or St Edward king and confessor (d. 1066),[11] but the latter's cult was greater than the former's by the late 13th century, and Edward I was actually named after the Confessor. What more appropriate than that Picot should choose the king's own patron saint, and certainly his namesake, as the dedication for his reparative chapel. True, the two chaplains were never founded. We know this because they do not appear in later times, and it looks significant that another chantry in memory of Walter

Lechlade was founded in the cathedral in 1292.[12] But the chapel is a different case. When John Leland visited Exeter in about 1540–3, he noted that the charnel chapel was 'made by one John Tr[esurer of] the cathedral church of Ex[cester]'. This fits Picot better than the other treasurers named John, who either lived before or after the charnel chapel is known to have existed. Leland's evidence is late and unique, but it accords with the other indications that the charnel chapel originated with Picot in the 1280s.[13]

The next mention of the chapel, the first definite one, occurs on 2 March 1322 when Walter Stapledon, bishop of Exeter, endowed a chantry priest to say services 'in the chapel which is situated in the churchyard (*atrium*) or cemetery of the major church of Exeter, commonly called "charnere"'.[14] This tells us that the chapel already existed, and simply relates to a chantry foundation inside it. It also introduces the habit, which remained virtually general down to the Reformation, of calling the building 'the charnel chapel' rather than by the name of a saint. St Edward, if he was the original patron, became forgotten. Stapledon's foundation was accompanied by an elaborate ordinance. The chantry priest was to be financed by the synodal and chrism dues belonging to the bishop from the archdeaconry of Totnes. He was to be appointed by Stapledon while the bishop lived, and afterwards by the dean or the chapter, and his stipend was to be £3 13s. 4d. a year. He was to say all the usual daily offices, daily prayers for the dead (*placebo, dirige* and commendation), and a daily mass in the early morning after the first cathedral masses (the Bratton masses) had been said at dawn. While Stapledon was alive the mass was to be either the normal daily mass or a votive mass in honour of the Holy Ghost, and after his death it was to be a mass of *requiem*. Intercessions were to be made at the mass for the souls of Stapledon, the other bishops of Exeter, and all the faithful departed. Four previous bishops had chantries founded in their memory in the cathedral, and Stapledon evidently wished to have the same, despite the anomaly that the chantry would be in the charnel chapel while his tomb was to be inside the main building. The first chantry priest, John de Lideforde, was appointed on 18 March 1323. In addition to his liturgical duties he was told to help the subdean (who was penitentiary of the cathedral) in hearing confessions and imposing penances.[15] A large number of people lived in the cathedral Close before the Black Death, including some 80 resident clergy and over 100 lay servants, and the subdean must have needed some help with his work.

From 1323, therefore, the charnel chapel housed a priest saying prayers at intervals throughout the day, and a daily mass. Apart from this, the chapel seems to have had no general public role with regard to the dead. The funerals of Exeter people were held in the cathedral itself, and there is no mention (despite much documentation) of any body resting or being buried inside the chapel, or any funeral taking place there or funeral offerings being made. Visitors to the graves in the cemetery may have used the chapel for private prayer, but even this is not recorded. Rather, the chapel was simply a chapel over a charnel house, as there were chapels over bridges or city gates, and like charnel chapels elsewhere it was to have a variety of uses during its history rather than a specialised function. Appointments of priests to Stapledon's chantry are virtually unrecorded after 1323, but they probably continued up to the Black Death of 1348–9 and then stopped. The plague caused a recruitment crisis in the Church since the fall in the number of clergy, followed by a rise of wages and prices, made it hard to attract men to serve as poorly-paid chantry priests when better benefices were available. Lists survive of the cathedral chantry priests (or annuellars as they were called) in 1359 and regularly after 1384,[16] and the Stapledon priest is not mentioned among them save for a single brief exception. On 14 December 1393 the cathedral chapter appointed Walter Marker as chantry priest in the charnel chapel, at a time when clerical recruitment was improving and other vacant chantries were being filled.[17] But

Marker did not stay for long; by 1395 he had moved to another post, and the charnel chantry was again suspended, this time until 1508.[18]

It is uncertain whether any other liturgical activity went on in the chapel during the second half of the 14th century. The building survived, however, for in 1391 the chapter forbade the playing of ball against its walls,[19] and in 1426 services in the chapel begin to be mentioned again. In that year the chapter gave permission for the chapel to be used by the city guild of skinners: one of several craft guilds which emerged in Exeter during the late 14th and early 15th centuries. As well as their economic functions, these guilds had religious interests, dedicating themselves to God or a saint and observing the appropriate Church festival as their feast-day.[20] The skinners were dedicated to Corpus Christi, and by 1413 they acted a play each year on the day of this feast, the Thursday after Trinity Sunday.[21] On Corpus Christi 1426 the skinners transferred the religious part of their celebrations to the cathedral and the charnel chapel, with the chapter's agreement. The choice of the chapel may not have been fortuitous. In London the skinners had already adopted the charnel chapel at St Paul's as their chapel by 1416, and three of their officers were eventually buried there beneath imposing tombs with effigies.[22] In Chester the craft was responsible for acting the Resurrection of Jesus Christ in the local cycle of mystery plays, with mentions of the dead and their graves.[23] As skinners were involved with carcasses and bones, there was a certain grim aptness in the choice of a charnel chapel for their religious devotions.

The celebrations of 1426 are recorded in an unusually elaborate memorandum in the cathedral obit accounts, which normally only list the payments of money at masses for the dead. The memorandum tells us that the skinners joined in the usual Corpus Christi procession held by the cathedral clergy in the Close and round the nearby streets, attended the high mass which followed it, and offered 9s. 3d. in money. On the following day they went to a second mass in the charnel chapel, and offered a further 2s. 7d.[24] There is no mention of the observance in the following year. But in 1428 10s. 6d. is recorded being offered by the skinners in the cathedral on Corpus Christi, and in 1429 9s. 9d., plus 11d. in respect of half the offerings in the charnel chapel. A note explains that the chapter let the skinners keep half their offerings in the charnel chapel on condition that these were used for ornaments for the altar there, implying that the skinners had adopted the chapel as their own place of worship. In 1430 10s. 5d. was offered in the cathedral and in 1431 7s., after which the entries, both about the cathedral and the charnel chapel, disappear from the obit accounts.[25] The skinners may have ceased their connection on the grounds that they got little in return for their offerings, or they may have gone on using the chapel without this being recorded.

The next to appear in occupation of the chapel are the vicars choral of the cathedral. In November 1451 their accounts of property and income in Exeter include a fine being levied on one of the vicars for absence from the 'mass of benefactors in the charnel'.[26] Similar fines are mentioned in subseqent years, sometimes for absence from the 'charnel mass', sometimes from the mass 'in the charnel'.[27] Being fines for absences, they occur irregularly, but they seem to relate to masses which were held every month, towards the beginning of the month. In one year the masses are always held on the first Wednesday, in others on the first Thursday, Friday or Saturday, the weekday varying from year to year.[28] This makes it virtually certain that the 'charnel mass' is the same as the 'kalendar mass' which vicars were also fined for not attending. The kalendar mass was a mass of commemoration for the members (living and dead) of the Exeter guild of Kalendars, a religious society of clergy, laymen and laywomen, who met from about 1200 once a month in the church of St Mary Major to celebrate the mass. The guild had property nearby, including a graveyard for burials, which gave rise to the street-name Kalendarhay, but in the middle of the 14th century the members seem to have transferred their property to the vicars choral (whose college was subsequently built in this area) in return for the vicars undertaking the monthly masses. The vicars had no chapel in their college, and as the masses were not strictly a cathedral activity, the charnel chapel (lying close to the college) was a good alternative choice. Charnel masses go on being referred to in the vicars' records down to 1542, and probably continued until the abolition of masses for the dead in 1548–9.[29]

In the early 16th century, the role of the charnel chapel grew to encompass daily, monthly and annual services, not to mention non-liturgical functions. This reflected a general revival of activity at the cathedral between about 1480 and the beginning of the Reformation in the 1530s.[30] Constitutionally the period saw Bishop Oldham endow the vicars choral with new property in 1508, so that meals could be provided in their college (hitherto the vicars had eaten with their canons). In 1528 a new house was provided to accommodate the chantry priests, and reforms were made to other groups of the cathedral clergy, including the adolescent secondary clerks and the choristers. New statutes were drawn up, new festivals and votive antiphons introduced and new pieces of music composed for services. The cathedral building began to be too small for all the activities going on. Three chapels, those of St Edmund, St James and St Mary Magdalene, had passed out of use in the 14th and 15th centuries, and it was necessary in the 1510s to build two extra ones, the Speke and Oldham chapels: the first major additions to the cathedral since the Black Death. The use of the charnel chapel also increased. Lying close to the west front, it became an obvious place to house liturgical and other activities which could not be accommodated inside the main building.

The first evidence for this enhanced role comes from a comprehensive inventory of the cathedral's goods, drawn up in 1506. The text was printed by George Oliver in 1861, in his cathedral history, but the original has since disappeared. It lists the cathedral's movable contents in a rough topographical order from east to west, continues with a catalogue of the library which lay in the cloisters, and ends by describing the 'chapel of St Edmund over the charnel in the cemetery' (capella sancti Edmundi supra ossilegium in cimiterio).[31] This phrase has puzzled some historians.[32] Does it refer to the charnel chapel, or to the chapel of St Edmund at the west end of the nave, which is not otherwise mentioned in the inventory? If the former is correct, did Oliver or his source misread St Edmund for St Edward — the dedication of Picot's chapel in 1286? These problems disappear when they are examined in the context of cathedral history. St Edmund's chapel in the nave is not mentioned in use liturgically after 1337, and probably ceased to be so used at the Black Death when clerical recruitment fell.[33] The chantry priests who had previously served it were transferred to other chapels,[34] and by 1506 it had no altar or ornaments and was hence left out of the inventory. The place may already have been occupied by the bishop's consistory court, as it was in later centuries, which would explain why it was not brought back into service as a chapel when space was again at a premium after 1500. The reference of 1506 must therefore be, as it appears, to the charnel chapel. As for the dedication, St Edward is unlikely to have survived or been known in 1506, since it is nowhere mentioned after 1286. St Edmund may be a mistake, through confusing the long-disused nave chapel with the charnel chapel, or the cult of St Edmund may actually have been transferred from the one chapel to the other. Whatever the case, the dedication to Edmund failed to stick. It is not recorded again, and from 1510 to 1515 ordinations of clergy in Exeter are regularly recorded taking place 'in the chapel of the Blessed Mary the Virgin inside the cemetery of the cathedral church of Exeter' (in capella beate Marie Virginis infra cimiterium ecclesie cathedralis).[35] Only the charnel chapel could have been referred to in this way, and it looks as though the dedication had been changed yet again — a practice which need not surprise us, as it occurs elsewhere in Exeter.[36]

The inventory of 1506 shows that the charnel chapel was well stocked with a chalice, service books, vestments and altar cloths, several of them given by John Major, one of the contemporary chantry priests.[37] Two years later, on 12 June 1508, Bishop Oldham revived the Stapledon chantry and reintroduced daily services in the chapel. Noting that no clergy could be found to staff the chantry because of the poverty of the stipend, he transferred the endowment of £3 13s. 4d. a year to the vicars choral, on condition that they celebrated mass there one by one in turn for a week at a time.[38] Oliver states that the cathedral treasurer, John Ryse, founded a second daily mass for his soul in the chapel on 18 March 1522 (perhaps 1523 modern style), but the source for this cannot be found and the institution is not confirmed by other records.[39] Ryse or his executors, on the other hand, certainly granted property in Preston Street to the cathedral chantry priests at some date before 1535, in return for them celebrating an annual obit mass in the charnel house for the souls of Ryse, his parents and his friends.[40] The choristers too became involved with the chapel at this time. In 1527 the chapter agreed that 'when the last antiphons at the cathedral and the charnel house were over', the boys should stand in the west porch of the cathedral and sing the psalm *De Profundis*, facing the grave of Laurence Dobell, rector of St Mary Major.[41] This reveals a regular daily visit by the choristers in the late afternoon to sing a votive antiphon in the charnel chapel.

Early 16th-century Catholicism was not only liturgical; its leaders also emphasised education and preaching, and these too figure in the charnel chapel on the eve of the Reformation. Cemeteries were obvious places for open-air sermons to large congregations. The charnel chapel of St Mary-without-Bishopsgate (London) adjoined an open-air pulpit and an elaborate two-storey gallery, built so that visiting notables could sit to hear the sermons.[42] The Exeter charnel chapel had an outside pulpit by 1534 when it was employed by Hugh Latimer on his preaching tour through the west country to explain the Church policy of Henry VIII. According to John Hooker, the late 16th-century historian of Exeter, Latimer preached

yn the charnell howse which was then standinge yn the churcheyard of the saide citee, out of which howse was a pulpytt yn the north wall towards the churcheyarde.[43]

Inside, the chapel was utilised in the 1530s and 1540s for the reading of theological lectures to the local clergy. Such lectures had been given somewhere or another in Exeter since the 12th century, and in 1283 Bishop Quinil had annexed the revenues of the parish of Newlyn in Cornwall to the cathedral chancellorship on condition that the chancellor gave regular lectures to the clergy on theology or canon law.[44] The lectures are mentioned intermittently up to the early 15th century, and either survived or were revived under Bishop Veysey in the early 16th century. By this time they were given by other well-educated members of the chapter, as well as the chancellor, and took place in the charnel chapel. Hooker informs us that Robert Tregonwell, canon from 1537 to 1543,

dyd rede the dyvinitie lecture yn the charnell howse to his great commendation and dyd meanteyne Luthers doctryne yn some poyntes as also miche dysprasid the corrupte state and arrogonicys of the pope,[45]

while Nicholas Weston, subdean from 1539 to 1547,

dyd rede the dyvinitie lecture yn the charnell house to the great proffet of his auditory and commendation to himselff.[46]

This function of the chapel is closely paralleled at Worcester. There the equivalent chapel and its chantry were adapted by Bishop Carpenter between 1458 and 1464 to house a library, staffed by a theology graduate, who had to read lectures to the local clergy and supervise them when they came to look at the books. The Worcester lectures, like those at Exeter, were still going on in the 1530s.[47]

The last references to the Exeter charnel come from a year or two afterwards. Leland observed the place on his visit, between about 1540 and 1543,[48] and the charnel masses (as we have noted) were still being held in 1542. The dates of the chapel's disuse and disappearance are not recorded, but probably took place between about 1548 and 1553.[49] In 1548 all chantries were abolished and their priests pensioned off, making redundant the various small chantry chapels inside the main cathedral building. Space became available inside for sermons and lectures, and the charnel chapel was no longer required for this purpose. In 1549 the new Protestant liturgy did away with the votive antiphons and requiem masses which had been the chapel's other main activities. It no longer possessed an obvious function. Protestants, like the dean Simon Heynes, may actively have wanted the building destroyed, seeing it as irretrievably associated with superstitious practices. Like minded clergy at St Paul's Cathedral organised the demolition of the charnel chapel there in 1548, and removed cartloads of bones from the charnel house for reburial at Finsbury Field.[50] At Exeter the building was also dismantled to ground level, and the charnel house filled in with material including pottery of the mid-16th century.[51] It is not clear what happened to stray bones after this date and whether another repository was found for them. When Hooker came to write about the history of Exeter under Elizabeth I, he mentioned the chapel two or three times, but casually and without much interest.[52] To a Protestant like himself it already belonged to a remote and irrelevant past.

REFERENCES

1. Henderson and Bidwell (1982), 151, 168–9. In general an excellent article, I dissent from it (as the following pages will show) with regard to the history of St Edward's chapel, the identity of St Edward and the exact date of the demolition of the charnel chapel.

2. 'Charnel' comes from the Latin *carnarium*, deriving from *caro*, 'flesh'. The Latin word originally meant 'a flesh-hook' or 'a larder', but in medieval usage it acquired the grimmer meaning of 'a mass grave'. The word entered the English language via French, and the earliest usages in documents north of the Channel, during the 13th and early 14th centuries, follow the chief French forms of 'charner' or 'charnere'. 'Charnel' became the dominant spelling later in the 14th century, and an adjective 'carnary' is also found. On the etymology, see Du Cange (1937), II, 176–7, and Latham (1981), fasc. ii, 284 (Latin); Toblers and Lommatzsch (1936), II, 275 (Old French); *OED* (1933), II, under 'carnary', 'charnel', and Kurath and Kuhn (1959), 'C', 173 (Middle English).

3. One was founded at Worcester Cathedral by Bishop William of Blois, between 1218 and 1236, and others are mentioned at St Paul's Cathedral (London) in 1282, St Augustine's Abbey (Canterbury) in 1287, and Malmesbury Abbey in *c*. 1296. They became quite common in English cemeteries during the later Middle Ages, probably due to density of burials which caused stray bones to rise to the surface or to be disturbed when new graves were made. A place to deposit the bones became desirable, so a house or crypt was built to contain them, called the charnel or charnel house, and this was often accompanied by a chapel. On charnel chapels in general, see Leland (1907–10), I, 184, 270; II, 107, 149; Cox (1913), 169–70; and Cook (1947), 37–8. Other evidence includes Beverley (Raine (1865), III, 179); Bury St Edmunds (*Calendar of Patent Rolls, 1292–1301*, 520); Canterbury, St Augustine's (Twysden (1652), 1942); London (Stow (1908), I, 167, 329–30; (Furnivall (1882), 75–6); Malmesbury (Brewer (1879), 124–5); Norwich (Lobel (1975), II, Norwich map 2); Winchester Cathedral (*VCH Hampshire*, II, map between 50–1, 59); and Worcester (*VCH Worcestershire*, IV, 411–12).

4. On the early chapels of Exeter, see Rose-Troup (1923), passim.

5. Owen (1974), 105. This is dated 1395 (*sic*). I prefer to read 1285, the year in which two other Exeter parishes (St Cuthbert and St Paul) were united (Exeter Cathedral Archives, Dean & Chapter (hereafter D&C) 2111). There is a reference to the vicar of St Mary Major borrowing the charter of union from the cathedral archives in 1411 (D&C 3550 f. 130ᵛ).

6. Rose-Troup (1923), V–VI, 19–20.

7. Ibid., 19–20, 34–7.
8. The earliest printed reference to St Mary Steps is in 1273 (Hingeston-Randolph (1889), 140).
9. London, Public Record Office, C 143/10/10; *Calendar of Patent Rolls, 1281–1292*, 222.
10. On the affair, see Rose-Troup (1942), 38–57. Although she states that Lechlade's body rested in the charnel chapel after the murder, I cannot find the fact in her sources and suspect this to be a conjecture, based on her belief that the 1214 chapel of St Edward was the charnel chapel.
11. For St Edward 'king and confessor', see *Ordinale Exon* (1909), I, 15, 267, 360.
12. Orme (1982), 17–18.
13. Leland (1907–10), I, 228.
14. Hingeston-Randolph (1892), 374–6.
15. Ibid., 148.
16. D&C 2587/1–2.
17. D&C 3550 f. 91.
18. Ibid., ff. 92ᵛ, 99ᵛ. The chantry is specifically noted as vacant in about the 1410s (D&C 3625 f. 86ᵛ).
19. D&C 3550 f. 72ᵛ
20. On the early Exeter guilds and their religious activities, see Youings (1968), 10–13.
21. Ibid., 10; Radford (1950), 241–2, quoting Exeter City Archives, Mayor's Court Roll, 1413–14 m 38d.
22. Stow (1908), I, 329–30.
23. Deimling (1916), II, 331.
24. 'Memorandum, that on the feast of Corpus Christi in the year of our lord 1426, the brothers of the fraternity of skinners of the city of Exeter first had and held the solemnity of their brotherhood in the charnel chapel in the cemetery of the cathedral church of Exeter, by licence of the dean and chapter. They went in procession with the choir of the said [cathedral] church and the rectors and chaplains of the city, going out by the west door of the church to the gate [i.e. Bear Gate] next to the house of the dean, and proceeding via Smithen Street to the High Street. They went along the High Street to the gate in St Martin's Street leading towards the cathedral cemetery, entered the cemetery as far as the corner of the treasurer's house, and went into the cathedral through the door by which they came out. Afterwards the brothers were present at the high mass of the cathedral and offered 11s. 10d., including 2s. 7d. which they offered at the mass celebrated in the [charnel] chapel on the morrow of the feast, which sum was divided among the canons' (D&C 3770 f. 202ᵛ).
25. D&C 3771.
26. VC, 22282 m 19.
27. VC 22235 m 2 to 22267 mm 2–3, passim.
28. On the history of the guild of Kalendars, see Orme (1977), 153–69.
29. VC 22267 mm 2–3. There is another reference to the charnel chapel in the fabric accounts of 1456–7, in which John Nott, one of the cathedral chantry priests, was paid 40s. 'for making a portion at the charnel' (*ad faciendum unum porcionem apud le charnere*) (D&C 2701). Was this a piece of building work, or a set portion of prayers?
30. On what follows, see Orme (1981), 88–9, 96–9; (1983), 83–4, 93–4; and (1986a) 31–2.
31. Oliver (1861), 375–6.
32. E.g. ibid., 217; Lega-Weekes (1915), 9.
33. I have found no reference later than *Ordinale Exon*, I, 277.
34. The priest of the Lechlade chantry was celebrating at St Paul's altar in 1385, and the priest of the Butler chantry (founded at St Edmund's altar in 1263: D&C 3672 f. 339ᵛ) at St Paul's altar in 1472 (Orme (1982), 13,18).
35. Exeter, Devon Record Office, Chanter XIII (The Register of Hugh Oldham), ff. 102ᵛ–122ᵛ. The Lady Chapel, the usual place for such ordinations, may have been unavailable because of the rebuilding at the east end to accommodate the new Speke and Oldham chapels.
36. As well as the change we have postulated in the case of St Mary Steps, the chapel in Exeter Castle was said to be dedicated to St Mary in 1486 but to the Holy Trinity in 1546 (*Calendar of Patent Rolls, 1485–1494*, 28; Snell (1961), 16.
37. Oliver (1861), 375–6.
38. D&C 2407.
39. Oliver (1861), 217.
40. D&C 195. The grant can be dated before 1535 because the men to whom it was made included James Northbroke who left the cathedral's service in that year (Orme (1980), 81).
41. D&C 3551 f. 39ᵛ.
42. Stow (1908), I, 167.
43. Devon Record Office, Exeter City Archives, Book 51, f. 342ᵛ. Similar open-air pulpits are a feature of the Breton churchyard 'close' chapels, commonly called charnel chapels and generally dedicated to St Anne (e.g. Guimilliau and Landivisiau).

44. On the history of theological lectures in Exeter, see Orme (1976), 52–3, with additions in Orme (1978a), 23.
45. Exeter City Archives, Book 51, f. 346ᵛ.
46. Ibid., f. 345.
47. On the Carnary library at Worcester, see Orme (1978b), 44–5.
48. Leland (1907–10), I, 228.
49. Henderson and Bidwell ((1982), 151, 168–9 wished to date the chapel's disappearance to the early 1540s, because it is not mentioned in the chantry surveys of 1546–8. The latter, however, are not complete, especially as regards the cathedral which managed to retain most of its chantry property (Orme (1979), 80–4).
50. Nichols (1852), 57; Stow (1908), I, 329–30.
51. Henderson and Bidwell (1982), 169.
52. Exeter City Archives, Book 51, ff. 342ᵛ, 345, 346ᵛ.

M

The Liturgical Furnishings of the Choir of Exeter Cathedral

By Veronica Sekules

The liturgical furnishings of the choir and high altar of Exeter Cathedral were complete by the time of the dedication of the high altar in 1328. Each one of these remarkable structures — the high altar reredos and the sedilia, the bishop's throne and the pulpitum — was conceived on a lavish scale. The designs and, perhaps above all, the sheer size of the furnishings signalled very clearly the importance which was attached to them, both as decorative and as functional objects. This paper sets out to examine why it was that these furnishings should have been given such precocious prominence in the rebuilding of the east end of the cathedral in the late 13th and early 14th centuries.

THE HIGH ALTAR REREDOS

The reredos of the high altar no longer exists, but was the most remarkable of all Exeter's liturgical furnishings.[1] Fortunately, much is known about it, largely from the fabric accounts,[2] but also from a few descriptions giving hints of its former appearance, and possibly also from surviving fragments.

In 1301–2 work began on the flooring of the chancel and in 1307, Bishop Bitton was buried on the lowest step before the high altar.[3] The altar account began as a separate section of the fabric rolls in 1316–7, the first two years being spent in the preparation of stone, principally from Beer quarry.[4] In 1318 John de Bannebiri was paid 100 shillings for constructing three vaults carrying the tabernacle of the high altar.[5] This was a considerable sum, £1 more than the woodcarvers were paid for the Bishop's throne, so this was likely to have been a substantial structure. It has been assumed, probably correctly, that accounts for the high altar tablature included those for the sedilia.[6] For the total scheme 48 images were made between 1321 and 1322. Three of these may have been for the tabernacles over the sedilia, the remaining 45 for the reredos.[7] Between 1321 and 1322, considerable quantities of colouring materials were bought for painting the sculpture: 12,800 gold foils, 2,900 silver foils, 2½ lb azure, 1 lb indigo, 4 lb verdigris, 14 lb vermilion and 2 lb cinople.[8] The whole composition was inscribed with 550 letters, which were undoubtedly identifying inscriptions.[9] Only two pieces of information survive giving us a hint about some of the iconography. The fabric accounts record that metal foils for the lily were purchased between 1321 and 1322, and this was presumably for inclusion with a figure of the Virgin in an Annunciation scene.[10] An inventory of 1506 also mentions silver-gilt crowns on the heads of Mary and Christ in 'frontispicio magni altaris', which implies that the pair were seated in majesty.[11] It is quite likely that a major part of the scheme was devoted to the life and glorification of the Virgin, to whom the high altar was partly dedicated. The prominence of the Annunciation would also have reflected the very high esteem at Exeter for the Archangel Gabriel, whose feast was accorded the same status as Easter and Christmas.[12] After the 1328 high altar dedication, Bishop Grandisson added to the permanent furnishings two silver-gilt figures of St Peter and St Paul, which stood to the left and right of the altar. He also donated a hanging pyx for the sacrament.[13]

In 1324–5, a final payment was made to Master John the goldsmith for the silver table.[14] This was undoubtedly the silver tabula, or retable, 'in frontispicio magni altari' mentioned in the 1327[15] inventory, which was also scantily described in the 16th century by John Leland, who said:

Bishop Stapledon made also the riche fronte of stonework at the high altar in the Cathedral church of Exeter and also made the riche silver table in the middle of it.[16]

By 1325, the whole composition was evidently complete, and was certainly so by 1327, the date at which the silver retable is mentioned in the inventory.

The reredos was set against a wall which was solid at least in its lower parts, for locks for doors behind the high altar were made between 1321 and 13. ¼, and a repair for three locks for three doors behind the altar is recorded in 1407.[17] These doors gave entry into a vestry beyond the high altar. At the Reformation, the reredos was stripped of all its images and the silver retable was removed. In 1638, the background stonework remained, rising from the sanctuary floor to the base of the east window. It was plastered over and Archdeacon Helyer commissioned a painted *trompe-l'œil* perspective.[18] This gives us at least the minimum dimensions of the reredos, confirming that the wall extended to the height of the east window. Archdeacon Helyer's reredos was replaced by another designed by John Kendall in 1818–22, and this in turn was replaced by Gilbert Scott in the 1870s.[19]

Evidence for the original appearance of the 14th-century reredos was examined by Percy Morris in two articles for the *Antiquaries Journal* for 1943 and 1944.[20] He noticed remains of attachments on the south side, to the sedilia (Pl. XXVIA), which are roughly chopped away in the upper parts. On the north side, at the east end of Stapledon's tomb he traced a base moulding in outline.[21] Percy Morris reconstructed the Exeter reredos as a composite, based on the design of the pulpitum and the sedilia at Exeter, and the Neville screen behind the high altar of Durham Cathedral, of some 60 years later.[22] John Carter's plan of 1797 confirms that the Exeter reredos was indeed attached to the east end of the sedilia.[23] It is very likely that from the design of the sedilia we can to some extent extrapolate the design of the reredos, always bearing in mind that what exists may differ considerably from the original, as in 1639 they were said to be dilapidated and in 1745 the pinnacles were pared down and stunted, then Kendall restored them in the 1820s, and in the 1870s Scott re-lengthened the pinnacles and inserted at least 1,400 pieces of new stone.[24] What Percy Morris's reconstruction does not take into account, however, is that we know that the reredos was built against a wall and was therefore not an openwork screen like the one at Durham. There is also the tantalising reference in the fabric accounts to the construction of the tabernacle upon three vaults. It implies at least a basic triple division and may indicate that the structure at the base was in deep relief. The triple division was clearly continued immediately above the reredos in the tracery design of the east window of the choir, which was either of six or of nine lights.[25]

Inside Stapledon's tomb against its east wall, Bishop and Prideaux and, later, Percy Morris, noticed remains of arcading and a portion of a cornice reset vertically, on which is carved a crawling figure of a king (Pl. XXVIB). The arcading they interpreted as pre-existing the tomb, which they took to have been built *c.* 1330, that is four years after Stapledon's murder. They suggested that the crawling king was part of the original south cornice to Stapledon's tomb which underwent, they postulated, restoration at some point in the medieval period.[26] However the king is in a markedly different style from the figures of angels carved on the north cornice, even bearing in mind that they have been recut. Analysis of the paint on the figure of the king seems to indicate a 17th-century date, and it is possible therefore that these fragments were placed here from the reredos when it was dismantled either at the Reformation, or when Archdeacon Helyer's screen was painted in 1638.[27]

One other fragment of the reredos may survive — the triple arches now built into the north wall of St Andrew's chapel (Pl. XIID). This curious structure has clearly been heavily patched and in this position for some time. Scott thought that it came from the reredos.[28] Percy Morris rejected this suggestion because the arches were made to rest against a flat wall surface (which he didn't accept for the reredos) and because the carving was too coarse in comparison with the sedilia. He preferred to suggest that it was an Easter sepulchre removed to make way for Stapledon's tomb.[29] According to this theory, the arches would have been in position for only three years between completion of the choir and erection of the tomb, and then removed and kept safe, but in damaged condition for 600 years. Quite apart from the unlikelihood of this having been the case, we know that Exeter followed Sarum in having a temporary sepulchre which was set up on Maundy Thursday and removed on the Friday of Easter week.[30] The St Andrew's chapel arches are certainly carved more crudely than the present-day sedilia, however, as Percy Morris himself pointed out, the bays are of the same width, and like the sedilia they are slightly faceted and projecting as if they were designed as a canopy for a large opening or niche. Both stylistically and in terms of their scale, they are also very like the principal arches of the bishop's throne. These arches thus demonstrably conform with the designs of the choir furnishings and it seems most likely that they are souvenirs from the 14th-century reredos placed in St Andrew's chapel following their removal by Archdeacon Helyer.

The reredos was built on a substantial scale, apparently as a series of niches for ranks of figures, 45 in all, rising upon three vaults up to the sill of the east window of the choir. At this date, between 1316 and 1325, such a grand structure, free-standing behind the altar and closing it off completely from the area behind, is exceptional and possibly unique. Very few comparable English 14th-century examples are known. Apart from the Neville screen at Durham, these include the lost screen at Peterborough, the stripped and restored reredos at Ottery St Mary, and the most complete, preserving some of its sculpture, at Christchurch, Hampshire. All of these post-date Exeter; the Peterborough screen seems to have dated from c. 1330 or later, Ottery is 1340–50, and Christchurch, c. 1350.[31] As Christopher Wilson has pointed out, the Ottery St Mary and Christchurch examples have such close links with Exeter, they may well reflect its design.[32] That at Ottery, with its basic triple division, may have been a very similar, though smaller version.

The design for the Exeter reredos seems to have developed from a type of low altar-screen which was well established by the 13th century. A representative example was constructed in the Angel Choir at Lincoln Cathedral, where a wall behind the high altar extended for the width of the choir. It contained doors giving access to a sacristy, but the structure was low enough to enable the shrine of St Hugh to be seen rising behind and above the altar.[33] A similar arrangement for showing numerous shrines may be seen in a 15th-century drawing of the high altar of St Augustine's Canterbury (Pl. XXVIc). The custom of placing saints' shrines raised at the back of altars, so that they could be seen from the choir, may be the key to the inspiration for the Exeter reredos.

Exeter had many relics, the majority of them reputedly donated by King Athelstan. The most significant were: a portion of the true cross, some of the hair of Christ, a bit of the body of John the Baptist, the head of St Stephen, part of the head of St Nicaise and the finger of St Mary Magdalene.[34] All the relics were disposed about the church at altars, within images, within processional crosses, the smaller ones collected into reliquaries. The most important, like the finger of St Mary Magdalene were, by 1506, collected in the Lady Chapel.[35] However, at the date of the erection of the reredos, by 1325, there was no relic so important and unique as to make Exeter a place of particular pilgrimage — there was no entire body, not even a local saint. Perhaps precisely because of this, the formidable group of holy images at the high altar, rising from the floor to the stained-glass window above, was intended to simulate the effect of a vast reliquary, in a grander and more lavish arrangement than that recorded to date in any other church. The Virgin, St Peter, and St Paul to whom the altar was dedicated were naturally particularly honoured here, but part of the purpose of this dramatic display was surely to give particular emphasis to the importance of the high altar as the centre of the liturgy, the more so as there was no rival holy site here. The great reredos could well have been a form elaborated, or even invented by Exeter for this very purpose.

THE BISHOP'S THRONE

The bishop's throne is another example of a furnishing which seems to have been specially elaborated at Exeter, in order to emphasise the bishop's status and authority. It was carved in 1316–17 by Robert de Galmeton and an associate, images were made for it between 1317 and 1320, and it was painted and inscribed with 250 letters in 1323–4, so as with the altar reredos, its decoration served a didactic purpose.[36] Of its images, six angels survive, five holding liturgical vessels for censing and anointing, the other with a book. Though it was a normal convention for the bishop to have the principal stall at the east end of the south side of the choir, next to that of the chancellor, there seems to be no precedent anywhere earlier than Exeter for a throne on this scale.[37] From here, the place of the bishop is visible even from the nave, and it is a clear symbol of his supremacy and authority. Bishop Stapledon, who commissioned the throne was Lord High Treasurer to Edward II, Professor of Canon Law at Oxford and had been appointed papal chaplain by Pope Clement V. He had justification for pretensions to grandeur.[38] However, there is some evidence for this being a tradition among bishops of Exeter and that foundations were perhaps being laid for a 'cult of bishops' in preparation for the time when one might be canonised.

Bishop Peter Quinil may have been working towards the promotion of a cult of bishops at Exeter. The design of his seal is revealing of his attitude to his status (Pl. XXVID). He is represented enthroned and beneath a canopy. Although there had been a number of 12th-century versions of this design, it is most unusual for an English bishop's seal of the late 13th century. Only one other comparable example is known, that of Anthony Bek of Durham, and his does not include a canopy.[39] The seal it most resembles is the contemporary Exeter Chapter seal showing St Peter enthroned beneath a canopy. It may be significant that the bishop shared the same christian name as the patron saint, but the comparison is more likely to have been intended to emphasise that Exeter bishops were invested with special authority directly from the patron saint. Significantly, the image of St Peter dating from c. 1304 in the great East window, shows the saint vested with the highest earthly authority, as Pope.[40] Another factor which may have been relevant was that the feast of St Peter's Chair on 22 February, traditionally the day on which St Peter was enthroned as Bishop of Rome, had the second highest grading at Exeter, a status shared only by Peterborough Abbey, whereas at other cathedrals, even at York which was also dedicated to St Peter, it was of lesser grading.[41]

Quinil was specially honoured after his death as the builder of the new work, and the rebuilding of the east end of the church itself may well reflect still wider ambitions at Exeter to enhance the status of its bishops.[42] A remarkable number of east end rebuilding schemes for English cathedrals during the 13th century were undertaken either shortly after the canonisation of a bishop, or at the time of petition to the Pope for a canonisation, with a partial, or sometimes a major intention to provide grand and spacious settings for their shrines. These included Old St Paul's, Lichfield, Lincoln, Chichester, Worcester, Salisbury, York and Winchester.[43] Miracles were attested at the tombs of other bishops, such as Bishop Walter of Suffield, the builder of the Lady Chapel at Norwich, who died in 1257, and Bishop William Button II of Wells, venerated from 1274, without, in either case, any formal approaches towards canonisation.[44] Lincoln almost had a triumvirate of bishop saints in the Angel Choir although only St Hugh was officially canonised, but Bishop Remigius had long been locally venerated and applications to the Pope on behalf of Grosseteste were current at the time of the dedication of its altar in 1280.

By the 1320s, Exeter was thus very much the exception among English sees, in not enshrining either the remains of a canonised bishop or even of a venerated one, but it does appear that successive bishops either held out hopes, or at least devised various methods for drawing attention to their status. Quinil's successor, Thomas de Bitton, continued the work of building the church and was buried in 1307 before the lowest step of the high altar in the presbytery.[45] He had instituted in 1300 a curious variation on a chantry, whereby he granted 40 days' indulgence for all penitents who would avail themselves of his ministry, or pray for his prosperity in life, or the repose of his and his relations' departed souls after death.[46] The Cathedral Customs, as collated by Grandisson, provide evidence of a tradition of continual reverence for both living and departed Bishops. Much was made of the censing of bishops during Mass, whether they were officiating or not, and this was done immediately after the censing of the high altar.[47] This was most unusual, the normal procedure being that the altars in the choir were censed, then the officiating priests, then the tombs of saints, then the dignitaries seated in the principal stalls.[48] One of the earlier Exeter customs expressly forbidden by Grandisson in his ordinal was the practice of censing the tombs of bishops in the choir or elsewhere in the church, which he permitted to continue only if they were canonised.[49] The reason for this injunction was undoubtedly to curtail the eager veneration for his predecessor, James Berkeley. He only officiated for 14 months from 1326 to 1327, but his cult was locally popular until the 1340s.[50] Presumably Grandisson was not prepared to promote Berkeley's canonisation any further, perhaps he was hoping that he might be a better candidate himself, or perhaps he was attempting altogether to stop the veneration of bishops at Exeter.

Bishop Stapledon's tomb is of great interest in the context of the aggrandisement of the status of bishops at Exeter. Its site, to the north of the high altar, is the equivalent of that of Bishop Niger at Old St Paul's, Osmund at Salisbury and Remigius in the Angel Choir at Lincoln. All were venerated as saints. Osmund was eventually canonised in the 15th century, but Niger and Remigius never were. I have suggested in an earlier volume of these Transactions that in the case of Remigius, the placing of his tomb next to the Tomb of Christ was a deliberate means of according him the honour of the Saviour's special protection. This related to a continental tradition dating back to the 9th century, and at Lincoln may well have been adopted precisely in order to draw attention to Remigius's blessedness.[51] In a less obvious way, Stapledon's tomb also conforms to this tradition, in that facing his effigy, a full-length portrait of the Resurrected Christ displaying His wounds was painted on the tester.[52] This confrontation would have had extra resonance when the Easter Sepulchre was erected nearby, or possibly against this tomb, on Maundy Thursday. It could even be an indication of an early desire to promote the canonisation of Stapledon, which in the end proved impossible. However, whatever was his posthumous fate, there is no doubt that, during his lifetime, Stapledon had the highest ambitions. That he should have commissioned the biggest bishop's throne ever known would not only be characteristic of these, but would evidently have conformed to long-standing ambitions of his predecessors on behalf of themselves and the renown of their cathedral.

THE PULPITUM (Pl. XXXIVa)

The pulpitum was built between 1318 and 1325 according to the fabric rolls, from which we learn that it incorporated 45 images, 11 panels with a Judgement, and a further 12 images in the two furthest panels.[53] These panels are arranged above the three great canopies which form the base of the structure on its western side, the centre one of which opens into the choir, and the two side ones originally providing space for altars. It thus takes the form of a substantial balcony. Passion scenes are most likely to have accompanied the Judgement, but all that survives are tiny traces of indecipherable carvings in the centre panel of the front, and a dove emerging from clouds in the side return panel on the south.[54]

The pulpitum is one of a group of early 14th-century great stone screens, erected in order to separate the choir almost completely from the nave. Other examples of similar date are at Lincoln, Southwell, St David's and formerly at Old St Paul's. None of these pulpita is likely to have pre-dated the Exeter one, and none took precisely the same form. The pulpitum of Old St Paul's probably dates from the mid- to late 1320s.[55] It did not take the balcony form and apparently did not have panels of religious scenes, but was adorned with a series of single figures placed in niches facing west along the nave. The Lincoln pulpitum, which is probably contemporary with the remodelling of the south transept, c. 1335, is very similar to the St Paul's design, with rich foliage and diaper background decoration for the figures.[56] An important forerunner, possibly the prototype for these two pulpita, was likely to have been that built for the new choir of Salisbury, c. 1260. It was made of purbeck marble, some 12 feet deep, and reputedly had statues of kings arranged in large niches facing west.[57] It also had smaller niches above them which possibly contained religious scenes, although there is no surviving record. The St David's and Southwell pulpita were probably built during the late 1330s, and are closer to the Exeter design in that they are without niches for statues, but instead incorporate side niches for altars within the west face. However, neither has panels above the openings for religious scenes. The basic structure of these three pulpita may relate to the Old Sarum pulpitum, as excavated by St John Hope, which had altars against its west face.[58] Panels of religious imagery were not uncommon on English pulpita, but generally also belonged to an earlier tradition, like the 12th-century examples formerly existing at Christchurch, Canterbury, and at Durham. In Germany, comparable examples survive from the mid-13th century, such as the west pulpitum at Naumburg, which incorporates a series of Passion scenes on stone panels above the opening arch. A similar structure, now only surviving in fragments, was at Mainz Cathedral, only this, like that at Exeter, was carved with a Judgement cycle.

The design for the Exeter pulpitum appears to be quite traditional; however, given the large-scale disappearance of these furnishings, it is not possible to be precise about derivations. Exeter introduced the balcony pulpitum as part of its general desire to create a set of dramatic furnishings for the choir. The preference here for the use of religious imagery is consistent with the overriding emphasis among the Exeter furnishings on the religious doctrine of the church. The Judgement of Christ is represented directly at the entrance to the choir. It sets the scene for the choir and iconographically it could be viewed as a pair to the reredos, with its triumph of Christ and the Virgin among a heavenly host. One would, as it were, pass through Judgement on entering the choir, and approach the Heavenly Court in Paradise displayed on the reredos.

CONCLUSION

The aggrandisement of the liturgical furnishings at Exeter: the deliberate stress on scale and height in the case of the throne, the high altar, emphasised with its innovative reredos and the pulpitum with its religious imagery, may be a manifestation of a deliberate policy to stress the importance of the liturgy at Exeter. What we know of the liturgy is primarily from Bishop Grandisson's ordinal, and the group of furnishings predate it by at least ten years. However, in codifying Exeter's liturgical practices and imposing on them a Sarum model, Grandisson did state that he was retaining Exeter peculiarities and it is possible to extrapolate a number of the distinctive features which predate his reform and indicate that certain aspects of the liturgy were always particularly elaborate.[59]

In 1275, Bishop Bronescombe instituted a statute that no vicar or other inferior minister or clergyman was allowed to officiate in choir, whatever his learning or emoluments, unless he could play a musical instrument or had knowledge of singing.[60] From this one can surmise that the extensive directions for singing in polyphony, which are evident in Grandisson's books, would seem not to have been entirely his initiative. Bronescombe also instituted the feast of St Gabriel in 1278 as a feast of major grading.[61] Exeter had more double feasts than any other English church — 65 as opposed to the 50 according to Sarum — and had one extra grade of double feast.[62] Again, the grading was probably rationalised by Grandisson, but the number of feasts was apparently inherited from earlier customs. There are other Exeter peculiarities, in addition to those pertaining to bishops mentioned earlier, such as genuflection to the altar at the *Incarnatus* in the Creed rather than inclination as practised elsewhere, and a distinctive sequence of liturgical colours.[63] All this suggests a possibility that the Exeter liturgy was elaborated to the extent of being an attraction in its own right, equivalent to that of a cult. No doubt this was motivated partly by the fact that, without an important relic or local saint, Exeter could not be a legitimate place of pilgrimage, and that instead it became of paramount importance to find other means by which to promote the status of the church. Lacking a glittering bank of shrines at the high altar, Exeter chose to magnify the authority of the Church and its ministers by an elaborated liturgy, and to surround them in the celebration of its rites with furnishings of equivalent splendour.

REFERENCES

1. There was also a small reredos for the Lady Chapel, which is generally believed to be an integral part of the building initiated during the episcopate of Bishop Bronescombe, and probably completed towards the end of Bishop Quinil's incumbency. It exists only as a shadow of its former self, as an arcaded screen in the wall behind the altar. Some authorities have claimed that much original work remains and that Kendall, who restored it in the 1820s, added only the outer bays. Although there is no apparent difference between the outer and inner bays and the entire arcade looks at the very least heavily recut, this reredos is related in design to the sedilia in the Lady Chapel, and markedly different in design to the new reredos that Kendall designed for the High Altar, so what exists may well be a complete restoration of the original.
2. Erskine (1981), and Erskine (1983).
3. Oliver (1861), 54.
4. Erskine (1981), 87–91.
5. Ibid., 111.
6. Morris (1943), 131; Bishop and Prideaux (1922), 56.
7. Erskine (1981), 144–5.
8. Ibid.
9. Erskine (1981), 145.
10. Ibid.
11. Oliver (1861), 320.
12. Ibid., 43–5; F. C. Hingeston Randolph (1889), xiv–xv, 243–4.
13. Oliver (1861).
14. Erskine (1981), 163.
15. Oliver (1861), 301
16. Morris (1943), 142; Bishop and Prideaux (1922), 59.

17. Oliver (1861), 388.
18. Morris (1943), 123.
19. Bishop and Prideaux (1922), 63–4.
20. Morris (1943), and Morris (1944).
21. Morris (1943), 126–7, 136; Pls XXIId, XXIIIc, XXVI.
22. Morris (1943), 141, 145–6; Fig. 4.
23. The plan was engraved for Carter (1797b).
24. Morris (1943), 137–8.
25. Brooks and Evans (1988), 74.
26. Morris (1943), 127–8; Bishop and Prideaux (1922), opp. 60.
27. I am grateful to Anna Hulbert for discussing this with me.
28. Morris (1943), 139; Bishop and Prideaux (1922), 57, agreed with Scott.
29. Ibid., 140.
30. *Ordinale Exon.*, Vol. 1, 320.
31. Christopher Wilson, 'The Neville Screen' *BAA CT*, III, (1980), 91–3.
32. Ibid, 95.
33. Stocker (1987), 96–9, 102.
34. Dugdale (1819), 528–31.
35. Orme (1986b), 28; Oliver (1861), 352–3.
36. Erskine (1981), 85, 94, 119, 147.
37. *Ordinale Exon.*, Vol. 1, 2; Sarum customs mention only the 4 dignitaries. Frere (1901), Vol. 1, 13.
38. Oliver (1861), 54–66.
39. I am grateful to T. A. Heslop for telling me about these seals.
40. Brooks and Evans (1988), pl. IV, 20.
41. Klauser (1979), 88. Sandler (1974), 155; Chambers (1877), 83.
42. Oliver (1861), 48.
43. This point is also raised by Peter Draper in 'Architecture and Liturgy' (1987), 87.
44. Kemp (1948), 117–8.
45. Oliver (1861), 54.
46. Ibid., 52–3.
47. *Ordinale Exon.*, Vol. 1, 63, 66, 196, 198, 304.
48. Frere (1901), Vol. 1, 113–24.
49. *Ordinale Exon.*, Vol. 1, 25.
50. Orme (1986b), 27; Orme (1986c).
51. Sekules, 'The Tomb of Christ at Lincoln Cathedral and the Development of the Sacrament Shrine: Easter Sepulchres Reconsidered' *BAA CT* VIII, 118–31.
52. The tester is illustrated in Coales (1987), Fig. 14.
53. Erskine (1981), 153, 157.
54. I am grateful to Eddie Sinclair and Anna Hulbert for showing me their work on the cleaning of the central panel of the pulpitum.
55. Work on the tower and steeple was underway in the early 1320s and in 1327 the choir moved to the new work; the pulpitum was likely to have been under construction during this period. Dugdale (1716), 24–5; VCH *London*, I, 412.
56. The Lincoln pulpitum was probably built at the same period as the remodelling of the south-west transept after the death of Bishop Dalderby. David King, 'The Glazing of the South Rose at Lincoln Cathedral', *BAA CT* VIII (1986), 134–5.
57. Hope (1917), pl. XIII, 55–6 n. 1.
58. Ibid.
59. Frere (1901), Vol. 1, xxxiii. I am grateful to David Chadd for advising me about Grandisson's liturgical reforms.
60. Jones (1817), 410.
61. Grandisson's use of polyphony is discussed in Harrison (1958), 109–11; I am grateful to David Chadd for this reference. For Bronescombe, see reference in n. 12.
62. Chambers (1877), 79–84; Browne (1906–16), 80.
63. Ibid.; the scheme of liturgical colours was set down by Grandisson (*Ordinale Exon.*, Vol. 1, 12–15), and purported to be according to the custom of the court of Rome, 'but on examination it will be found to embody other traditions, probably those of Exeter', Hope and Atchley (1918), 136–9.

Dating the Misericords from the Thirteenth-Century Choir-stalls at Exeter Cathedral

By Charles Tracy

The 13th-century misericords at Exeter Cathedral are the earliest complete set of choir-stall tip-up seats in England. Although their relevance to the study of medieval choir-stalls is only marginal, their treatment is justified because of the challenge they throw down to the accepted model of stylistic development in England in the 13th century. Authorities have dated the carvings variously over a span of 50 years, from 1220 to 1270.[1] It has also been held by some that the misericords were worked on intermittently over the whole period. A protracted manufacture is highly unlikely, however, and it is possible to date all of the carvings to the early 1240s. Some thought has been given to the dating problems more recently,[2] but the relevant stylistic ambience from which the Exeter carvings emanate has not, in my opinion, been successfully identified. It is the purpose of this paper to provide a credible stylistic context for the carvings as a basis for the arguments on dating. Moreover, the opportunity will be taken to place the lost Exeter choir-stalls in a wider historical context

In the great secular cathedrals, such as Exeter, the organisation of the seating in the choir mirrored the hierarchy of the chapter. The matter is dealt with in great detail in the 12th-century *Sarum Consuetudinary*, from Old Sarum, under the rubric *De Stallis Personarum in choro ecclesie Sarum*.[3] In the choir entry at the west end the dean had the right-hand stall, the precentor the left. At the east end the chancellor had the end stalls on the south side and the treasurer the opposite stall on the north. The four dignitaries had archdeacons sitting next to them and the other stalls were to be occupied by canons, priest-vicars and clerks, and the few deacons who were allowed to stand *in superiori gradu*. Below this upper rank was the *secunda forma* for junior canons, deacons and the *parvi canonici* and the rest of the choristers. The *Sarum Consuetudinary* was adopted by Bishop Brewer at Exeter in the 13th century and came to be used almost universally by English secular cathedrals.

The only 13th-century choir-stalls where we can examine the arrangements for the dignitaries is at Salisbury. Here we find that the seats of the returned-stalls get wider as they approach the centre until they reach the dean and precentor's seats which are 99 cm wide as against the standard centre-to-centre measurement of 67.5 cm. The last seats at the east end at 80 cm are also wider than usual. To underline the greater importance given to these dignitaries' seats some of them are also given special sculptural embellishment.

The choir at 13th-century Exeter probably occupied the crossing and part of the east end of the nave. This was the normal position in the Romanesque period.

In accordance with the constitution introduced by Bishop Brewer (1224–44), the body of ecclesiastics belonging to the cathedral amounted to a total of 24 archdeacons and canons, 24 vicars choral, 12 secondaries and 14 choir-boys.[4] At Exeter, the number of surviving 13th-century misericords (48)[5] corresponds with the tally of dignitaries, canons and vicars.[6] If there were 48 back-stalls, eight of which might have been returned against the pulpitum, the lateral stalls would have been no more than 13.7 m in length, hardly long enough to embrace the two bays of the nave arcade which spanned the crossing.[7] A row of sub-stalls on each side would have been required and a bench for the choir-boys in front.

Naturally enough, the provision of a new set of choir-stalls was a matter close to the heart of a cathedral's dean, a monastery's abbot or prior, and the high officials of such establishments. There is no evidence for individual or corporate lay involvement in the commissioning of choir-stalls in this period. In the late 12th century Samson, sub-sacrist at Bury St Edmunds Abbey, was arranging paintings and composing verses for his choir enclosure.[8] In 1220 Richard de Greneford, a chaplain at St Paul's Cathedral, agreed to provide the timber necessary for making the new stalls.[9] Similarly, at Peterborough, Abbot Walter of Bury St Edmunds (1233–45), gave ten marks towards the cost and much of the timber for the new stalls erected during his term of office.[10] At Gloucester Abbey Elias of Hereford, sacrist (d. 1237), rebuilt the central tower which had fallen down in 1222 and provided the monks with new stalls.[11] As a functionary of the abbey Elias was redistributing surplus income. Gloucester had no local saint but Rochester Cathedral was particularly fortunate at the beginning of the 13th century in reaping a considerable bonanza from the offerings at the shrine of William, the Scottish baker, converted into a local saint and martyr by carefully orchestrated publicity.[12] The funds accruing from this exercise subsidised the building of sacrist William de Hoo's new choir and its furnishings. At Westminster Abbey patronage of the building works and furnishings was the prerogative and concern of the king himself. In 1252–53 Henry III ordered that timber should be obtained for the roof of the new work of the church and for the stalls of the monks.[13]

It has traditionally been claimed that the 13th-century choir-stalls at Exeter Cathedral were fitted in the time of Bishop Brewer.[14] Before his election he was head of the cathedral chapter and, as bishop, he can be expected to have taken a greater interest in his church than someone appointed from outside. Such a man would have been well able to pay for new stalls himself. What is more, the provision of a new set of choir-stalls would be entirely consonant with his documented activities as constitutional reformer. During his episcopate he increased the revenues of the canons from his own resources, founded and endowed the office of dean,[15] consolidated the dignities of precentor, chancellor and treasurer, and built a chapter house. The fact that he was buried in the middle of the choir seems to suggest that he may have wished to be remembered in a special sense. It is extremely unlikely that the new stalls would have been set up by Brewer's successor, Bishop Blond (1245–57). Apparently a saintly and contemplative man, Blond has never been recorded as taking any interest at all in the rebuilding or embellishment of his cathedral church.[16]

It is possible that when wooden choir-stalls were first erected in cathedrals, and monastic and collegiate churches, in about the 10th century, they were places for standing and not seats, the only concession offered to the old and infirm being the permitted use of crutches. However, before long, seats seem to have been provided. They were only to be used during the Epistle and Gradual at Mass, and during the Responses at Vespers.[17] At all other times they were turned back out of the way. Peter of Cluny in 1121, referring to the conduct of services, says that at certain times: 'Here the seats are turned up'.[18] They must, therefore, have been generally adopted by this date. In some churches the occupant of the stall may have turned round to kneel and used the misericord as a desk, in others, they prostrated themselves against a low form in front of the back-stalls.[19] The term misericord appears in the constitution of the abbey of Hirsau in the first quarter of the 12th century.

English misericords of the 13th century use a simple semi-oval seat plan and small depth of moulding. Examples from the first half of the century are those from Christchurch Priory, Hants and Osney Priories, Oxon (the latter now in Kidlington Parish Church). The method by which they were usually housed into the seating at this time was by means of a projection of the back of the seat (or the adjacent standard) formed into the shape of a pin and upon which the seat was hung.

Bishop Brewer is supposed to have brought back patterns for the carvings from the Holy Land.[20] In particular, it has apparently been stated over and over again that his baggage included the design of the elephant carved on a misericord[21] (Pl. XXVIIA). There were no elephants in the wild in the various countries through which the crusaders passed, but there may have been individual specimens in *bestiaria*. It is possible that the elephant, and others of the animals represented, may have been copied from the embroideries which the bishop brought back with him and presented to the cathedral, as mentioned in the inventories. But the Exeter elephant constitutes a considerable advance in draughtsmanship when we compare it with the usual type of representation found in the Bestiaries. It is true that the animal's tusks are placed at the wrong angle, the legs have hocks like a horse instead of knees, and the feet are not properly toed, but, with the carefully drawn ears and the hump on its back, it is recognisably an African elephant. Illustrations of elephants in books were always full of errors. An important exception, however, was the drawing that Matthew Paris did of the animal which was presented to Henry III by Louis IX in 1255 — and even here the legs are not quite right as the knees have slipped down towards the ankle (Pl. XXVIIB). It seems more than likely that the accounts in the bestiaries are responsible for the misrepresentation of the legs. These books state that the elephant cannot bend its knees so that when it falls it cannot get up again. For this reason it always sleeps leaning against a tree.[22] Bestiaries are a prime candidate for the sculptor's model, particularly since so many of the other subjects found on the misericords are closely derived from these books. However, as far as the elephant is concerned, if we examine the bestiaries which the sculptor might have used, such as the 12th-century BL Add.MS 11283 or the 13th-century bestiaries, also in the British Library, Sloane MS 3544 and Harley MS 3244, the greater degree of realism in the Exeter elephant will be instantly recognised. Accordingly, we should keep an open mind as to the Exeter artist's source for his representation.

The problem of dating the Exeter misericords has, up to now, been approached in one of two ways. The first is exemplified in an article published in 1920,[23] although this was certainly not the first time that it had been put forward. In view of the coexistence at Exeter of traditional English 'stiff-leaf' foliage as well as other, more naturalistic leaf forms, the writer argued for a genesis of the carvings over a very wide time span (Pl. XXVIIc, D). Where the 'stiff-leaf' style occurs together with the so-called naturalistic leaf forms on the same misericord, we are told that the carving must have been worked on at two different periods. An attempt was made to put the carvings into a tidy chronology starting with the pure 'stiff-leaf' and ending with the maple and oak leaf which 'might well be found in the Decorated period'.

Since then this school of thought has become further entrenched, one author assigning different dates to many of the misericords from 1220–30 to 1260–70 on the same Darwinian criteria.[24] He admits that the local tradition has it that the misericords were carved between 1238, when Brewer returned from the Holy Land, and 1244, when he died. But he avers that the 'stalls' are entirely the work of one hand, and must have been carved over a long period. This dating theory takes scant account of the limitations of furniture making. The second dating hypothesis, put forward by Francis Bond, is altogether more sensible.[25] The traditional attribution to Brewer's episcopate is ignored, and it is suggested that the carvings must have been made sometime between 1255, when Louis IX's elephant was installed in the Tower of London, and 1279, the first year for which the cathedral fabric rolls have been preserved. Since there is no record in the fabric rolls of the stalls having been made in the late 13th century, the year 1279 is a reliable *terminus ante quem*.[26] As to the

existence at Exeter of naturalistic and conventional foliage at one and the same time, Bond
says:

It has sometimes been assumed that the two designs are of different date. This does not always follow.
Since the world began there have been young men and old men, progressives and retrogressives; the
latter would be sure here and there to repeat time-hallowed, if out-of-date, design, if only to save
thought.[27]

It is clear that the first so-called dating theory is little more than wishful thinking. Bond's
dating is, however, vulnerable to attack on its basic assumption that the elephant misericord
must have been based upon a sighting of Henry III's beast or at least access to Matthew
Paris's drawings of it.[28] However unlikely it may seem that an English artist could have
drawn such a life-like elephant in the early 1240s, the weight of evidence for placing the
other misericords at Exeter in this period forces us to accept no other conclusion.

Firstly, an attempt has to be made to place the carvings in their sculptural context. A
comparison with drawings is always likely to be helpful but the most useful stylistic
juxtapositions, upon which a secure dating can only be based, must come from the truly
comparable medium of sculpture. Since nearly all of the wood-carving of this period is lost
to us, we must look to sculpture in stone. The 'Stiff-Leaf' foliage is in the so-called 'small
embossed' style.[29] The main characteristics of this are, to quote Lady Wedgwood, that

the leaf forms have a restricted, usually convex, surface bounded by a rounded outline with no
exaggerated protrusions. The central and side lobes are reduced to equal proportions, and the whole is
capable of being inscribed within a pure trefoil ... they (the leaves) are displayed in evenly distributed
compositions, giving the effect of a mosaic of light and shade ... the stalks are of subsidiary
importance.[30]

The style appears to have been used first at Wells Cathedral in the nave after 'the Break'
(c. 1208–13). Thereafter, it moved north and eastwards via Worcester, Pershore,
Almondsbury and Gloucester to Bishop Northwold's choir extension at Ely, completed in
1252.

It is to the nave and the west front at Wells Cathedral that we are drawn for a comparison
with the woodwork at Exeter. The rather untidy and over-scale scrolling foliage on the
'Resurrection' tier is echoed in the handling of the Exeter misericords (Pl. XXVIIE). The leaf
forms are similar, particularly in the way the midrib dives into the hollowed-out central
lobe, and some of the leaves have a characteristic bump on them. There are parallels in the
animal carvings at Wells also. In the nave, the lion label-stops of early 13th-century date in
the north aisle remind us of the lion on the misericord at Exeter (Pl. XXVIIF, G). There are
also convincing juxtapositions with two Exeter misericord motifs in the spandrel dragons in
the nave at Wells (Pl. XXVIIIA, B). The double-bodied dragon had already been used at
Exeter on the tombs of Bishops Simon of Apulia, d. 1223, and Bartholomew, d. 1184. The
zigzag treatment of the hair in the central figure of the precentor's misericord can be found
on the standing figures on the west front at Wells.[31] As far as manuscripts are concerned,
two comparisons should be made. Firstly, the locusts figured in the English Apocalypse at
Trinity College, Cambridge (MS B.10.6, f. 9r), dated by M. R. James to no later than 1250,
are close in style, allowing for the difference in medium, to the Exeter, so called, 'Aristotle'
figure (Pl. XXVIIIC, D). Notwithstanding the absence of wings and use of human hands at
Exeter, both have the characteristics of the locusts described in Chapter Nine of the Book of
Revelations as 'horses prepared unto battle', with the heads of crowned men and tails with
scorpion stings. The second comparison is with the siren holding a fish in each hand. In a
Latin Bestiary in the British Library (BL MS Sloane 3544 f.28v) the image, which is almost
identical to the misericord, must derive from a source also known to the Exeter wood-carver

(Pl. XXVIIIE, F). This book was dated around 1300 by Einhorn,[32] but it is probably from the last three decades of the 13th century.[33]

In connection with the Exeter misericords Christa Grössinger, in an article on English misericords and their relationship to manuscript illumination, draws our attention to a dragon, c. 1265, on a spandrel at Stone church, Kent, executed by masons who are known to have worked at Westminster Abbey.[34] But none of the dragons at Exeter is particularly close in style, and the foliage at Stone and Westminster has little in common with Exeter. The only dated manuscript to which she refers is a Bible of 1254 from Salisbury (BL MS Royal B XII). In this there are several compositional parallels with the Exeter carving. But the style of the foliage, even allowing for the relative sophistication of the Bible artist, is not close enough to that of the misericords for our purposes. Motifs such as Atlas figures and dragons occur in each,[35] it is true, but they are not stylistically near enough for accurate dating. Grössinger seems to be following Bond's dating argument, although she suggests that, on the basis of the naturalistic leaf forms present at Exeter, the misericords may have been carved over a longer period of time. But, as has been rightly pointed out elsewhere,[36] the proto-naturalistic leaf forms are coeval with the main style. Indeed, as already mentioned, in several cases the two modes appear on the same misericord.[37]

It is surprising to find an imitation of real foliage attempted at Exeter in the early 1240s. However, I can only point to the unlikelihood of the choir-stalls having been made later than 1244 on the grounds of patronage. There is no other contemporary English botanically-observed foliage in any medium although the few isolated early instances of naturalistic decorative sculpture at Westminster Abbey, Windsor and Lincoln Cathedral have been dated 1240–50.[38] More helpfully, however, there are, I believe, convincing correspondences of other kinds between the Exeter misericords and English manuscript illumination of the third and fourth decades of the 13th century. In the British Library bestiary, MS Harley 4751, possibly from Salisbury, the treatment of the draped human form is close to that on the Exeter carvings. In both cases the garments are thick and plastic, and gathered in characteristically by a prominent cord around the waist (Pl. XXIXA). The same undergarment is also found gathered-up above the knees, and suspended from a waist belt (compare the Exeter 'Atlas' figure with the semi-naked figures on f. 69 of the bestiary[39]) (Pl. XXIXB). The same 'trough' folding is used in both monuments with characteristic V-shape falling folds on the torso and flying box-folds in the hems. Similar figures with bony rib-cages and pendulous female breasts as found in the carvings can be seen in the bestiary (e.g. the syren on f. 47). The treatment of water in the bestiary can be likened to that on the scene of the 'Swan Knight' at Exeter and, in the same vein, the tightly-curled volutes on the fleece of the goat in the bestiary remind us of the treatment of the lion's mane at Exeter. Finally, the water-spouts on the whale's back on f. 69 of the bestiary can be paralleled in many places at Exeter. The Harleian bestiary has been dated to 1230–40.[40]

The second book is Matthew Paris's *Life of St Alban* (Trinity College, Dublin MS 177 E.I.40), probably painted about ten years later.[41] In this the handling of the drapery is more stylised but the same conventions can be observed. The characteristic gathering in and folding over of the drapery at the waist can be observed. Of particular interest is the way that the undergarment is folded over the belt in f. 50 just as it is on the 'Atlas' misericord at Exeter. Although the *Life of St Alban* is evidently more remote stylistically from the Exeter sculpture than the Harleian bestiary, it is much closer than any parallels that might be put forward from English art of the 1250s.[42] Certainly, the Exeter carving has nothing in common with the earliest instances of botanically-observed foliage in England of the 1240s or the figure sculpture at Westminster Abbey of the 1250s.

There are two different sizes of misericord at Exeter — 56–61 cm wide for most of the stalls and, in four cases, seats 66 cm wide for the dignitaries. Three of the wider misericords are carved more intricately than the normal seats. The one with the figure holding a scroll in the centre, flanked by bishops, may have been intended for the precentor's stall on the north side of the choir where it is now. It has been suggested that the Exeter misericords were cut by stonemasons.[43] There is, it is true, a similarity between the 'precentor's' misericord and the carving on the Purbeck marble tomb of Bishop Marshall, d. 1206, in the cathedral (Pl. XXIXc, D). There are parallels, notably the figures in quatrefoil frames. But the techniques are evidently very different. That on the misericord, with its deeply grooved moulding and incisive linearity of design all heavily undercut, is a typical product of the wood-carver's chisel, whilst the foliage of the tomb is carved in one plane and concentrates on rounded mouldings and shallow relief. Perhaps this is an example of a deliberate archaising on the part of the wood-carver.

Bond was surely right to question the theory of a prolonged genesis. It is but a romantic notion that a wood-carver would single handedly take 40 or 50 years to complete a job that need not detain him for more than four years. It is reliably estimated that an experienced wood-carver could make a misericord like those at Exeter in no more than a month.[44] The presence of concentric rings on 25 of the misericords noted in 1870 has been cited as evidence that most of the carving is likely to have been the work of one man.[45] It is admittedly difficult, except in two of three cases, to identify with any certainty more than one hand at work. But it is unlikely that the master-carpenter did not have an assistant, especially as there was all the seating to be made. In any case, a protracted completion of some 40 or 50 years is to be ruled out on purely practical grounds. Each of the misericords with their oak hinges would have had to be fitted into position before the stalls could be erected. Moreover, it is unlikely that the misericords would have been carved *après la pose* as the working space for the craftsman would have been too cramped.

It is apparent, therefore, that the sculptor must have known Wells Cathedral and was able to draw upon a range of motifs dating from the late 1220s to 1239, the year of the consecration there. On the basis of the iconography he must have had access to bestiary books. Judging from his handling of drapery and his use of costume some of these books must have been quite up to date. As far as we can tell none of the carving at Exeter is of the 1250s or 1260s. The use of botanically-observed foliage at such an early date is surprising but on the grounds of patronage a date of before 1244 for the Exeter misericords is almost certainly inevitable. Moreover, Matthew Paris must yield the palm to the master-carpenter at Exeter for the first reasonably convincing depiction of an elephant in English art.

ACKNOWLEDGEMENTS

I would like to record my thanks to the Dean and Chapter of Exeter Cathedral for giving me access and for allowing me to take photographs with which to illustrate this paper. The fieldwork was paid for by the University of London's, Central Research Fund.

REFERENCES

1. Oliver (1821), 47, Freeman (1873), 34 and Bishop and Prideaux (1922), 31 follow the traditional attribution to Bishop Brewer (1224–44). Clarke (1920) 2, 3 suggested that some of the seats may have been carved as early as 1230 but others hardly earlier than 1260. The hypothesis of a protracted manufacture is followed by Remnant (1969), 34 and Grössinger (1975), 98. Bond (1910), 28 dates the choir-stalls to sometime between 1255 and 1279. Glasscoe and Swanton (1978), 10 assign them to the mid-13th century.

2. See Remnant and Grössinger, works cited above.

3. See Hope (1917), 115 and Tracy (1987), xx.

4. See Erskine (1976), 159–71. I am grateful to Mrs Erskine, the cathedral archivist, for advice on the 13th-century constitution.

5. In addition there are two more, one, clearly for a dignitary, of early 14th-century type and another belonging to the 15th century. The former was presumably made for Bishop Stapledon's new choir-stalls *c.* 1310 [see Tracy (1986), 99–103]. The latter was probably made after the fire of 1415 when, it is recorded in the cathedral fabric rolls, a payment of two shillings was made for repairs to the precentor's stall.

6. Abbots held stalls in some monastic cathedrals, such as those of Sion and Sherborne at Salisbury, that of Grestein at Chichester, those of de Lyra and Cormeille at Hereford, and Athelney and Muchelney at Wells. See Walcott (1868), 2.

7. These calculations are based on a supposed average seat width, centre to centre, of 67.5 cm. Hope suggests that at 12th-century Old Sarum, where there were 50 canons in 1227, the seating was confined to benches arranged axially on either side of the choir. He doubted if there would have been stalls and envisaged 25 men each side being easily fitted into a width of 40 ft representing the span of the crossing arches. See Hope (1917), 115, 116 and Pl. XIX. Cf. also excavation plans of St Augustine's Abbey, Canterbury, ibid., Pl. XIX. Joy (1976) suggests that the oak bench in the south transept at Winchester Cathedral may have been part of the 12th-century choir seating. See Joy (1976).

8. James (1894–8), 13.

9. Cook (1955), 33.

10. Sparke (1723), 119.

11. Hart (1863), 28.

12. See Anon, *The History and Antiquities of Rochester Cathedral*, Rochester (c. 1800), 10.

13. *Close Rolls* (1251–2), 280. See also Tracy (1987), 2 for Old St Paul's, Peterborough, Gloucester, Rochester and Westminster.

14. See n. 1.

15. The office of dean was founded in 1225. See Erskine (1976), 159–71.

16. For an account of Blond's episcopate see Oliver (1861), 37. Blond was succeeded by Bishop Bronescombe (1258–80) who initiated the work on the new eastern extension. For him a new set of stalls would have been premature as the ambitious new project comfortably outlasted his episcopate.

17. Thomas T. Wildridge, 'Misereres in Beverley Minster' (1879).

18. See also Tracy (1987), xx.

19. See Hope (1900), 110, and the Constitution of the Monastery of Hirsau, Germany, in Migne (1854), vol. 150, *Caput* xxix.

20. The legend is mentioned by Clarke (1920), 11. Brewer was absent on the Pilgrimage and on royal business in Germany from 1227 to 1235.

21. Work cited above, 12.

22. Clarke (1920), 14 quotes a passage from a letter in the *Spectator* for 12 August 1712 as follows: 'On Sunday last one (a preacher) who shall be nameless reproving several of his congregation for standing at prayers, was pleased to say, "One would think like the elephant you had no knees".'

23. Clarke (1920), 2, 3.

24. See Remnant (1969), 34.

25. See Bond (1910), 28.

26. Even though the accounts are only complete from 1299.

27. See Bond (1910), 204.

28. Matthew Paris, *Chronica Majora II*, Cambridge, Corpus Christi College, MS 16, f. 4^r.

29. Wynn Reeves (1952), 213, 417.

30. Ibid.

31. See for instance Courtauld Institute Illustration Archives, Archive 1, Cathedrals and Monastic Buildings in the British Isles, Pt 4 Wells (London 1977), 1/4/103.

32. Einhorn (1976), 337.

33. Personal communication from Dr Ronald Baxter, whose University of London Ph.D. thesis is entitled, 'A Study of the Latin Bestiary in England: Structure and Use'.

34. Grössinger (1975), 98–100. The spandrel at Stone church is illustrated in Gardner (1951), Pl. 38.

35. Grössinger (1975), 100.

36. See Glasscoe and Swanton (1978), 11.

37. For an interesting parallel to this intimate co-existence of conventionalised and naturalistic carving at Corcomroe Abbey, County Clare, Ireland, *c.* 1205–10, see E. Charles Nelson and R. A. Stalley, 'Mediaeval Naturalism and the Botanical Carvings at Corcomroe Abbey (County Clare)', *Gesta*, xxviii, 2 (1989), 165–74.

38. See Lethaby (1925), figs 33–4 and 52; Hope (1913), 56; and Cave, (1949), 7. None of the 'naturalistic' foliage at Exeter is botanically very convincing.
39. See Morgan (1982), Ill. 266.
40. Ibid., Morgan (1982), 124.
41. Dated by Morgan [(1982), 130] to c. 1240–50.
42. The dating of this manuscript is controversial but it is generally agreed to be no later than 1250. See Morgan (1982), 132.
43. Howard and Crossley (1917), 15.
44. Hugh Harrison of Herbert Read Limited has kindly provided an estimate of the man-hours needed to carve a typical Exeter misericord by a craftsman of today. This is about 4 weeks. I am grateful to him for advice on several aspects of the Exeter woodwork.
45. Clarke (1920), 6.

An Examination of the Polychromy of Exeter Cathedral Roof-Bosses, and its Documentation

By Anna Hulbert

When conservation work was undertaken by the writer in 1977–82 on Exeter's 14th-century roof-bosses, most of which had not been scaffolded for a century, the splendidly-preserved original polychromy provided many hitherto unremarked clues to the history of the cathedral. Internal evidence revealed during close examination of the layers of paint and gilding has greatly enlightened our interpretation of the fabric rolls, and the cleaned polychromy on several bosses has given us a fresh identification of their subjects. The superb quality and detail of the painters' work can only be fully appreciated from the scaffolding, and at the BAA Conference in 1985 it was possible to share the privilege of having worked so closely on these sculptures by showing many coloured slides.

THE INTERPRETATION OF THE FABRIC ROLLS

Although H. E. Bishop, E. K. Prideaux, and C. J. P. Cave have between them offered a convincing identification of the different groups of bosses and corbels referred to in the various rolls, little attention has previously been given to the building procedure, and in consequence some deductions regarding dating have been imprecise.

Vaulting could not be begun until the clerestory windows, with half-bosses at the apex of each, had been built; nor could the supporting centering be removed from beneath the newly-built ribs until a whole bay had been completed. When entries are found for payments for priming, painting, or gilding bosses, it is, therefore, highly significant whether the number of sculptures referred to includes the half-bosses in that part of the Cathedral, or only the 'great' bosses within the layout of the ribs.

Presbytery

In the Christmas and Easter terms of 1301–2, bosses were brought from 'Hamdon'.[1] Several of the heads in the tower and transept arches are either Ham Hill or the very similar Salcombe Regis stone, but the large number of carvings being produced at the same price and the·same time makes it likely that these entries refer to the extensive group of Ham Hill bosses in the presbytery. At the end of the midsummer term of the same year, the roll records a payment for the painting (*depinguendis*) of 49 bosses, 8 corbels, and other portions of the vault.[2] The materials are recorded: gold, silver, azure, and other colours. Although the medieval colour scheme was obliterated by Gilbert Scott's beige, green, dull red, and gold, microscopic examination of paint samples has revealed that the original polychromy was predominantly gold and azurite. Since the Presbytery includes an eastern half-boss, number 46A, to account for the odd number, the sculptures referred to correspond exactly to bosses 46–85 with their nine adjacent half-bosses, and the eight corbels below, on columns A–D, north and south sides (these are indicated on Fig. 1).

Gold and azurite were the most expensive and fragile of colours.[3] not to be put at risk while the heavy bosses had yet to be hauled into position. We may confidently conclude,

Ch. of SS Andrew & Katherine

FIG. 1. Bosses to which the
payment for painting in
Midsummer term 1301–2
probably refers

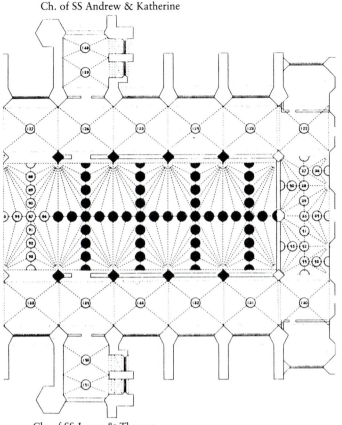

Ch. of SS James & Thomas

therefore, that this painting put the final touches to the completed four bays of the presbytery vault. However, other entries referring to different pigments and processes do not bring us to the same conclusion for their respective parts of the cathedral.

Choir

Many of the choir bosses are of Portland stone, which corresponds logically to the entry at the end of the midsummer term in the roll for 1303–4, for 18 great stones brought from Portland, and for carving 30 great bosses (numbers 86–115) and six aisle bosses (numbers 127–9, 135–7); the same entry refers to three main corbels, and there are three more among the payments during the Michaelmas terms of 1306–7 which could fit with those on the columns E–G north and south.[4] It is clear that the three large bays of the choir, together with the adjacent aisles, were about to be vaulted at this time (this is shown in Fig. 2).

The payments during the midsummer term of 1308–9 for priming (*primandum*) the bosses of the vault are of a different nature from that recorded for the presbytery.[5] They can only be interpreted in the light of the materials purchased, namely large quantities of oil and of red and white lead. These pigments are found in the priming and backgrounds of the bosses; moreover the process of priming the absorbent limestone would have consumed a

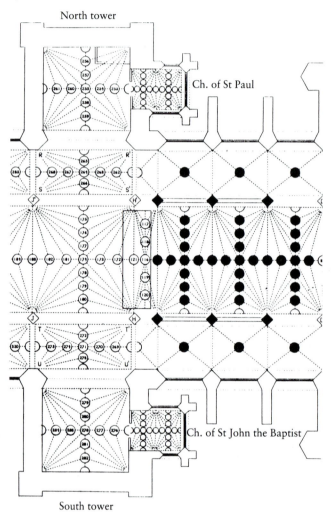

North tower

Ch. of St Paul

Ch. of St John the Baptist

South tower

FIG. 2. Bosses and corbels probably covered by payments in Midsummer term 1303–4 and Michaelmass term 1306–7

great deal of oil. Evidence from the crossing bosses which, unlike those of the choir, have suffered no overpainting, proves that the bosses were at ground level when primed, as the red lead backgrounds continue inside the joints in the masonry. The same could apply to the choir bosses.

Maybe the payment for finishing the choir, and for its gold and azurite, were on the missing roll for 1311–12, since the Michaelmas term of 1312–13 William of Montacute had begun work on further bosses and corbels which we may associate with the crossing.[6]

Crossing and Transepts

The building work in the Cathedral continued westwards, preparing the tower and crossing area to receive its vaulting. The roll for 1310–11 records the priming of the bosses of the

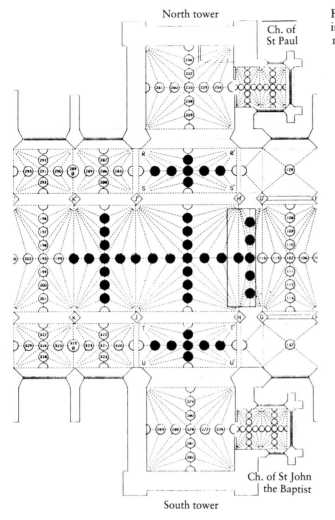

North tower

Ch. of
St Paul

FIG. 3.   Bosses probably referred to
in payments of Christmas term
1316–17

Ch. of St John
the Baptist

South tower

chapels[7] which have long been identified by Cave[8] and others, as those of the tower chapels
of St Paul and St John the Baptist: only scraps of medieval colour now survive there, though
the moulded capitals of St Paul's chapel retain a remarkable amount of brilliant pigment
and gold. Bishop and Prideaux conclude that 'priming' means the final colouring.[9] In the
same roll are payments for the metal rings around the Purbeck columns in the corners of the
towers;[10] and in the Michaelmas term of 1312–13 three marble capitals were carved.[11]
There are now only four Purbeck marble capitals with foliage carving in the cathedral, at the
four corners of the crossing at the level of the springing of the vault. William of Montacute
was paid during the same term.

The following Easter Richard Digon is named as a carver of bosses, producing two for
2s. 9d.[12] Between the Christmas and midsummer terms of 1312–13 it is possible that he may
have produced enough sculptures to account for the whole group attributed to his hand,[13]

filling the crossing and the four adjacent bays, as discussed by Bishop and Prideaux and by Cave.[14] Further preparations are unrecorded, as the rolls for 1313–16 are missing, but during the Michaelmas term of 1316–17 centrings were made, among other equipment for the 'high roof'.[15]

In the Christmas term of the same year comes the key entry: '*In xvij magnis clavis de petr' primand' apprestand' usque ad aurum*.'[16] The cost of priming these 17 great bosses, but not actually gilding them, works out at 1s. 2½d. each. Further entries for one and for 24 such bosses[17] at the same price (bar one halfpenny) although termed '*depictand*' must in fact refer to the priming: the total of 42 is exactly that of the great bosses in the crossing and east bay of the nave (numbers 172–93) the small western bay of the choir (116–21) and the two stone bays of the transepts (262–75) as is shown in Figure 3.

During conservation work in this area it was found that on every great boss the priming and background of red lead disappeared into the masonry joints under the medieval mortar. There can be no doubt that the bosses received their first painting at ground level. The surviving rolls do not give us an obviously associated entry for the purchase of red lead, but comparison with the records for the choir, already discussed, leave us in no doubt as to the methods and materials employed. Vermilion, which was more expensive,[18] was used here for the finishing touches: it gives a tidy edge to the gold leaf and extends over the top of the mortar joints. The gold leaf itself stops short of the plaster line, above which the stone is undercoated, the plaster having been stripped by Gilbert Scott. Huge quantities of '*pend-aunz*' stones for the infilling of the vault which carried the plaster were purchased 1317–19. (There is an entry for plastering for the Easter term of 1316–17,[19] but I suspect that this could refer to an area such as the nave aisles, the eastern bays of which belong stylistically to the same group.) It is not until the roll for 1320–1 that we find extensive purchases of vermilion and gold in quantities that suggest that they were used for these crossing area bosses.[20] Presumably, then, years between 1317 and 1320 must have been those spent in the actual building of the vaulting.

The above-mentioned entries for painting or priming the 42 bosses have sometimes been used to imply that the work in the crossing was complete by 1317.[21] In fact, like the entry for priming the choir bosses, these payments provide proof that the stones of the vault were still at ground level.

Towers

Amongst the entries of 1320–1 mentioned above, for the purchase of pigments, we find a great deal of white lead. At so late a date this cannot have been used on the 42 bosses of the crossing area: their white lead had dried some years before. The two transeptal towers each have nine wooden bosses; like those of the choir and presbytery they were repainted under the direction of Gilbert Scott. The payment for carving these wooden bosses occurs in the roll for the midsummer term of 1317–18, and that for priming them in the Easter term of 1319–20.[22] They could have been gilded at the same time as those in the adjacent stone bays of the transepts. Their medieval polychromy is now invisible, and the wooden vaulting is almost entirely stripped to the bare oak, but adjacent to bosses 258 and 259 the west face of the wooden ridge-rib retains its white lead. Although re-whitened at some stage in its history, there is no reason to suppose that the bottom layer is anything but medieval. Painting these vaults to match the whitened stone and plaster of the rest of the building doubtless accounted for some of the white lead acquired at this period.

ICONOGRAPHY AND INTERPRETATION IN THE LIGHT OF THE POLYCHROMY

During conservation work, some of the sculptures were found to represent subjects very different from those hitherto suggested. The most obvious example is boss 184 in the eastern bay of the nave (Pl. XXIXE, F). Prideaux and Shafto and Cave identify this as the lion breathing life into his still-born cub, the legend symbolic of Christ's Resurrection.[23] However, not only is the brown lion's head turned away from the smaller beast, but his claws have sunk into its hindquarters, so that painted blood flows from the wound (Pl. XXIXE). Moreover, the small grey beast is not a lion cub: its face has a human complexion and screams in agony (Pl. XXIXF). It is clearly intended for a manticore. A slightly different manticore, also fighting a lion, appears on the overpainted wooden boss 278 in the south tower; uncovering tests indicated that its face was also originally flesh-coloured.

In spite of the discovery of pink-veined ears and green scales or feathers on the open-mouthed beast on boss 188, with its red ochre lion-like body, no named fabulous beast has yet been suggested as a definite model. A detail is shown in Plate XXIXG to illustrate the care with which every hair has been delineated by the painter. The similar beast on wooden boss 280 originally had gold scales on its neck.

The bosses are mostly about 2 feet in diameter, those at the centre of each bay being about 5 inches wider,[24] so the reader will appreciate that little of this detail can ever have been visible from ground level. All the plates show the cleaned bosses before any retouching was begun. In many places the polychrome layer was loose and blistered, but had not actually been lost when the conservation team began work. After consolidation, the paint surface showed relatively little damage. Such a case was boss 174, which Prideaux and Shafto believed to be damaged to the extent of the stone being worn.[25] They are surely right in suggesting that it represents the *Miles Christi*, but it is only since cleaning that the heraldry, presumably anonymous by intention, and repeated on shield, gown, and caparison, can be described with absolute certainty: or, a bordure azure. Like Samson on boss 195 he is surrounded by three dragons, and cannot ever have resembled St George.

Moving further west down the nave, into the area vaulted during Bishop Grandisson's episcopate, we may note that in the Crucifixion on boss 202, the Cross itself is painted green.

The king on the central boss of the second bay of the nave, No. 195, is difficult to identify. He is seated on a branch like a tree of Jesse, but then so is Bishop Grandisson on boss 234, although Cave may be right in suggesting King David.[26] Prideaux and Shafto are certainly wrong in calling this Christ in Majesty,[27] for he has grey hair and wears stockings and black shoes with elegant red shoelaces. His crimson tunic is embroidered with tiny fleurs-de-lis. The flanking angels have gold hair, like Christ on 202, and all three faces are perfectly preserved without a single paint loss: they needed no retouching (Pl. XXXA)

The whole choir and presbytery, comprising bosses 46A–121, were repainted during Gilbert Scott's restoration of the 1870s. When paint samples from this area were mounted as cross-sections, evidence was found for three separate layers of paint, though the damaged state of the 1302 colour before the repainting has given us no one really clear sample. The bottom layer was obviously medieval, but usually the top two layers each had an identical white priming. The middle layer was approximately the same colour as the bottom layer but employed a different pigment. The clue to this sequence of repainting was found in notes by E. V. Freeman, where he says,

Not that the work here claims to be a literal reproduction, for neither are the corbels regilded nor do the colours above rigidly correspond to those formerly employed, experiment having proved in this as

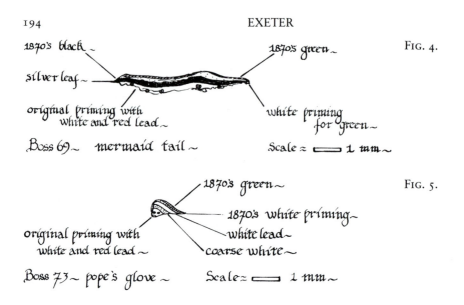

FIG. 4.

1870's black ~
1870's green ~
silver leaf ~
original priming with
    white and red lead ~
white priming
    for green ~
Boss 69 ~   mermaid tail ~   Scale ≈ ▭ 1 mm ~

FIG. 5.

1870's green ~
1870's white priming ~
white lead ~
original priming with
    white and red lead ~
coarse white ~
Boss 73 ~ pope's glove ~   Scale ≈ ▭ 1 mm ~

in other instances that an exact resuscitation of mediaeval colouring cannot be relied upon to commend itself to modern judgement.[28]

The crude blue with which the azurite was experimentally imitated must have presented a sorry travesty of the suble medieval polychromy, and some colours were utterly distorted: on boss 69 the middle layer on the tail of the mermaid is black, overpainted green (Pl. XXIXH; Fig. 4). The black was a mistaken reproduction of the original silver leaf, which had tarnished: traces of this are just visible in a microscopic cross-section.[29]

The fishy realism of a silver mermaid tail would have contrasted with the shaggy goat on boss 58, which seems to have been fantastic azuite blue.

On another boss in the presbytery, No. 73 (Pl. XXXB) the strange sight of a pope with green gloves may also be accounted for by Scott's recolouring: a paint sample examined under the microscope shows that the gloves were originally white (Fig. 5). This boss offers a further illustration of changes wrought during repainting. Plate XXXc is an infra-red photograph showing the middle layer of embroidery design, with gold crosses underneath the present brown spots on the Pope's chasuble. These may reproduce the bottom, medieval, embroidery pattern more closely than what is visible now.

The toughness of the 1870s recolouring, combined with a lack of time and funds, precluded a full examination of every overpainted boss, but enough has been learned to show us how different the choir and presbytery must have looked when first painted. Even the simple processes of conservation documentation are not without a wider value: on boss 75, repainted without prior repairs to the broken stone, the heavenly fiddler's bow appeared to have an oddly square end.[30] This musicological puzzle was solved as soon as close access was obtained.

SOME METHODS AND MATERIALS

There exist further clues in both the vaulting and the fabric rolls by which the building procedure can be considerably clarified. Many entries record the purchase of lead, mostly for roofing, and there is also mention of red sand for plumbing '*in rubea arena ad plumbem superfundend*'.[31] Such purchases are few as presumably it could be re-used.

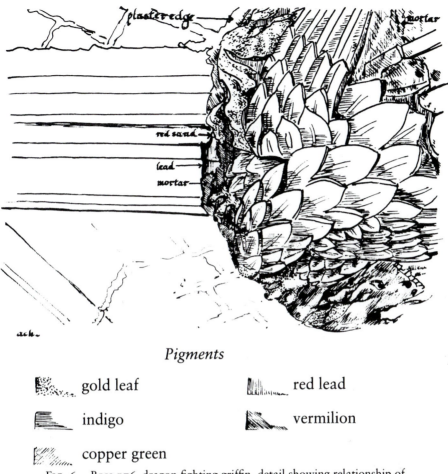

Pigments

gold leaf   red lead

indigo   vermilion

copper green

FIG. 6.   Boss 176, dragon fighting griffin, detail showing relationship of
colour and construction. See also Plate Cii

In the crossing area, lead can be seen in many of the masonry joints in the horizontal
ridge-ribs. These were evidently cramped with iron spikes set into molten lead. The joints
were plugged with red sand during this plumbing operation; later the sand was removed,
presumably at the same time that the centering was dismantled, and mortar pointing carried
out in the usual way. The stones of the arched ribs were merely bedded in mortar.

In spite of the red sand, of which traces remain, some of the lead dribbled out of the joints
while still hot. On boss 176, the dragon fighting the griffin, it has flowed over the red lead
painted background. Lime mortar pointing covers most of this dribble of lead, and
vermilion lies on top of the mortar. Scraps of red sand between the lead and the mortar
complete this panorama of medieval construction methods, all within a few square inches
on the east face of the boss adjacent to its southern rib (Fig. 6).

The pair of corbels K, north and south, below boss 193, marks the point where the
vaulting of Bishop Grandisson's episcopate takes over from that built under Bishop
Stapledon. These sculptures are particularly interesting as they have two layers of medieval

paint. On the head of the supporter king below the figure of the Virgin and Child on K south, a hairy eyebrow, similar to those on boss 183, can be discerned through a chip in the upper layer (Pl. XXXD): it may well be that these corbels were first painted by the artist who polychromed the crossing area bosses above and to the east of them.[32] The supporter king and the Tumbler on K north opposite, now dressed in indigo, with gold, red, and white embroideries, were both originally dark crimson. The dress and cloak of the Virgin, now gold and white respectively, were once azurite and crimson, evidently a crimson lake. Pockets of dirt separate the two layers.

It seems likely that the polychromy of these corbels would have been renewed by the painters of the bosses of the six western bays of the nave. The crimson lake of the Virgin's cloak is of particular interest, as most of the crimson on the crossing bosses, on grapes and other fruit, is a translucent iron oxide of high quality. On boss 264, however, crimson lake is found on the seamless robe of Christ, which in turn looks very like that of the Risen Christ under Bishop Stapledon's tomb-canopy. Used so sparingly and only for the holiest of persons it could well be some of the expensive 'cinopele' purchased during the midsummer term of 1320–1.[33]

Another material which the cathedral's builders found useful for small alterations to blocks of stone, and for running repairs to broken carvings, was pitch. The fabric rolls often specify its use for cement. Many purchases and plentiful traces remaining in the building testify to its usefulness. It seems also to have been used for damp-proofing the wall under the early 16th-century Resurrection painting in the Sylke chantry.

Three Styles of Polychromy Compared

A detailed account of the techniques and pigments that have been found on Exeter's bosses is in course of preparation. To complete the present brief survey we may outline the colour schemes favoured at different periods. The gold, silver, and azurite, against a scarlet background, employed on the bosses of the presbytery and choir, has already been mentioned.

In the crossing section, as we have seen, the backgrounds are red lead with a thin top coat of vermilion. Gold leaf is applied lavishly to the foliage, right up the sides of the bosses. Stems were copper green, now discoloured to a greeny brown. The blue on bosses 174 and 176, and evidently also on the dragon's wings on 185, is indigo, which pigment, together with more 'cinopele', was purchased for the altar in the Christmas term of 1320–1.[34] Although on corbel K south, the azurite is on the lower layer and the indigo on the upper one, the small quantities involved would scarcely have necessitated a special purchase.

From boss 194 westwards, not only do the ribs change from Caen to Beer Stone, but the polychromy shows considerable economy. The background colour is red earth, the edges of the leaves of the foliage being merely outlined with red lead. Gold is kept to the prominent bottom faces of the bosses, the sides being silvered. Presumably the silver leaf once bore a yellow glaze, but it has now tarnished. The blue on Bishop Grandisson's arms (boss 199) is an azurite mixture. Azurite was a far more expensive pigment than indigo, but there seems to have been very little blue of any kind in the nave. Bishop Grandisson's chosen burial place was under his west front figure screen, rivalling Bishop Stapledon's brilliantly polychromed new altarpiece and tomb at the east end, and Eddie Sinclair's discoveries (see above, pp. 116–17) may suggest that it was here, rather than in the nave, that the finest pigments were lavished.

ACKNOWLEDGEMENTS

The Dean and Chapter of Exeter Cathedral have commissioned the conservation work from 1976 onwards, which has made this study possible. The cathedral's surveyor and masons have provided many helpful observations, as have a number of scholars and specialists. Mr Peter Dare identified most of the different stones. The conservation team meticulously recorded every detail discovered in the daily log book. Ms Gillian Lewis and Ms S. Wakelin at the National Maritime Museum, Greenwich, Ms J. Darrah at the Victoria and Albert Museum and Dr A. Roy at the National Gallery, London, and Mrs Plahter of Oslo University, have generously assisted with the identification of paint samples. Warmest thanks of all are due to Mrs A. M. Erskine who made available manuscript notes from the fabric rolls prior to publication: without these, much valuable evidence might have been overlooked during work.

The plan used for Figures 1–3 is the work of Dr Anthony Clayden, Head of the Department of Graphic Design at Exeter College of Art and Design, and Mrs Helen Blackman and Mr Lee Davis of the University of Exeter Computer Unit.

REFERENCES

1. Erskine (1981), 20 and 22.
2. Ibid., 24.
3. Hulbert (1987), printer's omission slip for page 278. Note: two paragraphs are on this slip and the introduction is missing altogether.
4. Erskine (1981), 35 and 38. The 1304 carver seems to have been unusually well-paid. The second of these identifications should be made with caution, as the rolls for 1304–6 are missing.
5. Ibid., 47–8.
6. Ibid., 63. But compare also p. 49, when an entry for glass for the clerestory windows at Christmas 1309–10 suggests that the masons had finished at least part of the choir.
7. Ibid., 56.
8. Cave (1953), 9.
9. Bishop and Prideaux (1922), 48.
10. Erskine (1981), 59.
11. Ibid., 63.
12. Ibid., 67.
13. Ibid., 192–3.
14. Bishop and Prideaux (1922), 48; Cave (1953), 9. These interpretations of the status and achievements of the different carvers should be treated with caution.
15. Erskine (1981), 73–5.
16. Ibid., 79.
17. Ibid., 80 to 82.
18. Hulbert (1987), 277.
19. Erskine (1981), 82.
20. Ibid., 126, 128 and 130–1.
21. B/E South Devon (1952), 135.
22. Erskine (1981), 97 and 117.
23. Prideaux and Shafto (1910), 134; Cave (1953), 20.
24. About 60 cm and 73 cm.
25. Prideaux and Shafto (1910), 125.
26. Cave (1953), 40.
27. Prideaux and Shafto (1910), 149.
28. Freeman (1888), 95.
29. Dr Ashok Roy has very kindly confirmed the presence of silver by exmination with Energy Dispersive X-ray microanalysis.
30. Remnant (1986), pl. 53.
31. Erskine (1981), 60 and 79.
32. It is possible that the entry for carving six corbels in the midsummer term of 1317–18 refers to some in this area, although the number of corbels already paid for should have provided for the crossing — compare

Erskine (1981), 99, with p. 63 and p. 36 n. 3 — and it is only further west down the nave that we can find another group of six in the same style. The Purbeck columns of the nave, which carry such corbels, were not finally paid for until 1332: Erskine (1983), 250. I have not found evidence to support the statement of Bishop and Prideaux (1922), 48, that the corbels were carved *in situ*.

33. Erskine (1981), 131; compare Eastlake (1960), vol. I, 116–18, and Thompson (1935), 418 n. 11. The 'cinopol' used for the choir, Erskine (1981), 48, was a little less expensive.
34. Erskine (1981), 134.

Flying Angels and Bishops' Tombs, a Fifteenth-Century Conundrum

By Bridget Cherry

Among the relatively sparse 15th-century work in Exeter Cathedral are the two elaborate tombs of Bishop Branscombe and Bishop Stafford at the entrance to the Lady Chapel, the former a remodelling of an older monument, the latter entirely a work of the 15th century. The canopies, in a fully-fledged Perpendicular style, were clearly conceived as matching pair, but are not identical, and opinions have varied on their relative dates (Pl. XXXIA–D).

To understand how they fit into the general disposition of the tombs within the cathedral, it is useful to outline briefly the arrangements made for bishops' monuments from the time of the start of the late 13th-century building campaign.[1] In Bishop Branscombe's new Lady Chapel wall niches were provided, to which the earlier monuments disturbed by the new building work were transferred. The place determined by Branscombe for his own tomb was St Gabriel's chapel at the east end of the south choir aisle, adjacent to the Lady Chapel. He was buried there in 1280. In its present position between the two chapels the tomb lies in line with those of his predecessors.

His successor, Bishop Quinil (d. 1291) was buried in front of the high altar of the Lady Chapel, with a plain incised slab, restored to its original place in 1820.[2] After this the concept of the Lady Chapel as a special place for bishops' burials was abandoned, and the siting of the next tombs reflects the progress of the new building work. Bishop Walter de Stapledon (d. 1326) was buried in the place of honour to the north of the high altar, his elaborate tomb complementing the rich presbytery furnishings of the early 14th century. The short-lived Bishop Berkeley (d. 1327) had a tomb with a brass (now destroyed) on the south side of the presbytery, whereas Grandisson (d. 1369) was buried in his own little chapel within the west front. After him came Brantyngham (d. 1394) with a chantry chapel in the second bay of the nave, on the north side. This has entirely disappeared (as has the other chantry chapel in the nave, of the Courtenay family, apart from the effigies, now in the south transept).

By the early 15th century the major building campaigns had been completed, and attention appears to have turned to the regularising of the cathedral fittings, particularly the provision or replacement of screens dividing off the chapels of the transept and the east end.[3] The choice of the east end for the tomb of Bishop Stafford (d. 1419) can be seen as a further indication of this desire to refurbish this part of the building. The site which Stafford chose for his tomb was the chapel of St John the Baptist at the east end of the north choir aisle, the counterpart to the south-east chapel with Branscombe's tomb. Plans for the tomb were made during Stafford's lifetime; he endowed the chapel as a chantry with several manors in Dorset which were handed over to the Dean and Chapter in 1408.[4] In 1413 his cousin Canon William Langton was buried in the chapel according to his will: '*ex parte dextera vel sinistra tumbe Reverendi Patris Domini mei Edmundi Episopi Exoniensis*'.[5] The wording of the will perhaps suggests that the precise siting of Stafford's tomb had not yet been determined. Langton's fine brass showing a kneeling cleric survives, set in the floor of the chapel, i.e to the left of Stafford's tomb.

Stafford's own burial is described in the Chapter Act Book for 1419.[6] The funeral processed from the manor of Clyst, where he died, his body being conveyed to Exeter 'in a certain cart called Whyrlecole' with five horses trapped in black and with coats of arms, and was borne ceremoniously into the cathedral to be buried the next day '*in tumulo ab ipso Episcipo per vitam apparato*'. Unfortunately there are no references to the making of the tomb in the fabric rolls so the exact time of construction is uncertain. It has commonly been assumed that the whole of Stafford's tomb, that is both the effigy and the canopy, date from before 1419, indeed it has been described as 'the earliest surviving monument of a type which became a pattern for the whole C15'.[7] However it is by no means certain that the effigy and canopy were created together. The effigy is of alabaster, finely carved, the design distinguished by the 'gablette' or small canopy above the head, which, as Gardner has pointed out, relates it to several other alabaster effigies of the early 15th century — the Earl of Arundel (1416) at Arundel, the tomb of Henry IV (1413) and Joan of Navarre at Canterbury, and the tomb of Sir Ralph Green (1417) at Lowick, Northamptonshire.[8] The date range of these convincingly accords with an effigy commissioned a few years before the death of the bishop, who appears to have been following the lead set by royal and aristocratic patrons in commissioning work from the Nottinghamshire alabaster workers. The contract for the Lowick tomb, a rare survival which names the carvers, Thomas Prentys and Robert Sutton, interestingly specifies in addition to the effigy 'an arch of alabaster with pendants and cresting to be placed over the tomb'. The arch at Lowick is no longer there, and may never have been erected, and no alabaster arches are known elsewhere. The tomb of Henry IV at Canterbury has only a wooden tester (was this a substitute for something grander, never erected?). While the Stafford tomb may have been intended to have had a canopy from the beginning, it is easy to imagine there may have been problems in completing the monument if the alabaster workers were unable to provide a canopy and one had to be commissioned from another workshop. Certainly the style of the carving on the canopy, with its stiff little figures along the frieze, is far removed from the delicacy of the alabaster work.

The design of the canopy, with its single flattened four-centred arch, is also noticeably different in spirit from the western screen of the chapel. This is one of four screens of identical design, dividing off the north-east and south-east chapels, and the two transept chapels of St John and St Paul (Pl. XXXIB). The screen dividing the Lady Chapel from the retrochoir is of a similar but more elaborate design, although considerably restored.[9] The dating of these screens to the first third of the 15th century rests on two pieces of evidence: the arms of Stafford which appear on the screen to the south-east chapel of St Gabriel,[10] and two references in the fabric rolls of 1433–4.[11] The first mentions the purchase of 'ferramenta' from Denis Gabriel (presumably a smith) for stone screens in the cathedral, and the second refers to the sale of wooden screens which had been in the chapels of St John and St Paul. This suggests a gradual programme of improvement to the cathedral fittings to a unified design, begun at the east end under Stafford, but still in progress in the transepts in the 1430s, under the master mason John Harry. The detail of these screens is still very much in the tradition of the 14th-century furnishings, with knobbly foliage ornament and wilfully projecting little pedestals and canopies for small images, quite different from the more streamlined and subservient ornament of the tomb canopy. The stylistic innovations introduced into the cathedral architecture in the later 14th century by Robert Lesyngham (the redesigned east window and the north-west porch) appear to have made little impact on the conservative taste of the furnishing (a dichotomy not uncommon in other centuries).

As Pevsner indicated, the setting of Stafford's effigy, on a tomb chest decorated with shields and quatrefoils, surmounted by a canopy with a single, cusped, flattened arch with traceried spandrels, is of a type that became common in the 15th century and continued popular into the early 16th; well-known descendants include the drawing associated with the projects for the tomb of Henry VI, and the 16th-cenury Spencer tomb at Great Brington, Northamptonshire. The basic form of this type of canopy would appear to have been developed from the Perpendicular doorway with four centred arch in a square frame. If the Stafford canopy is of *c.* 1419 it would indeed be an early example of the type. But apart from the discrepancy with the chapel screen, which has already been noted, further puzzles arise when one compares the canopy with the matching one on Branscombe's tomb.

The Branscombe effigy is of the late 13th century, one of the finest of its date, still retaining much of its original colouring.[12] How it was originally displayed is unknown. The principle of using canopies over effigies was well established by the end of the 13th century, for ecclesiastical as well as secular tombs (Bishops Bingham and Bridport at Salisbury, 1246 and 1262; Bishop Aquablanca at Hereford, 1268). However, if there had been a canopy, it would seem odd for it to be destroyed, and it seems more likely that it was the absence of such a superstructure that inspired the remaking of the tomb in a manner that was felt to be in accord with 15th-century notions of the dignity appropriate for one of the cathedral's chief benefactors.

On the new tomb chest, presumably because it was rather longer than the older effigy, a pair of angels was added at the foot, possibly the angels referred to in the fabric rolls of 1442–3: *'in wire empt. pro angelis ad novam tumbam Walteri Primi. 2d'*.[13] The reference to a 'new tomb' at this time suggests that it was very recent, or still under construction. The purpose of the wire is obscure. Was it for some means of fixing, or for decoration? If for the latter, it could equally well have been intended for the other angels liberally distributed over the canopy. These, beneath their regrettably crude overpainting, have a striking family resemblance to those at the foot of the effigy — the same wavy hair framing the face, and the same long fingers. The abundance of angels was no doubt considered appropriate for a tomb sited in the chapel dedicated to St Gabriel, Branscombe's special patron. The canopy angels total 26 — two censing angels in the spandrels on the show side to the north (the spandrels to the chapel have foliage), and others on the terminals of the cusps and along the frieze. Some of the latter hold musical instruments, which are possible candidates for wire embellishment.

While the overall design of the Stafford and Branscombe canopies is very similar, the detail of the carved decoration is not, as can be seen especially in a comparison of the angel friezes. The Stafford angels are static, and not well suited to their horizontal position. They give the impression of designs adapted from standing or voussoir figures (Plate XXXID). In contrast the sculptor of the Branscombe angels has exploited the horizontal postures to good effect; the angels are shown in a variety of animated positions, kicking up their legs and twisting their heads upright, while the figures at each end reach out to grasp the corner shafts of the canopy, in a sophisticated integration of architecture and sculpture (Plate XXXIC). The Stafford canopy not only has fewer angels on the frieze, but has simpler ornament around the arch, with foliage instead of censing angels in the spandrels. The angels on the main cusps of the arch, which on the Branscombe canopy are carved in the round, on the Stafford canopy present a frontal view only, their rear quarters being concealed by the convenient device of wavy clouds. In short, much effort was expended on the Branscombe canopy, which was the work of a sculptor of high calibre. The Stafford canopy is a respectable but inferior companion, and it seems more likely that it was inspired by the Branscombe canopy than vice versa. If one accepts the date of *c.* 1442–3 for the completion of Branscombe's 'new tomb', then this rather than *c.* 1419 would mark the introduction into the cathedral of the 'perpendicular' style in furnishings, and the shift away from the traditional designs still employed in the 1430s for the chapel screens.

Around the Branscombe tomb chest is a rhyming verse which begins:

Olim sincerus Pater, omni dignus amore
Primus Walterus Magno iacet hic in honore

and continues for another ten lines to celebrate the Bishop's good works and piety.[14] Here again Branscombe's tomb is more elaborate than Stafford's which apparently inspired less literary attention, with an epitaph only four lines long, recorded by Leland.[15] This, however, is not surprising, given Branscombe's significance in the history of the cathedral. It is revealing that the Branscombe epitaph refers to him as 'the first Walter', an implicit reference to the later eminent Bishop with the same name, Walter of Stapledon (and is of course evidence that the verse could not have been composed in the late 13th century). It is perhaps no coincidence that the second Walter's tomb on the north side of the High Altar, although of a very different design in its general form, has one feature in common with the Branscombe canopy, a frieze of flying angels on its north side (Plate XXXIE). These are convincingly positioned horizontal figures, like those on the Branscombe tomb, although without musical instruments, and considerably larger. This tomb has suffered a number of later alterations, particularly on the side facing the presbytery, where the cornice was repaired and renewed in the 16th and 18th centuries, and again in 1805,[16] but the aisle side with the angel frieze appears to be original work.

The concept of a 15th-century sculptor drawing his inspiration from the iconography of an earlier bishop's tomb in the same cathedral would seem attractive. However, the story is more complicated, for the designer of the Branscombe canopy was also in touch with contemporary work elsewhere. The most striking comparison is with the tomb of John Holand, Duke of Exeter, formerly in the hospital of St Katharine-by-the-Tower, London, now in the chapel of St Peter ad Vincula in the precinct of the Tower of London. In its original position this tomb, like the Branscombe and Stafford monuments, occupied a screen-like position between its chantry chapel and the main body of the building. Holand died in 1447; the tomb bears his effigy and those of his first and third wives, but the size of the canopy and the arrangement of the coats of arms show that the third effigy is clearly a late addition.[17] The implication is that the monument was planned some time before Holand's third marriage in 1439, perhaps at the time of the death of his first wife, Anne Stafford, in 1432.

Although the Holand tomb is differently proportioned and more elaborately decorated than the Branscombe canopy, they have a remarkable number of features in common. Both have a single canopy arch with trefoiled cusping, and shield-bearing angels on the terminals. Both have small spandrels with censing angels, although the Branscombe canopy has tracery instead of trumpeting angels in the large spandrels. Both have a frieze with flying angels in horizontal postures. On the outside of the Holand tomb the frieze angels carry scrolls or support coats of arms, but below the soffit of the canopy there are also angels with musical instruments.

The detail of the sculptural style of the Holand and Branscombe canopies is difficult to compare as the former is heavily covered with whitewash (possibly concealing some restoration work), and the latter is disfigured by modern paint. However the general design and the common iconographic features are too close to avoid the conclusion either that one is dependent on the other, or that there must have been some common pattern available to both sculptors. Some of the motifs are not easy to parallel elsewhere. While spandrels with censing angels were already a common device on the great 14th-century canopied tombs such as the Percy tomb at Beverley and its derivatives, friezes of flying angels on medieval tombs are surprisingly elusive, despite the fact that this ancient motif can be traced back to depictions of Roman Victories. So far no other 15th-century examples have been located. Full horizontal figures of this kind obviously required more skill on the part of the sculptor than the more commonplace upright busts of shield bearing angels, found, for example, at Exeter on the later chantry chapel of Bishop Oldfield (1519).

How does one explain the connection between the London and Exeter tombs? It is tempting, but unconvincing to postulate some personal connection. Holand's first wife, Anne Stafford, daughter of the 5th Earl, was a cousin several times removed from Bishop Stafford of Exeter,[18] but it is the Branscombe rather than the Stafford canopy with which the Holand tomb is most closely linked. John Holand, Earl of Huntingdon and later Duke of Exeter, although born and brought up at Dartington in Devon, had a busy professional career as member of the Privy Council, Admiral, and Constable of the Tower of London, and there is no evidence that he spent any time on his Devon estates.[19] What one can conclude with reasonable certainty is that the model for this new type of tomb canopy in the Perpendicular style did not emanate from the conservative Exeter Cathedral workshop, still imbued with older decorative traditions, as the chapel screens show. The existence of the Holand tomb strongly suggests a London workshop as the source of the design, and perhaps even of the craftsmanship of the Branscombe monument. Holand was one of the most important men in England, and the tomb which he commissioned would be likely to attract the notice of those seeking a fashionably up-to-date design.

The conundrum which remains is how to account for the relationship between the 14th-century flying angels on Stapledon's tomb, those on the London monument, probably of the 1430s, and the Exeter ones probably of the 1440s. Elaborate hypotheses could be put forward: a London tombmaker was invited to Exeter to advise on a new up-to-date setting for the Branscombe and Stafford effigies, took note of the detail of the flying angels on the Stapledon tomb, returned to London, where he made use of this feature on the Holand tomb, then produced a design based on this grander tomb which was used for the Exeter monuments. Alternatively one recourses to the art historian's favourite device of lost common prototypes. Whatever the explanation, it is salutary to be reminded that interchange of artistic forms was not restricted to one location or to one century, and that the story behind them is often likely to be too complicated to be explained easily by the surviving evidence.

As a pendant it can be noted that the tomb canopy with richly decorated four-centred arch became a popular type in Devon parish churches, especially favoured in the 16th century for small monuments without effigies (as for example at Heanton Punchardon (1521) and Bishops Nympton (1540).[20] It would be far-fetched to derive these more rustic examples directly from the cathedral tombs. The tomb canopy with four centred arch was by then widespread all over England, while the distinctively Devonian use of lush foliage ornament reflects a local taste for lavish decoration which can be paralleled in contemporary woodwork. However the Carminow tomb at Ashwater, a remote village in west Devon, possibly to Thomas Carminow (d. 1442) is more closely related. It is clearly a reduced version of the Branscombe/Stafford canopy design. The tomb chest has cusped quatrefoils, the canopy a cusped and sub-cusped arch with tracery in the main spandrels, and foliage in the inner ones (as on the Stafford Canopy and the southside of the Branscombe canopy). There are shield bearing angels as terminals to the main cusps, and a parapet with quatrefoils (of identical, not alternating sizes as on the cathedral tombs), but on the frieze below, the sculptor has not attempted angels, only a band of foliage. The simplified forms are characteristic of a copy, perhaps based on a design provided by the workshop responsible for the cathedral tombs. It shows how progressive designs commissioned for important centres could occasionally find echoes in surprisingly out-of-the-way places.

ACKNOWLEDGEMENTS

I am most grateful to Mrs Audrey Erskine for her guidance over the manuscript sources.

REFERENCES

1. Bishop and Prideaux (1922), 118 ff.
2. Britton (1826), 102.
3. Bishop and Prideaux (1922), 131 ff.
4. Oliver (1861), 97.
5. Oliver (1861), 97.
6. Exeter 3550, Chapter Acts.
7. Pevsner (1952), 146.
8. Gardener (1940), 61.
9. Vallance (1947), pl. 62.
10. Bishop and Prideaux (1922), 131 ff.
11. Roll 2685.
12. Prior and Gardener (1940), pt III, ch. 4.
13. Roll 2690.
14. Oliver (1861), 45.
15. Oliver (1861), 57.
16. Britton (1826), 102.
17. Cherry (1990).
18. Oliver (1861), 94.
19. Emery (1970), 57–62.
20. Cherry and Pevsner (1989), Pls 51 and 52.

The Ring of Bishop Grandisson

By John Cherry

In the list of the rings found in the graves of English bishops published in 1930 by Charles Oman there is a gap between the ring found in the tomb of Archbishop Greenfield of York, who died in 1315, and the ring that belonged to William Wytlesey, Archbishop of Canterbury, who died in 1374.[1] This gap is unfortunate but the ring of Bishop Grandisson does give us some indication of the changes in fashion in the period.

The ring from the grave of Grandisson was found in the early 1950s during work in the chapel by the west door where Grandisson was buried in 1369 in accordance with the terms of his will. It is worth quoting the beginning of the passage in the will that deals with his burial and funeral.[2]

I, John de Grandisson, of the church of Exeter an unprofitable and unworthy Minister, being by the grace of God sound in mind and body, do make my will after this manner. I commend my spirit to my Creator, the Creator of all; but as to my body, which is corruptible and hath weighed down my soul, I will that it be buried without the West Door of the Church of Exeter, as quickly as can possibly be arranged in seemly fashion; without inviting my near kinsfolk or great Nobles, but only any neighbouring Bishop or Bishops. And I will that four wax tapers be set about my body, each of twenty pounds in weight, one at the head, one at the feet, and one on the right hand and on the left hand one. As for the other tapers, each of which is to be a pound in weight, let a pair be set on each Altar throughout the church; and let one of them there remain, and the others be distributed amongst the Parish-Churches of the City. I also forbid, under pain of Divine displeasure, all drinking of spiced wine in the Choir, by night around my body; but, if such things must needs be done, let it be in the Chapter house, or in some other place suitable for such a purpose; or, instead thereof, let a hundred shillings be distributed in common among all Ministers of the Choir who are present and recite the Psalter. I will, also, and bequeath, that, on the said day of burial, a hundred of the poorer people be provided with cloaks and hoods, if so many can be procured, made of thick cloth, white or grey; and that simple priests who attend on the day of my interment, as well as all Religious, whether men or women, receive, each of them, four pence. Also, if any Bishop, or Bishops, shall come to my burial, let them each receive for his expenses, as much as shall seem good to my Executors; together with a pontifical ring, or a plain mitre embroidered with gold thread, or some other fitting jewel, unless he has received one from me in my life time. . . . Also I desire that my familiars be clad not in black garments but in their own robes of the suit of the current year; and the priests and clerks of my Chapel in surplices and white capes, as they have been accustomed. And it is my wish that there should be a general distribution of bread to the poor not on the actual day of my burial, but on some other day, either before or after; and that, as far as shall be possible, not in money but in bread.

The history of this tomb is sad. In 1586 John Hooker records that Grandisson was 'buried in a tombe of ledd in the chaple in the west wall of his owne churche: his tombe was of late pulled up, the ashes scattered abroade and the bones of his carcasses bestowed no man knoweth where'.[3]

There was a cursory inspection of the contents of the tomb shortly before 1899. A further reopening in the 1950s was more exhaustive and it is recorded that much broken pottery was found, bones, English and German coins of Elizabethan date, a small piece of material about 2 inches square which might have been part of the orphrey of a chasuble, and a gold ring.[4] It therefore seems that when the contents were scattered before 1586 the grave was filled up with material from an adjacent rubbish heap, but two tiny objects remained which probably came from Grandisson's burial.

Medieval bishops often possessed large numbers of rings. Although Bishop Bitton, of Exeter, who died in 1307, was buried with a single gold ring set with a sapphire, his successor, Walter Stapledon, had a great many.[5] In a list of his effects delivered to Grandisson in June 1328 by the executors there were 91 rings. Of these one was broken, three of them were handsome, and the rest were ordinary, but the pontifical and best rings were stolen at the time of his death in London.[6] In his own will dated 1368 Grandisson mentions seven individual rings as well as the gift of a pontifical ring to any bishop attending his burial. He left his ring pertaining to the office of a bishop to the church in Exeter, and the only ring that is specifically described is the ring set with beautiful and thick sapphires in the form of a cross that he left to Philip de Beauchamp.[7] On the effigy of Bishop Oldham, died 1517, there are no less than seven large rings on the fingers, three on the right and four on the left. In addition there is a ring of extraordinary size worn over both thumbs.

The ring found in the tomb is made of gold with much smaller proportions of copper and silver.[8] It is quite a small ring — the internal diameter is 19 mm and the external diameter is 20.5 mm. It has an oval bezel with a chamfered edge. On the bezel the Virgin and Child are engraved reserved against an enamelled background (Pl. XXXIIA). Part of the enamel has been lost and reveals a cross hatched background. The folds of the Virgin's drapery are filled with red enamel. The background enamel is blue decorated with four pointed stars in reserve. The Virgin is crowned and holds the child with the left hand while her right hand points to the child. The child looks up at the Virgin and holds out a round object, possibly an apple, in his left hand. The engraving of the figures is of high quality and has been carried out with a chisel with a U-shaped tip. The hoop of the ring is rectangular in section. The outside (Fig. 1A) has an inset rectangular panel with an inscription reserved against an enamelled background. Although the exterior of the hoop of the ring is very worn tiny traces of white enamel remain. The inscription, difficult to read, begins with a cross and reads AVE MARIA GRACIA PLENA DOMIN — the angelic salutation at the Annunciation (Fig. 1). On the back of the bezel is the abbreviated inscription IHC XPC for Jesus Christ engraved across the long side of the bezel, each abbreviation with a cross above (Pl. XXXIIB).

The interest of the inscription on the outside lies not so much in the words but the way in which the letters are reserved in a rectangular panel. This way of enclosing the inscription is characteristic of Italian 14th-century signet rings. This may be illustrated from the drawing of a ring in the British Museum (Fig. 1B).[9] The style of the Lombardic lettering on this ring is close to that on the Grandisson ring. This way of treating the inscription is certainly Italian in origin, although this Italian manner may have been adopted on French rings.

Iconographically the child with the apple occurs throughout western Europe. He appears in English manuscripts of the early 14th century such as Corpus Christi Cambridge MS 53. The style of the Virgin and Child suggests a French rather than an Italian origin. The drapery of the Virgin and Child on the ring is shown by curving folds of changing thickness engraved and filled with enamel. The folds of the drapery are emphasised by shading. This drapery style also occurs on two enamelled objects of Parisian origin. The first (Pl. XXXIIE) is the reliquary of the Holy Thorn in the British Museum (MLA 1902, 2–10, 1). Here a similar style of drapery treatment may be seen on the shoulder of Simeon in the scene of the Presentation. The dating of the reliquary is not certain. If the king and queen are Phillippe VI and Jeanne de Bourgogne, a date in the 1340s would be reasonable.[10] Another example of the same style of drapery treatment may be seen on the ewer in the National Museum Copenhagen. It is clearest on the central figure in the game of 'frog in the middle' on the neck of the ewer. The ewer bears the hallmark of Paris and the similarity between the style of its enamelled decoration and the style of the illumination of Jean Pucelle enables it to be dated between 1320 and 1330.[11] From these comparisons the ring may have been produced in

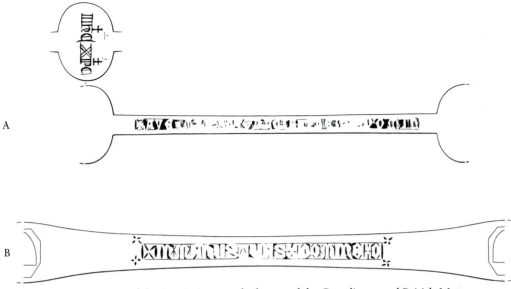

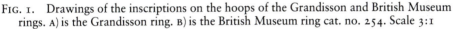

FIG. 1.   Drawings of the inscriptions on the hoops of the Grandisson and British Museum rings. A) is the Grandisson ring. B) is the British Museum ring cat. no. 254. Scale 3:1

Paris between 1320 and 1340, and the Italian treatment of the inscription suggests possible Italian influence on French ring making at that period.

The only other surviving evidence of a ring that belonged to Grandisson is the signet ring used to impress the back of his seals. A fine impression survives on the back of the seal on the Ottery charter of 1337 (Pl. XXXIIc).[12] It shows a half-length Virgin with long curving folds of drapery holding the child. They are placed above a shield which may have contained Grandisson's arms. Although this could be either a small seal or a ring it is more likely to be a ring since, owing to forgeries of his seals, the Bishop in 1354 commanded that no seals should be accounted genuine unless it bore 'the impression of our ring on the back'.[13] Rose Troup thought that the signet ring contained a fine intaglio with the Virgin and Child perhaps brought from Italy by Grandisson.[14] The inscription around the ring, *Ego sum Mater Misericordie*, reflects the beginning of the inscription on the thin plate of lead that Grandisson in his will ordered should be deposited with his body: 'Here lieth John de Grandison, the pitiable Bishop of Exeter, most miserable servant of the Mother of Mercy...'.[15] This will he sealed with an impression of his ring — perhaps the same ring he had used in 1337 to seal the Ottery charter. The sculptor of the ivories associated with Grandisson, in the British Museum and the Louvre, showed a knowledge of contemporary Italian painting. In particular a group by Ambrogio Lorenzetti has been cited as a source for the Virgin and Child on the Triptych (BM MLA 1926, 7–12, 1).[16] Grandisson was particularly devoted to the Virgin. This may be illustrated by his composition of a series of masses for the Blessed Virgin to be celebrated weekly through the year in memory of the seven joys of the Virgin and the references to the Virgin in his will, so that the occurrence of the Virgin and Child on his rings is not surprising.[17]

It may be noted that in his youth Grandisson was in Paris studying under Jean Fournier, later Pope Benedict XII, and, as chaplain to Pope John XXII, he probably resided at his court in Avignon. Grandisson was consecrated Bishop of Exeter at Avignon in 1327. It is known that he purchased objects from abroad, particularly Paris, since in his will he refers to the pastoral staff which he bought at Paris, the repair and improvement of Bishop Stapledon's mitre at Paris for 200 marks sterling, and the purchase of a gilt cross set with gems and the images of Mary and John bought at Paris.[18] William Bateman, Bishop of Norwich, also made similar purchases in France since he gave a cup of Avignon work of 1352 to his new foundation of Trinity Hall. John of Gaunt also bought a golden chalice made at Bordeaux and a golden retable made at Amiens.

Comparable examples of the Virgin and Child on the bezel of a ring with an enamelled background are not common. Another example, formerly in the Rosenheim collection, is now in the Victoria and Albert Museum (Pl. XXXIID).[19] The bezel is octagonal, with a frilled edge, and the triangular hoop is engraved with the inscription *Gaude Virgo Mater Xpi*. It is interesting to compare the iconography of the two rings. The Grandisson Virgin is half-length and she holds the child in her left hand. The child offers her an apple with his left hand. On the V&A ring the Virgin is enthroned while the child stands on the edge of the throne and puts his right hand around the Virgin's neck. The Virgin offers him an apple with her right hand. The engraving on the Grandisson ring is more linear and finer than on the V&A ring which is rather cruder. The treatment of the inscriptions are completely different since the V&A ring has individually engraved letters on the outer edges of its triangular sectioned hoop while the exterior of the Grandisson ring has a block type of inscription. Both use stars to key the enamel. The triangular shape of the hoop and the frilled edge of the bezel suggests a French origin for the V&A ring.

Both the Grandisson ring and the V&A ring are examples of a small group of rings with large enamelled bezels. Other 14th-century rings with enamelled iconographic bezels are in Scandinavia. Two with the face of Christ against an enamelled background occur in the Slagelse hoard, Denmark, deposited shortly after 1372. One of the two rings with enamelled bezels (D. 1776) is rather worn and therefore must have been made about or before the middle of the 14th century.[20] A notable feature of English rings of the later Middle Ages is the widespread popularity of enamelled bezels showing religious figures such as St Katherine, St Christopher, St George, or the Virgin — a class of rings often known as iconographic.[21] This type of ring provides a clear contrast to the ornamental rings of the 13th century which depend for their effect on the use of stones or the engraving of the hoop. Too much emphasis should not be placed on the role of the Grandisson ring in this change, but iconographic rings may have been derived from rings with large enamelled bezels. The pictorial quality of English iconographic rings may reflect the influence of continental enamelled rings such as that of Bishop Grandisson.

ACKNOWLEDGEMENTS

I am grateful to the following for their help: The Very Revd R. M. S. Eyre, Dean of Exeter, John Allan, Mrs Marian Campbell, Mrs A. Doughty, Mrs Audrey Erskine, Neil Stratford, and Dr P. Thomas.

REFERENCES

1. Oman (1930), 30. The only continental bishop's ring falling between these two dates is that set with a crystal belonging to Guillaume de Melun of Sens (d. 1336). A gold ring set with an amethyst was found in a tomb, identified as that of Bishop Trellick, who died in 1361, opened in August 1813 in Hereford Cathedral. M. H. Bloxam, *Fragmenta Sepulchralia* (c. 1840-50), 94 and James Storer, *Cathedral Churches* (London, 1816), vol. XI, Hereford (m).
2. Hingeston–Randolph (1894–9), 1511–21.

3. Hooker (1919), 232.
4. Anon. 'Two medieval bishops' tombs', *Friends of Exeter Cathedral*, 27th annual report (Exeter, 1957), 23–7. The ring has subsequently been published in *Age of Chivalry* (1987), no. 638.
5. For an account of the discovery of Bitton's ring by Dean J. Milles of Exeter see Evans (1956), 134–5.
6. Oliver (1861), 64–5. The inventory is quoted completely in Hingeston–Randolph (1892), 566.
7. Hingeston–Randolph (1892), 1518. Philip de Beauchamp was Archdeacon of Exeter and one of the executors of Grandisson. For further details, see Emden (1957), I, 136–7.
8. The exact proportions of metals in the ring are 79.1 per cent gold, 10.6 per cent silver, 10.3 per cent copper. The weight of the ring is 4.268 grammes. I am grateful to Mr Duncan Hook of the British Museum Research Laboratory for providing this analysis.
9. MLA 72, 6–4, 378. Dalton (1912), no. 254.
10. MLA 1902, 2–10, 1. *Les Fastes du Gothique*, exh. cat. (Paris, 1981), no. 190.
11. Cited above in n. 10, no. 183. An excellent colour photograph of the scene of 'frog in the middle' is reproduced in Gaborit Chopin (1982). This article contains an excellent discussion of the dating of the various pieces.
12. The Ottery charter is BL Add. MSS 15453.
13. Cited above in n. 2, 1135.
14. Rose Troup (1928), 273.
15. Hingeston–Randolph (1892), 1521.
16. The ivories are published with an extensive bibliography in *Age of Chivalry*, nos 593–5. The reference to Ambrogio Lorenzetti is by Saxl and Wittkower (1969), no. 33, pl. 11.
17. Troup, work cited at n. 15 above, 253.
18. Hingeston–Randolph (1892), 1513, 1515.
19. V&A reg. no. M8–1956. Rosenheim sale 9 March 1923, lot 96.
20. For the Slagelse hoard see Lindahl and Steen Jensen (1985), 123–82. This group of rings is also discussed by Lindahl (1985), 189–96. There is also at least one example in the Statens Historika Museum Stockholm (Steingraber (1957), pl. 62) and a gold ring with the head of Christ against an enamelled background in the Oslo Archaeological Museum.
21. For iconographic rings see Oman (1930), 23, and Cherry (Cherry (1981), 57). The term 'iconographic' was used by Dalton in 1912. It is not possible to indicate exactly when the type started. Most are generally assigned to the 15th century. The use of black letter inscriptions could indicate a late 14th-century date for their commencement. The Virgin and Child is a popular subject occurring on Dalton cat. nos 724, 725, 747, 757, 761.

Some Observations on Views of the Interior of Exeter Cathedral in the Nineteenth and Twentieth Centuries

By John Thurmer

This paper illustrates certain lost features of the cathedral. In the 19th century the restorations of Kendall and Scott are landmarks.[1] John Kendall worked extensively both inside and outside from early in the century to his death in 1829. Gilbert Scott restored the cathedral (mainly the interior) between 1870 and 1877. These observations therefore fall into three categories: pre-Kendall, Kendall's work and Scott's work.

PRE-KENDALL FEATURES

The Nave (Pl. Ci)

The watercolour is attributed, but without certainty, to Thomas Girtin, 1775–1803. This and a print of the late 18th century are the only known illustrations of the nave before 1834. In 1684 a 'cumbrous double range of pews of ugly horse-box stall type'[2] had been erected in the middle three bays of the nave. The pulpit was in the centre on the north side. It was used for 'lectures' or sermons other than the sermon prescribed after the Nicene Creed, which would have been delivered from the choir pulpit. All this was removed in 1834, after Kendall's death but consistently with his principles.[3] The pulpit was given to St James's Church, which was built in 1836 in the suburbs of Exeter and in the patronage of the Dean and Chapter, (rebuilt in 1878–85). The church and its contents were destroyed as a result of the Second World War. Though unlamented at the time, the pews do not deserve complete oblivion. The 17th century accepted without question that the cathedral consisted of two distinct major units — the choir and the nave. If the nave is used on its own, its focal point is the central bay, not the east end, which, with its shallow transepts formed by the towers, is the boundary between choir and nave. In the 19th century the Dean and Chapter, thwarted in its desire to remove the choir screen and throw the cathedral into one unit (see below), compromised by making the nave as much a conventional Victorian church as possible, with liturgical furniture concentrated at the east end. Various forms of this arrangement were in use from the mid-19th century to 1982.[4]

The Font

The font which appears in the watercolour was the gift of Dean Annesley and first used in 1687. It has undergone several changes of position and use. But it was restored to its original position in 1891.[5]

The Choir (Pl. XXXIIIA)

The photograph is of the 1860s.[6] The choir-stalls were erected in 1763, the work of the cathedral carpenter, John Gale.[7] The seats incorporated the 13th-century misericords but other information about the woodwork before 1763 is lacking. In his printed report to the

Dean and Chapter, Scott described Gale's stalls as 'wainscot-work of the last century —
costly enough, I doubt not, and well worked so far as mechanical handicraft goes — but
utterly devoid of all thought of appropriateness to its position'.[8] In 1870 Scott removed all
the choir woodwork, except the bishop's throne and the misericords.[9]

The cramming of the benches into the central space between the stalls indicates the
difficulty of providing seating for the general public.[10]

The Reredos (Pl. XXXIIIc)

This is a print of 1797. The 14th-century reredos lost its images and canopies at the
Reformation, but its solid stone background still stood, up to the base of the east window.
Up to 1638 it had a fabric royal arms stretched or draped over it. In that year, and as a result
of Archbishop Laud's Visitation of the Province of Canterbury, William Helyar, Archdeacon of Barnstaple, initiated and paid for its embellishment, painted by William Cavell,
lymner, directly onto the fabric of the reredos. There was some controversy about it,
because Helyar appealed to the Archbishop's Court of Audience;[11] but he was successful.
The painting survived the Commonwealth and appears, rather indistinctly, on prints of the
choir before 1817 when Kendall removed it. The stone is pitted with marks suggestive of
iconoclastic attack, but attack before, rather than after, painting, which, conservators
insist, is done directly onto the stone.

Had the reredos survived until Scott's restoration, what would he have done with it? As
late as 1973 it was described as 'extraordinary'.[12] But it was notable in two ways. It was the
main structure of the original reredos, and the painting an indication of Caroline theology
and taste. It has something in common with the frieze of the pulpitum, which also has
painting on previously carved stone, apparently of about the same date.

The design of the reredos suggests the entrance to a cathedral, with a great central door
and two side doors, like the cathedral's own west front. Across the main entrance and over
the altar table are the tablets of the commandments, flanked by the familiar figures of the
period, Moses and Aaron.[13] The iconography implies that, if the cathedral itself, or its
sanctuary, is the Holy Place, the Holy of Holies is heaven beyond, entered by obedience and
worship, centred in the Eucharist. There are also angels above, and St Peter, the cathedral's
patron, with his keys, on the north, balanced on the south by a figure less easy to identify. It
is either St Paul, the natural companion of St Peter, or St John the Evangelist, who was also
popular in Caroline iconography.[14]

KENDALL'S WORK

The Reredos

In 1817 Kendall was commissioned by the Chapter to dismantle the remains of the old
reredos with Helyar's painting and erect a new one. It is shown in a pre-Scott photograph
(Pl. XXXIIIB). The local newspaper described it as

in the pointed style of the fourteenth century; the centre, over the altar, is enriched by a canopy
entwined with ivy, and supported by columns. The principal flower, or finial, is composed principally
of the emblems of the united empire — the rose, thistle and shamrock. On each side are three
semi-hexangular recesses, surmounted by canopies highly decorated with the oak, vine, hop, rose and
palm....[15]

The arrangements of the altar conform to Canon 82 of 1604[16] in that the Ten
Commandments were inscribed on the central panel of the reredos, and the altar has 'a

carpet of silk or other decent stuff'. There are no ornaments, but the cathedral's Caroline silver candlesticks were put out at communion time with the rest of the plate. Communion benches occupy the space between the choir-stalls and the altar rail.

The Choir Screen

A photograph of before 1868 (Pl. XXXIVA) shows that the organ has lost its conical finials but still has pipes on the side. The heraldic devices on the screen have been replaced by Kendall's parapet. The sculpture above the central columns is a 'double rose and thistle of cumbrous and graceless sculpture'.[17] It filled a gap in the original carving in the early 17th century, and was no doubt a compliment to the royal house of Stuart, who from 1603 united the crowns of England and Scotland. The national symbols were removed when, through the generosity of Dean Earle (1900–18), the original work was restored by Edwin Luscombe, and restored so skilfully that it is virtually impossible to distinguish between the 14th- and 20th-century work.

Kendall embellished the stone walls of the outer bays of the screen with what Scott later called 'miserable surface tracery'.[18] Kendall's high altar, described above, can be seen through the opening. The screen altars were not restored until 1933.

The nave has stalls and chairs. Some people listened to what they could hear of the service in the choir,[19] and some services were held in the nave.

The Lady Chapel

This had housed the library since the cloisters and library chamber were destroyed in the Commonwealth. In 1821 the library was removed to the chapter house and Kendall restored it as a morning chapel. This is shown in Pl. XXXIVB. For some time it tended to be called 'the Old Library', but about 1830 the term Lady Chapel came back into use. An early service was instituted at this time — Morning Prayer was *said* in addition to being sung daily by the choir at 10.15 a.m.[20] In the photograph the east window is undergoing repair. In 1869 glass was inserted in memory of Bishop Phillpotts; it may be in preparation for that. The canopies under the window were erected by Kendall in 1823.

SCOTT'S WORK

The Reredos (Pl. XXXIIID)

Two features of Scott's restoration were highly controversial. First, the reredos. Scott dismissed Kendall's reredos as 'well-intended but ill-designed'[21] and demolished it (how quickly taste changes), relegating the Commandments to the ambulatory. He erected instead the sort of construction foreshadowed in his report to the Chapter (p. 2). It has three sculptured alabaster panels — the Ascension in the centre, flanked by the Transfiguration and the descent of the Holy Ghost, with surmounting cross and angels, all richly inlaid and jewelled. With it Scott designed a very handsome wooden pillared altar-table, covered normally with rich frontals.

W. J. Phillpotts, Archdeacon of Cornwall, Chancellor of the diocese and son of the previous bishop, petitioned Bishop Frederick Temple against the Dean and Chapter on account of the reredos. The point at issue was not the cross (which was legal by the Privy Council judgment in the case of Westerton v. Liddell, 1857) but the figures, which it was claimed contravened 3 and 4 Edward VI Cap. 10, 'An Act for abolishing ... divers books and images'. A subsidiary charge against the Dean and Chapter was that the new reredos has been erected without the Bishop's formal permission, known as a faculty. The Bishop held a Visitation Court and ruled reluctantly (on the advice of an assessor, Mr Justice Keating of the Court of Common Pleas) that the reredos was illegal. The Dean and Chapter appealed to the Provincial Court of the Arches and were successful, the appeal subsequently being upheld by the Privy Council.[22]

The judgment is of great ecclesiastical and artistic importance. It effectively established the legality of figure sculpture in the Church of England. On the basis of the Edwardian act Phillpotts had a good case, and the judgment was tantamount to legislation. But the act had not been systematically applied, and rigorous application in 1875 was not a practical possibility.[23]

The judgment confirmed the Chapter's independence of the ordinary jurisdiction of the Bishop, whose concern with the fabric was limited to ensuring conformity with the law. The reredos lasted until 1939, when it was supposed to have become unsafe; but taste had moved against it and it was dismantled.[24]

Scott's Choir Looking West (Pl. XXXIVc)

The other great controversy of Scott's restoration was the treatment of the *pulpitum* or organ screen. Though not a matter of litigation, this caused greater popular passion than the reredos. The dominant ecclesiology expected a church building open from end to end; a sort of sacred theatre, with the chancel like the stage. Cathedrals like Exeter were held to be large and grand examples of this model, and if they were not, they ought to be, and solid screens, where they existed, should be removed.[25] This view, which failed to understand the historical character of the greater churches, was widely and passionately held. Scott shared the dislike of screens and often removed them. But he had another principle also — namely, original architectural features should not be destroyed. He would not destroy the Exeter screen because it was original; and he maintained his view against strong pressure and violent abuse.[26] He was opposed to removing the masonry from the outer bays of the screen, but as a compromise he eventually consented to do this, so affording some view through the screen.[27]

Scott's Nave

The photograph of the great west window (Pl. XXXIVd) shows the glass inserted in 1766 by William Peckitt of York, 'the most celebrated mid-Georgian glass painter'.[28] The photograph is therefore before 1904, when this glass was removed to make way for a window in memory of Archbishop Frederick Temple, Bishop of Exeter 1869–85. The Temple window was destroyed in the bombing of 1942 and has been replaced by another.[29] Much of the heraldic glass in Peckitt's window was inserted in 1922 in the windows of J. L. Pearson's cloister room, a partial rebuilding of the cloisters begun in 1888. The pulpit was designed by Scott and is still in place. It commemorates John Coleridge Patteson, a Devon clergyman who became the first bishop of Melanesia and was murdered at Nakupu in 1871. Scott's choir-stalls and other furnishings were primarily intended for the popular second Evensong, which was held in the nave, and for which a voluntary choir (still in existence) was founded in 1881. There was clearly a sense of distinction between the two main parts of the cathedral. The cathedral choir sang the morning services and three o'clock Evensong (daily) in the choir; the voluntary choir sang the parish-type Sunday 6.30 p.m. Evensong in the nave. The railway age made possible an increased number of county and diocesan festivals, which used the nave. Scott's stalls for clergy and choir in the nave lasted until 1969, when they were replaced by movable furniture designed by Laurence King.

REFERENCES

1. For Kendall (1766–1829) see Colvin (1978), 488–9, and Erskine (1988), 77–80. He succeeded his father as stonemason to Exeter Cathedral. For Scott (Sir George Gilbert, 1811–78), his work at Exeter, see again Erskine (1988), 80–4.
2. Erskine (1988), 69.
3. Kendall had come under the influence of John Carter, the most learned student and defender of English Gothic fabric in his day, whose survey of the cathedral was published by the Society of Antiquaries in 1797. Kendall himself published *An Elucidation of the Principles of English Architecture usually denominated Gothic* (Exeter, 1818). A contemporary publication by James Scorer, *Graphic and Historical Description of the Cathedrals of Great Britain* (1816), described Kendall's principle as 'correctly imitating corresponding parts' (Vol. 2, 19), and such a principle seems to have extended to re-instating the 'Gothic' character of the cathedral.
4. In that year the Dean and Chapter put the movable nave altar in the central bay, with the seats in the eastern bays facing inwards. The liturgical requirements of the 1980s are not those of the 1680s, but they have something in common as against the 19th-century ecclesiologists. It may be noted also that this position of the altar comes nearer to the requirements of the 1559 and 1662 Prayer Books than most Caroline or Victorian practice.
5. Erskine (1988), 134.
6. Recently acquired by the Dean and Chapter.
7. Chapter Acts, 1763–70, 35.
8. Sir G. G. Scott, *Report to the Dean and Chapter* (1870), 2.
9. Dean Boyd used some of the 1763 panelling for the entrance hall of the Deanery, where it is still to be seen.
10. Secular cathedrals, like monasteries, were not places where lay people usually worshipped, and this seems to have been the case until the mid-19th century. The pews in the nave from 1683 to 1834 were for notables like the mayor and corporation. The choir-stalls were for the cathedral foundation. But from the 1840s there was a new enthusiasm for cathedral services. Influential works such as John Jebb's *The Choral Service of the United Church of England and Ireland* (1843) praised the cathedral service, sung by a robed choir of men and boys, as the ideal of Christian worship, which ought to be (and soon was) imitated in every church in the land. This liturgical revolution raised interest in cathedral worship, and the seating of congregations became a pressing matter. It is prominent in Scott's 1870 report. He criticised the intruding benches, and, like most of his contemporaries, would have preferred the lay congregation to be in the nave. But that raised the question of the screen; on which, see below.
11. The appeal is printed in *The Exeter Reredos. A Report of the proceedings of a Visitation ...* (Exeter, 1874), 141. No other record of the genesis of the Helyar reredos seems to survive.
12. Hope and Lloyd (1973), 28. Erskine (1988), 57–8.
13. The heads of Moses and Aaron are preserved on the stairway leading to the present archive library.
14. Addleshaw and Etchells (1948), 159.
15. *Trewman's Exeter Flying Post*, 2 Feb. 1819 (quoted in full in Erskine (1988), 79).
16. The Canons of 1604 had the authority of the Convocation of Canterbury and the Crown, and unless overridden by statute law were authoritative until the revised Canons were promulgated in 1964 and 1969; but some of the 1604 Canons were obsolete before that.
17. Oliver (1861), 214.
18. Report, 3.
19. Ibid., 4.
20. It was a sign that the cathedral was busier and more devout — those not free for a long sung service in the middle of the morning had their office early. In 1839 the College of Masters, later known as St Luke's, was founded in the Close, and its students attended the 7 a.m. service. With the subsequent increase of early celebrations of the Eucharist, this double Mattins did not survive; but when daily choral Mattins had to be abandoned in the 1950s, Mattins was again said daily in the Lady Chapel, usually at 7.30 a.m.
21. Report, 2.
22. Law Reports, Admiralty and Ecclesiastical, Vol. 4, 297–379, and Privy Council Appeals Vol. 6, 435–67.
23. Rather strangely the courts took no cognisance of the Helyar reredos which was in the cathedral for nearly two centuries. But they were much swayed by the precedent in the Court of the Arches of a judgment in 1684 in favour of the twelve apostles and St Paul painted at Moulton in Lincolnshire. There was, they said, no distinction in law between flat painting and sculpture. Both were legal providing they were not superstitious in content or use.
24. The Vicar of Heavitree, a Prebendary of the Cathedral, acquired it for St Michael's Heavitree, a large and essentially Victorian building. There it remains, and looks very splendid, having been carefully repaired and

conserved in 1988. Scott's altar-table was in Herbert Read's (Ecclesiastical Furnishings) workshop in 1942 and was destroyed in the bombing.

25.   Addleshaw and Etchells (1948), 214–17.

26.   Report, passim. It is said that the Chapter were in favour of removing the screen. This may be a deduction from the extent of Scott's arguments for retaining it, and from the subsequent compromise. Low Churchmen opposed the screen as popish; e.g. *The Cathedral Rood-Screen contrary to Protestantism and Common Sense — Four Letters to the Western Times by A Constant Reader* (Exeter, 1871). High Churchmen opposed it because it confused the orders of clergy and laity by seating them together in the choir; e.g. W. T. A. Radford, *Remarks on the Restoration of our Cathedral* (Exeter, undated).

27.   It is a pity that Scott's original view did not carry the day. He had a largeness of mind which makes his opponents look petty and blinkered, and conservation (his own word) was, within limits, the principle to which he held. Chapter Acts, 30 October 1871.

28.   B/E *South Devon* (1952), 143.

29.   B/E *Devon* (1989), 385–6 (written by C. Brooks).

ABBREVIATIONS AND SHORTENED TITLES

AASRP	*Associated Architectural Societies Reports and Papers*
Age of Chivalry	*The Age of Chivalry: Art in Plantagenet England 1200–1400*, Royal Academy Exhibition Catalogue, ed. J. Alexander and P. Binski
L'Apocalypse en français	*L'Apocalypse en français au xiiie siècle* (B.N.Fr. 430) Société des anciens textes français (Paris 1900)
Antiq. J.	*Antiquaries Journal*
Archaeol. J.	*Archaeological Journal*
Architectural History	*Journal of the Society of Architectural Historians of Great Britain*
BAA CT, 1–x	*British Archaeological Association, Conference Transactions (Medieval Art and Architecture at:)*
	I. *Worcester Cathedral* (1978)
	II. *Ely Cathedral* (1979)
	III. *Durham Cathedral* (1980)
	IV. *Wells and Glastonbury* (1981)
	V. *Canterbury* (1982)
	VI. *Winchester Cathedral* (1983)
	VII. *Gloucester and Tewkesbury* (1985)
	VIII. *Lincoln Cathedral* (1986)
	IX. *East Riding of Yorkshire* (1989)
	X. *London* (1990)
BAR	*British Archaeological Reports*
B/E	N. Pevsner *et al.*, ed., *The Buildings of England* (Harmondsworth various dates)
Bible	See *The Holy Bible*
Biblia (Pauperum)	*Biblia Pauperum*, see Henry (1987)
BL	British Library
BN	Bibliothèque Nationale Française
BP	Abbreviation for *Biblia Pauperum*, see above
Bull. Mon.	*Bulletin Monumental*
Cennini	Cennino d'Andrea Cennini da Colle di Val d'Elsa: *Il Libro dell'Arte*, D. V. Thompson, ed., 2 vols. Italian text and English translation (New Haven 1933)
Church Monuments	*The Journal of the Church Monuments Society*
CVMA	*Corpus Vitrearum Medii Aevi*
D&C (Exeter)	*Exeter Cathedral Archives, Dean and Chapter Act Books*
DNB	*Dictionary of National Biography* (Oxford 1908–9)
Douay Version	*The Holy Bible: Douay Version Translated from the Latin Vulgate and diligently compared with other editions in divers languages* (Douai A.D. 1609; Rheims A.D. 1582; London Burns and Oates, revised and annotated 1914; 1956)
Douce Apocalypse	*Apokalypse MS Douce 180 Vollstandige Faksimile-Ausgabe im Originalformat der Handschrift MS Douce 180 aus dem Bestiz der Bodleian Library — Oxford* (Graz 1983)

Dysson Perrins Apocalypse	*The Apocalypse in Latin, MS. 10 in the Collection of Dyson Perrins FSA*, Introd. M. R. James (Oxford 1927)
EETS es	Early English Text Society, extra series
EETS os	Early English Text Society, original series
(H)Eraclius	*De Coloribus et Artibus Romanorum* (in M. P. Merrifield (1967) Vol. I, 182–257)
Eton Roundels	See Henry (1990)
Exeter Cathedral Guides:	1. *A Guide to the Cathedral Church of Exeter with an Account of its Antiquities, Monuments &c.* (Plymouth-Dock 1818) 2. Bell's see Addleshaw (1899) 3. Pitkin Pictorial Guide: *Exeter Cathedral* (London 1976) Others as listed
FR	(Exeter Cathedral) Fabric Rolls, Exeter Cathedral Archives
(The) Holy Bible	see Douay Version
JBAA	*Journal of the British Archaeological Association*
JRIBA	*Journal of Royal Institute of British Architects*
JSAH (America)	*Journal of the Society of Architectural Historians of America*
Lausanne	'Portail peint de la Cathedrale de Lausanne': analyses pour une restauration', V. Furlan, R. Pancella, T. A. Hermanes, *Chantier* No. 12 (1981), 13–20
Migne	*Patrologia . . . Latina*, see under *Patrologia Latina*
MLA	Department of Medieval and Later Antiquities, British Museum
NBR	National Buildings Record (RCHME)
OED	*The Oxford English Dictionary* (Oxford 1933)
Ordinale Exon.	*Ordinale Exoniensis*, eds J. N. Dalton and G. H. Doble, 4 vols (Henry Bradshaw Soc., Vols XXXVII and XXXVIII [1909], vol. LXIII [1925], vol. LXXIX [1940])
Patrologia Latina	*Patrologia Cursus Completus . . . Series Latina*, ed. J. P. Migne, 221 vols (Paris 1844–64)
PDAS	*Proceedings of the Devon Archaeological Society*
Engravings	Most not separately listed here
PRO	Public Records Office
RCHME	Royal Commission on Historical Monuments for England
RDK	*Reallexikon zur deutschen Kunst-geschichte*, ed. O. Schmidt, K-A. Wirth and others, Vols I–VI– (Stuttgart 1937–73–)
SAHGB	Society of Architectural Historians of Great Britain; annual journal entitled *Architectural History* (see above)
Speculum Humanae Salvationis	*The Mirour of Mans Salvacioune: A Middle English Translation of* Speculum Humanae Salvationis: *A Critical Edition of the Fifteenth-Century Manuscript Illustrated from* Der Spiegel der menschen Behaltnis (Speyer, Drach *c.*1476), ed. A. Henry (London and Philadelphia 1986)
Strasbourg Manuscript	V. and R. Borradaile, *The Strasbourg Manuscript*, translation (1966)
TDA	*Reports and Transactions of the Devonshire Association for the Advancement of Science, Literature and Art*
TEDAS	*Transactions of the Exeter Diocesan Architectural Society*

Theophilus	(*De Diversibus Artibus*), J. G. Hawthorne and C. S. Smith trans. and eds, *On Divers Arts: the foremost medieval Treatise on Painting, Glass-making and metalwork* (Dover reprint 1979)
Trinity College Apocalypse	*The Trinity College Apocalypse*, introd. P. H. Brieger, 2 vols (London 1967)
VC	Exeter Cathedral Archives, Vicars Choral
VCH	*Victoria County History*
Warwick Archive	Warwick Archive of Moulding Drawings, c/o Dr R. K. Morris, History of Art Dept., Warwick University, Coventry

BIBLIOGRAPHY

Addleshaw, P. (1899) *The Cathedral Church of Exeter: A Description of its Fabric and a Brief History of the Episcopal See.* Bell's Cathedral Series, London 1898, 2nd edn rev., 1899

Addleshaw, G. W. O. and Etchells, F. (1948) *The Architectural Setting of Anglican Worship.* London

Alexander and Binski See under *Age of Chivalry* (Abbreviation)

Allan, J. P. and Jupp, B. (1981) 'Recent Observations in the South Tower of Exeter Cathedral', *PDAS* 39, 141–54

Aubert, M. (1964) *High Gothic Art* (Art of the World Series), trans. P. Gorge. London

Beacham, P. (1990) 'Local Building materials and Methods', in Beacham, P. (ed.) *Devon Building: an Introduction to Local Traditions*, 13–32. Exeter

Bedford, R. P. (1911) *St. James the Less: A Study in Christian Iconography.* London

Berland, Dom J.-M. (1980) *Val de Loire Roman.* 3rd edn, La Pierre-qui-Vire

Billings, R. W. (1843) *Architectural Illustrations and Description of the Cathedral Church at Durham.* London

Bilson, J. (1899) 'The Beginnings of Gothic Architecture. II. Norman Vaulting in England', *JRIBA*, 3rd series, VI

—— (1922) 'Durham Cathedral: The Chronology of its vaults', *Archaeol. J.*, 2nd series, XXIX

Bishop, H. E. and Prideaux, E. K. (1922) *The Building of the Cathedral Church of St Peter in Exeter.* Exeter

Blair, C. (1972) *European Armour.* London

Blake, D. W. (1972) 'Bishop William Warelwast', *TDA*, CIV, 15–33

Blakeway, J. B. (1825) *A History of Shrewsbury, II.* London

Blaylock, S. R. and Allan, J. P. (1984) 'Exeter Museums Archaeological Field Unit: Second Interim Report of Work in Exeter Cathedral (for 1983–1984)', transcript in Exeter Cathedral Library

—— (1985) 'Exeter Museums Archaeological Field Unit: Third Interim Report of Work in Exeter Cathedral (for 1984–85)', transcript in Exeter Cathedral Library

Blum, P. Z. (1969) 'The Middle English Romance "Iacob and Iosep" and the Joseph Cycle of the Salisbury Chapter House', *Gesta*, Vol. VIII, 18–34

—— (1991) 'The sequence of Building Campaigns at Salisbury', *The Art Bulletin*, LXXIII, 6–38

Boase, T. S. R. (1953) *English Art 1100–1216.* Oxford

Bock, H. (1961) 'The Exeter Rood Screen', *Architectural Review*, 130, 313–17

—— (1962) *Der Decorated Style.* Heidelberg

Bomford, D., Dunkerton, J., Gordon, D., Roy, A. (1989) *Art in the Making, Italian Painting before 1400.* National Gallery Exhibition. London

Bond, F. (1906) *Gothic Architecture in England.* London

—— (1910) *Wood Carvings in English Churches I. Misericords.* Oxford

—— (1914) *Dedications and Patron Saints of English Churches: Ecclesiastical Symbolism, Saints and Their Emblems.* London

Bond, F. B and Camm, B. (1909) *Roodscreens and Roodlofts*, 2 vols. London

Bonde, S. and Maines, C (1987) 'St-Jean-des-Vignes: An Augustinian Abbey in Soisson (*sic*), France' *Archaeology* (Sept.–Oct.), 42–9

Bony, J. (1958)   'The Resistance to Chartres in early Thirteenth-Century Architecture', *JBAA*, 3rd series, XXI, 35–52

—— (1979)   *The English Decorated Style: Gothic Architecture Transformed 1250–1350*, The Wrightsman Lectures 10. Oxford

Brakspear, H. (1913)   'Malmesbury Abbey', *Archaeologia*, LXIV

Brakspear, (Sir) H. (1931)   'A West-Country School of Masons', *Archaeologia*, LXXXI, 1–18

Britton, J. (1826)   *The History and Antiquities of the Cathedral Church of Exeter*. London

Brewer, J. N. (n.d.)   *The History and Antiquities of the Cathedral Church of Exeter*. London. (*c.* 1819–20; some engravings dated 1818)

Brewer, J. S. (ed.) (1879)   *Registrum Malmesburiense*. London, Rolls Series

Broderick, A. and Darrah, J. (1986)   'The Fifteenth Century Polychromed Limestone Effigies of William FitzAlan, 9th Earl of Arundel, and his Wife, Joan Nevill, in the FitzAlan Chapel, Arundel', *Church Monuments (The Journal of the Church Monuments Society)* Vol. I, Pt 2, 65–94

Brooks, C. and Evans, D. (1988)   *The Great East Window of Exeter Cathedral: A Glazing History*

Browne, C. B. (1906–16)   'Some Fourteenth-Century Customs of the Cathedral Church of St. Peter in Exeter', *TEDAS*, 3rd series, Vol. III, 80

Buckler, J. C. (1822)   *Views of the Cathedral Churches of England and Wales, with Descriptions*, London

Burrow, I. G. (1977)   'The Town Defences of Exeter', *TDA* 109, 13–40

Carpenter, S. C. (1943)   *Exeter Cathedral 1942*. London

Carter, J. (1794)   *Specimens of Ancient Sculpture and Painting Now Remaining in England Vol. 2*. London. Engravings by James Basire

—— (1797a)   *Vetusta Monumenta*

—— (1797b)   *Plan, Elevations, Sections and Specimens of the Architecture and the Ornaments of the Cathedral Church of Exeter*, with plates engraved by James Basire after John Carter, and Descriptions by Charles Lyttelton (1754), H. Engelfield and J. Windham. Society of Antiquaries of London

—— (1813)   *Some Account of the Abbey Church of St. Alban*, pls iv and v. London

Cave, C. J. P. (1949)   *Roof Bosses of Lincoln Minster*, Lincoln Minster Pamphlets

—— (1953)   *Medieval Carvings in Exeter Cathedral*, King Penguin, London

Chambers, J. D. (1877)   *Divine Worship in England in the Thirteenth and Fourteenth Centuries*. London

Chanter, J. F. (1932)   *The Bishop's Palace, Exeter and its Story*. London

Cherry, B., Pevsner, N. (1989)   *B/E Devon* for *The Buildings of England: Devon*, 2nd edn

Cherry, B. (1990)   'Some New Types of Late Medieval Tombs in the London Area', *BAA CT* x. London (1990), 140–55

Cherry, J., Ward, A., Gere, C., Cartlidge, B. (1981)   'Medieval Rings', *The Ring from Antiquity to the Twentieth Century*. London

Chierici, S. (1978)   *Lombardie Romane*, La Pierre-qui-Vire

Clapham, A. W. (1934)   *English Romanesque Architecture After the Conquest*. Oxford

—— (1955)   *St Augustine's Abbey, Canterbury, Kent*. Official Guide-book, London

Clarke, K. M. (1920)   *The Misericords of Exeter Cathedral*. Exeter

Clifton-Taylor, A. (1972)   *The Pattern of English Building*. London

—— (1989)   'Building Stones' in *B/E Devon* 2nd edn, 20–5

Coales, J. (ed.) (1987)   *The Earliest English Brasses*, Monumental Brass Society

Cockerell, C. R. (1851)   *Iconography of the West Front of Wells Cathedral with an Appendix on the Sculpture of other Medieval Churches in England*, Appendix B. London

Colchester, L. S. and Harvey, J. H. (1974)   'Wells Cathedral', *Archaeol. J.*, CXXXI, 200–14

Colchester, L. S. (ed.) (1982)   *Wells Cathedral: A History*. Shepton Mallet

—— (1987)   *Wells Cathedral*, New Bell's Cathedral Guides, London and Sydney

Colvin, H. (1978)   *A Biographical Dictionary of English Architects 1600–1840*. London

Colvin, H. M. (1983)   'The "Court Style" in Medieval English Architecture: A Review', *English Court Culture in the Later Middle Ages*, eds V. J. Scattergood and J. W. Sherborne, 129–39. London

Conant, K. (1966)   *Carolingian and Romanesque Architecture 800–1200*, 2nd edn. Harmondsworth

Cook, G. H. (1947)   *Mediaeval Chantries and Chantry Chapels*. London

—— (1955)   *Old St Paul's Cathedral. A Lost Glory of Mediaeval London*. London

Cornish, J. G. (1932)   'The Quarries of Salcombe Regis', *Devon and Cornwall Notes and Queries XVII*, parts 1 and 2, 30–4

Cotton, W. (1900)   *Bosses and Corbels in the Cathedral Church of St. Peter, Exeter*. Exeter

Cotton, W. and Woollcombe, H. (1877)   *Gleanings from the Municipal and Cathedral Records Relevant to the City of Exeter*. Exeter

Cox, J. C. (1913)   *Churchwardens' Accounts*. London

Cranage, D. H. S. (1912)   *An Architectural Account of the Churches of Shropshire*. Wellington

Dalton, O. M. (1912)   *Catalogue of Finger Rings*. London

Daras, C. (1961)   *Angoumois Roman*. La Pierre-qui-Vire

Dean, M. (1979)   *The Beginnings of Decorated Architecture in the Southeast Midlands and East Anglia*. Unpublished Ph.D. Dissertation, University of California, Berkeley

de la Beche, H. T. (1839)   *Report on the Geology of Cornwall, Devon and West Somerset*. London

Delisle, L. and Meyer, P. (1901)   *L'Apocalypse en Français au xiiie siècle*, Société des anciens textes français

Deuchler, F., Hoffeld, J. M., Nickel, H. (1971)   *The Cloisters Apocalypse*, 2 vols. New York

Draper, P. (1981)   'The Sequence and Dating of the Decorated Work at Wells', *BAA CT*, IV, 18–29

—— (1986)   'The Retrochoir of Winchester Cathedral: Evidence and Interpretation,' *JBAA*, CXXXIX, 68–74

Dru Drury, G. (1948)   'The Use of Purbeck Marble in Mediaeval Times', *Proceedings of the Dorset Natural History and Archaeological Society*, LXX, 74–98

Drury, H. M. R. (1947)   'The Reconstruction', *Friends of Exeter Cathedral Annual Report* 18

—— (1957)   'Exeter Cathedral, Devon', *Studies in Conservation*, 3, no. 1, 3–7

—— (1958)   'Report by the Surveyor to the Dean and Chapter', *Friends of Exeter Cathedral Annual Report* 28, 29–31

Du Cange, C. du F. (1937)   *Glossarium Mediae et Infimae Latinitatis*, ed. D. P. Carpenter, G. A. L. Henschel and L. Favre, II. Paris

Dugdale, Sir W. and Dodsworth R. (1655–73)   *Monasticon Anglicanum*

Dugdale, W. (1716)   *A History of St. Paul's Cathedral*, 2nd edn. London

—— (1818)   *The History of St Paul's Cathedral in London*. London

—— (1819)   *Monasticon Anglicanum*, II. London

Durrance, E. M. and Laming D. J. C. (1982)   *The Geology of Devon*. Exeter

Durkan, J. (1970)   'Notes on Glasgow Cathedral', *The Innes Review*, XXI

Durliat, M. (1964)   *Rousillon Roman*. 2nd edn. La Pierre-qui-Vire

Eastlake, C. L. (1960)   *Methods and Materials of Painting of the Great Schools and Masters*, I. New York. Originally published as *Materials for a History of Oil Painting*. London, 1847

Edmonds, W. J. (1898)   *Exeter Cathedral* (also 1897)
Ecles F. C. (1949)   'Repairs at Exeter Cathedral', *Country Life* 17 June 1949, 1442–4
Einhorn, J. W. (1976)   *Spiritalis Unicornis*. Munich
Emden, A. B. (1957–9)   *A Biographical Register of the University of Oxford to A.D. 1500.*
                               Oxford

Emery A. (1970)   *Dartington Hall*. Oxford
Erskine, A. M. (1976)   'Bishop Briwere and the Reorganisation of the Chapter of Exeter Cathe-
                               dral', *TDA*, 108, 159–71
—— (1979)   *Exeter Cathedral: Documentation of West Front and Image Wall,
                               1794–1839*, unpublished typescript, copy in Cathedral Library
—— (ed.) (1981)   *The Accounts of the Fabric of Exeter Cathedral, 1279–1353: Part I
                               1279–1326*, Devon and Cornwall Record Society, n.s. vol. **24**.
                               Torquay
—— (ed.) (1983)   *The Accounts of the Fabric of Exeter Cathedral, 1279–1353: Part II
                               1328–1353*, Devon and Cornwall Record Society, n.s. vol. **26**. Torquay
—— (rev.) (1988)   *Exeter Cathedral: A Short History and Description by the Rev. Vyvyan
                               Hope, M.A., F.S.A., and John Lloyd, M.A., F.S.A., F.R.S.L., revised and
                               extended*. Exeter
Evans, J. (1956)   *History of the Society of Antiquaries*. London
Everett, A. W. and   'The rebuilding of Exeter Cathedral *c.* 1270–1360', *TDA*, 100, 179–90
  Hope, V. (1968)
Fernie, E. C. (1976)   'The Ground plan of Norwich Cathedral and the Square Root of Two',
                               JBAA, CXXIX, 77–86
—— (1983)   *The Architecture of the Anglo Saxons*. London
Fernie, E. C. and   'The Early Communar and Pitancer Rolls of Norwich Cathedral Priory',
  Whittingham, A. B.   *Norwich Record Society*, XLI
  (1972)
Findlay, D. F. (1939)   *The Fabric Rolls of Exeter Cathedral, 1374–1514*, Ph.D. Thesis, Uni-
                               versity of Leeds
Fox, Sir C. (1955)   'The cleaning of the image-wall and porches of the West Front.' *Friends
                               of Exeter Cathedral, Annual Report* 21. Exeter
Freeman, P. (1888)   *The Architectural History of Exeter Cathedral*; new edn, ed. and with
                               additional matter by E. V. Freeman. Exeter and London
Frere W. H. (1901)   *The Use of Sarum*, 2 vols, Cambridge
Furlan, V., Pancella, R.,   'Portail peint de la Cathédrale de Lausanne; analyses pour une restaur-
  Hermanés, T. A. (1981)   ation'. *Chantier* No. 12, 13–20
Furneaux, J. (1849)   'A Paper on St German's Priory Church', *TEDAS*, III
Furnival, F. J. (1882)   *The Fifty Earliest English Wills*, EETS os, LXXVIII. London
Gaborit, S. R. (1978)   *Great Gothic Sculpture*, Reynals World History of Great Sculpture
Gaborit Chopin, D.   'Les Emaux Translucides Parisiens dans la première moitié du XIVe siècle'
  (1982)   *Archaeologia*. Paris
Gardner, A (1935)   *A Handbook of English Medieval Sculpture*. Cambridge
—— (1940)   *Alabaster Tombs of the pre-Reformation Period in England*
—— (1951)   *English Medieval Sculpture*. Cambridge
Gardner, S. (1984)   'The Church of Saint-Étienne in Dreux and its Role in the Formulation of
                               Early Gothic Architecture', *JBAA*, CXXXVII, 86–113
Gee, L. L. (1979)   '"Ciborium" Tombs in England 1290–1330', *JBAA*, CXXXII, 29–41
Gem, R. D. H. (1973)   'St German's Priory Church', *Archaeol. J.*, CXXX, 289–91
—— (1978)   'Bishop Wulfstan II and the Romanesque Cathedral Church of Worces-
                               ter', *BAA CT*, I, 15–37
—— (1982)   'The Significance of the 11th-Rebuilding of Christ Church and St Augus-
                               tine's, Canterbury, in the Development of Romanesque Architecture',
                               BAA CT, V, 1–19

Gethyn-Jones, E. (1979)	*The Dymock School of Sculpture.* London and Chichester
Givens, J. (1985)	*The Garden outside the Walls: Botanical Naturalism in English Gothic Sculpture*, unpublished Ph.D. dissertation, University of California, Berkeley
Glasscoe, M. and Swanton, M. (1978)	*Medieval Woodwork in Exeter Cathedral.* Exeter
Glenn, V (1986)	'The Sculpture of the Angel Choir at Lincoln', *BAA CT*, VIII, 102–8
Glorieux, P. (1952)	*Pour revaloriser Migne: tables rectificatives*, Mélanges de Science religieuse 9. Lille
Goodridge, F. F.	Translation of *Piers the Ploman*, see under Langland (1959)
Groen, C. M. (1978)	'The Examination of Five Polychrome Stone Sculptures of the late Fifteenth Century in Utrecht', *ICOMOS Committee for Conservation, 5th Triennial Meeting, Zagreb, Proceedings*
Grossinger, C. (1975)	'English Misericords of the thirteenth and fourteenth centuries and their relationship to manuscript illuminations', *Jnl. of the Warburg and Courtauld Institutes*, XXXVIII
Gundry, P. B. H. (1972)	'Report by the Surveyor', *Friends of Exeter Cathedral Annual Report* 41, 26–7
Gunnis, R. (1968)	*Dictionary of British Sculptors 1660–1851*, Revised edn. London
Halsey, R. (1985)	'Tewkesbury Abbey: Some Recent Observations', *BAA CT*, VII
Harrison, F. (1958)	*Music in Medieval Britain.* London
Hart, W. H. (1863)	*Historia et Cartularium Monasterii S. Petri, Gloucestriae*, Vol. I. London
Harvey, J. H. (1978)	*The Perpendicular Style 1330–1485.* London
—— (1984)	*English Mediaeval Architects: a Biographical Dictionary down to 1550*, revised. Gloucester
Hawthorne and Smith, (1979)	See under Theophilus in Abbreviations above
Hearn, M. F. (1971)	'The Rectangular Ambulatory in English Mediaeval Architecture', *JSAH (America)*, XXX, 187–208
Hellins, J. (1890)	'Notes on the Remains of Norman Work in Exeter Cathedral', *TEDAS* 2nd ser.
Henderson, C. G. and Bidwell, P. T. (1982)	'The Saxon Minster at Exeter', *The Early Church in Western Britain and Ireland*, ed. S. M. Pearce, Oxford BAR British Series, CII, 151, 168–9
Henderson, C. G. and Blaylock, S. R. (1987)	'The East Window', *Exeter Archaeology 1985/86.* Exeter
Henry, A. (ed.) (1986)	*The Mirour of Mans Saluacioune: A Middle English Translation of Speculum Humanae Salvationis: A Critical Edition of the Fifteenth-Century Manuscript illustrated from Der Spiegel der menschen Behältnis, Speyer, Drach c. 1476.* London and Philadelphia
—— (ed.) (1987)	*Biblia Pauperum: A Facsimile and Edition.* Aldershot and Ithaca. (See also under abbreviation BP)
—— (ed.) (1990)	*The Eton Roundels: Eton MS 177 'Figurae Bibliorum': A Colour Facsimile, with Transcription, Translation and Commentary.* Aldershot
Hewett, J. W. (1848)	*A Brief History and Description of the Cathedral Church of St Peter, Exeter*, Exeter
Hilberry, H. H. (1959)	'The Cathedral at Chartres in 1030', *Speculum*, XXXIV
Hill, D. I. (1986)	*Canterbury Cathedral* (New Bell's Cathedral Guides). London
—— (1889)	*The Registers of Walter Bronescombe (A.D. 1257–1280), and Peter Quivil (sic) (A.D. 1280–1291), Bishops of Exeter, with Some Records of the Episcopate of Bishop Thomas de Bytton (A.D. 1292–1307); also the Taxation of Pope Nicholas IV. A.D. 1291 — (Diocese of Exeter).* London and Exeter
Hingeston-Randolph, F. C. (ed.) (1892)	*The Register of Walter de Stapeldon, Bishop of Exeter.* London and Exeter

—— (1894–99)   *The Register of John de Grandisson, Bishop of Exeter A.D. 1327–1369*, 3 vols. London and Exeter

Hoey, L. (1984)   'Beverley Minster in Its 13th-Century Context', *JSAH (America)*, XLIII, 209–24

—— (1987)   'Piers Versus Vault Shafts in Early English Gothic Architecture', *JSAH (America)*, XLVI, 241–64

Hooker, J. (1919)   *Description of the Citie of Excester*, ed. W. J. Harte, S. W. Schopp and H. Tapley-Soper

Hope, V. (n.d., *c.* 1966)   *A Cathedral Miscellany*, unpublished MS and typescript in Cathedral Library

Hope, V. and Lloyd, L. J. (1973)   *Exeter Cathedral: A Short History and Description*. Exeter

Hope, W. St J. (1900)   *The Architectural History of the Church and Monastery of St Andrew, Rochester*. London

—— (1913)   *Windsor Castle, An Architectural History*, I, (London 1913)

—— (1917a)   'Quire Screens in English Churches with Special Reference to the Twelfth-Century Quire Screen formerly in the Cathedral Church of Ely', *Archaeologia*, LXVIII (1917), 43–110

—— (1917b)   'The Sarum Consuetudinary and its relation to the Cathedral Church of Old Sarum', *Archaeologia*, LXVIII (1917)

Hope, W. St J. and Atchley, E. G. C. F (1918)   *English Liturgical Colours*. London

Howard, F. E and Crossley, F. E. (1917)   *English Church Woodwork, 1250–1550*. London

Howard, F. T. (1933)   'The Building Stones of Ancient Exeter', *TDA*, 65, 331–5

Hulbert, A. (1987)   'Notes on Techniques of English Medieval Polychromy on Church Furnishings' *Jubilee Conservation Conference Papers; Recent Advances in the Conservation and Analysis of Artefacts*. Compiled by J. Black. University of London, Institute of Archaeology

Jacob, W. H. (1913)   'Winchester Cathedral Consistory Court', *The Antiquary*, XLIX

James, M. R. (1894–98)   'On the Paintings formerly in the Choir at Peterborough', *Proceedings of the Cambridge Antiquarian Society*, IX

Jansen, V. (1975)   *The Architecture of the Thirteenth-Century Rebuilding at St Werburgh's, Chester*, unpublished Ph.D. dissertation, University of California, Berkeley, University Microfilms, Ann Arbor 176–15, 235

—— (1979)   'Superposed Wall Passages and the Triforium Elevation of St. Werburg's Chester', *JSAH (America)*, XXXVIII, 223–43

—— (1982)   'Dying Mouldings, Unarticulated Springer Blocks, and Hollow Chamfers in Thirteenth-Century Architecture', *JBAA*, CXXXV, 35–54

Jenkins, A. (1806)   *The History and Description of the City of Exeter and Its Environs*. Exeter

Jones, J. (1757)   (delin., Coffin sculpt.), (Print of) *The Ichnography of the Cathedral Church of St Peter at Exeter*

Jones, J. (1817)   'Ancient Constitution, Disciplines and Usage of the Cathedral Church of Exeter', *Archaeologia*, XVIII, 410

Joy, E. T. (1976)   *Woodwork in Winchester Cathedral*. Winchester

Katzenellenbogen, A. (1964)   *Allegories of the Virtues and Vices in Mediaeval Art from Early Christian Times to the Thirteenth Century*. London 1939, repr. New York 1964

Kemp, E. W. (1948)   *Canonisation and Authority in the Western Church*. Oxford

Kendall, J. (1842)   *An Elucidation of the Principles of English Architecture, Usually Denominated Gothic*. London 1818, re-issued 1842

Kidson, P. (ed.) (1978)   *Lincoln: Gothic West Front, Nave and Chapter House*. Part 5 of *Archive 1: Cathedrals and Monastic Buildings in the British Isles*. Courtald Institute Archives, ed. P. Lasko. London

Kimpel, D. (1977)   'Le dévelopment de la taille en série dans l'architecture médiévale et son rôle dans l'histoire économique', *Bull. Mon.*, cxxxv, 195–222

King, D. (1986)   'The Glazing of the South Rose at Lincoln Cathedral', *BAA CT* viii

Kirschbaum, E. (ed.) (1968–76)   *Lexicon der christlichen Ikonographie*, 8 vols. Rome

Klauser, T. (1979)   *A Short History of the Western Liturgy*. Oxford

Krinsky, C. H. (1970)   'Representations of the Temple of Jerusalem before 1500', *Journal of the Warburg and Courtauld Institutes*, 33

Kurath, H. and Kuhn, S. M. (1959)   *Middle English Dictionary*, 'C'. Ann Arbor

Kusaba, Y. L. (1983)   *The Architectural History of the Church of the Hospital of St Cross in Winchester*. Ann Arbor

Langland   See under Abbreviations

Langland, W. (1959)   *Piers the Ploughman: William Langland Translated into Modern English*, trans. F. F. Goodridge. Harmondsworth

—— (1978)   *The Vision of Piers Plowman: A Critical Edition of the B-Text Based on Trinity College, Cambridge Ms B.15.17 with Selected Variant Readings, an Introduction, Glosses, and a Textual and Literary Commentary*, ed. A. V. C. Schmidt. London

Latham, R. E. (ed.) (1981)   *Dictionary of Medieval Latin from British Sources*, London

Leach, R. (1978)   *An Investigation into the Use of Purbeck Marble in Medieval England*. Crediton

Leedy, W. C. L. (1980)   *Fan Vaulting: a Study of Form, Technology and Meaning*. London

Lega-Weeks, E. (1915)   *Some Studies in the Topography of the Cathedral Close, Exeter*. Exeter

Leland, J. (1907–10)   *Itinerary in England and Wales*, ed. L. Toulmin Smith, 5 vols. London

Lelong, C. (1976)   'Recherches sur l'abbatiale de Marmoutier a l'epoque romane', *Comptes Rendues Acad. des Inscriptions et Belles-Lettres*, 704–34

—— (1979)   'Aperçus complémentaires sur le plan de l'église abbatiale de Marmoutier a l'XIe siècle', *Bull. Mon.*, cxxxvii, 241–7

Le Patourel, H. E. J. (1973)   *The Moated Sites of Yorkshire*, Society for Medieval Archaeology Monograph No. 5

Lethaby, W. R. (1903)   'How Exeter Cathedral was Built — I', *Architectural Review* xiii, 109–20; (part II, 166–76)

—— (1906)   'Restoration Work at Exeter Cathedral'. *Country Life*, 15.XII.1906

—— (1925)   *Westminster Abbey Re-Examined*. London

Lindahl, F. and Steen Jensen, J.   'Skattefundet fra Slagelse, 1883', *Aarboger Nord. Oldk. Hist.*

Lindahl, F. (1985)   'Middelalderlige fingerringe med ikonografiske motiver', *Konsthistoriska Studier* 8. Helsinki

Lobel, M. D. (1975)   *The Atlas of Historic Towns*. London

Lynam, C. (1905)   'Notes on the Nave of Chepstow Parish Church', *Archaeol. J.*, lvii, 271–8

Lysons, D. (1822)   *Magna Britannia (Vol) 1: History of the County of Devon*. London

Lyttelton, C. (1754)   *Some Remarks on the Original Foundation and Construction of the present Fabric of Exeter Cathedral*; printed as a preliminary to Carter (1797b) above

McAleer, J. P. (1984)   'The Façade of the Romanesque Cathedral at Exeter', *PDAS*, xlii, 71–6

Maddison, J. (1978)   *Major Building in the North-West Midlands and North Wales c. 1270–1400*, unpublished Ph.D. thesis, Manchester University

Maury, J. (1974)   *Limousin Roman*, 2nd edn. La Pierre-qui-Vire

Merrifield, M. P. (1967)   *Original Treatises dating from the XIIth to the XVIIIth Centuries on the Arts of Painting*, 2 vols. London 1849, Dover Reprint 1967

Milburn, R. L. P. (1949)   *Saints and their Emblems in English Churches.* London

Morgan, C. O. S. (1885)   'St Woolos's Church, Newport, Monmouthshire', *Archaeologia Cambrensis*, 5th series, II, 279–96

Morgan, N. (1982)   *Early Gothic Manuscripts I, 1190–1250.* Oxford

Morris, P. (1943, 1944)   'Exeter Cathedral: a conjectural restoration of the 14th-century altar screen', *Antiquaries' Journal*, XXIII, 122–47 and XXIV, 10–41

Morris, R. K. (1974)   'The Remodelling of the Hereford aisles', *JBAA* 3rd sereis, XXXVIII, 21–39

—— (1978a)   'The Development of Later Gothic Mouldings in England, *c.* 1250–1400 — Part I', *Architectural History*, 21, 18–57

—— (1978b)   'Worcester Nave: from Decorated to Perpendicular', *BAA CT*, I (1978)

—— (1979)   'Later Gothic Mouldings in England, *c.* 1250–1400, Part II', *Architectural History*, 22 (1979), 1–48

—— (1982)   'Late Decorated Architecture in Northern Herefordshire', *Transactions of the Woolhope Naturalists' Field Club*, XLIV pt I (1982)

—— (1984)   'The Architectural History of Wells Cathedral', review article of L. S. Colchester, ed., *Wells Cathedral, A History*, in *Transactions of the Ancient Monuments Society*, new series XXVIII (1984), 194–207.

—— (1990)   'The New Work at Old St Paul's Cathedral and its Place in English 13th-century Architecture', *BAA CT* x, 74–100

Muratova, X. (1989)   'Exeter and Italy: Assimilation and Adaptation of a Style: The Question of Italian Trecento Sources in the Sculptured Front of Exeter Cathedral (Fourteenth Century)', *World Art: Themes of Unity in Diversity, Acts of the XXVIth Congress of the History of Art*, ed. Irving Lavin, 1. Pennsylvania State University Press

Musset, L. (1974)   *Normandie Romane, II, La Haute-Normandie.* La Pierre-qui-Vire

—— (1975)   *Normandie Romane, I, La Basse-Normandie,* 2nd edn. La Pierre-qui-Vire

Nichols, J. G. (ed.) (1852)   *Chronicle of the Grey Friars in London*; Camden Soc., LIII. London

Nickel, H. (1972)   'A Theory about the Early History of the Cloisters Apocalypse', *Metropolitan Museum Journal* 6, 59–72

Oliver, G. (1821)   *History of Exeter.* Exeter

—— (1861)   *Lives of the Bishops of Exeter, and a History of the Cathedral.* Exeter

Oman. C. C. (1930)   *Catalogue of Rings.* London

Ordinale Exon   See under Abbreviations

Orme, N. (1976)   *Education in the West of England 1066–1548.* Exeter

—— (1977)   'The Kalendar Brethren of the City of Exeter', *TDA*, CIX, 153–69

—— (1978a)   'Education in the West of England', *Devon and Cornwall Notes and Queries*, XXXIV, 22–25

—— (1978b)   'The Medieval Schools of Worcestershire', *Transactions of the Worcestershire Archaeological Society, 3rd series*, VI

—— (1979)   'The Dissolution of the Chantries in Devon', *TDA*, CXI, 75–123

—— (1980)   *The Minor Clergy of Exeter Cathedral, 1300–1548.* Exeter

—— (1981)   'The Medieval Clergy of Exeter Cathedral: I, The Vicars Choral and Annuellars', *TDA*, CXIII, 79–102

—— (1982)   'The Medieval Chantries of Exeter Cathedral', *Devon and Cornwall Notes and Queries*, XXXIV and XXXV, 12–21

—— (1983)   'The Medieval Clergy of Exeter Cathedral: II, The Secondaries and Choristers', *TDA*, CXV

—— (1986a)   'Sir John Speke and his Chapel in Exeter Cathedral', *TDA*, CXVIII, 25–41

—— (1986b)   *Exeter Cathedral As it was, 1050–1550.* Exeter

—— (1986c)   'Two Saint Bishops of Exeter, James Berkeley and Edmund Lacy', *Analecta Bollandiana*, CIV, 403–18

Ostoia, V. K. (1972)   'Two Riddles of the Queen of Sheba', *Metropolitan Museum Journal* 6, 73–96

Owen, D. M. (1974) *John Lydford's Book*, Historical MSS Commission and Devon & Cornwall Record Soc., xx. London

Pevsner, N. (1952) *The Buildings of England, South Devon* (Harmondsworth 1952)

—— (1953) 'A Note on the Art of the Exeter Carvers', in Cave (1953), 25–32

Pevsner, N. and Metcalf, P. (1985) *The Cathedrals of England: Southern England.* Harmondsworth

Pickard, R. (1933) 'Weathering of Exeter's Walls and Buildings', *TDA* 65, 332–9

Plahter, L. E., Skaug, E., and Plahter, V. (1974) *Gothic Painted Altar Frontals from the Church of Tingelstad. Materials/Techniques/Restoration.* University of Oslo and University of Bergen

Portman, D. (1966) *Exeter Houses 1400–1700.* Univ. of Exeter

Prideaux E. K. (1912a) 'Figure Sculpture of the West Front of Exeter Cathedral', *Archaeol. J.* 69, 1–35

—— (1912b) *The Figure Sculpture of the West Front of Exeter Cathedral Church: A Complete Photographic Record with Notes.* Exeter

Prideaux, E. K. and Shafto, G. R. Holt (1910) *The Bosses and Corbels of Exeter Cathedral: An Illustrated Study in Decorative and Symbolic Design.* Exeter and London

Prior, E. S. and Gardner, A. (1905) 'English Mediaeval Figure-Sculpture', *Architectural Review* 17

—— (1912) *An Account of Medieval Figure-Sculpture in England.* Cambridge

Pycroft, G. (1882) 'Art in Devonshire. Part II' *TDA* 14, 278–316

RCHM(E) (1970) *An Inventory of the Historical Monuments in the County of Dorset, Volume Two: South-East, part 2.* H.M.S.O.

Radford, C. (1950) 'Three Centuries of Playgoing in Exeter', *TDA.* 82, 241–69

Radford, C. A. Ralegh (1960) 'The Romanesque Cathedral at Exeter', *Report of the Friends of Exeter Cathedral, Annual Report* 30, 28–36

Raine, J. (ed.) (1865) *Testamenta Eboracensia*, vol. iii, Surtees Soc., xlv

Rannie, A. (1966) 'Decorated Architecture in the Cathedral', *Winchester Cathedral Record,* 35

Remnant, G. L. (1969) *A Catalogue of Misericords in Great Britain.* Oxford

Remnant, M. (1986) *English Bowed Instruments from Anglo-Saxon to Tudor Times.* Oxford

Robinson, J. A. (1927) 'Links between Wells and Exeter, 1260–1340', *Somerset and Dorset Notes and Queries*, xix, 25–9

—— (1931) 'On the date of the Lady Chapel at Wells', *Archaeol. J.* lxxxviii, 159–74

Rocque, J. (1744) *Map of Exeter* [with perspective views]

Root, M. E. (1950) *Dunkeld Cathedral*, official guide, 2nd edn. Edinburgh

Rose-Troup, F. (1923) *Lost Chapels of Exeter.* Exeter

—— (1928) 'Bishop Grandisson, Student and Art-Lover', *TDA,* 60, 239–75

—— (1942) *Exeter Vignettes.* Manchester

—— (n.d.) *The Consecration of the Norman Minster at Exeter, 1133.* Exeter

Rossi-Manaresi, R. (1987) 'Considerazioni Tecniche sulla Scultura Monumentale Policromata, Romanica e Gotica', *Bolletino d'Arte*

Rossi-Manaresi, R. and Tucci, A. (1984) 'The Polychromy of the Portals of the Gothic Cathedral of Bourges', *ICOMOS Committee for Conservation, 7th Triennial Meeting, Copenhagen. (Proceedings)*

Russell, G. (1980) 'The North Window of the Nine Altars' Chapel at Durham Cathedral', *BAA CT,* iii, 87–9

—— (1983) 'Decorated Tracery in Winchester Cathedral', *BAA CT,* vi, 94–100

—— (1986) 'The Original West window of Lincoln Cathedral', *BAA CT,* viii, 83–9

Salzman, L. F. (1952) *Building in England down to 1540.* Oxford

Sandler, L. F. (1974) *The Peterborough Psalter in Brussels and Other Fenland Manuscripts.* London

Saxl, F. and Wittkower, R. (1969) *British Art and the Mediterranean.* Oxford

Schiller, G. (1972)   *Iconography of Christian Art* Vols I and II, trans. by J. Seligman. London
Schmidt (1978)   See under Langland (1978)
Secret, J. (1968)   *Perigord Roman*. La Pierre-qui-Vire
Sekules, V. (1986)   'The Tomb of Christ at Lincoln Cathedral and the Development of the Sacrament Shrine: Easter Sepulchres Reconsidered', *BAA CT*, VIII, 118–31

Smith, J. T. (1807–09)   *Antiquities of Westminster*. London
Smith, J. T. (1963)   'The Norman Structure of Leominster Priory', *Transactions of the Ancient Monuments Society*, N.S., XI, 97–108
Snell, L. (1961)   *The Chantry Certificates for Devon and Exeter*. Exeter
Somers Cocks, J. V. (1977)   *Devon Topographical Prints 1660–1870: A Catalogue and Guide*. Exeter
Southerdon, F. (1913)   'Researches on Atmosphere Pollution in Exeter, and the Action of Coal Smoke upon the Fabric of Exeter Cathedral', *Journal of the Royal Sanitary Institute*, **34**, No. 9, 402–8
Sparke, J. (1723)   *Historiae Anglicanae Scriptores varii*, II. London
Spence, J. E. (n.d.)   *A Short Guide and History to the Church of St German's*. Plymouth
Stalley, R. (1981)   'Three Irish Buildings with West-Country Origins', *BAA CT*, IV
Steingraber, E. (1957)   *Antique Jewellery*. London
Stewart, D. J. (1868)   *On The Architectural History of Ely Cathedral*. London
Stocker, D. (1987)   'The Mystery of the Shrines of St Hugh', *St Hugh of Lincoln*, ed. H. Mayr-Harting, 96–99, 102. Oxford
Stone, L. (1972)   *Sculpture in Britain: The Middle Ages*, 2nd ed. The Pelican History of Art. Harmondsworth 1955, revised edn 1972
Stow, J. (1908)   *Survey of London*, ed. C. L. Kingsford, 2 vols. Oxford
Svanberg, J. (1983)   *Master Masons*
Swanton, M. (1979)   *The Roof Bosses and Corbels of Exeter Cathedral*. Exeter Cathedral
Swanton, M. (ed.) (1991)   *Exeter Cathedral — A Celebration*. Exeter
Taylor, H. M. and Taylor, J. (1965)   *Anglo-Saxon Architecture* Vols 1 and 2. Cambridge
Theophilus   See under Theophilus in Abbreviations
Thompson (1933)   See under Cennini in Abbreviations
Thompson, D. V. (1935)   'Trial Index to some Unpublished Sources for the History of English Mediaeval Craftsmanship', *Speculum* **10**, 4, 410–31
—— (1956)   *The Materials and Techniques of Mediaeval Painting*. London 1936, Dover reprint New York and London 1956
Thurlby. M. (1984)   'A Note on the Former Barrel Vault in the choir of St John the Baptist at Halesowen and its place in English Romanesque Architecture', *Transactions of the Worcestershire Archaeological Society*, 3rd series, IX, 37–43
—— (1985a)   'The Romanesque Elevations of Tewkesbury and Pershore', *JSAH*, (America), XLIV, 5–17
—— (1985b)   'The Elevations of the Romanesque Abbey Churches of St Mary at Tewkesbury and St Peter at Gloucester', *BAA CT*, VII, 36–51
—— (1988)   'The Former Romanesque High Vault in the Presbytery of Hereford Cathedral', *SAH*, XLVII, 185–9
Tidmarsh, W. G. (1932)   'The Permian Lavas of Devon', *Quaternary Journal of the Geological Society*, **88**, 712–75
Toblers, A. and Lommatzsch, E. (eds) (1936)   *Altfranzosische Worterbuch*, II. Berlin

Tracy, C. (1986)   'The Early Fourteenth-Century Choir-Stalls at Exeter Cathedral', *The Burlington Magazine*, CXXVIII, 99–103
—— (1987)   *English Gothic Choir-Stalls 1200–1400*. Woodbridge

Traver, H. (1907)   *The Four Daughters of God: A Study of the Versions of this Allegory, with Special Reference to those in Latin, French and English*, Bryn Mawr College Monographs, 6, Bryn Mawr

Tudor-Craig, P. (1952)   See under Wynn Reeves (1952)

—— (1976)   *One Half of Our Noblest Art: A Study of the Sculpture of Wells Cathedral*. Wells

Twysden, R. (1652)   *Historiae Anglicanae Scriptores X*. London

Ussher, W. E. A. (1902)   *The Geology of the Country Around Exeter, Memoirs of the Geological Survey, sheet 325*

Vallance, A. (1947)   *Greater English Church Screens*. London

Walcott, M. E. C. (1868)   *Sacred Archaeology. A Popular Dictionary*. London

Watson, A. (1934)   *The Early Iconography of the Tree of Jesse*. London

Wayment, H. (1984)   *The Stained Glass of the Church of St Mary, Fairford, Gloucestershire.* Society of Antiquaries Occasional Paper (New Series) 5. London

Webb, G. (1956)   *Architecture in Britain: The Middle Ages*. Harmondsworth

Whittingham, A. B. (1951) 'Bury St Edmunds Abbey. The Plan, Design and Development of the Church and Monastic Buildings', *Archaeol. J.*, CVIII

Wildridge, T. T. (1879)   *Misereres in Beverley Minster*

Willis, R. (1846)   'The Architectural History of Winchester Cathedral', *Proceedings of the Archaeological Institute of Great Britain* 1–81; reprinted in R. Willis, *Architectural History of Some English Cathedrals*, I. London 1972

—— (1980)   'The Neville Screen', *BAA CT*, III, (1980), 91–3

Wilson, C. (1985)   'Abbot Serlo's Church at Gloucester, 1089–1100: Its Place in Romanesque Architecture', *BAA CT*, VII, 52–83

Winkles, B. (1838–42)   *Winkles's Architectural and Picturesque Illustrations of the Cathedral Churches of England and Wales*, 3 vols

Woodforde, C. (1937)   'A Group of Fourteenth-Century Windows Showing the Tree of Jesse' *Journal of the Society of British Master Glass Painters*, 6, 184–90

Woodman, F. (1981)   *The Architectural History of Canterbury Cathedral*. London

—— (1983)   'The Retrochoir of Winchester Cathedral: a new interpretation', *JBAA*, CXXXVI, 87–97

Worth, T. B. (1878)   *Exeter Cathedral and its Restoration*. Exeter

—— (1880)   *Worth's Hand-Book to Exeter Cathedral with Plan*. Exeter

Wynn Reeves, P. (1952)   (P. Tudor-Craig, now Lady Wedgwood), *English Stiff-Leaf Sculpture*, unpublished University of London Ph.D. thesis

Youings, J. (1968)   *Tuckers Hall, Exeter*. Exeter

THE PLATES

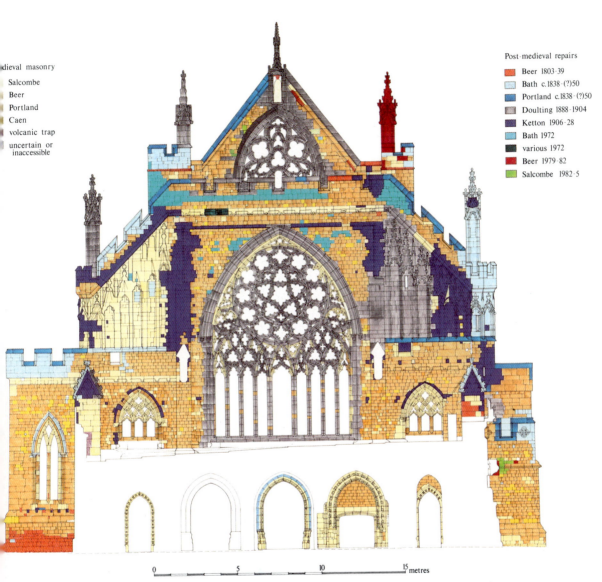

Post-medieval repairs
- 🟥 Beer 1803-39
- ⬜ Bath c.1838-(?)50
- 🟦 Portland c.1838-(?)50
- ⬜ Doulting 1888-1904
- 🟪 Ketton 1906-28
- 🟦 Bath 1972
- ⬛ various 1972
- 🟥 Beer 1979-82
- 🟩 Salcombe 1982-5

dieval masonry
- Salcombe
- Beer
- Portland
- Caen
- volcanic trap
- uncertain or inaccessible

0   5   10   15 metres

A. Exeter Cathedral, the west front, showing geology of medieval builds and of
post-medieval repairs (see note * on page 115)

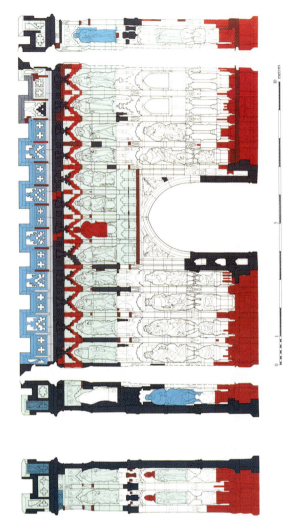
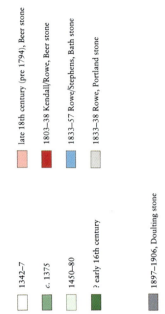
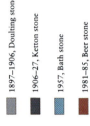
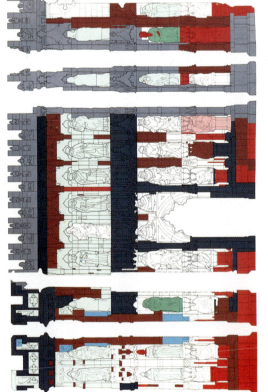

1342–7	late 18th century (pre 1794), Beer stone
c. 1375	1803–38 Kendall/Rowe, Beer stone
1450–80	1833–57 Rowe/Stephens, Bath stone
? early 16th century	1833–38 Rowe, Portland stone
1897–1906, Doulting stone	
1906–27, Ketton stone	
1957, Bath stone	
1981–85, Beer stone	

B. Geology and phasing of image screen, after completion of conservation in 1985

Ci. Exeter Cathedral, interior of nave in late 18th century, looking east. Watercolour attributed to Thomas Girtin (1775–1803)

Cii. Detail of Griffin on boss 176, in the central crossing, after cleaning and retouching. See also Hulbert, fig. 6

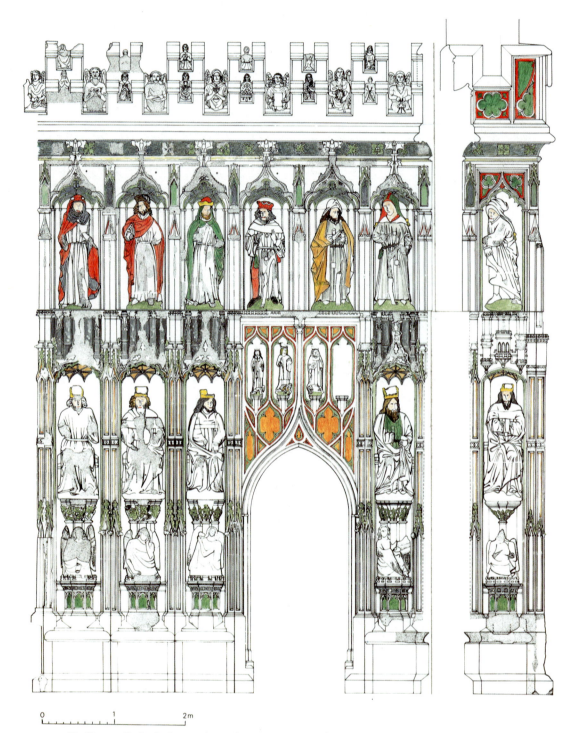

D. Exeter Cathedral, west front, image screen, north sector. Evidence from the analysed
paint fragments has been used to colour relevant areas

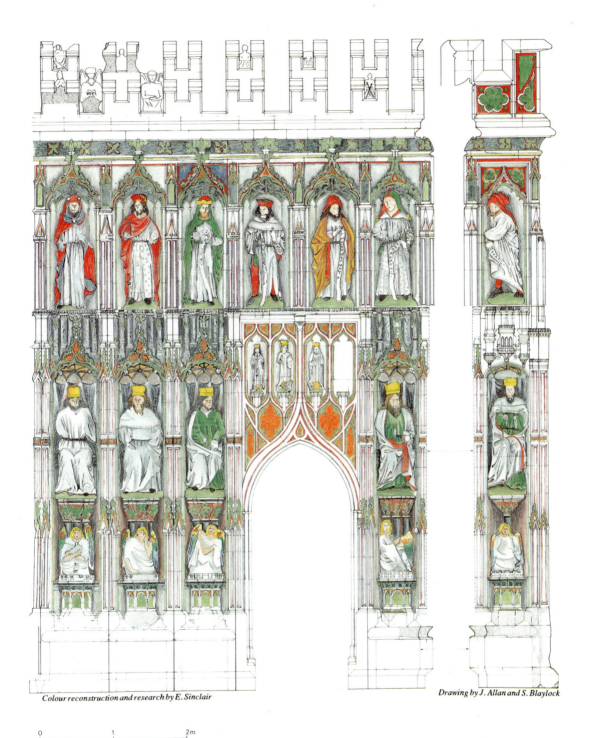

Colour reconstruction and research by E. Sinclair

Drawing by J. Allan and S. Blaylock

0   1   2m

E. Exeter Cathedral, west front, image screen, north sector reconstruction of colour,
based on evidence from paint analysis and comparative material

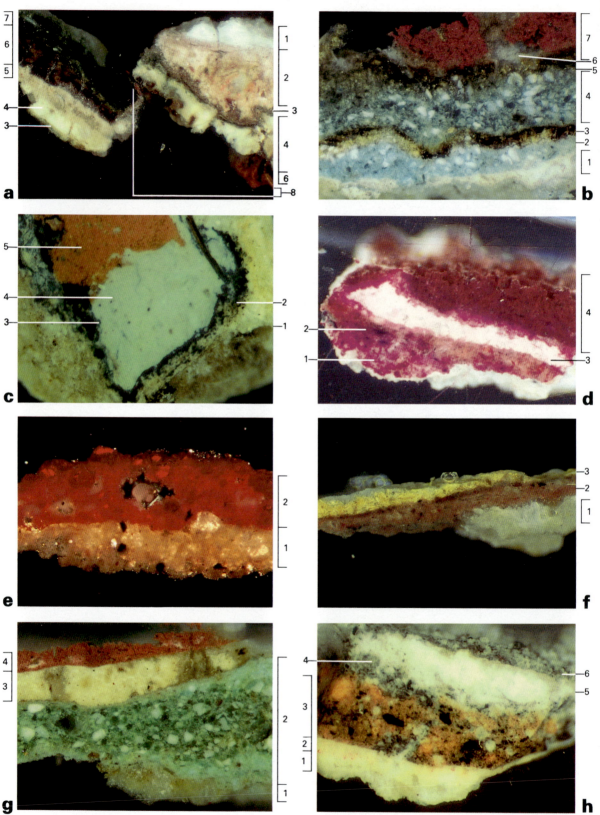

F. Photomicrographs of paint cross-sections. With the exception of e all are photographed in reflected light.

a. Sample 459. Magnification × 60. From the central doorway, north spandrel: angel's wing.
Paint has separated; right fragment of paint is upside down, and fits below left fragment.

1. Lead white.
2. Pink primer, containing iron-oxide red, red and white lead and chalk.
3. Oil-rich discoloured green.
4. White.
5. Pink primer.
6. Discoloured green glaze.
7. Copper green glaze.
8. Iron-oxide red.

b. Sample 64. Magnification × 40. Soffit of canopy C6.

1. White ground.
2. Indigo and lead white.
3. Oil-rich sealant with lead white.
4. Azurite and lead white.
5. Oily layer.
6. Dirt deposit.
7. Iron-oxide red.

c. Sample B 21/2. Magnification × 40. From weathered hole in pilaster between B 21 and B 22. Stained with Amido Black 2 for protein. (Oil was also identified in layer 3 in a separate test, indicating the use of an emulsion.)

1. Stone.
2. Dirt.
3. Blue-black stain indicating possible sealant layer.
4. Lead white.
5. Red lead.

d. Sample 341. Magnification × 40. Drapery of figure B 6. Stained with Acid Fuchsin for protein.

1. Lead white and chalk, stained magenta.
2. Pink primer, stained magenta.
3. Lead white, stained around edges.
4. Iron-oxide red.

e. Sample 224. Magnification × 60. Collar of figure C 6. Thin section, as seen in transmitted light, through crossed polars.

1. Lead white, with inclusions of calcium carbonate white and carbon black.
2. Vermilion and lead white.

f. Sample 347. Magnification × 40. Crown of figure B 7.

1. Stone.
2. Pink primer consisting of iron-oxide red, chalk and carbon black.
3. Orpiment.

g. Sample 113. Magnification × 60. Trefoil on canopy C 8.

1. Calcium carbonate.
2. Verdigris and lead white.
3. Lead white and calcium carbonate white.
4. Iron-oxide red.

h. Sample 166. Magnification × 40. Beard of C 3.

1. Calcium carbonate.
2. Pale pink flesh colour, consisting of lead white and vermilion.
3. Ginger beard, consisting of red lead, carbon black, iron-oxide red and white lead.
4. Carbon black and lead white, possibly not paint but sooty deposit.
5. White.
6. Sooty deposit.

I. Exeter Cathedral, general view of eastern arm from south-east
© *Conway Library, Courtauld Institute of Art*

II. Exeter Cathedral, eastern arm with retrochoir and Lady Chapel, north elevation. Plate engraved by James Basire after John Carter
(Carter 1797b)

III. Exeter Cathedral, north tower, nave and image screen, north elevation. Plate engraved by James Basire after John Carter (Carter 1797b)

IV. Exeter Cathedral, interior, choir and presbytery, looking east
© V. Jansen

VA. Exeter Cathedral, St James'
Chapel south wall, detail of angle of
former Romanesque chapel(?) left
exposed in rebuilding after 1942
bomb damage

VB. St German's Priory (Cornwall), nave, south arcade
from south aisle

VC. Tewkesbury Abbey,
south-east crossing pier, detail

VD. Exeter Cathedral,
fragment of
Romanesque capital
now set against the east
wall of the cloister

VE. Exeter Cathedral, interior, north
transept west wall and north nave aisle

VIA. Exeter Cathedral, interior, north transept arch to east chapel

VIB. Exeter Cathedral, interior, south transept arch to east chapel

VIC. Ottery St Mary (Devon), interior, north tower, east wall

VID. Exeter Cathedral, Romanesque keystone

VIE. Exeter Cathedral, interior, south transept arch to east chapel, detail

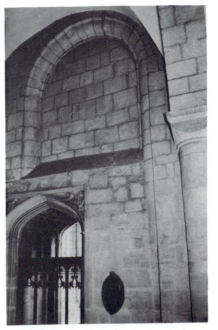

VIIA. Exeter Cathedral, interior, south choir aisle, west bay, south wall, detail

VIIB. Gloucester Cathedral, interior, north choir aisle, west bay, north wall, detail

VIIC. Winchester, St Cross, interior, north choir aisle

VIID. Gloucester Cathedral, chapter house, interior, dado arcade, detail

VIIE. Exeter Cathedral, exterior, south tower, capital, detail

VIIIA. Exeter Cathedral, chapel of St Gabriel,
east window

VIIIB. Exeter Cathedral, north transept chapel of
St Paul

VIIIC. Exeter Cathedral, blind tracery to Chapel of St Andrew

IXA. Exeter Cathedral, chapel of St John the Evangelist, north-east corner (coursing outlined)

IXB. Exeter Cathedral, join of the chapel of St Gabriel and the Lady Chapel

IXC. Exeter Cathedral, exterior wall, eastern bay of presbytery, south (break indicated)

IXD. Exeter Cathedral, interior, Lady Chapel, piscina, sedilia, and part of tomb recess

IXE. Exeter Cathedral, interior, presbytery, triforium on south

XA. Wells Cathedral, stairs to chapter house

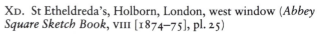

XB. Merton College Chapel, Oxford, north

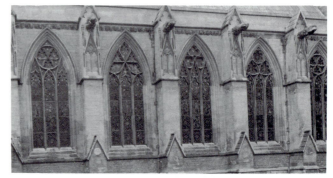

XC. Tintern Abbey, choir looking east

XD. St Etheldreda's, Holborn, London, west window (*Abbey Square Sketch Book*, VIII [1874–75], pl. 25)

XIA. Exeter
Cathedral,
pulpitum, west
face (detail)

XIC. Exeter
Cathedral,
pulpitum, west
side, bases
(Purbeck marble)

XIB. Exeter Cathedral, pulpitum, north-west
corner

XID. Exeter Cathedral, pulpitum, east bay,
vault

© *Conway Library, Courtauld Institute of Art:*
P. Draper

XIIA. Exeter Cathedral, pulpitum, north-west
bay, vault
© *Conway Library, Courtauld Institute of Art:*
P. Draper

XIIB. Exeter Cathedral, bishop's
throne, canopy (detail)

XIIc. Exeter Cathedral, tomb attributed to
Sir Robert Stapledon

XIID. Exeter Cathedral, St Andrew's chapel,
north wall, canopy

XIIIA. Exeter Cathedral, west front, centre porch and door to Grandisson chapel (right)
© *Conway Library, Courtauld Institute of Art: P. Draper*

XIIIB. Exeter Cathedral, north porch, entrance (detail)

XIIIC. Winchester Cathedral, feretory screen (detail)

XIIID. Winchester Cathedral, feretory bay, north side (detail)

XIVA. Exeter Cathedral, nave, south side (detail)

XIVB. Exeter Cathedral, nave, north side (detail)

XIVC. Exeter Cathedral, north transept, north window (detail)

XIVD. Wells Cathedral, Lady Chapel, window (detail)

© Conway Library, Courtauld Institute of Art: C. Wilson

XVA. Exeter Cathedral, Chapel of St John the Evangelist, east window and Lady Chapel (left)

XVB. Exeter Cathedral, presbytery, high east window exterior

XVC. Exeter Cathedral, presbytery, high east window interior showing sill, mullions and north jamb

XVD. Exeter Cathedral, presbytery, high east window exterior, showing sill and south jamb

XVIB. Exeter Cathedral, west front, image screen, the south sector
c. 1890 (unnumbered photograph, Exeter Cathedral Library)

XVIA. Exeter Cathedral, west front, image screen, the
north sector in 1984 (after conservation)

XVII. Exeter Cathedral, west front, sculpture in the south porch. (a) south side: the Annunciation (b) north side: the Adoration of the Magi

XVIII. Exeter Cathedral, west front, John Carter's drawings compared to surviving sculpture. (A) drawing of figure C10 (BL Add. MS 29931 f. 72); (B) figure C10 after stripping in 1984; (C) figure C28 after conservation in 1982; (D) drawing of the medieval figure B10 (BL Add. MS 29931 f. 78), destroyed early 19th century, replaced by E. B. Stephens 1857; (E) drawing of figure C33 (BL Add. MS 29931 f. 76); (F) figure C33 after stripping in 1985

By permission of the British Library

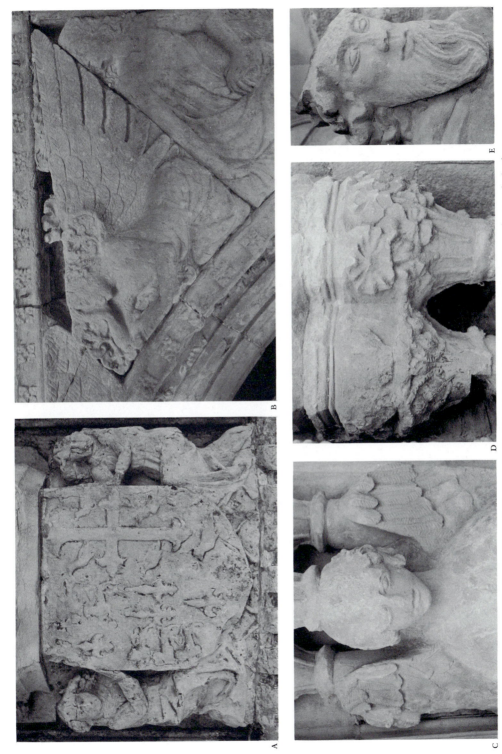

XIX. Exeter Cathedral, west front, (A) shield at base of niche C16; (B) south spandrel of great west doorway in 1984 with mortar stripped from joints; (C)–(E) details of replacement and recarving by John Kendall: (C) A34 replaced in 1817; (D) capital of A35 showing medieval foliage (left) and recarving by Kendall (right); (E) head of figure B35 (15th century) showing eyes recut in Kendall's style (cf. (C))

XX. Exeter Cathedral, west front, (A)–(D) details of the B-register figures:
(A) B19 head; (B) B12 dexter arm; (C) B27 torso; (D) B30 typical draperies of
B-register sculpture; (E)–(F) typical C-register draperies: (E) C21 (south); (F) C21
(north) and C22; (G)–(I) C-register heads, hair and headgear: (G) C29; (H) C2; (I) C5

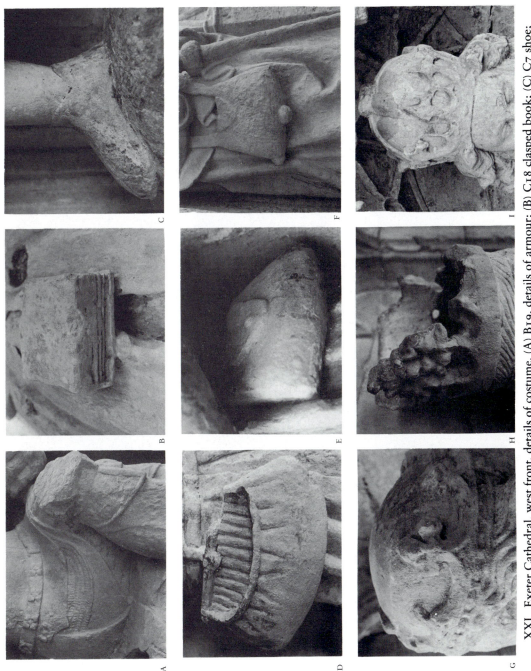

XXI. Exeter Cathedral, west front, details of costume. (A) B19, details of armour; (B) C18 clasped book; (C) C7 shoe; (D) C6 purse; (E) C4 purse; (F) C20 purse; (G) B12 crown; (H) B6 crown; (I) C17 crown

XXII. Exeter Cathedral, west front, details of architecture and sculpture. (A) quatrefoil behind canopy of C35; (B) string course behind canopy of B35; (C) string course at base of the southern buttress exposed on the removal of shaft A34/35 in 1979; (D) canopies B22/23, junction of shafts; (E) Figure B1, upper block removed during conservation in 1983, showing flat rear face; (F) Figure C24, hollowed rear face; (G) canopies B11/12 shaft removed to show jointing of canopy blocks; (H) canopy C3 showing form of secondary canopy and outline of primary canopy (finial modern); (I) canopy C12, showing soffit vault, recarved rib exposed in central foil of secondary canopy and joint between soffit (right) and secondary hood (left)

XXIIIA. Exeter Cathedral, chapel of
St Edmund. North and west faces
Photo: author

XXIIIB. Exeter Cathedral, chapel of
St Edmund. North and east walls
Photo: author

XXIIIc. Exeter Cathedral, chapel of St Edmund.
Interior, entrance (south) wall and arch
Photo: author

XXIIID. Exeter Cathedral, chapel of
St Edmund. Vault, from below facing west
Photo: author

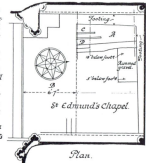

Wall A is built of Salcombe stone roughly squared & coursed, stepped, as shewn in the sections below. At the South end of it are two lengths of chamfered plinth 2ft 4ins and 3ft long, at C and D respectively

Wall B is random masonry built of local trap rock and is the foundation of the North wall of the Norman Cathedral. For a height of 1ft 10ins at the bottom it rests on wall A, which otherwise is not bonded to the return walls.

The foundations were exposed during alterations to St Edmunds Chapel, May 1936.

Footing

C
D   A
18" below foot
Rammed gravel
5' below foot

B
6·7'

St Edmund's Chapel.

Plan.

Scale of feet

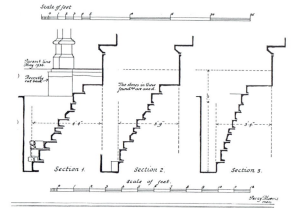

Present line May 1936.
Recently cut back

The stones in these foundⁿˢ are axed.

4·4'
5·9'
3·4'

Section 1.   Section 2.   Section 3.

Scale of feet.

Percy Morris mens

XXIVA. Exeter Cathedral, chapel of St Edmund. Excavation, May 1936, as recorded by P. Morris
Photo courtesy of Exeter Cathedral Library

XXIVB. Exeter Cathedral, chapel of St Edmund. Junction of north nave aisle wall and east wall of chapel
Photo: author

XXIVC. Exeter Cathedral, chapel of St Edmund. East window
Photo: author

XXVA. Exeter
Cathedral, chapel of
St Edmund. Excavation
of 1936, in west half of
chapel, viewed from
south
Photo courtesy of
J. Edward Norris

XXVB. Exeter
Cathedral, chapel of
St Edmund. Excavation
of 1936, viewed from
north-east
Photo courtesy of
J. Edward Norris

XXVC. Exeter
Cathedral, chapel of
St Edmund. Base of
flying buttress, top of
pier buttress (east wall
of chapel), pinnacle, and
entrance to roof-space
over chapel vault
Photo: author

XXVD. Exeter
Cathedral, chapel of
St James and St Thomas.
East windows (from
J. Kendall, 1818,
Pl. XIV)
Photo courtesy of The
Society of Antiquaries of
London

XXVE. Exeter
Cathedral, chapel of
St Edmund. Interior,
base of east wall with
bench
Photo: author

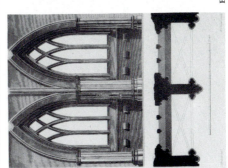

XXVIA. Exeter Cathedral, sedilia

XXVIC. St Augustine, Canterbury, layout of shrines at high altar, after a 15th-century drawing, in Dugdale's *Monasticon*

XXVIB. Exeter Cathedral, tomb of Bishop Stapledon, figures from high altar reredos built into east end of canopy

XXVID. Exeter Cathedral, seal of Peter Quinil, Bishop of Exeter, 1280–91, and second seal of Cathedral, *c.* 1280.

Photos courtesy of Society of Antiquaries, London

XXVIIA. Exeter Cathedral, Elephant misericord
Conway Library, Courtauld Institute of Art

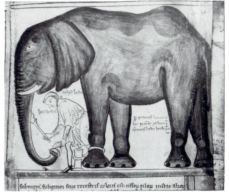

XXVIIB. Matthew Paris, *Chronica Majora*, Corpus Christi College, Cambridge MS 16, f. 4r
Permission of Master and Fellows, Corpus Christi College, Cambridge

XXVIIC. Exeter Cathedral, 'stiff-leaf' foliage misericord

XXVIID. Exeter Cathedral, misericord using simultaneously both conventional and naturalistic foliage

XXVIIE. Wells Cathedral, west front 'Resurrection' tier, detail
Conway Library, Courtauld Institute of Art

XXVIIG. Exeter Cathedral, lion misericord

XXVIIF. Wells Cathedral, label-stop in nave north aisle, west label-stop, Bilson bay 17/15

XXVIIIA. Exeter Cathedral, two-bodied dragon with foliage
tail misericord

XXVIIIB. Wells Cathedral, dragon in
spandrel of nave arcade, north side.
Bilson pier 9
Conway Library, Courtauld Institute of Art

XXVIIIc. Exeter Cathedral, 'Aristotle' misericord
National Monuments Record

XXVIIID. English Apocalypse, detail.
Trinity College, Cambridge. MS B.10.
6. f. 9r
*Permission of Master and Fellows Trinity
College, Cambridge*

XXVIIIE. Exeter Cathedral, 'siren' misericord
Conway Library, Courtauld Institute of Art

XXVIIIF. Latin Bestiary, detail, British
Library, Sloane MS 3544, f. 28v
Copyright Warburg Institute

XXIX. Exeter Cathedral, details. (A) Knight in combat with a dragon misericord; (B) 'Atlas misericord; (C) 'precentor's' misericord; (D) detail of Bishop Marshall's tomb; (E) Boss 184, 1316 paint: lion digging claws into Manticore; (F) Boss 184, 1316 paint: screaming human face of Manticore; (G) Boss 188, 1316 paint: fabulous beast with pink-veined ears; (H) Boss 69, 1870s paint: mermaid tail with green overpaint

Copyright: A, B, D, Conway Library, Courtauld Institute of Art; E–H, A. C. Hulbert

A

C

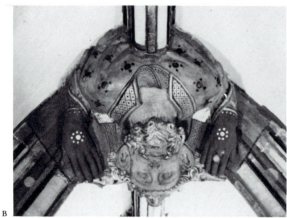

B

D

XXXA. Exeter Cathedral, boss 195, mid-14th century colour unretouched

XXXB. Exeter Cathedral, boss 73, Pope with 1870s overpaint

XXXC. Exeter Cathedral, boss 73, infra-red photograph

XXXD. Exeter Cathedral, corbel K. south, supporter king with two medieval paint layers

Copyright: XXXA–D, A. C. Hulbert

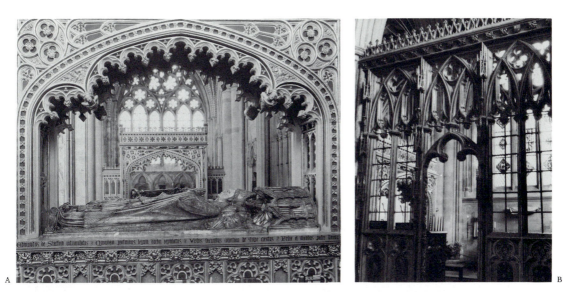

XXXIA. Exeter Cathedral. Tomb of Bishop Stafford, looking south to tomb of Bishop Branscombe

XXXIB. Exeter Cathedral. West screen to Branscombe chapel

XXXIC. Exeter Cathedral. Angel frieze on the canopy of Bishop Branscombe's tomb, north side

XXXID. Exeter Cathedral. Angel frieze on the canopy of Bishop Stafford's tomb, south side

XXXIE. Exeter Cathedral. Angel frieze of the canopy of Bishop Stapledon's tomb, north side
Copyright: A, D, E, George Hall; B, C, Bridget Cherry

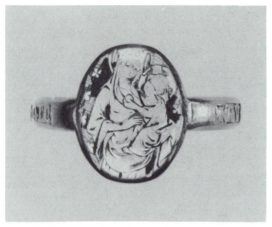

XXXIIA. Bezel and hoop of Grandisson ring
Photo British Museum

XXXIIB. Back of bezel and hoop of Grandisson
ring
Photo British Museum

XXXIIC. Impression of Grandisson ring from
the Ottery Charter
Photo British Library

XXXIID. Bezel of the ring from the
Rosenheim collection
Photo Victoria and Albert Museum

XXXIIE. Holy Thorn Reliquary. Scene of the
Presentation in the Temple and the Flight into
Egypt
Photo British Museum

XXXIIIA. Exeter Cathedral, choir, view to west
Photograph before 1870

XXXIIIB. Exeter Cathedral, choir, view to east,
Kendall's reredos

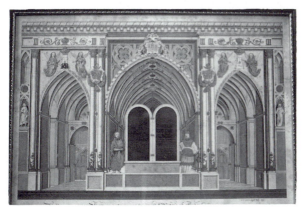

XXXIIIC. Exeter Cathedral, print of 1797 showing the
17th-century reredos

XXXIIID. Exeter Cathedral, Scott's
reredos and high altar. Photograph
of c. 1875

XXXIVA. Exeter Cathedral, the screen and organ from the nave, before 1868

XXXIVB. Exeter Cathedral, interior, the Lady Chapel *c.* 1869

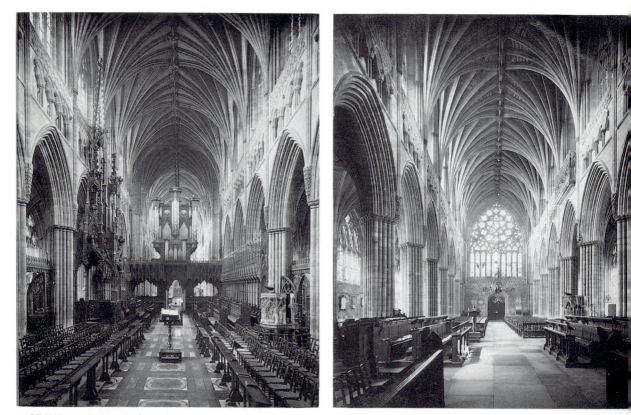

XXXIVC. Exeter Cathedral, the choir interior, looking west *c.* 1880

XXXIVD. Exeter Cathedral, interior, nave looking west